TZINTZUNTZAN

Mexican Peasants in a Changing World

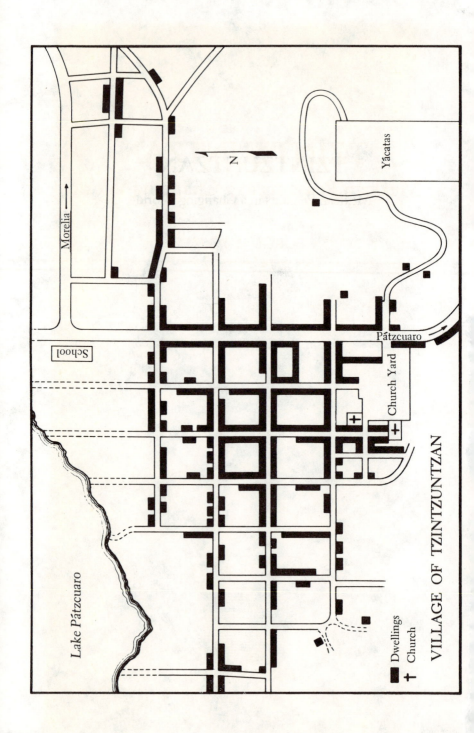

Lake Pátzcuaro

Morelia →

N

School

Yácatas

Pátzcuaro

Church Yard

■ Dwellings
✝ Church

VILLAGE OF TZINTZUNTZAN

TZINTZUNTZAN
Mexican Peasants in a Changing World

GEORGE M. FOSTER
University of California, Berkeley

WAVELAND
PRESS, INC.
Prospect Heights, Illinois

For information about this book, write or call:

Waveland Press, Inc.
P.O. Box 400
Prospect Heights, Illinois 60070
(847) 634-0081

Contents

AND CHILDREN. SIBLING RELATIONS. MARRIAGE.
FRIENDS AND NEIGHBORS. THE COMPADRAZGO.
BAPTISM. LESSER COMPADRAZGOS. IDEAL AND
REAL COMPADRAZGO BEHAVIOR. COMPADRAZGO
FUNCTIONS.

RISES. OUTSIDE SOURCES OF AID. ATTITUDES ON
ECONOMIC PROCESSES.

Preface, 1967

The initial field work on which this study is based took place between late 1944 and mid-1946, when I spent altogether about eight months in Tzintzuntzan, Michoacán, Mexico, dividing my time between the village and teaching duties at the National School of Anthropology in Mexico City. Sr. Gabriel Ospina of Bogotá, Colombia, then a graduate student at the National School, spent about fourteen months at Tzintzuntzan during this period, working as my research associate. Our findings are described in *Empire's Children: the People of Tzintzuntzan*, published in 1948 by the Smithsonian Institution, my employer during the periods of field work and manuscript preparation. For various reasons I was not able to return to Tzintzuntzan until 1958, when a short visit convinced me the time was ripe for a new study. Since then I have spent from a few weeks to as much as three months in residence each year, for a total of about eight additional months.

During this second period of investigation I have built on my early knowledge, on the one hand emphasizing the changes that have occurred over twenty years and on the other hand searching for insights into the personality of the villagers which would facilitate meaningful relating of individual behavior and belief to underlying basic cultural patterns. As field work progressed I came to believe that social and cultural change are governed, much more than is usually recognized, by subconscious assumptions which add up to a particular view of how the several universes about man determine and limit the amount and kinds of activity in which he can engage. This growing conviction about the importance of what has been called "world view" or "cognitive orientation" ultimately decided the form and content of this book. In order to make two decades of change in Tzintzuntzan intelligible, I found it essential first to describe the village and its occupants, then to sketch the character of the people, and finally to relate this character to major social and cultural institutions. Only then did I feel change processes could be seen in proper perspective.

The result is a book consisting of two rather disparate sections: the first, an analysis in theoretical terms of the character of the people and of their principal institutions, and the second a rather detailed account of twenty years of change, and of how many among these changes stem from pre-existing personality and cultural forms. In the first part many descriptive data have been omitted; some readers may feel too many. But for the interested specialist in ethnography or Mexican life, these data can be found in the earlier monograph, and in subsequent publications listed in the bibliography. And, I hope, a sparsity of detail may reveal with greater clarity the hypotheses which I feel are the principal contribution of this book.

In describing a community at least some of whose members are literate, and which is a part of a modern nation, a degree of anonymity is essential, lest the information friends have given in confidence embarrass them. Most names in this book are those by which people go in real life. The villagers are proud that an anthropologist feels their community is important enough to study, and they are pleased that many people in the United States know about it, and that some come to the village and ask for them by name. In a few instances, however, I have thought it desirable to conceal true identities by using fictitious names. These are Alonso, Arias, Barragán, Cabeza, Caro, Castellanos, Córdoba, Enríquez, Gómez, Herrera, Horta, Huerta, Luna, Marcos, Martín, Matos, Medellín, Méndez, Miranda, Molina, Noriega, Pánfilo,

Paz, Pelón, Prieto, Reina, Rivera, Romano, Torres, Villalba, Zúñiga, and Zurita. Needless to say, given names used with these surnames are also pseudonyms.

All prices are expressed in Mexican pesos, unless otherwise indicated, and are written with the dollar sign. During the period of the restudy 1959–1966 the peso exchanged at 12.50 pesos to 1.00 dollar. During the initial period of field work in the mid-1940's, the peso exchanged at 4.85 pesos to 1.00 dollar.

An author is indebted to many people and institutions. National Science Foundation Grant G-7064, and annual grants from the Research Committee of the University of California (Berkeley) have supported research since 1959. My wife, Mary, has spent most of the recent periods of study with me, and her company, insights, and stimulation are what make field work fun and worthwhile. Dr. Michael Maccoby has given much aid and encouragement, reading and rereading early versions of the manuscript. Major reorganizations in mode of data presentation, and emphases on specific points, are the consequence of his meticulous help.

To Gabriel Ospina, I owe special debts: for his great contribution during the original field period, his aid in setting up shop for the subsequent work, and for his supervision of the 1960 project census (actually carried out by Sr. Benjamín Gurrola). In 1951 the Mexican Government and UNESCO established in Pátzcuaro *El Centro Regional de Educación Fundamental para la América Latina* (commonly called CREFAL), to train Latin American personnel in community development skills. Professor Ospina, an original CREFAL staff member, made Tzintzuntzan a pilot project village. Thus, not only was he able to acquaint me with occurrences over these years, but he himself was responsible for many decisions that influenced the villagers' lives. Professor Lucas Ortíz Benítez, Director of CREFAL, and Dr. Aníbal Buitrón, Subdirector during most of the period of field work since 1958, and the scientific staff of the institution have helped in many ways.

It is a pleasure to acknowledge the courtesy of the Mexican Government which, over more than a generation, has permitted me to carry out anthropological studies, and to bring students to

Mexico for training and research. The Instituto Nacional de Antropología e Historia, and its Director, Dr. Eusebio Dávalos Hurtado, have always lent me support in my work, for which I am grateful.

It is impossible to acknowledge by name all of my Tzintzuntzan friends. But I would be remiss in friendship obligations — which the reader will note are enormously important in Tzintzuntzan — if I failed to point out that a very significant degree of my insights into how the community works comes from the good fortune of living in the home of Doña Micaela González, with her husband Don Melecio Hernández, her daughters Dolores and Virginia Pichu, and her nephew Amado González. The friendship of this remarkable family, and the dedicated and unqualified support of its members, have played a major role in enabling me to describe how a Mexican peasant community functions.

Several graduate students from Berkeley have worked with me in the lake area: Jean Cooke (in Tócuaro), Richard and Susan Currier (in Erongarícuaro), William Iler (in Tzintzuntzan), Susan Ripley (in Pátzcuaro), Cynthia Nelson (in Erongarícuaro), and William and Barbara Smith (on the island of La Pacanda). Miss Nelson and Mr. Smith subsequently returned to their villages for year-long studies which formed the basis of their doctoral dissertations. Through the research of these colleagues I have seen the culture of Tzintzuntzan in a wider local perspective than would otherwise have been possible, and they have also called my attention to specific points of theoretical importance.

A number of the theoretical ideas found in the first part of this book have previously received treatment in article form, especially Foster 1961, 1963, 1964a, 1964b, 1965a, 1965b, 1965c, and 1966. In some cases I have quoted rather extensively from these sources without using quotation marks, making only minor changes in the original text. This is particularly true in the second half of Chapter Two, "The Dyadic Contract," which comes from Foster 1963.

GEORGE M. FOSTER

Preface, 1979

The writing of *Tzintzuntzan* was completed in 1965, although a few facts from 1966 were added prior to publication in 1967. My theoretical interpretations—particularly the Image of Limited Good—were thus based on the village and the behavior of its people as I knew them in 1945–1946 and again during the period 1958–1965. These 20 years were not without change. At the same time, Tzintzuntzan, highly traditional in 1945, was still basically conservative in 1965; continuity in custom and world view, rather than change, was the striking impression. Although *Tzintzuntzan* deals extensively with change and innovation during these 20 years, the overall picture is one of a conservative and traditional peasant village that was bewildered by the rapid changes taking place about it—uncertain as to how it too could participate in these changes.

Since 1965, usually accompanied by my wife Mary, I have made annual visits to the village of from one to three months, most recently in March 1979; not infrequently, when the opportunity offered, I have managed an extra short trip or two. Among the many tasks I have assigned myself is the keeping of a formal record of material and physical changes in the village, the taking of a complete census in 1970, and the recording of births, marriages, and deaths. I have also noted examples of the striking changes in the cognitive orientation of many villagers, their growing "openness," their ability to participate in national affairs.

When Mary and I returned to the village in 1958 to renew fieldwork after a lapse of 12 years we were struck by the relative lack of visible signs of major change. We felt that we were able to take up where we had left off; we "knew" the culture, discovering that we still fitted into it comfortably. In contrast, the 13 years from 1966 to 1979 have been a time of almost unbelievable change. Had we not been in the village during these years, and had we returned only in 1979 after a long absence, it is doubtful that we would have "known" the culture in the same way we did in 1958. The signs of economic progress are today everywhere: television sets, propane gas stoves, hi-fi consoles, trucks and automobiles, new schools, new markets, city clothing, comfortable houses, and stores selling a wide variety of consumer articles. Accompanying these material changes has been a striking shift in world view, particularly among the members of the younger generation. No longer are they bound by the psychological shackles of the Limited Good outlook. They recognize opportunity, believe that with hard work they can exploit it, and demonstrate through their collective achievements the accuracy of this perception. Increasingly well-educated, these young people in aspirations and outlook are broadly Mexican and not narrowly Tzintzuntzeño.

Hand-in-hand with the acceptance of progress, the villagers have clung to many traditional values, often recasting them in new form, thus invigorating a life they have all known well. This is particularly evident in the florescence of the fiesta system in which, almost unique in Mexico, ritual life today is more interesting and more impressive than two decades ago. Social forms—the compadrazgo for example—likewise continue to have great symbolic meaning, and traditional customs are closely adhered to.

In recent years colleagues who know of my continuing research in Tzintzuntzan have asked that I bring them up to date on changes. Several papers have partially dealt with these requests, e.g., Foster 1969, 1973, 1979, and especially Kemper and Foster 1975. Because of this continuing interest in the village, I am particularly grateful to Elsevier for reissuing *Tzintzuntzan* and for giving me the opportunity to add an epilogue in which I summarize and analyze important developments in the village since 1965.

Preface, 1988

Since the second version of *Tzintzuntzan* was published in 1979, nine years have gone by. During this time, I have made biannual visits to the village for periods from ten days to one month. In addition, Doña Micaela González (in whose home my wife, Mary, and I live when in Tzintzuntzan), her daughters Dolores and Virginia Pichu, and the school teacher María Flores, have thrice visited us in our Berkeley home. These contacts have enabled me to continue general ethnographic research, particularly in the area of ethnomedicine, to monitor basic patterns of change and modernization, to note the effects of Mexican currency devaluation and monetary inflation, to copy parish and municipal vital statistics records and, with Robert Kemper and Stanley Brandes, to take a 100 percent census in February, 1980 — the fourth since 1945.

The pattern of progress and modernization described in the 1979 Epilogue continues, but it has slowed slightly in recent years because of *la crisis*, the economic depression that has afflicted Mexico since the early 1980s. The value of Mexican currency, which had fluctuated in the twenty to twenty-six pesos to the dollar range during the late 1970s, suddenly began to plummet in early 1982, reaching the figure of 1450 pesos to the dollar in July, 1987. Simultaneously, inflation climbed to an annual rate of over 100 percent. In the new Afterword, I have dealt especially with these two phenomena: first, the remarkable economic and cultural development of the village in recent years, as well as extending back to 1945; and second, the consequences of these recent national economic problems as they affect village life. These seem to me to be the most important events of recent years. For readers interested in ethnomedicine and related topics, attention is called to the following articles:

Foster, George M. 1981. "Old Age in Tzintzuntzan, Mexico." In *Aging: Biology and Behavior,* edited by J.L. McGaugh and S.B. Kiesler, pp. 115-137. New York: Academic Press.

_____. 1982. "Responsibility for Illness in Tzintzuntzan: A Cognitive-Linguistic Anomaly." *Medical Anthropology* 6: 81-90.

_____. 1984. "How to Stay Well in Tzintzuntzan." *Social Science & Medicine* 19: 523-533.

_____. 1985. "How to Get Well in Tzintzuntzan." *Social Science & Medicine* 21: 807-818.

_____. 1987. "The Validating Role of Humoral Theory in Traditional Hispanic-American Therapeutics." *American Ethnologist* (In press).

Above left: *Doña Micaela González, in whose home I have lived during visits since 1958.*

Above right: *A penitent during Easter Week ceremonies, hooded, with leg irons, carrying a dish in which people place coins.*

Doña Otilia Zavala, a potter, glazing her pots prior to the final firing. The big kiln is in the background.

CHAPTER ONE

The
Peasant
Community

PEASANTS IN AN INDUSTRIAL WORLD

It is a paradox of our century that, at a time when some men confidently reach through outer space, others live in small, isolated communities where the way of life is only now beginning to change from that of the time of Christ. For half the world's people are peasant villagers who eke out a bare subsistence from exhausted soils, uneconomic handicrafts, or from fishing or tending scrub cattle. Envious of the more fortunate peoples they see and hear about, they are nonetheless bound up in a cocoon of custom where the traditions and values of earlier generations still are seen as the safest guideposts in life. To the educated urbanite, with his good job, comfortable home, and social security, it may appear that the great challenges facing mankind lie in eliminating war, conquering disease, using leisure time constructively, and landing men on the moon. These are all exciting goals.

But most critical of all challenges is incorporating the culturally and economically marginal peasant villager into the modern world, where he will have access to the material and intellectual opportunities now enjoyed by his more fortunate countrymen. A preindustrial planet with a sparse population can tolerate social systems marked by great differences in wealth and freedom. However morally wrong one may feel such extremes to have been, past civilizations demonstrated the vitality to weather the conflicts they engendered. But it is doubtful that a heavily populated industrial world can indefinitely survive contrasts of the present magnitude: on the one hand, a biblical style of life with a very narrow margin of security, and on the other, the affluent society. Because of scientific communication media, formerly isolated peoples become merely marginal. They may remain as deprived as formerly, but now they see there are differences. They are increasingly dissatisfied with their lot but, sadly enough, it is extremely difficult to convert this dissatisfaction into purposeful seeking after new opportunities. For in addition to the obvious economic problems faced by developing countries, social, psychological, and cultural barriers hold back peasants, even when new opportunities may be had for the asking. The literature on development is replete with instances in which peasant farmers have rejected new fertilizers and hybrid seeds, their wives hide their children from public health vaccinators, and adult literacy courses go unattended. To the technical specialist the peasant seems, more often than not, to be suspicious, uncooperative, lacking in gratitude for proffered help, unable or unwilling to recognize opportunity.

Today's villagers are not being ignored by their national governments. Through community development programs, public health services, agricultural extension guidance, and spreading school systems, peasants increasingly are offered the opportunity to raise levels of living and better prepare themselves to participate in a life whose boundaries are beyond those of the village. Today's peasants remain problems, not because of neglect and unconcern on the part of more fortunate peoples, but because the combinations of factors which simultaneously motivate people to change, which loosen the fetters of traditional social organizations, which

4

instill new values, and which create optimum economic opportunities, have only partially been determined. We know, for example, that peasant farmers will adopt new crops or improved cultivation practices if there is a ready market, when the appeal of better health through better food falls on deaf ears. And we know that immunization programs and health education are more effective when tied to curative services than when presented on their own merits. It has been demonstrated that illiterates can quickly learn to read and write when there is sufficient motivation, such as the desire to communicate with absent relatives, or the wish to offer village handicrafts to urban peoples. It is not that peasant villages are completely resistant to change; some have made rather notable progress in recent years. Rather, the problem is that change does not come rapidly enough to narrow the gap between town and country, and to meet the rising aspirations of people who are still, in spite of everything, psychologically separated from the modern world of which they are a part.

As a social anthropologist I have been concerned for a good many years with the problems involved in drawing peasant peoples into effective participation in national life, with the search for the key factors in personality, culture, social forms, and economic conditions which favor modernization. No discipline in itself combines the research methodology and theoretical framework to give the answers we need. Economics, sociology, psychology, agronomy, medicine, education, all have their strengths, and their limits. One of anthropology's strengths is that a single community is intensively studied, and sometimes kept under observation for a long time, so that the real behavior of people can be recorded and worked into theoretical models which explain their behavior. These models, which have predictive value, can then be tested, over the years, against what actually does happen. Cultural models which explain and predict dynamic processes with some accuracy are, of course, enormously useful in planning specific developmental strategies.

In this book I hope to give the reader some idea of the style of life in a Mexican peasant community, the personality of the people, and the common patterns which pervade society's basic institutions. The behavior that is described is interpreted according to a model of world view, with its axiom that a healthy society is one in equilibrium. The implications of this model are examined with respect to problems of social and economic change, and tested against the real changes (as well as the stabilities) that have been observed over twenty-two years.

The scene of the story I am about to tell is Tzintzuntzan, a Spanish-speaking mestizo village 230 miles west of Mexico City, on the shores of Lake Pátzcuaro. Although at the time of the Spanish Conquest of America Tzintzuntzan was a great city, capital of the Tarascan Indian Empire, it is today a simple peasant community of 2,200 inhabitants, nearly indistinguishable in outward form from many other highland Mexican pueblos, and similar in psychology and mode of life to rural communities in many of the world's newly developing countries. Since it represents, I am convinced, a generic style of life, the lessons we learn from Tzintzuntzan must be pertinent, in greater or lesser degree, to the developmental problems experienced in a large part of the world.

PEASANT SOCIETY

My theme is peasants. But what are peasants, and what is a peasant community? If the conclusions to be drawn from this study are to have general validity, it is essential to place Tzintzuntzan in a wider context, that of a societal type. Probably every reader has his own image of a peasant village. It may be the adobe walled, redtiled roof clusters of houses nestled against the eroded hillsides of Mexico, the whitewashed walls of Southern Europe, the dung-colored cubes on the dusty Near Eastern plains, or the hamlets of India shaded by great trees. Whatever the outward form, all these settlements share features that make them peasant. Many writers argue that practicing agriculture for a livelihood is the key to peasantry. It is true that most peasants are farmers. But by no means all of them are, and Tzintzuntzan is a case in point. And, of course, many cultivators are not peasants. American farmers have never been peasants, and it seems stretching the point to speak of a contemporary peasantry in industrial Western Europe. At the other end of the spectrum of technological complexity the agricultural peoples of indigenous Africa south of the Sahara are felt, by most anthropologists at least, not to be true peasants; at best we call them "semi-peasants." Neither do the long-settled, skillful farmers of the pueblos in the American Southwest qualify as peasants. In these, and other technologically simple agricultural areas, an essential ingredient is missing.

This ingredient is an organic nexus to urban life, a tie with political, economic, and cultural dimensions. Peasants, as Kroeber put it, are class segments of a larger population with urban centers: "they constitute part-societies with part cultures" (1948:284). That is, in contrast to primitive tribal groups, they are in no way autonomous, culturally self-sufficient units. They can be understood only in a broader setting. Throughout history peasants have been a peripheral but essential part of civilizations, producing the food that makes possible urban life, supporting the specialized classes of political and religious rulers and educated elite who carry what Redfield called the "Great Tradition," which gives continuity and substance to all advanced culture sequences.

Thus, although peasant communities are primarily agricultural, the criteria of definition should be structural and relational rather than occupational for, as in much of Mexico, peasants also may earn their living from such work as fishing, pottery making, and from weaving tule mats or cotton or wool cloth. It is not *what* peasants produce that is significant; it is *how* and *to whom* they dispose of what they produce that counts. When settled rural peoples exchange a significant amount of their production for items they cannot themselves make, in a market setting that transcends local transactions stemming from village specialization, then they are peasants.

Historically speaking, peasant communities have grown up in a symbiotic spatial-temporal relationship with the more complex components of their greater society, i.e., the preindustrial market and administrative city. In this relationship, economic dependency invariably produces political, cultural, and often religious dependence as well. Peasant society thus represents the rural expression of national, class-structured, economically complex preindustrial

7

civilizations, in which craft specialization as well as agricultural production stimulate trade and commerce, and in which market disposition is the goal behind a significant part of the producer's efforts. Because peasant society changes slowly, it survives for a long time in an industrializing world. But since it is not a function of the modern manufacturing city, ultimately it will disappear.

This view of peasant society has varied implications. One of the most important is that the peasant is essentially powerless in large areas of life, because the basic decisions affecting villagers are made by members of other classes. Political activity is narrow in scope, for major control is exercised from national or provincial centers. Economically, peasants are dependent on forces that operate well beyond their local boundaries; only rarely, and under special circumstances, are prices for their products set by village factors. In Latin America and the Mediterranean, at least, in religion there is no local autonomy, for obligations and observances are set and guided by dogma and doctrine that far transcend even national boundaries.

In other words, peasants obey; they do not command. They wait to be told, but they do not make major decisions themselves. They are at the end of the lines of communication and authority that radiate from cities. Before injustice, the arbitrary, and the incomprehensible they must be passive acceptors, for they lack the power and knowledge to be otherwise.

In a culture historical sense peasant society is also the end of the line; it accepts far more than it gives. Its Little Tradition, to again use Redfield's expression, is a function of the Great Tradition of its cities. For, if we examine the cultural content of any peasant community, the striking finding is how many of its elements represent simplified, folk manifestations of ideas and artifacts whose origin is the city of an earlier historical period: costume, furniture, social forms, religious beliefs and practices, language, to name a few. Peasant communities continually incorporate into their fabrics significant parts of the sophisticated, intellectual components of the life of the cities with which they have contact. Peasant society is only in a very special sense a "grassroots" creation, produced by rural cultural vigor and inventiveness.

Peasant societies are what they are — and thus stand in contrast to truly primitive tribal societies, which are more nearly grass-roots products — precisely because, throughout history, they have replenished and augmented their cultural forms by imitating customs and behavior of other members of their wider society. But, since peasants comprehend imperfectly what they see in cities, the urban-inspired elements they acquire are reworked, simplified, and trimmed down so they can be accommodated to the less complex pattern of village life. And, because this process is slow, by the time urban elements are successfully incorporated into village culture, urban life has been changed, and has progressed, so that villagers have always been doomed to be old-fashioned. No matter how hard they have tried, what they may have believed to be the last word (as well as what they have not consciously recognized as urban-inspired) has invariably reflected city forms of earlier generations and centuries.

In Mexican peasant communities the time lag and simplification process is particularly well exemplified in contemporary folk medical practices (the term "folk" rather than "peasant" is used here because many of these beliefs are found in cities, especially among the lower classes; they are therefore "popular" as well as peasant). At the time of the Conquest of America scientific Spanish medicine had developed from the humoral pathology of Hippocrates and Galen, had been reworked and elaborated by Arab physicians, and had been introduced into Spain by Arab civilization. This system's focal point was the classification of foods, herbs, medicines, illnesses, and many other things according to paired qualities of heat or cold, and moistness or dryness, in varying degrees. Thus, "hot" and "moist" sweet basil (*albahaca*) was described as C_3H_2, i.e., *caliente* to the third degree and *húmeda* to the second degree. "Cold" and "dry" vinegar was described as F_1S_2, or *frío* in the first (and least) degree, and *seco* in the second degree.

Humoral pathology was brought by physicians, by churchmen, and by other educated people to America, where its concepts and practices filtered down to the masses, blending with indigenous elements to form contemporary folk medicine in all its variant forms. But the complexity of scientific humoral pathology could

9

not be maintained by illiterate, uneducated people who had to transmit the system by oral tradition. So, for this or other reasons, the qualities of dryness and moisture disappeared entirely, and the degrees of temperature were lost, or so modified that differences are expressed only as hot vs. very hot, and cold vs. very cold.

PEASANTS ARE MARGINAL PEOPLE

The peripheral, dependent position of peasants seems to produce the conditions responsible for their view of life, and the behavior that, because they hold this view, they consider appropriate. Peasants have not understood, and they do not understand, the rules of the game of living that prevail in cities, to which they are bound, and for this ignorance they are at the mercy of personal and impersonal urban controls. One is reminded of the protagonist in a Kafka novel: in spite of a just position, good intentions, and hard work, capricious forces prevail which he cannot understand, against which he is powerless, and which ultimately may spell his doom. Peasant and protagonist are buffeted about by powers and authorities whose purposes and meanings are incomprehensible and unpredictable, forever obscure and unknowable; both are lost souls, wandering in a maze whose meaning they cannot fathom.

Perhaps we can better grasp the peasant view of the city if we consider the ways in which human beings classify experience. Probably all people dichotomize their universes into the unknowable (and hence uncontrollable) and the knowable (and hence, at least potentially, controllable). To Western Man the division is between the natural and supernatural, the former capable of being known through the senses, and the latter to be known only through divine revelation. Man increasingly exercises control over the former; with respect to the latter, by the nature of things, he sees himself forever in a subordinate position. Some tribal peoples regard areas of Western Man's unknowable-uncontrollable as just as tangible, just as knowable, and just as subject to manipulation as is the material world around them. They beat drums to drive away the monster that threatens to devour the sun in an eclipse; they play flutes to aid the sun in rising each morning; with magical spells and incantations they actively intervene in the affairs of the invisible world, and they expect their powers to work to their welfare.

Peasants, on the other hand, can be thought of as classifying both the supernatural *and* the urban sides of life as equally unknowable and uncontrollable, places inhabited by beings with enormous powers for good and evil, whose motives and actions are exercised capriciously and unpredictably, against which man has no certain defenses. Magical spells or other positive acts of intervention are useless in the face of these conditions. Whether dealing with the saints or the city merchant or ruler, rural man must plead and supplicate, propitiate and fawn; if the heart of the power is moved to compassion, the peasant may achieve what he wishes. But the peasant will never know *why* the heart has been moved, or why compassion is forthcoming on one occasion and denied on the next. The knowable, by contrast, is limited to the tight little world which abuts the peasant and his village.

Lacking any real understanding of how their greater world works, and incapable of taking frontal action against the extra-village forces that control them, peasants have had to be content with local rules of the game of living — their cultures — which provide them with behavior norms which spell some defense in a world they see, quite rightly, as hostile and threatening. A peasant culture, like every other culture, is based on and validated by a value system, which may be thought of as representing common views and understandings shared by all members of the community on the way life is lived. Only a few of these views exist at a conscious level; the really significant ones are deeply buried. For values and world view, as I see them, consist of implicit premises about reality, of subconscious assumptions which are so taken for granted that they never intrude upon conscious thought. Yet all behavior is a function, a consequence, of this world view of which people are no more aware than they are of the grammatical rules of which their speech is a function.

TZINTZUNTZAN'S IMPLICIT ASSUMPTIONS

If, therefore, we wish to understand *why* people behave as they do, if we wish to probe into a society more deeply than by simply describing them, our task is to discover the implicit premises, the unquestioned postulates, which give rise to behavior. In Tzintzuntzan — and by extension other peasant communities — I believe a great deal of behavior can best be explained if it is viewed as a function of the assumption that almost all good things in life, material and otherwise, exist in limited and unexpandable quantities. If the most valued expressions of "good" such as wealth, friendship, love, masculinity, and power exist in finite, constant quantities, it logically follows that someone's improvement with respect to any of these forms can be only at the expense of others. This view — that individual improvement can come only at the cost of others — seems to me to be the key to understanding why Tzintzuntzeños behave as they do. It also explains why they often seem so conservative in their views, so timid in accepting the opportunities a changing world increasingly offers them.

The belief that someone's improvement in position is a threat to others leads to an equilibrium model of the healthy society. A person who acquires, or is believed to have acquired, more than his traditional share of good, must be pulled back to the level of all, lest the temporary imbalance in the distribution of good become permanent, and lead to serious consequences. And a person who falls behind with respect to his traditional share of good is also a threat to the community: his envy of others who have lost nothing may bring them misfortune. Traditional behavior in Tzintzuntzan is pointed toward maintaining an equilibrium with respect to good, a state of balance or a status quo in which people *must at least feel* they are neither threats to, nor threatened by, others. For, since a perfect equilibrium is obviously impossible, the *illusion* of equilibrium must gloss over inequalities that cannot otherwise be handled. This is why Tzintzuntzeños find it difficult to discuss wealth and other differences dealing with "good" except euphemistically. The mere utterance of words that imply such differences is unsettling. When, in my naïveté, I sometimes asked, "Who are the wealthiest men in town?" the answer was always the same: "There are no wealthy men; *here we are all equal!*" Or when I asked,

"Which men are the most *macho?*" (i.e., the toughest, most masculine), the answer was always: "Here there are no *machos*; we are all equal!" Just as North Americans believe a sound democracy (synonymous with a healthy society) must depend on a large middle class to which everyone belongs, or can reasonably aspire, and are made uncomfortable by the thought that some people belong to less privileged classes (and a few to more privileged classes), so are most Tzintzuntzeños made uncomfortable by the thought that any villager is other than "equal." *"Here we are all equal"* is the verbal assurance that all is well, that the traditional equilibrium that has spelled security still prevails.

The behavior of peasants which seems to reflect this view of the healthy society emphasizes secrecy and the concealment of possession, lest envious people be tempted into aggressive acts. And it encourages attacks upon those who seem, in any way, to stand out from the crowd. Hence, the ideal man attempts to maintain parity with others, but to avoid calling their attention to any real or suspected change for the better in his position, lest they invoke negative sanctions. Tzintzuntzeños are marked, to use Erich Fromm's term, by a "hoarding" personality type, in which secrecy, suspicion, and fear are the dominant characteristics.

At least in economic matters these implicit assumptions about the conditions of life, about the limitation of good, accurately reflect reality as it has existed in Tzintzuntzan during the last four centuries or so, and the forms of behavior engendered by this appraisal of circumstances have produced a viable community. But these assumptions less and less reflect reality in a changing world and in an industrializing nation. Consequently, the personality and behavioral characteristics of the "ideal man" of traditional Tzintzuntzan, inculcated in him by training and life experiences, ill fit him for participation in a world in which opportunities for and demands on the individual are far different from those experienced by his father. As the urban and industrial sectors of his country have progressed, the Tzintzuntzeño increasingly has found himself outside the mainstreams of Mexican life, looking enviously upon his more fortunate countrymen, but handicapped in his efforts to join them because his view of how the world works is badly outdated.

PEASANT BEHAVIOR INCREASINGLY OUTDATED

What is true of Tzintzuntzan seems true of peasant communities in other parts of the world. Today's planners, and particularly economists, often speak of the "irrational" behavior of traditional village peoples. In a strict sense they mean, of course, "irrational" because motivated by forces different from those which move "economic man." This is a justifiable use of the word. But the narrow economic sense frequently leads us to think that the behavior of people who do not partake of a rational, scientific tradition is illogical, with the implication of being "not very clever," and even perhaps implying a lower intelligence. This is an unjustified conclusion. Since the normative behavior of every group depends upon its particular world view, its assumptions about its several universes, all behavior must be rational and sense-making. Irrational behavior can be spoken of only in the context of a cognitive view which did not give rise to that behavior.

When the assumptions that underlie the behavior of a specific group are fairly accurate, in that they reflect the real conditions with which people must cope, we say that the society is well adjusted to its environment. It has the means to meet the basic threats to its life, and to bring a significant measure of satisfaction to its members. Thus, the world view which I believe has guided peasant behavior for thousands of years has, until recently, been rather accurate. And although I do not share a common view that traditional rural life is the repository of the basic morality, values, and virtues of a nation lost to its city dwellers, there is no doubt that the test of time has shown that peasant society worked well. Its members' (subconscious) comprehension of the rules of the game that prevailed were reasonably true, so that traditional behavior protected people, and brought them significant degrees of joy and happiness along with sorrow, suffering, and grief.

14

But in a rapidly modernizing world, the rules of the game of living change much more rapidly than does the cognitive view that guides behavior. So when peasant peoples are pulled into the social and economic contexts of whole nations, on an unprecedented scale, some of their traditional behavior seems illogical to others because the social, economic, and natural universes that increasingly set the conditions of their life are quite distinct from those revealed to them by their traditional view. That is, their cognitive orientation provides moral and other precepts that produce behavior inappropriate to the new conditions of life, which they do not yet grasp. For this reason, when the world view of many among a nation's people is out of tune with reality, these people will behave in a way that appears irrational to those who are more nearly attuned to reality. Such people will be seen as a drag (as indeed they may be) on a nation's development, and they will be cutting themselves off from the opportunity to participate in the benefits that economic and social progress can bring.

To return to Tzintzuntzan, much of today's behavior seems irrational when viewed against the conditions of life that now prevail in Mexico. The villagers are therefore seen as a "problem" by their government. Mexican agricultural production has doubled in recent years; that of Tzintzuntzan has remained static, and possibly even declined. Yet almost no use is made by farmers of fertilizers, insecticides, and hybrid seed which would greatly increase their production. This is "irrational," and to many outsiders, maddening behavior. Mexico has developed an impressive industrial economy since the end of World War II, but Tzintzuntzan potters have rejected all efforts to teach them more efficient and improved techniques of manufacture. Again, irrational and (to their teachers) maddening behavior. Medical and public health services are now available on a scale undreamed of even ten years ago, yet all too often scientific help is sought only when the resources of the local curer have failed. School enrollment has increased significantly, yet a quarter of school-age children are not registered, and many more attend classes in desultory fashion. The maws of two hundred pottery kilns denude

CHAPTER TWO

The
Historical
Roots

THE PHYSICAL SETTING

Lake Pátzcuaro, lying at an elevation of 6,700 feet, has the form of a crescent moon, its two tips pointing east to embrace Tariaqueri Hill, on the north slopes of which, at water's edge, lies Tzintzuntzan. The surrounding country is serrated with volcanic cones rising to 12,000 feet, produced by an ancient thermal activity that continues, though abated, to modern times. In 1759 Jorullo volcano appeared out of a field, on the south slopes of the mountains ringing Lake Pátzcuaro, and nearly two hundred years later, in 1943, Parícutin broke out with equal lack of warning, in the high sierra to the west of the lake.

The lake climate is temperate: mean monthly temperatures range from 54°F. in January, the coldest month, to 68°F. in May, the hottest month. The highest daytime temperatures approach 90°F. during the hot season, but nights are always pleasantly cool. Rarely, in cold years, the temperature has fallen briefly below freezing. Rainfall averages 40 inches annually, concentrated between mid-June and mid-October. The land was originally well wooded, but in recent years, as populations have increased, timberlines have risen higher and higher on mountainsides, and deforestation has become a critical problem. The same increasing human pressure on the land has also largely eliminated the formerly abundant game — deer, opossums, rabbits, pigeons, and quail.

Although only a little of the agricultural land around Lake Pátzcuaro is really fertile, and much is thin and stony, the temperate climate and favorable rainfall make possible good crops of maize, wheat, beans, squash, garden vegetables, and fruits. The lake produces an abundance of fish, and livestock thrive. The climate is also healthy for human beings. Formerly there was a good deal of malaria around the lake, but the World Health Organization and Government of Mexico campaign of the late 1950's has eliminated this disease. Otherwise there are no major health threats that cannot be met with good diet coupled with environmental sanitation and other preventive measures. With modern agricultural techniques to exploit fully the forests and fields, and with modern medical controls and services, a population of modest size could live very well indeed in the Lake Pátzcuaro basin. But as in most of the newly developing world, health services have outpaced agricultural services, and the result is an exploding population which threatens the very modest living enjoyed by people today. Without extensive emigration, coupled with a much reduced birth rate, the future for the Pátzcuaro area, including Tzintzuntzan, is not promising.

Tzintzuntzan, in climate, rainfall, natural resources, expanding population, and general appearance is much like the other lake villages. Its one-story adobe houses with red-tile roofs are arranged in a neat checkerboard plan marked by east-west and north-south cobbled streets. Village activities cluster about three foci: the enormous churchyard lined with four-hundred year old gnarled olive trees, flanked by an ancient Franciscan monastery, the parish church, a large chapel, and a recently restored "open

18

chapel" dating from colonial times; the Morelia-Pátzcuaro highway which, just outside the churchyard, is lined with stands where local pottery is sold to tourists, and where the village basketball court and municipal offices are located; and the plaza, farther north, with iron bandstand, ultra-modern health center, stores, and bus stop.

THE PEOPLE

The people of Tzintzuntzan, like all people, take it for granted that their way of life is the normal way. Through travel, and from strangers who come to the village, they know there are other modes of life, which have attractions they often intensely envy. But they find it difficult to put themselves in other people's shoes, and they evaluate, criticize, condemn, and approve behavior on the basis of the traditional norms unconsciously acquired in being born into the pueblo and growing up surrounded by its customs. They believe Michoacán is unusually blessed for its climate and beauty, and that they are among the luckiest people on earth for being *Cristianos,* and knowing God, Christ, and the Virgin Mary who, in return for their devotion and prayers, will protect them from harm.

In spite of the very low standard of living of most families, people find joy in a wide variety of phenomena and events. My friends have commented on the pleasure they derive from hearing birds sing, tending potted plants in their patios, seeing verdant cornfields ready for harvest, breathing the pure air of the country after a visit to Mexico City, making pots, catching fish, going to distant fiestas, walking behind their mules on long trading trips to the *tierra caliente.* They obviously enjoy each other's company at baptismal and wedding dinners, when friends and neighbors join to eat turkey *mole,* and to drink beer and tequila during a relaxed afternoon. They derive satisfaction from the meticulous fulfillment of the obligations they recognize — to friends, relatives, *compadres,* to the Virgin and the saints — and they enjoy equally seeing their expectations fulfilled as a consequence of this proper behavior.

Tzintzuntzeños also feel sorrow and pain, despair and hopelessness, hostility and anger, fear and apprehension. A child dies because of lack of money to take it to the doctor; a friend proves to be false; there is not enough to eat; neighbors gossip maliciously and criticize, appear to delight in misfortune, and fail to bring help when aid is needed. Fitting the situation, people laugh or they weep, they rage or they withdraw, they sense exhilaration, or they feel overwhelmed. Whatever the mood, it always seems to me Tzintzuntzeños feel with an intensity that bespeaks enormous reserves of vitality. No village event is too minor to be a subject of interest, no personal tragedy so great but that it contains elements of humor, no community catastrophe so final but that life will go on.

Yet behind this seemingly placid front, Tzintzuntzan, like other peasant villages, is a troubled community. The villager who looks about him cannot but be impressed with the enduring qualities of traditional values. Above him, to the east, on a long artificial platform, rise five stone pyramids on which stood temples with perpetual fires, the visible heart of Tarascan religious practices, to recall to him his indigenous American roots. Within the village he is reminded of his Spanish heritage: colonial monuments three to four hundred years old, clustered around a churchyard the size of three football fields. The twentieth-century villager worships the same God in the same building that his ancestors did in the sixteenth century, and until fairly recently his life has not been so very different from that of these distant forebears. Traditional ways and traditional reverences suggest security.

But today's villager knows the past is gone; at the same time he is unsure of the future. For a generation he has had a hard-surfaced road with buses to take him to market towns and distant cities, and potable water and electricity. His children have a full primary school (even though often they do not take advantage of it), and his wife has the services of a new health center, where a trained midwife will deliver her children. He owns a radio, and he has viewed television. Since 1964 he has even been able to telephone to points in the distant world. There is a 50 per cent chance that he has worked as a *bracero*, an indentured farm

20

laborer, in the United States. Yet in spite of these physical points of contact with the mid-twentieth century, the Tzintzuntzeño is not yet in the modern world. He is caught between the past and the present, unable and unwilling to turn back, but beset by doubts about the road before him. Before we consider in detail his contemporary situation, let us examine briefly the historical events that have brought his village to its present state.

TZINTZUNTZAN — ONCE A GREAT CITY

The Tzintzuntzan of today is a fairly typical Mexican peasant community. But it differs historically from most peasant villages in that it has not always been peasant. Until the early years of the sixteenth century it represented the urban end of the continuum of command and influence. It was a great city, the center of the vast Tarascan Indian Empire. Surrounding peasant villages, and towns hundreds of miles away, feared its power and puzzled about its capricious and arbitrary ways. Tarascan villagers and townsmen of that time hastened to pay their tribute, and they trembled lest the wrath of the Tzintzuntzeños descend on their heads for some cause which they could not possibly hope to understand. Tzintzuntzan's priests exercised religious hegemony over wide areas, setting the standards and orthodox forms of cult and ritual. Provincial and local caciques paid obeisance to these leaders, and demonstrated their faith and fealty by bringing wood to Tzintzuntzan to feed the perpetual fires that burned in the temples atop each of the five pyramids that overlooked the city. They, and commoners who came to the huge periodic markets, carried back with them the artifacts and ideas of a great urban center, to incorporate them as best they could into the simpler fabric of provincial life.

By the year 1500 the Tarascan Empire covered the modern state of Michoacán, and parts of adjacent states to the north and west. Although Tarascan civilization was less complex than that of the Aztecs and their predecessors, it nonetheless represented one of the major foci of pre-Columbian culture in Mexico. Militarily the Empire was so strong the Aztecs were never able to subjugate it. The bulk of the Indians lived in towns and villages where they grew the basic indigenous American crops of maize, beans, squash, and many fruits and vegetables. In the absence of domestic animals, other than the turkey and a native stingless bee, lake fish and wild game provided meat. Skilled craftsmen made superlative pottery, cotton cloth was woven, mats were made of tule reeds, and artisans worked gold, silver, copper, precious stones, lacquer, and feathers into ornaments and decorative objects. Local craft specialization and regional agricultural production were important enough to support major markets which Rea, impressed by brilliant night illumination, compared to the sight of a burning Troy (1882:112).

Tzintzuntzan, at the time of the Conquest, must have been an impressive sight. The first chroniclers estimated its population at about 40,000, scattered in numerous *barrios* around Lake Pátzcuaro. Its five pyramids — *yácatas* in Tarascan — each capped by a temple, overlooked the town proper with its palace buildings, quarters for the wives and concubines of the Emperor, dwellings of political officials and nobles, and homes and workshops of craftsmen and artists. In every way Tzintzuntzan was a great city, the cultural, political, and religious focus for a vast area with urban elements, on the one hand, and peasant communities, on the other. Its ways were canons of proper conduct, sought after and imitated by peripheral peoples as best they could. Its economy sound, its soldiers brave, its gods seemingly all-powerful, Tzintzuntzan's future as a great city appeared assured.

But the same seemingly capricious forces that the modern Tzintzuntzeño sees underlying all life willed otherwise. In the short space of eighteen years, beginning in 1522 when the last Emperor, Tangaxoan, surrendered voluntarily to the Spaniards, the Empire was destroyed. Its ruler was killed, the priests and nobles were stripped of their rank and influence, and the city itself was reduced in status to an Indian village. Other Mexican cities were made religious and administrative centers for the country, and trade and commerce flowed toward them. Rarely in history has a community changed its typology so rapidly, been shifted from one end to the other of the urban-rural continuum.

With its political, religious, and economic elite wiped out, little remained besides farmers, fishermen, and potters — the stuff of which peasant society is composed everywhere. The Tzintzuntzan of today thus represents more than four hundred years of existence at the end of the line that radiates from cities, commanded and controlled from the centers that replaced it, content with the crumbs of culture that have filtered down from these new foci of power and influence.

THE CONQUEST'S FIRST YEARS

The significant historical events since the Conquest that have formed the modern village can be summed up in a few pages. Initially the Spaniards assumed Tzintzuntzan would remain their administrative center, and accordingly it was given the title and rank of Ciudad de Michoacán. At the end of 1525 or the beginning of 1526 several Franciscan friars arrived, to build a church and monastery; members of this order remained to exercise religious control over the surrounding area until 1766, when a secular priest replaced them. By this time pagan religious forms had been almost entirely eliminated. There have been no "idols behind altars" in Tzintzuntzan for a long, long time.

Following the pillaging of Michoacán in 1530 by Nuño de Guzmán, the deposed and seemingly mad president of the first *audiencia** of New Spain, the lawyer Don Vasco de Quiroga was sent in 1533 to restore peace. Much influenced by Sir Thomas More's *Utopia*, he established in many pueblos a "hospital" which was, in fact, the center for a communal way of life, where Christian virtues were imparted, where new and improved arts and crafts were taught, and where the sick and aged were cared for. Although until recent years *el hospital* played an important role in the ceremonial life of Tzintzuntzan, we know very little about the extent to which real life conformed to the idealistic plans drawn up by Don Vasco.

We do know that the lands of each village, and its hospital,

* An administrative and judicial tribunal that formed a basic part of Spanish government in America.

23

were communally held. Households were to be composed of an extended family consisting of up to a dozen married couples, with the oldest male the patriarch. The plan was for boys to marry at fourteen, and girls at twelve years of age. Each household was allotted a garden, the produce of which belonged to the family, but field production became community property.

Each male was trained not only in farming, but also to follow a trade such as weaving, pottery, masonry, or blacksmithing. Work was to be rotated: adult males to spend two years working in the fields, and then to be replaced by others, while they came to the hospital to work as artisans. Everyone was supposed to eat in a communal dining room, where meals were prepared in turn by the women. All luxury was taboo. Clothing was white, adequate for the climate, but without ornamentation. A hospital proper was provided for the sick, and there was a school "for Christian and moral instruction." With the exception of the rector, a Spanish ecclesiastic, all the officials were Indians, elected by turn. The hospital, obviously, was an all-purpose community center in a rigidly directed society.

Don Vasco has become an almost mythological culture hero in the Tarascan area, and he popularly receives credit for introducing practically all Spanish colonial elements. He is said to have assigned to each of the villages the craft that is followed to this day: pottery in Tzintzuntzan and Sante Fe, woodcarving in Tócuaro, hat-making on the island of Jarácuaro, copper working in Santa Clara, and so on. There is certainly an element of exaggeration in these accounts for, as more than one Tzintzuntzeño has remarked to me, "There are so many potsherds of the type made by *los antiguos** that pottery must have been made here before Don Vasco came." Moreover, it is difficult to believe that, apart from religious and ceremonial life, the hospital functioned as originally planned. Certainly there are few places in the world where people have a stronger concept of private property, manifest in agricultural lands, homes and gardens, domestic animals and produce, than among the Tzintzuntzeños and all

* "The ancient ones," i.e., people living prior to the Spanish Conquest.

24

the villagers of the lake area. Nor do many places show less sense of village cooperation and community action for group welfare, and more sense of individualism in all behavior. This hardly sounds like the heritage of a successful and smoothly functioning communal way of life. Whatever the true nature of Don Vasco's hospitals, history is clear about his other activities. Following his ordination in 1538 he became the first bishop to come to Michoacán, taking up residence in Tzintzuntzan in 1539. Tzintzuntzan had been named See of the new bishopric of Michoacán by Pope Paul III in 1536. Shortly after his arrival the new bishop correctly recognized the restricted possibilities for a Spanish town: the site had a poor water supply, and it was cramped between hills and the lake. So the following year, 1540, he moved his bishopric ten miles south to Pátzcuaro, a hamlet of a dozen houses with the status of barrio of Tzintzuntzan, taking with him the bells destined for the cathedral that was never built, the organ, and even the royal title of City of Michoacán. It was a catastrophic blow from which Tzintzuntzan could never recover.

LATER DECLINE

After the loss of the bishopric the population must have dropped to a size that could be maintained from the limited surrounding agricultural lands, from fishing, and from the manufacture and sale of pottery. In 1639 Rea counted 200 family heads, which suggests a population of about 1,000. Mestization of the population began in the earliest years of Spanish contact, for when Don Vasco moved the bishopric to Pátzcuaro both Indians and Spaniards are reported as objecting to the action. Two centuries later Tzintzuntzan had 45 families of Spaniards, 52 of mestizos and mulattoes, and 150 of Indians (Villaseñor y Sánchez 1748, p. 16). The surrounding area likewise was undergoing mestization, and over the centuries Tarascan speech died out in the peripheral areas of what had been the Empire, and the hard core of native language and culture shrank until it centered on the shores and islands of Lake Pátzcuaro, the sierra immediately to the west, and the Cañada, a pleasant valley north of the sierra through which today runs the Mexico City–Guadalajara highway.

Tzintzuntzan, in microcosm, represents this regional erosion of Tarascan speech and culture. By about 1850 I estimate the non-Tarascan population (defined as monolingual Spanish speakers) equalled or exceeded the Tarascan population, and for the next hundred years the latter declined, reaching only 12 per cent in 1945. Thus, although Tzintzuntzan's nearest neighbors are Tarascan hamlets, and although it reflects elements of Tarascan culture lacking in purely mestizo communities, the village has been essentially Spanish and mestizo for at least four generations, and the non-Indian element has been important for much longer.

Under the rule of Porfirio Díaz in the latter quarter of the nineteenth century peace and order prevailed in rural Mexico, and a number of cultural improvements were introduced into the country. Even before Porfirio Díaz' first term, a school for boys was functioning in Tzintzuntzan, for the governor's report for 1869 mentions it. A few years later a girls' school was opened. The railroad reached Pátzcuaro from Morelia in 1886, and for many years thereafter a steam launch linking the lake villages to a dock near the new station provided Tzintzuntzan with its easiest egress to the outside world, an opportunity that appears to have attracted very little local interest.

THE RECENT YEARS

Nevertheless changes were taking place. On October 2, 1930, Tzintzuntzan was separated politically from Quiroga, five miles to the north, and with a number of Tarascan and mestizo villages and hamlets as dependencies was set up as a "Free and Independent" municipio. The first major cultural impact of modern times occurred shortly thereafter, in the spring of 1931. General Lázaro Cárdenas, then Governor of Michoacán, sent a Cultural Mission consisting of teachers specialized in plastic arts, social work, music, home economics, physical education, and "small industries," and a nurse-midwife and an agricultural engineer. Sixty rural school teachers were brought from surrounding villages to

26

receive training in drawing and painting, singing, soap making, food preserving, dress making, elementary hygiene, group games, and other simple techniques and activities that could be taught elementary school children.

In retrospect it is hard to tell whether the villagers or the team members were more surprised by what they encountered: both agree it was a remarkable clash of cultures. The mayor was charged with finding sleeping quarters for the eight members of the mission and for the sixty rural teachers, and with rooms for cooking and eating, and the teaching of crafts and activities. He did well, but couldn't quite meet the goal, so that a number of people slept on table tops and on school benches. The social worker was in charge of preparing meals, and each week she went to Pátzcuaro in the steam launch to bring supplies, for the demand far exceeded the ability of local resources to supply necessities.

Most villagers were reluctant to cooperate, to help find living quarters, and to aid staff members and rural teachers. They wondered, too, if the female teachers, who wore a bloomer uniform, were men or women. In spite of such difficulties, however, the Mission had a big effect. A number of the more progressive families agreed to whitewash their houses, to improve the appearance of the village, and the present plaza, then a barren wasteland with a few houses, was cleaned up, sidewalks were marked out, flowering jacaranda trees were planted, a fountain (for which for years the villagers had yearned) was built, even though it lacked water, and space was cleared for a bandstand. At the end of the first month there was an open house exposition of arts, crafts, sports, and civic betterments, to which General Cárdenas came as guest of honor. He professed to be so pleased that he asked the Mission to remain a second month, and promised a gasoline pump to draw water from the springs in Ojo de Agua, a Tarascan hamlet at the east end of town, so that water would play in the fountain. The engineer was placed in charge of this operation, and he designed clay pipes to be made and fired by the local potters. The pipes were laid, the pump was installed, and everyone gathered for the longed-for spectacle: Tzintzuntzan with its fountain, just like big cities. But the system was inadequate. Either the pipes burst, or the water seeped out through the thousands of rough joints, and not a trickle emerged in the fountain. This episode is still quoted to prove that technical specialists are not really to be trusted.

Nevertheless, and in retrospect, villagers believe that the Cultural Mission was the turning point in community life. Their curiosity had been aroused, and they were less fearful of outsiders. Changes now began to come more rapidly, above all as the consequence of General Cárdenas' personal interest; he was now president of Mexico (1934–1940), and he saw in Tzintzuntzan a symbol of the indigenous glory of pre-Conquest Michoacán, his native state. A master potter spent a year trying to teach people to use new colors and glazes, and to try the wheel. He was unsuccessful, but potters remembered him, and a generation later, spurred by new market demands, they began to search for tattered scraps of paper they still had on which were written the formulas he had given them.

Electricity was brought from Pátzcuaro in 1938 and running water — this time with iron pipes — was installed about the same time. To complement the fountain, which now had its water, an iron bandstand, handed down from the Plaza Carrillo in Morelia, was erected. All these moves were opposed by a sizable chunk of the population. Surveyors appeared, stakes were driven along the old Calle Nacional, and into the country north and south of the village, and men were asked if they would like to work in building a highway. Many suspected a communist plot, but a few bold souls accepted employment, and when others noted the good wages, there was a rush to obtain jobs. By 1938 the road was graded, and in 1939 it was paved. Tzintzuntzan was now an hour from the state capital, Morelia, instead of a very long day's walk or ride, and twenty minutes from Pátzcuaro, its chief market outlet, instead of a three-hour burro or foot trip. In 1939 the new and modern *Escuela Rural 2 de Octubre*, named to commemorate the date of Tzintzuntzan's independence, opened its doors, and for the first time village children had ready access to the full six years of primary schooling.

With the paved highway many tourists began to come, especially to see a large painting in the church, a Descent from the Cross, popularly but doubtless erroneously attributed to Titian. When the church was destroyed by fire during Holy Week in 1944 it was said that American tourists, aided by three villagers, had come at night, stolen the painting, and then set fire to the building to make it look like an accident. All the villagers are convinced that the painting is now on display in a great museum in New York City. This does not make them especially hostile to Americans (although I see that it made our entrance into the village late in 1944 more than ordinarily difficult). They simply look upon the event as the way people behave: their three fellow villagers, whose names are no secret, and who still live, saw a chance to make a bit of money, and quite naturally, rich and powerful people from cities — in the United States or Mexico — are going to want treasures for their museums.

World War II hastened change. Although two men had gone to the United States as early as 1910, lived there a number of years, and survived to return, and another larger group had gone about 1922, some of whose members remained and were lost track of, it was not until war demands for field hands brought into being the bracero program that large numbers of field hands began to travel widely. The first to go were apprehensive; the rumor-mongers said they were to be thrown into front-line trenches, cannon fodder to save American lives. When it was realized that this was not happening, and when men returned with what to them were enormous sums of money, a rush began that grew until the program was terminated, at great social and economic cost to the village, at the end of 1964. By 1960 two hundred men — almost 50 per cent of the adult males — had visited the United States at least once, and a number had returned year after year.

This exposure, more than any other event, seems to me to have changed the village. It is a mistake to assume that the attitudes and views of every bracero are vastly modified by his American experience. Many return and take up their old ways with no apparent change whatsoever. But new attitudes and ideas are there. It was a bracero, and not a stay-at-home, who once astonished me by asking, "Doctor, what can we do to bring industry to Tzintzuntzan?" He had noticed the same thing another bracero had observed: "In the United States, even in little towns, like this, I saw tall smokestacks, and at the bottom of the smokestacks, lots of people were working. Here our villages have no smokestacks."

In other ways bracero influence is also significant. Only by working in *El norte* can most people expect to accumulate enough capital to break out of their economic bonds. Most of the new and greatly improved houses, which make the village more attractive, and a healthier place in which to live, are the result of bracero savings. And all except one of the village's several trucks came from bracero wages. American clothing for men and women, brought back initially by braceros, has revolutionized costume in twenty years. The old white trousers (*calzones*) for men are nearly gone, and the heavy Tarascan wool skirt (*telar*) with numerous petticoats and blouse, still widely used in 1945, has passed into oblivion.

The most recent major outside cultural influence on Tzintzuntzan began in 1953, when CREFAL selected the village as one of its pilot communities. The major projects were a pottery cooperative, to simplify a number of the arduous tasks of this profession, and to introduce improved techniques such as the wheel, templates, oil-fired kilns, and new glazes; a weaving cooperative and workshop, to teach young men to make textiles; a carpentry cooperative, for manufacturing furniture; an embroidery cooperative, to give a source of income to unmarried girls; and a chicken raising and egg program, to bolster family incomes. The results of this program have been variable, in general less successful than had been hoped for. CREFAL personnel consider their Tzintzuntzan program to have been a failure, which it was in a narrow sense, and Tzintzuntzeños are critical of the work that was attempted. At the same time, the continuing contact of villagers with the modern influences of a major training center, and with a great number of intelligent and interested people with varying backgrounds and personalities, cannot help but promote changes in outlooks and desires. New ideas are like freshly planted seeds: they need time to germinate. And, just as the full influence of the original Cultural Mission was not apparent for many years, so will it take time to measure the influence of CREFAL.

CHAPTER THREE

Tzintzuntzan
and Its People

VILLAGE DIVISIONS

Before describing the behavior of people, and attempting to con-struct a model to account for this behavior (Chapters Five and Six), it will be helpful to tell something about the population and composition of the village, the forms families take, how people earn a living, and the levels of living that are possible from Tzintzuntzan's very primitive productive techniques. The first thing that strikes a visitor to the village is that it is laid out according to the common Spanish chessboard plan, with five major streets running north and south, and four that cross them at right angles from east to west (see Frontispiece map). At the time of the Conquest, and for some years thereafter, Tzintzun-tzan was divided into twelve *barrios*, roughly translated into English as "ward," a division of a community which in post-Conquest Mexico usually has its own church or chapel.

The number of barrios was gradually reduced during colonial times, and a few survived into the early years of the present century, when they still had important ceremonial roles which will be mentioned when we describe religious activities. Wards are now gone, their place taken by four *cuarteles* which, however, mean so little to people that most cannot even tell in which they reside. Rather, informal appelations known to everyone describe the several sections of the village.

El Rincón ("The Corner") is a cluster of a score of houses at the extreme west edge of town, separated by open fields from the other sections. Although the distance is slight, it is enough to influence greatly standards of living, for the water pipes and electric lines which lace the rest of the village have not been extended this far. Rincón inhabitants therefore must continue the dreary process of hauling water in jars, and illuminating night activities with feeble kerosene lamps or candles.

El Centro is the imprecisely bounded central section of town that includes half or more of the houses. Within the Center, *La Plaza*, *La Alameda*, and *La Carretera* ("The Highway") may be named to indicate more precisely the site of a house. *Pueblo Nuevo* ("New Town") is a tightly packed group of small and poor houses just north of the church, all inhabited by potters. This was formerly church property, but sixty years ago the priest opened it to landless potters so that they might have their own dwellings. East of the highway, largely confined to both sides of Calle Victoria, is *Yaguaro*, another neighborhood of potters and other poor people.

Beyond Yaguaro lies *El Ojo de Agua* (The Spring; literally, "The Eye of Water"), a separate community of 170 Tarascan Indians, named after the spring which is the source of Tzintzuntzan's potable water system. Although El Ojo physically adjoins Yaguaro, and it is impossible to tell by looking where the boundary lies, it is considered to be a discrete settlement in Church and government records, and both Indians and Tzintzuntzeños fully recognize the separation. Moreover, it has its own chapel, that of the Virgin of Guadalupe, a feature that marks none of the separate sections of Tzintzuntzan proper.

33

In addition to El Ojo de Agua, Tarascan settlements come close to the west edge of town, just beyond El Rincón. First comes *Ichupio*, then *Tarerio*, next *El Espíritu*, and finally *Ucasanástacua*. Collectively known as *La Vuelta*, with a total population of about seven hundred, the farthest is little more than an hour's walk along the lake shore. Thus, all the settlements close to Tzintzuntzan are Tarascan in speech and culture. This, as will be seen shortly, not only has important effects on the population composition of Tzintzuntzan itself, but is reflected in other aspects of life as well. The relationship is reciprocal, and Tzintzuntzan is important in the lives of these hamlets.

THE TARASCAN INDIAN ELEMENT

Although each hamlet of La Vuelta has its own chapel, there are no resident priests, so the Indians must come to Tzintzuntzan for Mass, and for baptisms, marriages, and burials. Tzintzuntzan is also the only local center with stores, and it is the most convenient place at which to catch buses for Pátzcuaro and Morelia. As a consequence Tzintzuntzan, to the casual visitor, looks much more Indian than it actually is, for Tarascans nearly always can be found in the churchyard, in the plaza waiting for buses, and in stores making their purchases. At Sunday Masses, Indians are always conspicuous by their numbers, distinguished by a style of dress which has been abandoned in Tzintzuntzan itself.

This continual but temporary presence of Tarascans in Tzintzuntzan is one reason the village is often described in guide books and Mexican Government publications as an Indian pueblo. Another reason is doubtless the obvious strong Amerindian biological admixture in most Tzintzuntzan mestizos. Moreover, until a generation ago Tzintzuntzeños, and particularly the women, wore Indian costume. But still another reason helps account for the misconception that Tzintzuntzan is Indian. Since the village was once the capital of an important Indian empire, one which in the minds of Mexicans has a romantic connotation comparable to that of the Noble Redskin of North Americans, it is an important indigenous symbol of modern Mexican nationalism which glorifies the Indian roots of the country. Hence, many

34

Mexicans seem anxious to maintain the fiction that Tzintzuntzan, with its ancient pyramids, and its fine colonial monastery and churches, is still an Indian community. Tzintzuntzan is not, and has not been for generations, an Indian village. On February 17, 1960, it had a population of 1,877, the age-sex distribution of which is shown on page 36. Of these, only 213, or 11.4 per cent of the population, were able to speak Tarascan, as compared to 12.6 per cent in 1945. At first glance these figures suggest that Tarascan families are reproducing themselves at almost the same rate as Spanish-speaking families. This is not so. Examination of places of birth of Tarascan speakers shows that only 87 were born in town. The other 126, or 60 per cent, immigrated from the Tarascan communities, including 66 from Ichupio alone.

In 1945 Tzintzuntzan was also maintaining its Indian component through immigration, although the tendency was less marked, since only 42 per cent of Tarascan speakers had been born outside the community. Thus, the village holds a small Indian element not through natural reproduction, but because of immigrants who replace, almost at a constant speed, those who are abandoning their maternal tongue. For Tzintzuntzan, surprising as it may seem, represents opportunity that is lacking in the nearby lake shore settlements: stores, school, proximity to the church, and the convenience of electric lights and running water. Were it not for this steady immigration, Tzintzuntzan would some years ago have ceased to have Tarascan speakers.

The pattern of loss of Tarascan speech is simple: marriage customs and prestige values put pressure on Indians to abandon their tongue. The Indians know that using the Tarascan language marks them (in the eyes of the lake region mestizos) as social inferiors, so many bilinguals try to conceal the fact that they are fully competent in Tarascan as well as Spanish. Marriage patterns are even more important in destroying the language. For whenever one spouse is Tarascan and the other Spanish-speaking (true in 46 families, as against only 39 in which both spouses are Tarascan), the language of children invariably is Spanish. Thus, whenever a Tarascan marries a non-Tarascan (true of nearly 60

35

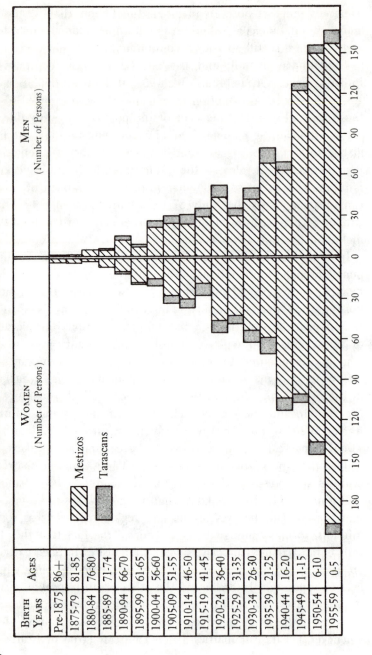

AGE-SEX POPULATION DISTRIBUTION IN TZINTZUNTZAN, 1960

WOMEN
(Number of Persons)

MEN
(Number of Persons)

Mestizos

Tarascans

BIRTH YEARS	AGES
Pre-1875	86+
1875-79	81-85
1880-84	76-80
1885-89	71-74
1890-94	66-70
1895-99	61-65
1900-04	56-60
1905-09	51-55
1910-14	46-50
1915-19	41-45
1920-24	36-40
1925-29	31-35
1930-34	26-30
1935-39	21-25
1940-44	16-20
1945-49	11-15
1950-54	6-10
1955-59	0-5

per cent of marriages involving Tarascans), he ceases to be a progenitor of his native tongue.

But even having both parents speak Tarascan is no guarantee that children will continue to speak the language. Of the 32 Tarascan couples with children living with them at the time of the census, in 14 the children spoke only Spanish, and in three more the older children spoke Tarascan but the younger children spoke only Spanish. In other words, whatever the parentage of a child born in Tzintzuntzan, the odds are he will reach adulthood speaking only Spanish. Moreover, in those homes in which Tarascan couples have recently moved from the hamlets with very small children, as the children grow older, associate with Spanish-speaking children, attend school (where of course all instruction is in Spanish), and become aware of the social values attached to the Spanish language, many of them will cease to speak their childhood tongue.

This is the process of losing a language. In 1948, impressed by the erosion of Tarascan speech, I wrote that within a few years the language would be dead in Tzintzuntzan. But the steady immigration had not entered my calculations, and it now looks as if the attractions of Tzintzuntzan will continue to draw Tarascan speakers from nearby lake shore villages, and that their proportion may hover around 10 per cent for a long time to come.

OCCUPATIONS

Whether Tarascan or mestizo, the average villager has a precarious existence. For Tzintzuntzan is a poor community, and its resources and productive techniques are inadequate to provide a level of living that its inhabitants increasingly will demand. Land, particularly, is in short supply. Except for limited lake shore *milpas** of rich alluvial earth, fields are stony and steep, and soils are thin. A 1960 agrarian census lists only ten men and two women with more than five hectares of agricultural land, and the largest holding is only fourteen acres. This is significant when compared to similar figures for other landowners in the munici-

* *Milpa:* a field for maize, beans, and squash; by extension, and loosely, an agricultural field.

37

pio, a good many of whom own twenty to fifty hectares. In addition to Tzintzuntzan's twelve "large" landowners, an additional fifty to sixty people own less than five hectares. An additional dozen hold *ejido** memberships, but because of the distance of the lands — about five miles — most exercise their rights through sharecropping arrangements with farmers from nearer villages.

The table opposite shows how the occupations of the 376 family heads in Tzintzuntzan are distributed.

The table reveals a number of important points about economic life in Tzintzuntzan. A total of 206, or 55 per cent of the families earn all or a major part of their income from making pottery. But pottery accounts for even more income, for in addition to these primary producers nine farmers work a bit of pottery in the off season, seven rescatón traders deal primarily in transporting pottery, and 15 pottery stands are on the highway (of which only five appear as primary occupations, and the remainder as secondary, or unlisted since run by non-family heads), for a total of 33 additional pottery sources of income, so that nearly 65 per cent of Tzintzuntzan families benefit directly from pottery.

By contrast, and because of limited agricultural lands, only 49 family heads, or 13 per cent, earn all or a major part of their income from farming. Adding the 35 whose primary income is from pottery, and the seven whose primary income is from fishing, the number rises to 91, or 24 per cent of Tzintzuntzan families that receive some income from agriculture.

Fishing — almost entirely in the hands of Tarascans — is even less important. Only 24 men list this as their primary occupation and of these only five list themselves as full-time workers. The others combine fishing with other occupations, for a total of 6 per cent of village families. Counting two more men who are primarily potters, and five who are primarily farmers, the total

* Ejido lands are communally held by groups of villagers organized into Agrarian Communities. Members enjoy the use of specific fields for life, may pass them on to their heirs, and may rent and sharecrop them. But they cannot legally sell them.

38

Occupations of Family Heads in Tzintzuntzan

Occupation	Numbers	Occupation	Numbers
Potters		*Carpenters*	
Full time, males	84	Full time	2
Full time, females	17	Carpenter & day laborer	3
Potter & day laborer	52	Carpenter & mason	1
Potter & farmer	36	Carpenter & barber	1
Potter & fisherman	2	Carpenter & pottery retailer	1
Potter & *petate* (reed mat)		Total	8
maker	1		
Potter & pottery wholesaler	1	*Masons*	
Potter & pottery retailer	1	Full time	2
Potter & barber	1	Mason & day laborer	1
Potter & public employee	1	Total	3
Potter & store owner	1		
Potter & carpenter	1	*Public employees*	
Potter & mason	8	Full time	12
Total	206	Employee & weaver	1
		Total	13
Farmers			
Full time	25	*Pottery wholesalers*	
Farmer & day laborer	6	(*rescatones*)	7
Farmer & potter	9		
Farmer & fisherman	5	*Pottery retailers*	
Farmer & petate maker	2	(highway stands)	5
Farmer & pottery wholesaler	1		
Farmer & pottery retailer	1	*Store owners*	5
Total	49	*Petate makers*	3
Day Laborers			
Full time	26	*Butchers*	2
Day laborer & pottery			
wholesaler	2	*Priests*	2
Day laborer & petate maker	4		
Total	32	*Baker*	1
Fishermen		*Fruit stand owner*	1
Full time	5		
Fisherman & farmer	7	*Midwife*	1
Fisherman & day laborer	9		
Fisherman & pottery		*Mechanic*	1
wholesaler	1		
Fisherman & petate maker	1	*Housewives, no other*	
Fisherman & net weaver	1	*occupation*	13
Total	24	Grand total	376

39

is only 31, or 8 per cent of the families with income from fishing. A *jornalero* is an individual paid a daily wage for his work, which may take many forms: helping large farmers, helping the owners of fishing canoes, aiding a mason or a carpenter, or working on the highway, to name the most common tasks. This term, therefore, means little when applied to primary occupations. The table does show, however, that 32 families, or 9 per cent, are almost entirely dependent on wage labor, and that an additional 71 family heads sometimes work as day laborers. Many in the latter category are braceros who, while in the United States, work for hourly wages.

The remaining occupations are numerically less important. The category "Public Employees" includes school teachers, and municipal officers such as the mayor, the town secretary, the judge's secretary, the treasurer, and so forth. Except for teachers they sometimes have other occupations. Not counting the 13 housewives without other occupational listing, we find that 162 family heads (45 per cent of the total) have multiple occupations and 201 (55 per cent of the total) have single occupations. In fact, the table does not fully show the extent to which occupations are multiple. One storekeeper is also a baker, rescatón traders may do a bit of retail marketing, and masons and carpenters put their hands to almost any task.

If occupation is examined from the standpoint of household units rather than family heads, the doubling up of sources of income is even more striking. Several men's wives have pottery stands on the highway, a few girls work as maids in Mexico City for weeks or months at a stretch, and a number of potters augment their income by selling firewood.

The primary productive techniques of Tzintzuntzan are simple, and even today, in the face of a remarkable economic growth in Mexico, they are changing little. Basically the methods were set after the Spanish Conquest, when a series of technological improvements and new crops and animals were introduced. The most important new techniques, which significantly improved indigenous production, were the primitive Mediterranean wooden plow drawn by oxen, threshing with the hoofs of horses, large fish seines, pottery glaze, and the simple round kiln that permits temperatures high enough to fuse the glaze, and wool weaving on the flat-bed loom. The most valuable animals and crops introduced were cattle, horses, burros, mules, sheep, goats, hogs, chickens, wheat, garden vegetables such as cabbage, carrots, onions, and garlic, and fruit trees, principally the apple, pear, and peach.

POTTERY MAKING

Potters bring clays from several different beds on mule or burro back, pulverize them, mix a "red" and a "white" variety in approximately equal amounts, add water, knead, and thus produce damp balls of material ready for working. Sand or other gritty tempers are not used. All pots are made with one or the other of two basic molding techniques. Plates, pot lids, cups, bowls, and casseroles are formed from a single pancake of paste spread over a convex mold with a handle that gives it a mushroom appearance. This is a widespread central Mexican technique, used in pre-Conquest times, although it appears that the handle on the mold was not added until after the Spaniards arrived; in other villages large molds of this type even today lack the handle. Pots and water jars are formed with a pair of concave molds into which paste pancakes are pressed, after which the edges are trimmed smooth. Then the two halves are joined and the juncture is smoothed from within until the mark of the joint is obliterated.

Regardless of method of forming, after drying vessels are removed from their molds and smoothed, first with a volcanic stone and water, and then with a wet cloth. Two firings are necessary. The adobe kiln is a primitive Spanish type, circular, with a subterranean firebox, a stone grate at ground level, and a chamber for pots above the ground. Most are from three to five feet in diameter, rising two to three feet above the ground. Pots are arranged carefully in the upper chamber, larger vessels holding smaller ones. When filled, the kiln is covered with potsherds to hold in the heat during the firing. Firing usually is begun in the early evening, the potter building the heat gradually, as moisture is expressed from the green ware. Maximum temperature, reached after about three hours, is maintained for another hour, after which the firebrands are scraped from the firebox and the kiln cools during the night. The intensity of heat is judged by the brilliance of the flames seen under the potsherd covering; for this reason the night-time firing is preferred.

The following day the fired vessels are glazed. The natural litharge, purchased in stores and said to come from Monterrey, formerly was ground on a hard metate into a very fine talc-like powder. Today the glaze is purchased ready ground. Since glaze fuses indiscriminately to the pot to which it has been applied, or to an adjacent pot, loading the kiln for the second firing is the most difficult operation in the entire process. Large pots go at the bottom, close to but not touching each other. Middle-sized pots rest on them, separated by tiny potsherds which permit separation after firing. And the smallest pieces go inside large pots, again carefully balanced and separated by bits of sherds. The second firing requires higher temperatures than the first, to about 900°C., but otherwise the technique is the same.

Tzintzuntzan potters make a very wide variety of wares; I know of no other Mexican village that produces more. The bulk of production is utilitarian ware in four basic types: *ollas* (wide-mouthed pots for cooking or grain storage); *cántaros* (narrow-mouthed globular water jars); *cazuelas* (casseroles); and *comales* (tortilla griddles). Each set is made in a series of fourteen named sizes. Much more elaborate artistic ware is also made today in increasing quantities and styles to meet domestic and foreign tourist demands. For many years Doña Andrea Medina and her children, especially Natividad Peña, have made *loza blanca*, a white-glazed ware with designs of animals, birds, fishing scenes, and people, which has brought considerable fame to Tzintzuntzan. Also traditional is a red-slipped burnished ware with painted ornamentation known as *tinaja*, since it is used to hold water. Although this ware corresponds to no archaeological pieces, the technique is certainly pre-Conquest. With competition for the tourist trade, new forms and glazes are appearing. Bernardo Zaldívar has developed a handsome near-black glaze on which he paints designs in white. Faustino Peña has learned to make a good green glaze, and a number of potters, following the lead of Teófilo Zaldívar, are now utilizing an oxygen-reducing-smudging process to turn the burnished red-slipped ware black, giving a surface similar to the famous black pottery of Coyotepec, near Oaxaca City.

AGRICULTURE

The principal field crops are maize, beans, and squash — the pre-Conquest trio — and wheat. In recent years steel plows have become common for parts of the agricultural process, but no farmer is without his *arado de palo*, a wooden instrument with an iron share of a design that goes back to ancient Egypt. This is a more sophisticated instrument than it seems at first glance, for by means of wedges and replaceable "ears" the depths to which it plows, and the width of the furrow it cuts, may be considerably varied. Whether a farmer uses a steel or wooden plow, he draws it with oxen; mules are unknown in this capacity and so, too, for all intents and purposes, is the tractor. For maize a farmer plows his field back and forth, and then crosses it at right angles, for the wooden plow, lacking a moldboard, does not turn up the soil. Crossing is essential to break up clods. Then the field is plowed in furrows one *vara* (ca. 32 inches) apart in the original direction, the spacing being determined by the width of the wooden yoke, so that with one ox walking in the most recent furrow the next furrow automatically forms at a constant distance. Finally, and to sow, the field is again crossed, which gives a series of squares each 32 inches across.

In the ideal sowing operation a farmer is assisted by a friend — perhaps a compadre with whom he exchanges labor — who brings his own ox team. As the farmer cross plows, forming the squares, a boy with a bowl of seed follows, dropping three maize grains at each point where furrows intersect. A second boy carrying beans follows, dropping one at each point and, where squash is included, a third boy does likewise with squash seeds. The second ox team and plow cover the furrow and seeds. Sowing begins with the first rains, in June. During the summer there are three major cultivations, and a bit of incidental hand weeding may follow as well. Roasting ears are ready by the end of September, but harvesting does not take place until December except if, in the rich lake shore milpas, wheat is to be planted, in which event the maize is cut a bit moist to permit the new plowing. Beans are harvested with maize, and threshed as needed from the end of November until Christmas by being beaten with poles until the kernels fall to mats placed beneath the plants.

Winter wheat usually is planted in fields that have lain fallow since the preceding December's maize harvest. The single plowing is done beginning in mid-August, and by mid-September fields are ready for broadcast sowing, immediately after which the farmer plows the field again so the seeds are mixed with earth and thus largely protected from birds. No subsequent cultivation or care is required. Wheat is harvested with a serrated steel hand sickle in April and May, the stalks tied in small bundles, and carried to the farmer's house to be stored until threshing. Although in recent years a few farmers have paid for machine threshing, most men still erect a temporary threshing floor by roping off a circular area in the street in front of their houses, piling wheat to a depth of a foot or so, and running horses around and around (reversing directions periodically) until near the end of the day the chaff can be separated by throwing grain and straw into the evening breeze with a wooden paddle.

Garden crops are planted in large patios and in lake shore milpas, but most people purchase a majority of the vegetables they consume, except for *chayotes,** which are found in most yards of any size. Except for a very little irrigation, accomplished with a primitive Spanish scoop, drawing water from canals cut in from the lake, farmers are dependent on rainfall for maturing of crops. Although summer rains are usually good, Tzintzuntzan farmers are subject to the same harrowing vagaries of weather as are farmers in other parts of the world.

* *Chayote:* A Cucurbitaceae, *Sechium edule,* sometimes called "vegetable pear" in English.

44

Almost all fishermen are Tarascan Indians. The principal net is the *chinchorro*, a large seine up to 500 feet in length of a type introduced from Spain after the Conquest. Since the lake shore is muddy and tule grown, the net is cast from a small one-man dugout canoe, and pulled into a long, boxlike wooden canoe, also cut from a single huge log, anchored in the mud by means of a pole driven into the shallow lake bottom. The principal catch is Lake Pátzcuaro's famous indigenous white *pescado blanco*, a fresh water smelt of the genus *Chirostoma*; the bony but delicately flavored *akúmara* (*Algansea lacustria*); and the North American large-mouth black bass, locally called *trucha*, or trout, introduced in the early 1920's. Small fish are taken in gill nets and in the *cuchara* ("spoon"), an outsized dip net called *mariposa* ("butterfly") in tourist literature which, because of its graceful appearance with two spreading wings has practically become the trademark of the Pátzcuaro region. Since huge dip nets are not indigenous to the New World, and since they are common in southern Spain, it seems likely that this net, like the seine, is an introduction. The gill net, on the other hand, may very well be indigenous.

Lake Pátzcuaro is famous among anthropologists because it is one of the very few places in the world where the spear thrower, primitive man's pre-bow and arrow hunting weapon, still survives. This two-foot stick with groove down the top is grasped in the right hand, supporting a 10-foot cane spear tipped with a barbed iron trident. When thrown by a skillful hunter it kills ducks at ranges up to 100 feet. Only rarely, and by accident, however, does it bring down a flying bird. A great communal duck hunt is held each year on October 31, after migratory birds reach the lake from the north, with hunters from all lake shore villages.

TULE REED WEAVING

The weaving of tule and straw figures has come to be a major industry not only in Tzintzuntzan but even more so in nearly all the Tarascan lake villages. The art is modern in this area. In 1945

Gabriel Ospina found that Don Plácido Pablo, a Tarascan Indian living in Tzintzuntzan, could weave ornamental petates as well as the utilitarian floor coverings. Don Plácido was hired by us to weave special petates, and the human and animal figures he also knew how to make, for the little museum that was being fitted out at the yácatas. Orders were placed by visitors who came to see us, and presently Don Plácido was working full time at this occupation. Others began to imitate him, and with the mushrooming of the tourist trade and the demand for popular arts all over Mexico, this product has come to be a major source of income for scores of lake dwellers. Although most of the work is done by Tarascans, who control almost all the tule beds, a few mestizos have become competent weavers.

LEVELS OF LIVING

Such are the principal productive processes by which villagers earn a living. In addition, many families keep a few pigs and chickens, some of which are sold when cash is needed, and a number of families have a head or two of livestock wandering in the hills, "banked" for an emergency such as serious illness, when they can be sold to pay bills. Animals, particularly large animals, are potentially a good investment, since they increase in quantity and value through reproduction. They are, in modern parlance, a growth-type investment, but like other growth investments, they carry greater than average risks. Pigs sicken and die, although less so than formerly, now that people are beginning to vaccinate against cholera. Cattle also die, and those which roam freely on communal lands are subject to theft as well. In spite of registered brands, for which each owner pays a rather high fee, rustling is not uncommon. Free-roaming cattle also cause a good many disputes: they break into a neighbor's field and damage his crop, he takes them home, the owner then must pay him to release them, and hard feelings are inevitable. Nevertheless cattle, and to a lesser extent pigs, are the economic and psychological equivalent to a city dweller's savings account. They form the biggest source of ready cash a family has to draw upon in time of need.

46

A number of families have plots of land too small to be farmed economically alone, and widows and other single women are also owners. Such lands are sharecropped, usually on an *a medias* or halves basis, by farmers who have the equipment — particularly the all-important team of oxen — to farm more land than they own. The owner furnishes land and seed, and the sharecropper does the plowing, planting, and cultivating. Both owner and sharecropper share harvest costs, and the crop is split evenly.

A living, it is clear, is earned by nearly everyone in bits and pieces. Every family member is alert to the possibility of picking up a few extra pesos here or there, and rare is a person who, in addition to his primary occupation, does not try his hand at other tasks.

The only thing all occupations have in common is that they scarcely produce enough for a family to live on. Unfortunately, since most people are self-employed, it is difficult to estimate levels of income, but enough data are at hand to show the very narrow economic margin that characterizes the lives of most villagers. A laborer earns from $5 to $8 for a full day, plus a noon meal if he is helping a farmer in his fields.* Craftsmen such as masons and carpenters earn from $15 to $20 daily. Public employees — the mayor, secretary, judge's secretary, and policeman — earn $4 to $6 daily, and they may legally keep a part of some of the fees for services, such as performing marriage acts. School teachers are much the best paid of public servants. In 1965 the principal received $1,615 monthly, and the other teachers, depending on rank and years of service, from $740 to $1,008. Income of potter families depends on intensity of work and numbers of workers. From $50 to $100 weekly is the usual range, with the minimum figure nearer to the average.

A petate maker can weave two large mats in a day, which sell for $7.50. If he buys reeds, at $2 a bundle, income is cut to $5.50. Farmers' incomes are impossible to calculate, but even the largest landowners live modestly, and many supplement their incomes with small stores, *nixtamal* (see pages 51–52) mills run by

* All monies are expressed in Mexican pesos, unless otherwise indicated, and are written with the dollar sign. See Preface for exchange figures.

their wives, or by other secondary occupations. Storekeepers, too, judging by the level of living of local owners, for the most part have small incomes. During recent years several owners of highway pottery stands have made profits which, by traditional standards, are breathtaking. So unusual is this progress that villagers refuse to believe that it is the consequence of shrewd merchandising. Apart from these, only some of those men who have gone to the United States as braceros have significantly raised their standards of living.

Productive processes and income can be translated into levels of living by considering them in relation to the prices of commodities commonly purchased by villagers, and by noting the kinds of housing and furnishings possessed by families. As the following prices show, a family with several children will be hard put to to balance a budget of $50 to $100 a week, let alone accumulate capital goods.

Beef and pork, kilo	$10.00
Beans, liter (depending on season)	1.50 – 2.50
Maize, liter (depending on season)	.45 – .75
Chickens, each	10.00 –20.00
Black bass, kilo	5.00 – 6.00
Milk, liter	1.00
Cotton shirt	13.00 –20.00
Cotton trousers	10.00 –30.00
Man's hat	20.00 –40.00
Cotton dress	45.00
Rebozo	35.00–150.00
Huarache sandals	20.00
Man's shoes	70.00
Woman's shoes	25.00

QUALITY OF HOUSING

Houses in Tzintzuntzan vary greatly in size, comfort, hygiene, and convenience. The poorest are one-room hovels with dirt floors, lacking light, water, ventilation other than the door, sanitary facilities, beds, and other conveniences. A few of the best houses at the other end of the scale offer comforts not usually associated with peasant life: several rooms, glass windows, tile floors, electric lights, shower baths, latrines, running water (actually a single tap in the patio), kerosene or gas stoves, innerspring mattresses, and even an occasional television set. Most houses fall between these extremes. The frequency of occurrence of some of the characteristics that make for comfort and hygiene in living, as reported on the 1960 project census, is as follows:

Trait	Percentage of Houses
One room	22
Two rooms	45
Three or more rooms	33
Raised cooking hearth (includes stoves)	74
Raised bed	64
Electricity	50
Water tap in patio	48
Latrine	42
Radio	38
Tile or cement floors	34
Electric iron	30
Watch or clock	22
Sewing machine	20
Glass windows	4

In an attempt to classify homes on the basis of comfort, convenience, and sanitation, a twenty-point scale was devised which allotted two points each for electricity, water, a latrine, a raised hearth, a hard floor, and a raised bed, however primitive; an additional point was allotted for a kerosene or gas stove, a glass window, a radio, a sewing machine, an electric iron, a watch or clock, a store-bought mattress, and whitewashed exterior walls. Fifteen per cent of the houses rated 16–20 points; 22 per cent fell in the 11–15 point category; 27 per cent fell in each of the 6–10 and 1–5 point categories; and 9 per cent fell in the zero category, representing homes with no improvements whatsoever.

These differences can be stated in another way. An "average" house has two rooms with a porch facing an enclosed patio separated from neighboring yards by a high adobe wall. The rear wall of the house backs up to the street, and is pierced by a double door large enough, when its two leaves are open, to permit passage of loaded pack animals and oxen. One or two windows, with solid wooden shutters, open to the street. These houses will normally have electricity, a water tap in the patio, and some type of raised bed. Many will have a latrine, at least one room with a hard floor, and a radio. The kitchen will probably be a separate small building almost certainly with its raised cooking hearth which has space for the *comal*, the pottery griddle on which tortillas are baked, and depressions for clay pots and casseroles in which all other cooking is done. Wood is the only fuel in these kitchens. The *metate* stone for grinding *nixtamal*, the maize grains from which *masa* dough is made, from which tortillas are patted out, stands to one side of the hearth, and crude wooden shelves hold several dozen pottery vessels of local manufacture, a few china plates, and several metal spoons. Knives and forks usually are not used in eating. Frequently there is no table, for the edges of the hearth serve this purpose in food preparation, and diners sit on low wooden chairs and hold their plates on their laps.

Porch railings, which are built of adobe, support pots with geraniums, shasta daisies, larkspur and other flowers, and medicinal and cooking herbs. Farther back in the patio are larger flowers such as hollyhocks, cannas, roses, and bougainvillaeas, and if space permits, pear, peach, fig, or *zapote* trees, chayote plants, and a few stalks of maize around which twine squash vines. Discreetly tucked behind the kitchen, but usually without any other enclosure, is the simple wooden-seated latrine. Although hardly elegant, houses like these are snug against the wind, and attractive with red-tile roofs, whitewashed adobe walls, and flowers and patio greenery. By peasant standards they offer a good deal of comfort.

The poorer houses, by contrast, are more likely to have only one room that serves for sleeping, cooking, and living. This room almost certainly will have a packed earth floor, and only its door to provide ventilation. Everyone in all but a few of these houses sleeps on reed mats on the floor, rolled up and thrust into a corner during the day. The hearth in 60 per cent of these homes consists of the pre-Conquest three stones on the floor on which are placed the tortilla griddle and bean pot, used to prepare most of the food of these families. Latrines, electric lights, and running water are rare in these homes — they occur in only about 5 per cent — as are the luxuries that tend to accompany them, such as radio, electric iron, sewing machine, and clock.

The top 15 per cent of the homes usually have three or more rooms, and in addition to the amenities described for the average house they are likely to have a watch or clock, a sewing machine, an electric iron, and a radio. Few had glass windows in 1960, but the number is increasing rapidly as this becomes a prestige item. The same is true of shower baths and bottled-gas stoves: of the latter there were only two in 1960, but six years later there were already eighteen. In a good many of these homes there is at least one store-bought bed and mattress.

Actually, the distribution of the comforts and conveniences described does not follow a precise pattern, and we cannot assume that a house with three rooms will automatically have electricity, running water, a latrine, and a hard floor. A number of one-room houses, for example, are owned by progressive young men who are just getting started, and they may have conveniences and even luxuries usually associated with much larger houses. On the other hand, elderly people may have rather large houses that are lacking in most comforts. Families that live in good houses near one of the several public fountains or water taps sometimes have no water; their owners see no reason to pay for a patio outlet when a few extra steps will take them to the same water, at no cost. Houses with electricity and water may lack latrines, and houses that have watches and radios may still make do with dirt floors. Progress and improvements do not come in a standard, predictable sequence, and the combination of elements which each house shows often seems due more to chance than to design.

THE DAILY ROUND

Regardless of relative degrees of home comforts, the daily round of activities in all families is much the same. After the evening meal the housewife warms a large pot of water, throws in a handful of lime, stirs it until it dissolves, and then adds as much maize as she thinks her family will eat the next day. Over the dying ashes of the fire the maize heats and expands to form nixtamal. Early the next morning — usually by 5 o'clock — the village's four nixtamal mills begin grinding, and there are always early risers on hand with their buckets of maize anxious to beat the crowd. After grinding, nixtamal becomes a dough, masa. The careful cook regrinds this little by little on her metate, stopping to scoop up the resulting varves from each stroke of the *mano*, the cylind-'cal grinding stone which she holds in both hands. Small daubs of dough are patted into tortillas, an operation that takes about fifteen seconds for each. Tortillas are first cooked briefly on one side, then turned and cooked on the other side for a longer time, and finally turned back to the first side for finishing, swelling at this point like a toad's belly, for a total of from a minute and a quarter to a minute and a half. A good worker who is not interrupted can make and cook four liters of tortillas — 65 or 70 — in about an hour; this meets the needs of an average family. In contrast, thirty years ago before mechanical mills were introduced, hand grinding of the nixtamal alone required an additional two hours of backbreaking work, time which was found by arising two hours earlier than at present. Nothing has liberated the Mexican country woman like the mechanical nixtamal mill. Moreover, she is spared the rheumatic shoulder pains which almost all older women complain of, and which they attribute to the severe physical effort of grinding nixtamal. And today the task of food preparation is lightened even more in some families by a small tortilla press which reduces the time needed to make tortillas to half or less that of the hand process. Many husbands object to this press, just as they initially objected to the mill, on the grounds that the tortilla tastes less good.

Not all wives rise at 5 o'clock, but most will be up by daybreak. Since many feed their families a breakfast of rewarmed tortillas from the preceding day, nixtamal mills still are seen doing a brisk business at 10 o'clock in the morning. Perhaps two-thirds of the families have only two formal meals a day. Men arise at daybreak and, often fortified only by a shot of tequila or aguardiente (distilled sugar cane juice), leave immediately to cut wood for the day's needs. Returning about ten they have *el almuerzo*, consisting of beans and tortillas, sometimes bread as well, and probably black coffee liberally sweetened with sugar. Then they set to work making pottery, or drive pack animals to the clay deposits. Families that have a mid-morning meal usually eat the main meal about five in the afternoon. This consists of broth, to which fresh lake fish may be added, or perhaps boiled rice, which is called "dry soup." This is followed by beans, tortillas, and several times a week by meat or fish. Poorer families rarely have meat more than once a week, buying it on Fridays if they go to Pátzcuaro to sell pottery.

Although the twice-a-day meal pattern probably owes its origin to poverty, many families follow it by choice, since it interferes less with productive activities than does a three-times-a-day pattern. On the other hand, a number of really poor families spread their limited diet over three meals, perhaps hoping to dull the pangs of hunger that are often with them. When the men in farming families are working long hours in the fields, three meals a day are common. Beans, tortillas, and bread are eaten upon arising, and probably sweetened coffee will be drunk. The housewife, after her morning chores, spends a great deal of time in preparing a substantial noon meal with the inevitable beans and tortillas, and with meat or fish, usually prepared in a vitamin-rich sauce of onions, tomatoes, garlic, chiles, and herbs. This meal is carried to the field where the men are working, so they will not lose time returning home, a fire is built to reheat the food, and husband and wife and field workers eat together. In these families a bite usually is consumed in the evening: coffee, an herb tea, or the maize gruel *atole*, probably a *taco* or a tortilla with beans, or perhaps cheese. Fruit, seasonally consumed in large quantities, is not considered to be part of a meal. It is eaten when available as a between-meals snack.

Whatever the occupation, the members of a family usually are at work early. During the agricultural season farmers are away before light, often walking several miles to their fields. From February to November children must be sent off to school by 9 o'clock, but stragglers are seen long after the opening hour. With the home at least partially cleared of people, the housewife is free to visit the store for her few daily purchases, to wash clothes — usually in a cement tank called a *pila* or on a large flat rock in her patio

— to drop in to visit with a neighbor or compadre, to visit the church to arrange flowers on the altars or, in more than half of the homes, to continue with her pottery work.

With dusk the pace of work slows, the family gathers in the kitchen, and if it is the custom, a light meal is eaten. With electricity people stay up later than formerly. Women may sew, or attend to other household chores, such as ironing, but men are more apt simply to sit and talk. In spite of good lighting it occurs to very few people to read. Post-adolescent boys roam the streets, usually in gangs, often singing in front of the houses of their girl friends, and older men gather in bars and stores for a few drinks. On Saturdays and Sundays there is a movie, attended by as many as two hundred people. But by 10 o'clock most lights are out and houses are quiet. In homes lacking electricity people retire earlier.

On Sundays this rhythm is broken. Most people arise little if any later than during the week, since they like to attend the early 6:30 Mass, leaving the later 10 o'clock Mass for the Tarascans who, since they must walk several miles, cannot come so early. Arising early is not seen as a hardship; sleeping arrangements usually are so lacking in comfort that lying abed late is hardly a luxury. Literally everyone in Tzintzuntzan attends Sunday Mass, and on weekdays perhaps a fourth of the women also go. After breakfast people devote time to household chores, but the major economic activities such as agricultural work, fishing, and pottery making are prohibited by the Church. Patios are swept, kitchen pots may be rearranged, a husband will repair a plow or fix a broken pot mold, and children will play in the streets. Those people who have not bathed Saturday afternoon will do so Sunday morning, for a weekly bath is the rule for almost everyone. Women usually take a sponge bath from a basin in their bedrooms. Large numbers of men, and increasing numbers of women, now patronize the public shower baths. After bathing, or concluding minor household tasks, husbands and wives may stroll to the plaza, make purchases, and visit with friends and relatives. Five o'clock rosary draws a considerable number of villagers, although fewer than the Masses. After dark the evening is much like that of any other day, one in which to relax and to prepare for the next day's activities.

54

CHAPTER FOUR

*Interpersonal
Relations: Family
and Compadrazgo*

NUCLEAR AND JOINT FAMILIES

In the preceding chapter we learned a little about the physical form of Tzintzuntzan, of relations between Tarascan Indians and mestizos, and of the ways in which the villagers earn their livings. In this chapter we turn to those aspects of the social structure of the village which have to do with family organization and role relationships, and with friendship and *compadrazgo* (godparent) patterns. The structure and function of the Tzintzuntzan family reflects the common Hispanic American village pattern. The nuclear, bilateral unit is simultaneously the ideal and the most common household even though, as we shall see, there is a significant tendency toward "jointness." I have concluded that the 1,877 people who lived in the village in 1960 can be assigned to 376 families. The determination of what is a family is not always a simple matter, and in Tzintzuntzan, as in other communities, there are gray areas where it is difficult to classify family relationships according to a single scheme. To begin, I have arbitrarily said that a married couple, with or without additional dependents, and irrespective of living arrangements with respect to other couples, is the basis of calculating families. There are 333 of these nuclear families. But not everyone lives as a member of or attached to a couple, and there are 43 "families" in which the composition includes no married people. These consist of seven widowers and 23 widows, some with and others without minor children, and 13 additional extremely mixed households.

The 376 families in Tzintzuntzan do not all have separate houses, each with its door to the street, as in an American small town. Some of the couples live in varying degrees of dependency on one another; in anthropological parlance they are joint families. The 333 married couples, for example, live in only 277 houses. Of these, 233 have their own homes, but the remaining 100 couples occupy only 44 dwelling units. Most of these joint families (34 cases) are composed of two couples, usually parents plus a married son (28 cases) but occasionally parents with a married daughter (2 cases). In eight households there are three married couples, and in two there are four. Most of these joint households, of course, have additional persons such as minor children, widowed parents, elderly aunts or uncles, and rarely more distant relatives. It is noteworthy that in only one instance do three generations of married couples live under the same roof, and in only seven instances do pairs of married brothers live together. The 277 homes occupied by one or more married couples, plus 43 occupied by families with no married couples, give us a total of 320 dwelling units in the village.

To say that 100 couples live in joint families in no way means that living arrangements are the same in all cases, or that identical processes have formed these households. There are, in fact, three degrees of "jointness," as evidenced by cooking arrangements. In 12 dwelling units, for example, families have physically separate kitchens, so that they can be said to be joint only in the sense that they occupy a common plot of land. In 16 additional homes there is a single kitchen, but the family units cook separately and maintain distinct food budgets. In only 16 instances do two or more couples participate in communal cooking based on a single food budget.

Joint families are primarily the result of marriage customs. In the usual pattern a man brings his bride to his father's house where the new couple lives for a year or two, until the first child is born, after which they separate, the son setting up his own home. For a couple with several sons, this means that during their middle years they are almost certain to live under a joint arrangement, for as the older married sons move out to set up their own households, the younger sons marry and bring their brides home. Frequently the last son to marry remains on in the parental home, inheriting it upon the death of his father. In 16 instances of a married son living with his parents, the young husband is 24 years of age or less, and has been married fairly recently. Most of these young couples will soon set up independent households. But in 21 cases the married son (or sons) are older than 24, and usually have several children. These joint families appear to represent a predilection for this type of living, and can be considered as more or less permanent. An ethnic factor is also involved, for in 15 of the 44 joint families one or more of the members is Tarascan; although they, too, usually prefer the single-family household, the Indians obviously show more preference than mestizos for joint households.

It may be pointed out, by way of summary, that only 13 per cent of the households are joint, but since by definition joint households are larger than single households, this 13 per cent accounts for 22 per cent (with 421 people) of the village population. Thus, despite a stated ideal of each married couple achieving independence and living alone with its children, there actually is a strong current of jointness, and it is a rare individual who has not, at some time in his life, been a member of a joint family.

FAMILY STRUCTURE

Whether a villager lives in a simple or a joint family, his primary ties are structured through his blood relatives. The fact of birth gives him his first point of reference, from which as long as he lives in the village he can never disengage himself. Blood descent is traced equally through the father's and mother's lines, and this dual affiliation is expressed in the Spanish custom whereby a person's surname — always compound — is made up of the patronyms of both parents. Thus Juan, the son of Pedro Morales Rendón and María Estrada Zavala, is Juan Morales Estrada. Patrilineality is evidenced by the priority of the father's patronym, and by the fact that with each new generation the parents' matronyms are sloughed off. But the system fulfills the function of identifying every individual in the eyes of the community as a full member of two family lines. The particularistic character of the kinship system is further emphasized by the fact that at marriage a woman does not merge her identity with that of her husband by assuming his patronym, as is done in Mexican cities. María Estrada Zavala remains María Estrada Zavala, and does not become María Estrada de Morales, as she would in more elevated social circles. Throughout her life she continues to be called by her maiden name, and commonly, at least until middle age, she is identified as the daughter of Jaime Zavala rather than as the wife of Pedro Morales. She inherits equally (in theory and often in fact) with male siblings; she may register property in her name; and she may buy, sell, or take court action without her husband's consent.

Although about a third of the married couples live in some type of joint family, the wider kinship ties of the extended family are usually not very important. Still, whatever the degree of feeling, all relatives must formally be classified, and both mode of address and behavior will, usually, be in accordance with this classification. With relatively minor differences, kinship terminology (which is basically Spanish) follows the English pattern, and no distinction is made between the father's and the mother's lines.

The principal structural difference as compared to the American system is a formal distinction between the sex of cousins, and between first cousins and more distant cousins, and the absence of the cousin "once" (or "twice") removed. In the ascending generation parents' cousins (ego's cousins once removed) and grandparents' cousins (ego's cousins twice removed) are simply lumped with uncles and aunts. In the descending generation the children and grandchildren of cousins (ego's once and twice removed cousins) are lumped with the children of siblings as nephews and nieces. Relative age is very important in determining, in a particular case, how people construe their kinship, and there are instances in which second cousins — who would be *primos* if they were of approximately the same age — look upon themselves in the uncle/aunt-nephew/niece relationship, and use the corresponding form of address.

In theory anyone addressed with a kinship term merits the formal third person personal pronoun *usted*, including parents. In many families this rule is rigorously adhered to, but informants feel that, in recent years, there has been a considerable relaxation in practice, and many children now address their parents with the informal second person *tú*. Age mates and younger relatives (and younger villagers at large) are, of course, always addressed as *tú*.

FAMILY ROLES AND BEHAVIOR

Villagers are in general agreement about ideal role behavior within the family: the husband is dominant, owed obedience and respect by his wife and children even after the latter reach adulthood. The wife should be faithful and submissive, frugal and careful in managing family resources, and kind and loving with her children, who reciprocate in kind. Siblings are expected to display the fraternal virtues of affection and mutual economic and moral support, both while they live under the parental roof and after they set up independent households. Real behavior, of course, runs the gamut from patterns approaching the ideal to patterns quite unlike it. By examining in turn the forms of interaction between spouses, parents and children, and siblings, we can see something of this wide range.

In spite of the ideal pattern of a dominant, authoritarian husband and father, husbands and wives frequently live in relative equality. Almost all men turn their earnings over to their wives for safekeeping and spending, expecting, however, to be given money for cigarettes, drinks, or other male expenses when they request it. Cash is kept in a locked chest (women more often than

59

men carry a ring of keys), or in a pot tucked behind the wood-pile or placed on a beam where it looks like one among dozens of old vessels and molds. Care is taken to ensure that no one outside the family knows where money is kept. In addition to these working funds, many women try to keep an *alcancía*, a piggy bank in which spare coins are dropped from time to time, to be kept for an emergency.

Some husbands, however, insist on keeping all money themselves, doling out daily expense money to their wives in small quantities. This is a frequent source of irritation between spouses. These are the really dominant husbands. Micaela describes such a man as *muy delicado y cumplido*, very correct and proper, but touchy and difficult. These husbands also hold a tight rein on their wives and children, and don't permit them to mix indiscriminately with other people. The wife of such a man is expected to talk with other women only to the extent necessary to make purchases and to have her nixtamal ground at the mill. Daughters are closely watched, sent to Mass, but not allowed to loiter afterward, or to stroll the streets or visit friends. Life with such men is not easy, but women feel that a wife must accept her husband as he is, vices as well as virtues, and that she must put up with what fate has brought her. For better or worse a woman should — although she often doesn't — submit to her husband's will, and a wife who keeps running back to her father is looked upon with scorn. A father's authority is seen as terminating with his daughter's marriage, and should she return to him he is under strong compulsion to send her back to her husband, except in cases of flagrant abuse.

Most married couples fight from time to time, but these fights are not brought to court; it is assumed a reasonable amount of friction is normal, and a woman who cannot keep her husband's temper within bounds is thought, by men and women alike, probably to deserve the abuse he may heap upon her. Wife beating is common, and some women even believe that a good husband should occasionally beat his spouse simply to remind her who is boss. Men, too, are much afraid of being accused of being dominated by their wives, and some beating is certainly due to the desire to impress one's associates with his *machismo*, or the desire to avoid the charge that a wife has the upper hand.

By no means all men beat their wives. "In all of my married life Vicente never beat me," says Nati. "If he ever did, I would die." And she probably would. Neither could she remember her father having beaten her mother. Like Nati and Vicente, a great many spouses appear to achieve real understanding and love. Smoothly running homes are not subjects for gossip, so it is probable that an observer gets a warped sample of domestic relationships. Relatively few women are rumored to have been unfaithful to their husbands, and even fewer have left them to live with another man. Among a few of the younger married men there is a certain amount of visiting prostitutes in Pátzcuaro, but after these early years I have the impression that most husbands settle down and are faithful to their wives as well. Sexual prowess, although not ignored in Tzintzuntzan, seems less a male concern here than in many other parts of Mexico.

Although the view is impressionistic, I have often thought that in pottery-making families domestic relations run rather smoothly. Potting, more than any other occupation, requires the intimate, smoothly integrated, continuing cooperation of husband and wife, and of the older children as well, if the family's economic needs are to be met. Potter spouses spend much more time in each other's company than do those in farming and fishing families, and continuing friction would seriously jeopardize the productive process. Moreover, the quiet, sedentary nature of much of the work encourages talk and an interchange of ideas and feelings not possible in the other occupations. If pottery making does, in fact, encourage domestic bliss, it is an important compensation for the miserably low incomes that characterize most of these families.

In all families the divison of labor between husband and wife is clearly spelled out. Women do the cooking, shop for food, wash clothes, keep house, tend the children, feed chickens and pigs, take a hot noon meal to their farmer husbands working away from home, or assume a major responsibility in making pottery. Twenty years ago husband and wife often drove a pottery-loaded mule or burro to the Friday Pátzcuaro or the Sunday Quiroga market, where the wife sold the ware while the husband visited with friends and had a few drinks. Since much more pottery is now sold through middlemen, wives today are less often in a position directly to receive money. Husbands expect to carry out all productive and economic activities that must take place outside the home, such as gathering firewood for cooking and kilns, bringing pottery clays, caring for horses, mules, and cattle, working in fields or fishing, or working for a cash wage.

PARENTS AND CHILDREN

When asked about relationships between parents and children, informants are equivocal. On the one hand they think of the ideal patterns that are expected to prevail, and if they are parents they have an image of themselves as loving and just in exercising authority. On the other hand, when these same parents recall their childhood, they emphasize the ways in which they suffered. Usually there was not enough food, and they were often hungry; clothing, too, was skimpy and ragged. But particularly, they say, they suffered because of their relationships with their parents, who failed to understand them. Fathers always seemed to have beaten their children, and even today most parents concede that their offspring must be physically coerced "to teach them to be good." Beating, in fact, is generally seen as the only sure way in which a moral lesson is imprinted on young minds. Through beatings, as well as moral lessons, children are supposed to learn that they owe unquestioned obedience to their parents, and especially to their fathers, whose word should be accepted as law. If a father finds a grown son drinking in a bar, and is minded to do so, he can strike him and send him home, without the son raising an arm to defend himself. Good sons, until middle age, are not supposed to drink in their father's presence under any circumstances, and often at fiestas I have seen married men refuse hard liquor and content themselves with beer until their fathers left the party.

After early childhood a good deal of formality and tension characterize father-son relationships. Fathers and sons do not become good friends again, if at all, until the younger man is married, and has his own home and family. Then the tensions often relax. Daughters, on the other hand, are felt to be much more affectionate with their fathers than are sons, but at the expense of close ties with their mothers. Although mothers and daughters must work together in most of the household chores, there is constraint in exchanging confidences. Sons feel much more at ease with their mothers, and will often confide in them on matters they would not dream of discussing with their fathers. Although young men go to the United States against their mother's wishes, a good many, upon hearing that she was seriously ill, dropped everything to return home, even though this has sometimes meant, for those lucky enough to have obtained immigration papers, forfeiting this much-prized right freely to enter the United States.

Both parents profess to prefer that their daughters not marry. Men are unpredictable, except in the sense that they will probably turn out badly, and a girl with a comfortable home, they reason, is foolish to sacrifice comfort and security for almost certain suffering. Consequently many mothers repeatedly warn their daughters that men are all wicked, and that they would be well advised to stay home, safely unmarried. But the concern is not entirely for the girl's welfare, for parents consciously and unconsciously recognize that a half-grown daughter is too valuable an asset to afford to lose at an early age. With a houseful of younger siblings she in fact is a second mother, without whose aid the real mother can scarcely cope with family chores. Natalia Paz was kept at home for years in this capacity of surrogate mother and maid, dutifully avoiding her urge to run off with Valentín, whose patience, in the face of extreme frustration, has always amazed me. Eventually she eloped, and though she was estranged from her parents for a year or so the reconciliation — as is always true — took place and they became good friends again.

Children are expected to show obedience to their parents as long as they live. A good many do, from love and affection. Bonifacio Zúñiga, age twenty-three, and his younger brother Pedro, are self-supporting; not only this, but most of Bonifacio's bracero earnings have gone to his parents who have, with the advice of the boys,

63

remodeled their old house into one of the most comfortable and elaborate homes in town. Yet neither boy goes out at night without telling his father his plans and asking permission. One night Pedro got rather drunk at María Horta's saint's day fiesta, stayed out late, was verbally chastised next day by his father, and was refused permission to accompany me to Morelia.

But people also feel that much of the attention children show old parents stems from their fear of being disinherited, for if a father has not distributed his property it is politic to be obedient. "That's why it's best not to distribute one's property until about to die," says Micaela. "Once children inherit they forget all about parents and pay no attention to them."

Are there instances of sons striking parents? A few men are named. Perhaps the most remarkable case is that of José Méndez who, when his mother remonstrated with him for his drunkenness, struck her. Almost immediately a *borrascón* of air, a small tempest, struck him, and he was queer ever after, seeming half drunk always, even when he was not. After his mother died, and he was past 50, he married for the first time, but died shortly thereafter. "He was never happy after he struck his mother," says Micaela. "Things never went right for him." Roberto Prieto, age 28, struck his father Miguel, age 63, when the latter sold a house which Roberto felt was partially his, since his earnings had helped buy it. My neighbor Epigmenio Molina struck his aged mother because she objected to his heavy drinking. He chased her around his patio, she screaming at the top of her lungs, until the neighbors came to the rescue. Informants also recall a few other times when sons struck parents, but agree the event is very rare.

Morality tales teach children what happens if they do not show proper respect to their parents, and to older people in general. Micaela quotes her grandmother as having witnessed the following episode which is alleged to have taken place in Quiroga many years ago. A girl raised by her grandmother, upon reaching adolescence, began to misbehave. Her grandmother seized a stick of firewood to beat her, but the girl, now well grown, forced it from her hands and started to chase her around the paths in the little town plaza.

Soon she caught up with her, and grabbed her flying hair so hard it all came out. But just at this instant her feet began to sink into the ground and she was rooted, motionless, left hand with her grandmother's scalp and right hand with the upraised stick. Slowly she sank deeper and deeper, giving off such an intense heat that those who came to help could not get near. For ten days she remained, gradually sinking, both arms frozen in position, piteously calling for water. Finally the priest came, sized up the situation, and said, "This girl is condemned by God." Then he "terminated the condemnation" by making the sign of the cross, and the girl immediately disappeared into the ground.

SIBLING RELATIONS

Male siblings, following the general hierarchic pattern of the community, are accorded more authority than female siblings. The eldest brother is a father surrogate, and can command his younger siblings of both sexes to do what he wants. Jesús Calderón takes it for granted that he can ask his fifteen-year-old brother, Enríque, to run errands for him, and it doesn't occur to Enríque to refuse, even though he may grumble. Elder brothers are expected to exercise discipline in the absence of fathers, and they are the ones who normally determine the division of property left by the deceased parent. The eldest sister — even if older than the eldest brother — ranks below him, but otherwise she has considerable authority over younger siblings, and especially younger sisters. She is a mother surrogate and, in past years at least, when both parents were away selling pottery, she would be in effective charge of a household of younger children. This functional relationship is sometimes reflected in modes of address. Younger children may call an elder sister *mamá* and she, in turn, may call them *hijo* or *hija*. Natividad Peña, to this day, sometimes calls her younger brother Faustino hijo, even though he is forty-five years of age, the father of seven children, and her compadre as well.

The youngest child in a family is called *la gorda del perrito*. As a housewife nears the end of the morning's tortilla making, she prepares a thick, outsize tortilla known as a *gorda* ("the fat one") to feed the dog; hence it is *la gorda del perrito*. And just as the final tortilla is a *gorda*, so is the final child. The child *gorda* is generally thought to be less scolded and more spoiled by parents, and older siblings often resent this preferential treatment.

Brothers are expected to share with fathers the responsibility of guarding their sisters' good name. Once when Natividad Peña was about fifteen her very strict father permitted her to go to the store, accompanied by her six-year-old brother, Faustino, whom she led by the hand. Returning, a boy she knew joined them, and they laughed and talked as they walked along. Upon reaching home her father came to the door and, furious with the boy, drove him away with stones. Then he beat both Nati and Faustino with a rope, she for her shameless ways with men and he, in spite of his tender years, for not having watched over his sister's morals.

Small children are often jealous of newly arrived siblings, but in general young brothers and sisters play together without undue friction, and older sisters particularly may spend a great deal of time caring for younger siblings, carrying them about in *rebozos** when they are very young, helping to teach them to walk, and keeping an eye on them when they begin to toddle. Friction is more apt to develop among adult siblings, especially when there is an inheritance problem. Most people agree that it is a rare estate that is divided without causing hard feelings among the heirs, and in some cases the family home is literally torn apart so that adobe bricks, roof beams, tiles, and door and window frames can be divided among the children.

When adult siblings leave town for good they often lose all contact with their remaining brothers and sisters. Ramón Barragán thinks his two brothers, who went with him to the United States in 1926, still live in Pennsylvania, but he has had no word from them in many years. One sister lives three miles away in Patambicho, but Ramón couldn't remember her husband's name when I asked him. Another sister is married across the lake in San Gerónimo, and Ramón can't think of her husband's name,

---

* *Rebozo*: a shawl, a basic part of the costume of Mexican women of the lower socio-economic levels.

either, but he does recall that the man once came to Tzintzuntzan "wanting to kill me."

In other instances, adult and married siblings retain a strong liking for each other. Doña Andrea Medina's children always help each other when there is a family fiesta or a crisis such as illness or a legal problem. Her grandson, Gaudencio Rendón, age twenty-four, before going to the United States for the first time as a bracero, made a two-day trip to San Angel, near Uruapan, simply to say goodbye to his younger married sister, Teresa. So the picture is very much that of other societies; siblings who like each other continue to be good friends and to enjoy each other's company. Those who do not, go their various ways.

MARRIAGE

From time to time a neighbor drops in or a family member returns home with the always exciting news: "Fulano has 'robbed' Fulana." A young man has eloped with a village girl and, expectably, marriage will follow. There are the inevitable questions: how and where did it happen? Had the two young people been *novios* — sweethearts? How will the girl's father react? Will he be angry, refuse to accept the boy's father's offer of "peace"? And when will the boy's father, accompanied by his *compadre* (in this instance, the baptismal godfather of the son), go to the girl's home formally to ask pardon? Occasionally, it is true, one hears that the young man's father or godfather has formally asked for the hand of the girl, but these instances are decidedly in the minority. In either case, the steps that lead to the setting up of a new family are cause for gossip, excitement, and pleasure.

The events that precede either the elopement or the formal petition are much the same. Today, through school contacts, where classes are coeducational, young people have ample opportunity to come to know each other well. Some parents still attempt to maintain the fiction that girls, prior to marriage, are carefully watched, so that they have no opportunity to come to know village youths. Traditionally a young man lay in wait for a girl as she went to a spring or well to draw water; this was almost the only opportunity he had to initiate relationships. But with the introduction of a potable water system in the late 1930's, and the simultaneous extension of schooling through the full six years of the primary grades — which few scholars finish before fourteen or fifteen years of age — patterns began to change. In today's world, the careful watching of daughters by jealous and fearful parents is pretty much a thing of the past. Still, most parents refuse to admit that their daughters have suitors, and no young man would think of attempting to visit his novia in her home, or even of passing her door to leave a message.

A widespread feeling expressed verbally and in other behavior is that girls are at the mercy of men, as far as sex is concerned. Should a man, for example, come upon a woman alone, be she married or unmarried, in a home or a field, it is thought she would have little choice other than to submit to his overtures. If the girl is unmarried, and the youth honorable, he would then "rob" her and they would be married. Marriageable girls and younger married women also express reluctance, even in broad daylight, to walk alone through the village. It is difficult to tell to what extent these patterns are based on the fact that a girl may really be attacked by a man, and to what extent they simply represent a stylized but not particularly accurate view of relationships between the sexes.

In the act of *robo*, of elopement, and consistent with the stated belief that women are always at the mercy of men, there is a fiction that the young man forcibly carries off the girl against her will and that, once abducted and dishonored, she has no recourse but to marry him. In fact, in nearly all cases the young couple are in complete agreement, and the act itself is the culmination of careful planning. "So she says she was carried off?" snorts Natividad. "Why, I saw it happen right here in front of my house. She was going along a yard ahead of the boy, so anxious was she to go with him!" The suitor usually is accompanied by one or two of his friends, normally unmarried age mates, to help ward off possible counterattacks. But this danger, too, is mostly fiction. Many people tell of seeing elopements, but no one can remember when anyone went to the aid of the girl. This is seen as interference in others' affairs, something that would certainly be resented by the parties concerned.

After her "robbery" the girl is "deposited" in the home of a relative, a godfather, a friend of the suitor, or even in his own home, if the act was undertaken with his parents' knowledge, as it occasionally is, where in theory her virtue is protected. In fact, sexual relations — if not previously consummated — are initiated immediately, for this is the act which makes the elopement irreversible. A father, however much he may detest the suitor, knows that his daughter is now unsalable to another; he is at the mercy of the stripling who has carried her off. It is a galling position in which to find one's self, and the fact that he, the father, previously had placed his wife's father in exactly the same situation in no way mitigates the anger. He can only seek to show the proper offended dignity, and then gracefully accept the inevitable. *Aunque me siento que las tripas me hiervan, tengo que acceptar*, said Valentín Rivera, speaking of the robbery of his younger daughter. Although he "felt his guts boiling" he had to accept the inevitable.

When the boy's father learns of the event his first act is to advise the municipal authorities of what has happened; in this way he protects himself against the possibility, however remote, of a formal complaint. Next he goes to the father of the girl and asks when he can come formally to his house to *hacer las paces*, to make peace, to apologize for his son's conduct, and to arrange for the marriage. The ceremony of *las paces*, the peaces, usually takes place two or three nights later, always at the home of the girl. The boy's father is accompanied by his compadre and perhaps a few friends and relatives as well. The girl's father will be found supported by his compadre (his daughter's baptismal godfather) and relatives and friends. Wives of the principals are likewise present. Sometimes the making of peace is cold and formal, and the girl's father may say he doesn't approve and will have nothing to do with the marriage. Rarely, he will refuse to attend the wedding ceremonies. More often the peace-making ceremony is a rite of social solidarity, in which public recognition is given to the act of elopement, and when plans are formulated for the civil and religious ceremonies.

During a recent six-year period fifty-eight marriages between previously unmarried people were initiated by robbery, and only ten followed upon a formal request. The latter is considered the proper form, in spite of its relative rarity, and usually characterizes families that are financially better off. The priest is sometimes asked to make the request, on the assumption that his implied approval will make it difficult for the girl's father to refuse. Other times a boy's baptismal godfather, or even his father, will ask.

Whether initiated by robo or by request, marriage in Tzintzuntzan is always validated by both a civil and a religious ceremony. The former comes first and is a legal prerequisite to the second. Either in the town hall or, for a somewhat higher fee in the home of the groom, the mayor or his secretary reads the official secular act which says marriage is a social (and not a religious) contract between two adults who wish this relationship, that it is dissoluble either through death or divorce, and that it is the only moral way of establishing a family and of propagating the human species. The emphasis on the social nature of the contract, and mention of divorce as one way to dissolve a marriage, are of course in direct opposition to Church teaching.

After the secular act is read and the requisite forms are signed, the bride and groom and their fathers call on the priest to inform him of what has transpired, and to record their intention to be married in the church. After this visit the wedding party returns to the groom's home for a mole dinner enlivened by adequate supplies of beer, tequila, and rum. If the bride has been "asked" she returns home with her parents; if "robbed" she continues living with her husband until the religious ceremony.

Most villagers believe that people are not really married by the civil act. They look upon it rather as Americans view a marriage license: as an expression of intent. Church marriage takes place from three weeks to two months after the civil ceremony, always preceded by the reading of the banns in Mass on three consecutive Sundays. Marriage godparents are selected, usually by the groom or his father, but frequently in consultation with the bride's father. They are expected to offer a rather elegant breakfast following the marriage Mass, and to give the groom the thirteen pieces of silver (now silver pesos), the *arras*, which he gives the bride. A day or two before the wedding the groom's family goes with the bride to Pátzcuaro to purchase her wedding outfit, or to buy the materials which a local seamstress will fit to the girl. The groom's baptismal godfather also is expected to buy the bride her wedding shoes.

The marriage act is read inside the church door, or in front of the altar, just prior to Mass, after which principals and guests go to the wedding breakfast at the home of the new godparents, where they are served small glass dishes of jello, cups of hot chocolate, glasses of milk, and quantities of white bread. A godfather who is able to afford the expense is expected to hire a band to provide music for dancing, or at the very least to share the expense with the groom's father who, later in the day, offers the elaborate turkey mole wedding feast whose expenses, with beer and tequila, will run from $300 to $500. With payments to the priest (up to $100) and to the civil authorities ($25 or more) and $100 to $200 of clothing for the bride, plus a couple of hundred pesos for music, the groom's father is faced with serious expenses.

The wedding dinner is always an event of much gaiety and fun, with joking and storytelling, and repeated clearings of the table to make room for more arrivals. Either before or after the meal the bride and groom, their parents, and the new marriage godparents, and other godparents and compadres who may wish to, withdraw to a room where the marriage godparents mumble advice to their new godchildren about the meaning of Christian marriage, and the obligations of each to the other. Then the godparents kneel in turn and embrace the parents of the couple, saying the ritual words: "Formerly we were friends; now we're going to be compadres. Here, and in the presence of God, we will respect each other as God commands." Only if the embrace, the *abrazo* is given, is the compadrazgo legitimized. The other compadres may also embrace the marriage compadres, thus extending the ties to a considerable number of people. The full extent of this relationship is described later in this chapter.

Tzintzuntzeños do not marry particularly early. A sample of 137, representing all first marriages during the years 1959 through 1963, show that although one girl married at the age of 14, two at 15, and seven at 16, most were in the age range 17–20, and more were married from 21–25 than from 14–16. Except for one 40-year-old woman who married a 35-year-old man, both first marriages, no girl older than 25 married for the first time. This suggests that a girl not married by this age is likely to live out her years as a spinster.

Apart from one 16-year-old, no males married at less than 18 years of age, and the range 19–23 accounted for about two-thirds of all first marriages for men. Men continue to marry for the first time through 29, but except for the instance mentioned above, no male in this sample married after that age.

Although Tzintzuntzeños like to think of themselves as a rather tight little community, about 40 per cent of the marriages involve a partner from another community. From 1959 to 1964, 65 marriages were recorded in which both husband and wife were from Tzintzuntzan. In an additional 20 the brides came from other places, and in two the groom was an outsider. Since weddings take place in the home of the groom, instances in which Tzintzuntzan girls marry out are not recorded in the local records (unless the groom is from another settlement in the municipio). Not having evidence to the contrary, we can assume that about as many girls marry out as are brought in — say 22 during the period in question. Almost all the marriages involving an outside partner are with spouses from nearby communities such as Pátzcuaro, Quiroga, lake villages, and settlements in Tzintzuntzan municipio; only occasionally does one see in the records Mexico City and other more distant places as the place of birth of one of the partners.

The elopement pattern of marriage, with occasional delays before civil and religious ceremonies, suggests that a good many girls must be pregnant at the time of marriage. Birth statistics indicate that they usually are not. Of 32 marriages from 1959 through 1962 for which the birth of children subsequently was recorded, in only two cases did first births occur after less than nine months. One bride was clearly six months pregnant at marriage, while the other gave birth eight and one-half months after the civil ceremony. Most first births occurred between one and two years following marriage; only 10 of the 32 were first births recorded in less than a year. It is possible, of course, because miscarriages are frequent, that in some instances of long intervals between marriage and birth of the first child, the girls suffered early miscarriages and then again became pregnant.

Newly married people almost always experience embarrassment and perplexity in addressing their parents-in-law. Except that they are invariably spoken to with the formal "usted," there is no fixed rule. Most young people say they try hard to avoid situations in which they must use either a name or a kinship term. Daughters-in-law are supposed to say "mamá" and "papá" in direct address, but frequently they use circumlocution to avoid this. María Hernández, for example, after six years of marriage and five children, still refers to her husband's mother as "the mother of Jesús" rather than as "my mother-in-law." Sons-in-law, too, may try to avoid calling their parents-in-law by kinship terms, or they may try combinations of address to ease the embarrassment which always seems to prevail. Jesús Calderón, for example, when he must use a direct term of address, calls his father-in-law, Melecio, *Papá Mele*, combining the kinship term and nickname in an affectionate, semihumorous form.

No special forms mark relationships between siblings-in-law. Those who feel a natural affinity for each other participate in family gatherings on much the same terms as blood relatives. Those who dislike each other try to follow the same avoidance patterns that would govern their behavior were they not related. Normally they address each other by given names, unless they are or become compadres, in which case the formal address that characterizes this institution will generally be used.

Structurally, what do Tzintzuntzan marriage customs imply? The first thing to remark is that, in contrast to many parts of the world, marriage is not really viewed as a contract involving two families, validated by the appropriate exchange of goods and services. The groom's family is seen as perhaps profiting slightly for a year or two, since the bride's services and some of her husband's earnings accrue to his parents. But more than counterbalancing this temporary advantage is the great economic loss of

73

paying for the wedding ceremony. As far as weddings are concerned, families with many daughters are envied, and families with many sons are pitied. That neither family feels it must be compensated for a loss is indicated by the absence both of a dowry and a bride price exchange.

The prevalence of the elopement system in itself negates any concept of real contractual alliance between families, for normally the parents of neither of the young spouses are consulted, nor do they have significant control over their children's choice of a mate. At the same time, the ubiquitous robo is not the threat to a social and economic system that it would be if large amounts of real property, and above all, land, were involved. Since a majority of families own very little, if any, agricultural land, and have only slight amounts of material wealth to pass on, there is neither need to nor thought of conserving a patrimony through judicious marriage alliances arranged by families. Marriage is looked upon, like all other social relationships, as a dyadic tie in which the partners immediately concerned make their choices, without outside interference or advice.

FRIENDS AND NEIGHBORS

A family, with its lineal and collateral branches, is obviously the primary device for stating position within the community: it offers everyone a series of shared understandings of statuses and roles, and provides a manipulative system of social ties. But people see their families as merely a first step in the never-ending process of building and maintaining a full network of viable ties to others. Neighborhoodship and friendship provide additional systems within which an individual customarily manipulates relationships to his advantage. The mere fact of existing, geographically speaking, of living in a given location, places a person in a neighborhood system marked by bonds of common interest. A suspicious character in the street is a matter of concern to all, as is a householder's vicious dog or an arroyo periodically made impassable by flash floods, thus preventing passage to the nixtamal mill. Although a person can select his neighborhood, once settled he has little control over the composition of the group that surrounds him.

Consequently, although neighborhood interaction is a good basis for friendship, not all neighbors are friends, and some can be very annoying indeed. Neighborhoodship, by comparison with kinship, is a flexible system, which offers many manipulative opportunities.

An even more flexible institution is friendship. Two people, neighbors or simply fellow villagers, begin to see they have interests in common and that they like each other. They drop in at each other's homes; they offer food; they exchange favors; they invite each other to fiestas; they develop a degree of *confianza*, of mutual trust, which is the basis of true friendship. The principal strength of friendship as a social interaction system is that a person has almost complete freedom in seeking out and establishing the ties that he desires, unfettered by the formalities of birth or other pre-existing associations. Manipulative opportunities are maximal, and restrictions are minimal.

Only in the bonds between pairs of adolescent boys, and to a lesser extent between girls, do we find friendship to be in any way formalized. Palship, or "best friend" ties frequently develop between teenagers, and the companions appear inseparable. An exchange of goods — knives, tops, or gadgets that adolescents treasure — usually marks the establishment of this friendship, and continuing exchanges occur as long as the ties are recognized. The relationship may last only a short time, or it may endure until one friend is married, at which time it may cease to be functional or, if the unmarried friend is asked to baptize the first child, it may be transformed into the compadrazgo. During a best-friend relationship partners spend much time with each other, and exhibit jealousy when they fear the other may be losing interest in them.

THE COMPADRAZGO

The flexibility of friendship ties, although recognized as desirable to a point, is also seen as a flaw in the system. It is nice to be able to pick associates, but once they are picked, and tested, and found acceptable, the lack of formally defined obligations and expectations, backed and validated by ritual sanctions, is found disturbing. For unless there is substance in the structure, it is felt,

75

a friend can turn on one without warning, can cease to be a friend, and he cannot be criticized for such action. He is merely taking advantage of the flexibility of friendship for his personal interests. Friendship, then, however close the bonds appear to be, always has some unpredictability that Tzintzuntzeños find disconcerting. Between the absolute formal rigidity of the family and the absolute flexibility of friendship, there is a gap. In other societies this gap is filled by such institutions as voluntary associations, and by the mutual obligations recognized between colleagues in professional or occupational fields. But in Tzintzuntzan there are no voluntary associations, other than the basketball team, for the church societies, which might seem to qualify, are in fact controlled and directed by the priest, and a sense of association between members is essentially lacking. Tzintzuntzeños feel the need for an institution that has the formality and continuity of kinship, but which permits the freedom of choice of friendship. They find it in the compadrazgo.

The basic principle of the compadrazgo is ritual sponsorship of a person or persons (occasionally of things) by another person or persons, with consequent formal ties among a number of people, which last during the lifetimes of the principals. In Tzintzuntzan there are five traditional occasions on which compadrazgo ties are formed: the baptism of a child, its confirmation, its first communion, its marriage, and the rite known as *de la corona* ("of the crown"). Although the first four are associated with the sacraments, and the fifth is validated by a minor religious act, only the first two are *de grado*, i.e., of the first importance, in the sense that they establish impediments to marriage between the people immediately involved, and their children as well.

In all forms of the compadrazgo the terminology is the same. The sponsoring persons, the godparents, usually a married couple, but occasionally an unmarried pair, and sometimes a single individual only, are known and addressed as the *padrinos* (*padrino* = godfather; *madrina* = godmother). The sponsored person, the godchild, a single individual except in marriage, is called *ahijado* ("godson") or *ahijada* ("goddaughter"). In addition to these ties, the godparents *and* the parents of the godchild also enter into a

76

new formal relationship: they become *compadres*, or co-parents. A male in this relationship is called and addressed as *compadre*, while a female is called and addressed as *comadre*. In Tzintzuntzan, as in much of Hispanic America, the compadre ties, in a functional sense, are more important than the godparent-godchild ties, and in some instances the child is little more than a means of establishing a compadrazgo relationship which the adults desire.

BAPTISM

For baptism, a godfather and a godmother (rarely, only a godmother) sponsor an infant, thus becoming its spiritual parents. Since baptism normally occurs before expiration of the forty-day period during which a new mother is not supposed to leave her home, she is unable to attend the baptism of her child; even if the act is delayed beyond the *cuarentena* she does not go to the church. The father, too, often does not attend his child's baptism. The godparents carry the child in its new clothing to the church and stand in the baptistry, the godmother holding the head and the godfather the feet, while the priest performs the baptism. Upon emerging from the church the godfather throws handfuls of coins known as the *bolo* to the assembled children, and returns the child to its parents. Later in the day the parents prepare an elaborate meal, at which the new godparents are the guests of honor. During this fiesta the godparents and parents retire to a room where they embrace each other in turn, recite the phrase about first having been friends and now, in the sight of God, they become compadres; thus the new relationship is formalized.

In theory, baptismal godparents are substitute parents who, in case of death or incapacity of the real parents, assume such responsibility as is indicated by circumstances, to and including complete care of the child. In fact, such responsibility never seems to be shown. Godparents are required to buy the baptismal clothes, which cost from $50 to $100, to pay the baptismal costs to the priest, to provide the bolo, and to deliver the *batea*, a ceremonial tray with bread, chocolate, sugar, candles, cigarettes, a bottle of alcohol, and a cake of soap, to the child's mother when they come to the fiesta. If the child dies an *angelito*, a "little angel," before reaching an age permitting mortal sin, the god-parents are expected to provide the coffin, the burial shroud, the rockets that punctuate the procession to the cemetery, and occasionally music.

A padrino, as we have seen, is also expected to accompany his compadre, his godson's father, in asking for the hand of a girl in marriage or, as much more often happens, in going to "make peace" after the youth has eloped with the girl. And, as previously noted, godparents give their godson's bride her wedding shoes. Godparents are expected to exercise a considerable moral influence over godchildren, correcting them and even punishing them, if need be. Godchildren formerly knelt and kissed the hand of their padrinos when meeting them, and even today they show a good deal of respect. Godsons are not supposed to drink in the presence of their godfathers, and godparents are assumed to have the right and obligation to intervene in any situation in which their godchildren are behaving improperly.

The compadrazgo belongs to a generic type of social relationship often labeled by anthropologists "fictive kinship." In fictive kinship systems people customarily address each other and act toward each other in ways that closely parallel true kin behavior forms. Yet the distinction between real kinship, based on blood ties, and pseudo-kinship, based on contract, seems always to be recognized in legal, as against social, usages. In Tzintzuntzan this distinction is particularly clear in inheritance rules: the blood lines through both the father's and the mother's sides of the family always determine the inheritance of major tangibles such as land, houses, and capital items. I know of no instance in which a godson or goddaughter has inherited significant amounts of property from a godparent.

LESSER COMPADRAZGOS

For confirmation, which takes place at any time after baptism, and sometimes even on the same day, the parents select a single godparent of the same sex as the child. Although this is a *de grado* compadrazgo, one of the first importance, the godparent's formal obligations are limited to the small confirmation fee expected by the Church. For first communion a male child should, in theory, have a godfather and a female child a godmother. In fact, since the catechism normally is taught by unmarried girls, most children, regardless of sex, have only a madrina. The new godmother becomes comadre to the parents of the child, and they become her compadres.

The minor "crown" (*de la corona*) compadrazgo belongs to the general type sometimes called "evangelical" in other places, in which the rite is carried out to cure a sick child, or in the hope of preventing feared illnesses. Few Tzintzuntzeños today seem to hold this belief. Rather, the compadrazgo is sometimes seen as a device to formalize a developing friendship, if no more important sponsorship is feasible, but perhaps more often it descends to the level of a joke, carried out on the occasion of major fiestas, when the new padrino is apt to purchase a small toy for the godchild.

The marriage compadrazgo has been described on an earlier page.

IDEAL AND REAL COMPADRAZGO BEHAVIOR

A formal description of compadrazgo relationships gives little real understanding of how the system works, for possibly in no other area of culture in Tzintzuntzan is the gap between ideal and real behavior so great. If the ethnologist asks informants about how people bound by the compadrazgo behave toward each other, he gets the same stock replies from everyone. The compadrazgo is the most sacred of all relationships; compadres must treat each other with absolute respect and formality at all times, and they must ever be alert to help each other in time of need. A compadre must always be addressed as "Compadre," rather than by his given name, and a comadre must be addressed similarly as "Comadre." If the partners previously had used the informal *tú* mode of address, they must now change to *usted*. Familial incest taboos also apply to compadrazgo partners, so a man knows that even if his wife is alone with her compadre he has nothing to fear. Compadre partners are selected only on the basis of common interest, the desire of friends of long standing to cement in ritual fashion the affection they hold for each other. Although family members occasionally may be selected, compadres usually are not taken from among close relatives. All these are the things people say, in response to direct questions.

Yet as with the family, real compadrazgo behavior frequently deviates greatly from the ideal. Far from always being a close and sacred relationship, compadre ties often are routine in the extreme. They may become tenuous, and sometimes they are broken to the point where compadres do not even speak to each other.

Nearly all informants will, if pressed, tell about compadre relationships that have gone sour. Sometimes they have simply cooled to the point where punctilious formality marks the limited intercourse that prevails, and at other times downright hostility is evidenced. Valentín Rivera and his son Gregorio passed Vicente Zúñiga, Valentín Rivera's compadre and baptismal godfather of Gregorio, as he stood on his doorstep. Although Vicente had recently tried to encroach on the lands of the indigenous community by erecting a wall, and was pretty well detested by everyone (villagers, including Valentín, had gone in a group to tear down the wall), Valentín felt he must greet him. *Buenos días, compadre,* he said. No reply. So in a louder voice he repeated the greeting. Vicente just turned his head away. So almost in a shout, Valentín said to his son, "It seems as if I must have spoken to a burro" (which of course could not be expected to answer).

In spite of the theoretical rule that says the informal *tú* address must become *usted,* perhaps 15 or 20 per cent of the compadres continue to use the informal second person personal pronoun. This is a consequence of several factors. When siblings serve as padrinos to the children of their brothers and sisters almost invariably they continue their previous informality. When one couple in a compadrazgo relationship is considerably older than the other, and has always addressed the younger pair as *tú,* they may continue to do so, while the younger pair, of course, continues to address the older couple as *usted.* Confirmation madrinas usually are considerably younger than the parents of a child, since they tend to be girls in their middle teens. Consequently, they, too, are apt to continue to be addressed as *tú,* sometimes calling the child's parents *usted*, and sometimes *tú*. It is clear that age differences that are basic in determining village modes of address often override the formal rules of the compadrazgo. Again the relative conservatism of people is a factor. Families that are culturally more Tarascan, or essentially traditional in outlook, are more apt to honor the stipulated forms of address; people who feel themselves less Indian and more modern are more relaxed about compadrazgo terminology, and more embarrassed by what they consider to be stilted and artificial behavior that results when the compadrazgo intervenes in long-established relationships.

Ideal, and often real, patterns of compadrazgo behavior are expressed on both a ritual and a commercial level. Major ceremonial occasions in the life cycle are highlighted by the compadre's participation, as we have seen. When a family offers a ritual meal, compadres are the guests of honor who sit at the head of the table, who are served first and most attentively, and who are treated with exaggerated decorum. Members of the family sit farther down the table or stand apart, and eat only after the compadres are served. Compadres also enjoy showing their affection for each other, and when a person is to be honored on his saint's day, it is usually a compadre who organizes the early morning *mañanitas* serenade. The feeling that compadres are tightly bound to one another, that they respect the feelings of mutual friendship that go with the ideal institution, and that they can be counted on in time of need, are sources of immense satisfaction to Tzintzuntzeños.

COMPADRAZGO FUNCTIONS

In addition to basic social cohesion, the compadrazgo often cements commercial ties. In former years muleteers carried pottery on journeys that sometimes lasted up to a month, passing through distant towns in the *tierra caliente*. They tried to establish compadrazgo relationships in each town where they stayed so as to have a place to pass the night and a support in case of trouble with local authorities. Long-distance muleteering is a thing of the past, but a related pattern persists, in that a number of potters have established compadrazgo relationships with pottery merchants in Pátzcuaro, to whom they deliver most of their wares. Moreover, within the village pottery merchants who have highway stands or who carry goods to Mexico City buy much of their merchandise from compadres. There is a strong feeling that a satisfactory commercial relationship is bolstered by a baptism or a confirmation.

One reason for the attractiveness of the compadrazgo is that it offers almost unlimited manipulative opportunities. Unlike kinship, an individual has a good deal of control over who is and who is not a compadre; he can consciously seek out those relationships which, whatever the reason, he sees as meaningful. Almost everyone, to some extent, appears to use the compadrazgo to strengthen or solidify position within the community, but some make much more conscious use of the manipulative possibilities than do others. When asked directly, most people say good friends make the best compadres, and that relatives usually should not be taken. Although I have not made a careful count, my data suggest that about one-third of primary compadrazgo relationships are with members of one's own family: siblings, first cousins, uncles and aunts, and occasionally parents. Of the other two-thirds, almost all are people of roughly the same socioeconomic status, and usually, but not always, from within the community itself. Most adults have one or two compadres from other villages, but the meaningful ties for the most part, now that muleteering is past, seem to be with Tzintzuntzeños.

A few people consciously attempt to enlist as compadres people of supérior social and economic status who can be of help in various ways. The Córdobas have several lawyer compadres from Morelia and Quiroga. Why lawyers? It's a pugnacious family, says Micaela, and it is helpful to have compadres who are able to help them out of their scrapes. Pánfilo Castellanos is conscious of the advantages, too. His compadres include a lawyer in Morelia, a physician in Pátzcuaro, and the local priest (who only with the greatest reluctance accepts such charges). Within the village itself Pánfilo shrugs his shoulders at most compadrazgo ties, and even, in the marriage of his eldest son to a village girl, refused to address the parents — whom he likes — by compadrazgo terminology, to the great distress of his more conventional wife. Most people, however, do not look for patrons as compadres. They hope to find good friends whose loyalty can be counted upon in time of need, whose company they can enjoy at fiestas and social gatherings, and who will cause them no trouble or worry.

Two features of the compadrazgo facilitate acquiring an optimum number of compadres of the latter type. The first is the rule that compadres not repeat. That is, for each of one's children there is normally a different set of compadres for baptism, confirmation, first communion, and marriage. And godparents for one occasion are not expected to serve as godparents to the same person or persons on subsequent occasions.

The second feature of the compadrazgo in Tzintzuntzan which enables one to acquire an optimum number of compadres, and the compadres one wishes, is that of extending the primary relationships to additional relatives and compadres of those involved in the act itself. This extension, or "blanketing-in," applies only to baptismal and marriage compadres. For each ceremony the pattern is slightly different.

In marriage, both the bride and groom come equipped with two parents, four grandparents, eight great-grandparents, and their padrinos *de grado*, i.e., of baptism and confirmation. All these people may establish compadrazgo relationships with the others in the list to whom they are not already so tied. Actually, of course, at the time of marriage a good many of these people will be deceased, and of the total of eighteen persons for both bride and groom, it would be a rare event when either would have the potential number present at the wedding ceremony. Nevertheless, through the single act of marriage up to thirty-six people become eligible to acquire additional compadres, some as many as a dozen, or even more. The collective number of potential new compadrazgo relationships resulting from a wedding is absolutely staggering.

The pattern is the same for baptism. When an infant is christened both its mother and father bring to the ceremony (figuratively speaking) a wide range of relatives including parents and grandparents, and their own baptismal, confirmation, and marriage godparents. The new baptismal godparents may also have living parents. The primary tie, of course, is that between the child's parents and the baptizing godparents, but by extension all the other people present may be brought into secondary, but nonetheless valid compadrazgo relationships.

But not all eligible persons present at a wedding or christening will want to form compadrazgo relationships with all the others. The individuals involved will see some of the potential new ties as very desirable, and others as equally undesirable. How is it decided just what new relationships will be established? The device is the abrazo, the ceremonial embrace, which all new compadres must give each other, and without which no compadrazgo is properly sealed. The persons present simply decide if they want to go through the embrace with all eligible people present. If so, they await their turn. If there are some candidates with whom they prefer not to establish ties, they conveniently remember an errand which needs attention at just this moment, and quietly slip out, thus avoiding an undesired entangling alliance.

In the early years of married life most people feel it desirable to build up a sizable group of compadres, so the general rule against repeating compadres, and the "blanketing-in" option are very desirable. But a person can maintain compadrazgo relationships with only a certain number of people — after the optimum point has been reached they become superfluous, and even a nuisance. Hence, there is a pronounced tendency for parents who continue to have many children increasingly to ask siblings and other close relatives to sponsor new baptisms and confirmations. In this way, expenses can be reduced and new ties now no longer particularly desirable are avoided. Strange situations occasionally result from this desire to stop proliferating compadres. Saúl Zurita is compadre to his own father and mother since, with his wife Paula, he baptized his newest baby brother. Modesto, the father, fulfilled Church requirements, and simultaneously avoided the expense and nuisance of elaborate ritual relationships he now does not want. Saúl continues to address his father as papá, with *usted*, and Modesto continues to address his son as *tú*, with no compadre-compadre nonsense to mar the relationship. This instance, although unusual, is not unique.

It is apparent that kinship, the compadrazgo, and friendship-neighborhoodship fulfill important and different functions in maintaining the community's stability, and in bringing security to each citizen. Kinship is basic, of course, since it gives the individual his first point of reference to his society, one which, as long as he remains in the community, he can never escape. The formal definition of kinship ties, and the precise placing of every person with respect to every other person in the extended family, is likewise to be seen as the starting point for all other village ties. But the kinship system of Tzintzuntzan is truncated as compared to those societies with clans, lineages, or functional extended families. The family in itself can accomplish only so much in structuring the ties each person needs to live in his community. Hence the importance of the compadrazgo, of fictive kinship, which has the religious validation and the formal structure of real kinship, combined with much of the flexibility of friendship, in that a person has great latitude in building this structure around him. It can accomplish much of what kinship accomplishes, and in many areas it does it more easily. In a traditional peasant society like Tzintzuntzan it is an ideal institution for extending the family.

CHAPTER FIVE

How
People
Behave

A COMMON MISCONCEPTION

In the preceding chapters, we have learned a good deal about the people of Tzintzuntzan, their history and environment, their work, and the formal aspects of their social relations. But in spite of these descriptions we can hardly say that we know them, for little has been said about what people think, what they feel, what their goals in life are, how they view the world about them, and what they believe prudent and desirable behavior to be. In this chapter we arrive at a new level of description and analysis, which continues through the following five chapters. I wish first to direct attention to people's overt behavior, and then to attempt an interpretation of character, and of the conditions which villagers feel are essential to maintaining a stable society. Finally I will try to show how the pattern which underlies these stability-promoting conditions is reflected and reiterated in the structure of religion, of decision making and conflict resolution, and in views about health and illness.

In describing the behavior of people in Tzintzuntzan I am faced with a problem encountered by many other anthropologists and social scientists who have written about peasants: the picture that emerges does not conform to a belief cherished by many that in rural life one finds embodied the natural and primeval human virtues shared by all humanity prior to the development of urban life, with its vices of individualism, competition, secularism, and lack of social cohesion. This discrepancy between what many people want to believe, and what emerges from the pen of most students of peasant life, can be explained as due to the durability of an intellectual theme in Western civilization.

Caro Baroja recently has traced the history of this theme, showing how, since early Greek times, city intellectuals have praised country life and its virtues, which they find in happy contrast to the moral corruption and artifice found in cities (1963). It is almost as if man, ever since inventing urban life, has felt guilty about it, and by way of apology feels compelled to insist that the fundamental virtues of his society can still be found in all their purity in the ways of the country. We are, in fact, faced with the opposition between one of man's most intensely cherished dreams — the beauty and idyllicism of rural life — and the hard data of contemporary social science research. Seeing in rural life a repository for a nation's fundamental morality is much more than the simple history of an idea, and an expression of a hope that man's nature is perfectible. It is an idée fixe that has guided many national political policies, and it intrudes as well into professional fields. American agrarian policy, for example, is based fundamentally on this assumption, and doctrinaire community development theory assumes the same thing. So to understand the real nature of life in traditional communities is a practical as well as a theoretical matter.

Those who hold to the idyllic view of rural life are shocked to read accounts which suggest that in many ways peasant life is quite the opposite of what they want to believe. To say such things seems almost wicked, for it appears to strike at the heart of man's image of his good society. The ancient assumption about rural life's virtues is therefore maintained by some who insist that reports that conflict with this view lack scientific objectivity and that, in addition, they simply reflect the personality of the writer who projects his own confused feelings about the world onto the peoples he studies.

Most scholars who have lived among peasants, whether in Mexico, South America, Spain, Italy, Egypt, or India do not share the Rousseauan view of rural life, but they usually have been genuinely fond of the people they have known. After overcoming initial suspicion, almost always present, they have found warm friendships, a sense of humor, an enjoyment of life, a spirit of rugged independence, and other personal qualities among the people that they find attractive. They have also, most of them, found suspicion, distrust, lack of cooperative behavior, and criticism of others. They have found villagers to be not so very different from urban dwellers, in the sense that they represent a wide range of temperament and behavior, and that they can hardly be characterized as all good or all bad in the traits they display. Above all they have found that the villagers' behavior conforms to broad cultural patterns, that it is a logical and sensible function of a total way of life.

Objective scholars — including those who have lived among peasants — who describe the personality and behavior of any group of people, mean to pass judgment, to evaluate behavior, only in the sense that they see it furthering or not furthering the goals, aspirations, and well-being of the people themselves. But in describing peasants, scholars writing in English are handicapped because the common words that apply to personality almost all carry evaluative connotations. "Cooperative," "friendly," "outgoing," "loyal," "thrifty," "hard-working" are all words that imply approbation. "Competitive," "uncooperative," "suspicious," "critical," "gossipy," and similar words imply criticism. Thus, there is no doubt but that a great deal of peasant behavior can accurately be described by these adjectives that carry negative connotations. In traditional peasant life, this happens to be a very logical and rational form of behavior; because it has promoted the viability of peasant societies over many millennia, it should be thought of as "good." But in the changing circumstances in which peasants now find themselves, it is less and less satisfactory in bringing people the security and opportunity they desire. In this sense, such behavior is "not good." The behavior, and the words used to describe it, are constant. The evaluation reflects the circumstances of time and history, and of the reader and his language.

BASIC FEATURES OF TZINTZUNTZAN CHARACTER

I find that behavior in Tzintzuntzan conforms in general to patterns outlined by other social scientists in Mexico and elsewhere: to name a few, Oscar Lewis in Tepoztlán (1951), Michael Maccoby in a village in Morelos, Mexico (1964), Ozzie Simmons in Lunahuaná, Peru (1959), Friedmann in Calabria and Lucania (1958), Banfield in the south Italian village of Montegrano (1958), Hamed Ammar in Egypt (1954), Carstairs in a Hindu community (1958) and S. K. Dube in Hyderabad State, India (1955). Life in these communities is described as marked by suspicion and distrust, inability to cooperate in many kinds of activities, sensitivity to the fear of shame, proneness to criticize and gossip, and a general view of people and the world as potentially dangerous.

These are, of course, not the only characteristics of personality. In Tzintzuntzan — and in the other communities, too, I am sure — family and friendship loyalties are often firm, as deeply entrenched and enduring as those found in any other society. People reveal a strong sense of humor: at fiestas, and in their daily contacts, they joke and clown, and they laugh wholeheartedly at the same incidents that amuse me. Enormous reservoirs of personal strength exist, upon which people draw for support in the face of adversity. The villagers derive great satisfaction from their religion, in their belief in the power and love of God, Christ, and the Virgin Mary. Tzintzuntzeños sense the beauty in the world around them, and they take pleasure in the tasks they do. Few are lazy, and many feel a puritanical satisfaction in hard work; if because of illness or age they cannot work, these people feel deprived. People seem to be at least as content, and at least as glad to be alive as people in my own society. Perhaps, on average, they are happier. There is no record of a suicide and no one, in my hearing, has ever said he felt depressed, although at times people certainly are. A person is sad, at the death of a parent, a spouse, or a child, but people seem not to think of themselves as either happy or unhappy, in the generalized sense in which many Americans do.

The ability to describe village behavior with any confidence comes only after long residence in the community, for Tzintzuntzeños, like other peasants, are a reserved people who do not immediately extend their friendship. Since an untrue friend may betray one, the villagers feel it safest to proffer friendship only after reasonable doubt about insincere motives is removed. When Gabriel Ospina and I first came to Tzintzuntzan we assumed that the reluctance to accept us, and even the overt hostility displayed toward us, was a natural consequence of fear about the motives of strangers from a different world. Only with the passage of time did we come to see that this caution is one of the basic forms of behavior in all interpersonal dealings.

Withdrawal, and concealing true feelings behind a mask, is one of the principal defenses peasants have used throughout history, between themselves and in facing strangers. Consequently, people listen to words, but they listen equally with all the senses, trying to read meaning into any clues that are forthcoming. Observational powers with respect to what seem to me trivial details of dress and behavior are acute. Adolfo Delgado has noticed that an American movie star is left-handed; Micaela was impressed because Barbara Smith crossed her rebozo in reverse fashion; and when I show a movie I took years ago in Tzintzuntzan, people comment on a chicken, a dog, the expression on someone's face, or some other detail which I, in scores of viewings, have never noticed.

After appraising people, the villagers give voice to their conclusions by describing them with the same adjectives used by social scientists. In a positive evaluation of others the words most frequently heard are "respectful," "correct," "honest," "not quarrelsome," and simply "very good." Generally lacking are such evaluations as "cooperative," "public-spirited," "generous," "kind," and "trustworthy." A good man is seen as one who minds his own business, who cares for his family, who meticulously fulfills his obligations to others, who respects their personality and dignity, who is not frivolous, who does not take advantage of his fellows, who avoids quarrels, and who does not presume. But a good man does not have to make a positive contribution to the group's welfare (except in the nearly obsolete *mayordomía* system); in fact, he is good precisely because he tends to avoid participation and contact, and not because he seeks positive intervention, which suggests ulterior motives.

PREVALENCE OF CRITICISM

With these preliminary remarks in mind, let us examine some behavior characteristics of the villagers. Of those an outsider sees, none is more striking than criticism. Criticism (and gossip and rumor) are laws of life. No one is spared, within or without the village, and no one is given the advantage of a doubt. The worst is automatically assumed, unless and until overwhelming evidence to the contrary is forthcoming. Even then, so deep is the suspicion and mistrust of others, it is difficult for people to believe that no hidden meaning underlies even the most casual acts. In everyday conversation, one hears many more adjectives that evaluate people negatively than those which evaluate them positively. A person is "critical," "gossipy," "abusive," "quarrelsome," "greedy," "conceited," "thick-skinned," "stingy," "nosy," "a nobody," "a drunk," "a thief." Juan is *orgulloso*, he won't cooperate in village affairs, lend money to friends, or help others; he's "stuck up." Eliseo Miranda is *egoísta*, he is selfish, refuses to share. A CREFAL professor gave him potatoes of a new and superior variety, which he was to plant, and then give seed potatoes to others. But he kept them all to himself, and gave none away. Ignacio is *muy alegativo*, abusive, he quarrels over the smallest matters and uses his position to abuse and take advantage of others. José is a *ladrón*, for he steals beans and maize across the low wall that separates his patio from those of his neighbors.

Consuelo is always *chismeando,* she gossips continually, maliciously, without foundation.

Manuela Torres remarks that Aurelia Medellín, well past seventy, has aged greatly in recent months, and that she suffers from a cardiac condition. Manuela seems genuinely astonished, and only half convinced, when I tell her I have recently taken Aurelia to see a Pátzcuaro doctor, and he has said she is in remarkably good health, considering her age. Aurelia had been living with her youngest son, Gaudencio, and his wife, María Antonia, in a town a hundred miles away. Manuela counters my evidence by saying she was recently there and saw how María Antonia treated Aurelia. "This girl is very bad," she says. I express surprise, since I also had been in the town, and had had a very different impression of Gaudencio's wife. Yes, she treated Aurelia rudely, didn't want to walk with her, refused to let her come along when she strolled in the plaza with her husband, and for this reason, Aurelia is not well. Manuela feels, like most mothers-in-law, that María Antonia is trying to separate mother and son. The CREFAL pottery professor, says Juan Guillén, really didn't want people to learn new pottery techniques; he only pretended he did, since that is what he was paid for. Once, in a small pottery firing experiment I worked out with Julio Calderón (pages 252–254) we bought green ware from one of the village women and arranged for her to glaze it for us. Because of defects in the experiment, which involved an oil-fired kiln, the pots turned out badly. "She didn't want you to succeed," said Primo, the father of Julio. "She purposely put too much binder in the glaze so it would remain white. Don't go to her again; she's only trying to deceive you." Primo was quite sure he spoke the truth.

People justify much of their criticism of others by saying "He is very egoísta," he's very egotistical. A person who is egoísta, who has the quality of egoísmo, is selfish, thinks only of his own welfare, refuses to share knowledge or other things with his neighbors. Eliseo Miranda, who refused to share the seed potatoes given him by CREFAL, is egotistical. Narciso Luna knew of a hardware store in Tlaquepaque (Jalisco) which sold a particular glaze unavailable locally. When other potters asked him

92

for the address, he said he had lost it. No one believed him. "He's egotistical," they said. Micaela refuses to give my address freely to villagers who ask for it — a protection not altogether unappreciated since the usual letter is a plea to arrange papers so they can come as immigrants to the United States. She is egotistical, say the villagers; she refuses to share with them. Several years ago Teodoro Zúñiga produced a new black burnished ware by the oxygen reducing process, a technique he apparently learned from Oaxaca potters in Mexico City, although he claims to have invented it himself. He refused to divulge the secret to others, and only after some time had gone by did the process leak out. He, and the other potters who first caught on, are all egotistical; they refuse to share. Few, if any, adults have not been at one time or another accused of egoísmo.

Rumor — a concomitant of criticism — rules in Tzintzuntzan. In the fall of 1963 the body of a newborn infant, the umbilical cord still attached, was found in an arroyo near town. Whose was it? Nobody knew. Lola Pichu, as Representante del Ministerio Público, recorded the finding in her books, then had the body buried, assuming the incident closed. Someone passing in a car presumably had disposed of the body in this remote place; had it been a local girl her condition would have been noticed. Then, to everyone's surprise, two "secret police" agents came from Pátzcuaro, looking for the guilty party. Then, obviously, the villagers concluded, it must be a local girl after all. Tongues started wagging. The three village midwives all gave negative reports: they had delivered no one in secret. Then someone remarked casually that a sixteen-year-old girl from Ichupio, a niece of Jaime Martín, had not been seen for several months. Another girl from La Vuelta was also named as not having appeared for some time. The answer was clear. They had remained indoors to conceal their illegitimate pregnancies, given birth, one of their babies was thrown away (no one bothered to speculate about the other), and now again they were out and about. The two girls were taken to Pátzcuaro for questioning, and given a medical examination, returning home with a clean bill of health, their virginity better attested than that of any other village girl.

The following Sunday Father Fuentes spoke of the event, preached about the evils of calumny, reprimanded his parishioners for starting rumors, and told them to say only what they knew, and not what they thought, to be true. But he, I suspect, was no more hopeful than I that behavior would change.

Criticism is directed equally at outsiders with whom villagers have contact. CREFAL students who collected eggs when the chicken ranching scheme was functioning were accused by all of short changing the sellers, of weighing their thumbs, as it were, along with the eggs, so that they would make a few pesos of personal profit.

Medical doctors, in spite of the dependence villagers have come to have on them in recent years, are also usually suspect; it is taken for granted their only interest in a patient is for the money that can be squeezed from him. Nevertheless, a good many people have submitted to surgical operations. But a member of the family always insists on being in the operating room — and this permission is granted by local surgeons — to check on the doctor's acts. With a family member present, it is reasoned, a doctor will not be able to take advantage of the patient, or skimp or omit or hasten the operation. Should the operation turn out badly, there will be a witness to affirm that "he did everything humanly possible."

Because of the distrust and suspicion that underlies the rank criticism that pervades daily life, people usually are very reserved, and reluctant to reveal their innermost thoughts. *La vida es una lucha*, life is a struggle, is an expression often heard, and guards must be kept up at all times. Revealing thoughts, or intentions, or information, lowers one's guards and makes him vulnerable to the malevolent acts of others. With all the good times people have, and the fun and friendliness the anthropologist observes, there is much loneliness in the character of people. Simple friendship and warm feelings without ulterior motives often come with difficulty, and though many people have good friends, most have very few intimate friends. Even within close families there is reserve, and although families are the principal economic productive units, and within them there is often much love and affection, the social rites of other societies emphasizing this oneness are poorly developed. Families never sit down to eat together at a table. Father and older sons eat quietly in the kitchen, each holding his plate on his lap, conversing little. Wives and daughters snatch bites as they make tortillas and serve food to the men, standing beside the raised hearth or squatting over the three firestones.

Even though no home is without one or more small altars, these are not centers of family rites. Any member of the family, as the spirit moves him or her, may light a candle to one of the saints or to the Virgin whose image stands there, perhaps without revealing his problems to others in the family. Mass does not reflect, as do church services in the United States, the feeling of family solidarity associated with a religious service. Women and babies occupy the right side of the church (facing the altar) and men the left side. Boys go with their age mates to the front of the church, on the left, and girls to the front, on the right. Mass divides, not unites, the family. Even in death the path is lonely. There are no family plots in the cemetery, and each corpse is placed in the most convenient spot, as determined by the mayor on an ad hoc basis. Husband and wife do not lie together in death; their earthly remains may be on opposite sides of the small cemetery, where each can continue to guard his counsel.

Distrust, loneliness, and reserve are also reflected in other forms of behavior. Since people find it difficult to believe that others can behave with lack of selfish interest, they are not given to banding together in associations, and this lack of sense of association severely cripples the community in many ways. People are reluctant to cooperate in other than the most traditional civic affairs, such as religious fiestas and national patriotic observances, and even here they are watchful, fearing that others will in some way use the situation for personal advantage. This same lack of sense of association has also affected adversely every effort of CREFAL personnel to form cooperatives, in pottery making, in weaving, and in carpentry. Suspicion and distrust limit members' ability to work together, for they fear others will extract more from the situation than they.

An overriding suspicion of the motives of others also presents a serious problem in local government, because many of the people who might best serve their community are averse to seeking political office. They know that as soon as a man is elected he will be attacked through criticism, slander, perhaps witchcraft, and even assassination. They know this to be true, because they criticize and slander all officials, sure they are defrauding the community (they sometimes are), utilizing office for personal gain. Jesús Peña was mayor in 1942. He was elected again the following year, but almost immediately he fell ill with a crippling arthritis coupled with other aches and pains. He could scarcely hobble to the office on crutches, and doctors could do him no good. Finally, desperate, he consulted a *curandero* (a folk medical curer) who told him he had been bewitched, and that he — the curandero — was unable to break the spell. Jesús saw the handwriting on the wall, resigned office, and within a few weeks was as healthy as ever.

SENSITIVITY TO PUBLIC OPINION

In a community in which suspicion and distrust are common, and in which criticism is forthcoming on the slightest pretext, it is to be expected that people will be inordinately sensitive to real and imagined slights and insults, and to public opinion. In Tzintzuntzan fear of "what people will say" is a much more potent instrument in making a smoothly functioning society than are the combined forces of law and the moral teachings of religion. "Correct" behavior is the best way to reduce criticism to the lowest possible levels, and no finer thing can be said of a person than that he is *muy correcto*, very correct.

From early childhood one learns to be "correct." Children, when confronted with a family friend or a stranger, are told *dále la mano*, i.e., step up and shake hands. All through life hands are shaken at the slightest pretext, in greeting or saying goodbye to friends, a hundred times a day. This is a demonstration of "correctness," of good intentions and good feelings. Children are taught, too, never to walk in front of others, if it is possible to avoid doing so, since this presumes on the dignity of the person

96

so offended. If there is no alternative, the child learns to say "with your permission," before so doing, thus showing he recognizes, and regrets, the possible offense he may be guilty of, and wishes to show he is taking an action only with the permission of the person he seems to threaten. Even when someone breaks away from a group he will say *con su permiso ya me voy*, with your permission I'll be running along. The departure is contingent upon the assurance that no one is offended by the action.

At fiesta meals certain guests are expected to bring tequila, rum, or beer; bottles are set on the table, and small glasses are provided, usually in quantities insufficient for each diner to have his own. A thirsty guest doesn't simply drink when the spirit moves him, since this might seem to presume on the tolerance of others. If it is beer he will pick up his bottle, look around the table, invite others to drink with him by saying *salud*, and wait until the others also lift their bottles, thus assuring him that he is not presuming in drinking alone. Should the diner desire hard liquor he turns to the person who brought the bottle and asks if he will not do him the honor of pouring a drink. But he will not take this drink; instead he insists that all of the others first have a round before he himself satisfies his thirst. At such fiestas not all guests arrive simultaneously, and not all diners eat at the same speed, so that the successive plates of soup, rice, and turkey mole reach individuals at different times. One rarely waits for the others, but before dipping into a new dish he courteously asks permission of his neighbors to do so, and only then does he feel he can continue to eat without fear of offending.

"Correct" behavior that will lessen the occasions on which one is criticized, or protect one from the danger of malicious rumors, is a general goal. Women are embarrassed if a neighbor suddenly drops in and finds them without an apron; it is "correct" for all women to wear this garment. Micaela is clever with her hands, and skillful in improving her house. Her abilities include laying cobblestones, which she happily does in the privacy of her patio. But when it is a question of the street outside, reluctantly she decides she will have to hire a peon, for fear of "what people will say" if she were seen doing this work.

"Correct" dress is given much attention; correctness means in most instances not dressing above village norms. For this reason, male city attire, with coat and tie, are looked at askance. Such costume can be described by any of three words: *catrín*, the usual Mexican word for city costume; *tacuche* (from Tarascan *takusi*, a piece of cloth); and *curro*, meaning "sporty" or "flashy." The first two words are powerful persuaders to conformity, but are not offensive; the last is a club. Primo Calderón, returning from the United States many years ago after a long residence there, presumed to dress in city fashion. A few suggestions that he was *entacuchado* sufficed; coat and tie were hung in a closet and never worn again. Even Bernardo Zaldívar, liked and respected for his effective work as town mayor, has been reluctant to wear city clothes. Several years ago Gabriel Ospina gave him a used suit coat which pleased him immensely. But when he wore it his friends chided him, "Ay, Bernardo, you're dressed very curro." He was so embarrassed he took it off, saving it only for the pottery-selling trips he makes to Mexico City.

People sometimes are reluctant to take a relative as compadre: "they" will say it is done to avoid expense. Jesús Molinero, in spite of his poverty, struggled to fulfill the duty expected of every able-bodied man, sponsoring a fiesta. He would have chanced divine wrath by failing to comply, but he couldn't face adverse public opinion. Gregorio Méndez beat his wife Carmen because her mother bought her a new and badly needed dress. "They will say," he said by way of explanation, "that I am unable to clothe my wife." On the ninth night after a death in a family great quantities of the hominy-like *pozole* dish are prepared to feed friends who have come the preceding nights to pray. Macaria Gómez doesn't think much of the custom, but when her husband Pánfilo died she complied because of what people might think: "they would say he didn't leave me anything, not even livestock that could be sold." She couldn't bear to think that people would feel Pánfilo had not been a good provider.

People are also sensitive about much of the treatment they receive from outsiders. They resent (quite properly, I think) the fact that most city people assert superiority by addressing them with the informal second person personal pronoun *tú*, as they would in addressing children, rather than with the formal *usted*. People are apologetic about themselves. "We are very humble" is an expression constantly heard and, when I drop in on potter friends, and in answer to my question as to how they are, they are apt to reply, "Well, here we are, in all of this dirt and mud."

With sensitivity, it is clear why so much emphasis is placed on "respect," and why the person, villager or outsider, who shows respect is himself liked and respected. In dealings between friends there are countless assurances that each is treating the other "with the respect you merit," for respect is seen as one of the few inalienable rights to which a man is entitled; therefore it is a precious commodity, to be guarded jealously.

Yet even with assurances of respect, a person is doubtful if they are really meant, since he knows his own protestations are not always genuine. One wishes *not* to be suspect, and to really merit the respect that may be shown him. So in a multitude of situations he urges others to do something such as to eat or come to visit *con confianza*, with confidence, with the certainty that the proffered food or hospitality is given without ulterior motives which must be fathomed. In a world in which everyone is suspect, everyone hopes against hope that he will be recognized as above suspicion.

Tzintzuntzeños, although never hesitant to criticize others, are, as we have seen, enormously sensitive to criticism. This applies as much to self-criticism as to the criticism of other people. Apparently, in order to merit respect, a person must feel that his own behavior is above reproach. Whatever the reason, whenever something goes wrong the blame is felt to lie in circumstances beyond one's control. Scheming people, the weather, bad luck, fate, all may be invoked by way of explaining failure. The one thing never heard is, "I made a mistake." A goat must be found for every untoward event. As María Flores once said:

> *El trabajo no es perder,*
> *Sino hallar a quien culpar.*

That is, the problem is not in failure, in losing; the work consists of finding someone to blame for the failure. Success, for reasons that will be forthcoming, is not seen as due to superior skill or hard work; lack of success, therefore, can hardly be due to lack of these personal qualities. To blame one's self is as unthinkable as to accept the blame of others.

The relationship between proneness to criticize and sensitivity to public opinion is recognized by some people, and it is expressed in the saying:

> El que peros pone, peros tiene.
> "He who gives 'buts' will receive 'buts.' "

A pero, a "but," is the expression of a real or imagined defect or shortcoming in someone, but it really is seen as revealing more about the speaker than the object. Micaela illustrated the expression by saying "Fulano (i.e., John Doe) is a very good person, pero ("but") he has such and such defects." A person who "puts peros" is always qualifying his kind words, trying to call attention to defects in others, damning with faint praise. And a person who does this constantly can expect a return in kind; he will "have peros" himself.

FRIENDSHIP QUALITIES

In a community such as Tzintzuntzan, where distrust, suspicion, criticism, and sensitivity are so widespread, we should not be surprised that friendship displays paradoxical qualities. On the one hand, absolute loyalty is seen as the primary virtue in personal relationships. Yet at the same time, friendship is seen as fragile and brittle, as unpredictable and uncertain. As the following illustrations show, real loyalty often overrides all other considerations in friendship relations. Yet the same people who exercise such loyalty may, on other occasions, be anything but loyal to each other. Shortly after the 1964 elections when Gustavo Díaz Ordaz was named president of Mexico I talked about politics with Bernardo Zaldívar, a former mayor and an active politician. He said the village overwhelmingly supported the Government's winning PRI party slate "because the deputies in this party are our friends, and naturally we support them." Bernardo, like the other villagers, saw support of the candidates as stemming, not necessarily from merit or qualification for office, but from the personal relationship with them.

Friendship is also illustrated by another event. José Castellanos became an ambulance driver for Social Security in Morelia. On one occasion he was bringing several children for tuberculin tests when he crashed his ambulance against a tree, badly cutting his head. Without waiting to see if the children were injured, he took off on a wild flight that finally, several days later, brought him to Tzintzuntzan. But rather than risk apprehension at home — in fact, the police did come there — he asked Macaria Gómez to hide him, and for several months he remained hidden in one of her rooms. He had no feelings of guilt for irresponsible driving, nor was he interested in whether he had injured or killed the children. Nor did Macaria and her family have guilt feelings in concealing a man wanted by the authorities. Had one of the children been a close relative, and the driver an unknown person, they would have been indignant at a system that allowed a criminal to escape. As it was, Jóse was a good friend, pursued by the authorities, and obviously it was their obligation to protect him. Yet five years later, for reasons having nothing to do with this incident, the two families, formerly so close, were not on speaking terms!

In the face of a stated ideal, and behavior such as that of Macaria and her family toward Jóse, loneliness and doubts, and uncertainties and disappointments are seen as constant threats to friendship. On one occasion Macaria loaned money to the son of her good friend Consuelo when he needed help to get to the United States as a bracero. When he returned he repaid the loan, but did not give her the present which, as a friend who had helped in time of need, she felt she was entitled to expect. *Un bién con un mal se paga*, a good deed is repaid by a bad one, she remarked philosophically, to explain her disappointment. The frequency with which this expression is heard reflects the common expectation that, although one good turn ought to deserve another, the other is not necessarily forthcoming. Children, hearing this aphorism countless times, soon learn that friendship and disillusionment are closely bound together.

That friendship is fragile, and to be viewed with caution, is illustrated by an experience of Adolfo Delgado. Once he bought a pair of trousers in Pátzcuaro in a shop where he knew the proprietor, paying without question $75 which, because of his friendship, he assumed was the best price he could get. Later he noticed the same garment in another store with a $35 price tag. *Entre los compañeros más se amuela*, he said in recounting the experience: "One suffers most because of friendship."

In view of what has been said on the preceding pages, the reader may well wonder if there is *no* form of village solidarity, of village cohesiveness, of trust, in which people close ranks for a common good. There is such a form but, as the following example shows, it is of a specialized type, negative in character. The death register for Tzintzuntzan has the following notation for a day nearly thirty years ago:

Francisco Zúñiga, son of Bonifacio, dead by a gunshot.
Estanislado Villalba, son of Jóse María, dead by a knife wound.

I asked Micaela what had happened. "Who told you this story?" she asked, with considerable heat. Relieved when I told her I had simply noted from official records that both men had died by violence on the same day, and realizing my knowledge of the event would not threaten the village, she launched into a long tale of jealousy over a woman, of drunkenness, of a fight, in which each man was slain by the brother of the other one. Both murderers, by a curious quirk of fate, had recently become our compadres when we had served as godparents to their daughters graduating from primary school.

Later in the day I asked Primo Calderón how the two men had died. He grunted, said they got drunk one night, killed each other, bodies were found the next day, and that's all there was to it. Vicente Rendón confirmed Primo's story: they got drunk and killed each other for unknown reasons. Wenceslado Peña said the same thing. But, since Micaela had said Francisco had actually been taken into Wences' house to die, I pressed him with a lead-

102

ing question. Well, yes, some people said Rudolfo, the brother of Estanislado, was the one who actually killed Francisco. And well, maybe it was Genaro, the brother of Francisco who, seeing his brother wounded, stuck his knife into Estanislado. Come to think of it, they carried Francisco in and he died right in the room in which we were sitting!

The authorities came from Pátzcuaro to investigate, but the case was clear. The bodies were found together on the street, neither family cared to press charges, and the subject was hushed up without further inconvenience from outside meddling. Everyone in town knew of the event, but not a word of it had been breathed in my presence, even in discussing murders which, in other cases, were freely talked about; the only puzzle, in the minds of the people I asked, was which of their fellows had betrayed the community by revealing the incident to me. But cooperation of the *omerta*, the Sicilian conspiracy of silence, requires no positive action; it merely implies the unspoken agreement to say nothing to outsiders. The ability to protect the community through silence provides no base on which to promote community welfare through positive action.

BASIC FEARS

The fear shown in the above story is but a specialized case of a much more general syndrome. For in fact, timidity and fear, of the known and the unknown, of the real or only the suspected threat, mark everyone's behavior. People fear poverty, old age, the death of their spouses, of their children, and above all their own deaths while still young, because this will leave their small children alone in a hostile world where no one will tend them the way parents should. Gossip is feared, eavesdropping is feared, envy is feared, anger is feared, fierce dogs are feared, and sleeping alone is feared. House doors usually are kept closed all day long, and at night they are wedged shut with heavy poles. Vicente Rendón's bedroom is bisected by a stout ten-foot post that props the shutters of his window that opens to the street. Nearly all homes have dogs that are beaten and abused, taught to hate man, and trained to attack anyone who comes to the door.

One hears of mysterious strangers from *por ay* — from where? "from there," a vague and unspecified locality. They are always in cahoots with local people who tip them off as to when a family is away, when it has had an economic windfall, or when circumstances are favorable for robbery. It is always difficult to approach Mariano Cornelio's house because of his mob of snapping dogs. But they protect him, to some extent he says, although not completely. A year ago strangers came from por ay, poisoned their predecessors, and stole two dozen chickens. They had local accomplices who knew his property, possessions, and family habits, but Mariano doesn't say who they are. This is in keeping with local character. Although a few close friends have told me the names of fellow villagers who have robbed them, I have found no court record of a Tzintzuntzeño formally charging another with theft.

Micaela's street door is always carefully shored up with posts at night. A door with a broken lower panel lies under a shed, evidence she says of strangers from por ay who one night tried to break in. Only because of the stout posts were they unable to accomplish their mission. Two months ago, in nearby Quiroga, she says, a man sneaked into the patio of a wealthy storekeeper, concealed himself until the family retired, then opened the door and admitted ten accomplices. They bound and gagged the mother, who was the only one who awakened, and quietly removed a television set, a radio, and all the stock of the store, loading it into a truck which they drove off into the night.

Lola is much frightened by strange men who say they are from Quiroga who wander through the village asking if there are pigs for sale; obviously, she reasons, they are looking for likely homes to rob. One day she returned home to find one of these men talking outside her door. He engaged her in conversation, asked about pigs (there were none), said he had a hangover and was going to find a friend to give him money to buy a drink. Lola saw her chance. She reached into her pocket, gave him fifty centavos, and told him to "cure" himself with her compliments. She felt the price was cheap to get this unsavory character away from her house.

Fear of eavesdropping conditions behavior. Salvador Cuiríz was remodeling the new house he had purchased, building a kitchen and dining room on the south side of the patio. I asked if putting them on the north side, so the sun would strike their windows, would not make them much more pleasant rooms. He agreed, but pointed out that his north wall is alongside the public baths and wash tubs, and if his kitchen were adjacent, people would overhear family conversations. The lot to the south is vacant, so no immediate problem, and even when built upon, with a single family there will be far fewer people to overhear what goes on. And, since he can eavesdrop on them, the dangers are balanced. Micaela debated for years putting a new kitchen adjacent to the street; she also feared eavesdroppers. Finally she did so, but cautioned us to talk in a low voice. We said we thought the twelve-inch adobe wall pretty well stifled sound, but she was unconvinced. She agreed to an experiment. While we talked in loud voices, Lola went outside and listened. Not a sound, said Lola; absolute silence within. Everyone was greatly relieved.

In Tzintzuntzan sleeping is often quite communal. A single bed may be used simultaneously by four or five people of various ages. What seems impossible crowding by standards of people who sleep one, or at most two, in a bed, is a source of comfort and security in the village. Sleeping alone may be an unpleasant, lonely, and therefore frightening experience. The warmth of other bodies in bed, the sounds of breathing, the turnings and stirrings of others, are all reassuring. Crowding, far from being a nuisance, is a positive value. When relatives and friends drop in from other towns they are — according to sex — added to the appropriate bed, much as in the United States a housewife adds an extra place at the table when guests unexpectedly arrive.

A basic fear is also revealed in a reluctance to provoke anyone's hostility and anger. "Avoid trouble at almost any cost" is a primary rule guiding most people in their relations with others. One day while walking to El Rincón with Doña Andrea Medina we saw a drunk staggering along in the same direction half a block ahead, and making slow progress of it. "Why don't we turn up here so we can avoid him," she said. "It's very unpleasant to meet drunks." So we jogged a block south, then west, then north again, thus bypassing a likely troublemaker.

One fall Vicente Rendón seemed in an unusual hurry to thresh the beans gathered in the patio of an unoccupied house. Why the rush? The woman in the house next door had been stealing a few plants at a time; he could see the trail in the dust where she dragged them over the low wall separating the properties. What was Vicente going to do? Denounce her to the authorities? No, he planned nothing. He simply wanted to finish threshing as soon as possible, get the beans under lock and key, and remove the temptation. The loss was slight, and there was no need to anger a neighbor, however unneighborly her behavior.

No one in town appears to be fonder of her siblings and their large families than Natalia Paz, now sixty, and the oldest of seven children. Yet, I once learned almost by accident, she had harbored a grudge for many years against her next younger brother, Julio, because of an inheritance problem. All children, including daughters, are entitled to inherit equally. Her father, upon his death, indicated that Julio, his eldest son, was to be responsible for the precise division of the large town lot he had owned. When the time came to divide, Julio excluded Natalia and her sister on the grounds that they were married and their husbands already had houses. Natalia felt that, for the years of hard work she had put in helping raise her younger siblings, and the postponement of her marriage because her mother couldn't spare her, she was entitled to her share. Yet, in spite of her feelings of antagonism Natalia rarely allows them to show; to avoid trouble and open conflict is even more important to her.

At a deeper, psychological level, attitudes toward food reveal a deep-seated fear of the outside world. Food, when it comes from unknown hands and unknown sources, arouses great anxiety. This is particularly true of meals eaten in cities away from home. If villagers find a small restaurant or market stall where the proprietress seems friendly, they will return again and again, often at considerable inconvenience, rather than risk the dangers of eating in an unknown restaurant. Tales abound of finding parts of human bodies and other unattractive elements in food served in

106

big cities. Once villagers were eating a stew in a market place in Mexico City. They asked the proprietress about a lump of bone and meat. "That's the head of the lamb you are eating," she said. "Ay, Mamá," said the woman's small son. "That's not *cabeza de borregito*, that's the head of the dog we killed yesterday."

Many years ago Natividad Peña, her husband Vicente Rendón, and their daughter Chelo rode into Mexico City with me, staying in a small hotel in the center of town. Upon our return to Tzintzuntzan they showed me a photograph they had had taken. "We look terrible," said Nati. "I am naturally ugly, but I look uglier in this picture. It's because we hardly ate a thing all the time we were in Mexico City. We were afraid of what might be in the food they gave us in restaurants." Then they told stories of finding cat meat in *mole*, disguised as chicken, and of their belief that dog, horse, and burro meat are freely served in Mexico City. They even told a variant of the following story in which Micaela claims to have been a participant.

When she was about ten, Padre Avilés took several village girls, including Micaela, to Mexico City to visit the Shrine of the Virgin of Guadalupe. They stayed in a small hotel in Colonia Roma, where they found the food rather poor. One day Padre Avilés was served a *torta*, meat fried in egg batter. He looked inside and there — Micaela graphically held up her hand and simulated lopping it off at the wrist — was the hand of a newborn infant. Padre Avilés said to the girls, "You'd all better look inside your tortas," and sure enough, each had a bit of the baby. So they went to the garden where Padre Avilés said to the hotel owner that it wasn't right to eat infants. "No, you don't understand," replied the owner, "these are stillborn foetuses that were never baptized, so it's alright to eat them." "I'm sure he must have been a Jew," said Micaela, searching for an explanation for this extraordinary logic. "Yes, of course, Jews do things like that. Once there was a troup of *húngaros* (Hungarians, i.e., gypsies — Jews, Hungarians, and gypsies are all the same to Micaela) camped at Santa Fe, across the lake. That night a woman died in childbirth. There was no crying, no noise. But all that night fires roared, and the gypsies were seen putting casseroles on the

fire. There was no burial, nothing, and the next day they left."
Obviously the woman and her infant had been cooked and eaten.
Another psychological aspect of fear is expressed in a wide-spread folk medical etiology. *Me dío un susto* ("I was frightened") is one of the most common explanations of illness. Fright may come from almost any source: an encounter with the devil or an evil spirit, a highway accident, gunfire, a sudden surprise, unexplained noises in the night. One night I was returning from Mexico City to Pátzcuaro when the sleeping car left the rails and rolled over on its side, fortunately without injuries to the passengers. "Weren't you frightened?" I was asked by the villagers. They found it hard to believe that serious illness didn't follow such a terrifying experience.

PRAGMATISM

Behavior in Tzintzuntzan is not based on an assumption of a fundamental orderliness in the universe, in which law and regularity govern the systems within which one lives. Consequently, immutable standards of comportment are not found. In determining a particular course of action the questions asked are not "what behavior conforms to canons of ethics or the logic of a system," but rather "what is most likely to work?" People are pragmatic, in personal relations, in medical practices, in decision making, and in all other activities.

When action is called for, an ad hoc appraisal is made of the situation, according to which a particular form of behavior will follow. Ideas about health and illness conform in theory to a beautifully logical system (Chapter Nine) in which the treatment appropriate to every diagnosis is quite clearly seen. Yet the treatment called for on the basis of logic is constantly modified on pragmatic grounds; something else has been done in the past, and the patient recovered, so now that experience will be called upon in the case at hand. Hypodermic injections conform to no traditional practices, yet obviously they cure people, so there is no compunction in overriding any sense of system to use this treatment.

Falsehoods, in theory, are recognized as sins, yet major and minor falsehoods are the order of the day. A friend or relative, child or adult, must be told something to force or persuade him to a course of action. Will the truth or a lie be more efficacious? The decision will be pragmatically decided, and the morality of truth versus falsehood will not enter the deliberations. Children are constantly told falsehoods — El Doctor and Mariquita will carry you away if you don't stop crying — is one of the most common, much to our annoyance. An envious younger sibling who sees an older sibling going off on what looks like a pleasant excursion will be told it is being taken to a doctor who will hurt it by sticking needles in its arm. The same techniques also are used to manipulate adults. One day I arrived at Faustino Peña's house, invited to eat pozole in honor of his saint's day. Eucario Cabeza, his compadre, who had brought the liquor, was just barely vertical, and his wife and the others were embarrassed about what I might think. "Come and lie down, Eucario," his wife said. "Father Huacúz is coming." Slowly the implications began to sink in. "Father Huacúz coming?" he repeated slowly. "Yes, he's just down the street. We can see him. He'll be here any minute." So, slightly protesting, Eucario allowed himself to be led off to a bedroom where he quickly fell asleep.

This pragmatic approach to manipulating people, or coping with interpersonal problems, obscure the line between truth and falsehood to the point where most people do not think in this way at all. Will an answer work? Will it please? Will it be the simplest solution? These are the questions asked.

EXPLOITING ADVANTAGE

Although a person is seen to have an inalienable right to "the respect which he merits," he does not expect absolutely just, fair, and impartial treatment from other people, from foreigners, from the government, from — in a word — the "system." In looking back over his life experiences he sees no pattern of an abstract justice; the good and bad have come to him in quixotic, unpredictable fashion that conforms to no apparent absolute standard. And, just as a person knows that he may not expect absolute standards in treatment to be extended him, he sees no reason to show them to others. An opponent or enemy may be accused of being egotistical, abusive, treacherous, quarrelsome, or dishonest, but he is unlikely to be accused of not playing fair. In all contests, physical, economic, or social, it is assumed that opponents will use any means at their disposal. A murderer hopes to shoot from ambush; surprise is one of his resources. "To hit below the belt," in a figurative or literal sense, is hardly understood. Standards of moral appropriateness other than what works best do not often enter calculations. Witness the following story:

Nabor Córdoba has threatened to kill Eusebio Herrera, who is married to José Enríquez' daughter, Aurelia. The reason is a quarrel over an inheritance in which Nabor seems to have justice on his side, but to hold no aces. Nabor's great-grandfather and Aurelia's grandfather, Santiago, were the same person. When Santiago died his three sons were living together in his house, the one now occupied by José Enríquez, the second son. Nabor's grandfather, Juan, the youngest son, was to have inherited the property, the older sons, according to custom, receiving other properties and monies. But Juan died young, his widow remarried and moved out, and José simply remained, de facto owner, paying taxes over the years and maintaining the house. Micaela admits that Juan's three daughters, of which the youngest is Nabor's mother, have the best legal claim to the property. José Enríquez also apparently recognizes this, for the two oldest daughters are said to have accepted $200 from him to release their claims. Nabor's mother refused the offer, and the matter was dormant for some time.

Then early in 1964 Eusebio, who had bought part of the property from his father-in-law, Juan, and whose wife Aurelia would receive the balance, claimed that Nabor's sister had insulted him. This was the excuse José Enríquez was looking for; he feigned anger and said because of this he would now give his niece — Nabor's mother — nothing, and that the property would go to Aurelia and her husband Eucario. Nabor feels his mother (and he and his siblings) are being done out of what is rightfully theirs, and being a tough customer, he doesn't plan to take it passively. Micaela agrees that Nabor is in the right, but accepts Eusebio's position as one in which, obviously, he can't surrender his "possession is nine points of the law" advantage. Absolute standards of justice occur to no one. *El que tiene pico más suelto se queda como albacea*, says Micaela by way of justification: "He who has the most active beak (i.e. can smell out opportunity) ends up as executor."

Lack of absolute standards based on a system that renders impartial and fair justice is also reflected in the relative absence of guilt feelings in encounters with the law. If one is caught and punished the feeling is one of regret and anger, but guilt feelings seem usually not to attach to the act that led to apprehension. When José Castellanos crashed his ambulance and fled, he showed no sense of responsibility to his small charges, and his only expressed feeling was of bitterness at having had the bad luck to lose a good job.

Lack of standards conforming to a sense of equal treatment for all is reflected in still another common form of behavior. Many people in positions of power abuse their position to the utmost, using it to extract personal gain. Many other people assume it natural to utilize any minor advantage that may fall their way. The mayor who sells bracero permits at high prices, for example, illustrates this behavior. He is criticized unmercifully for his dishonesty, but many of his critics would do the same thing had they the opportunity, and the remainder would agree that if he asked for a consideration of, say, $50 rather than $500 it would be all right. Small advantages accruing from a favorable position are assumed to be one's right; it is only excessive abuse that arouses anger. In a recent year the mayor wanted to sell the limited number of permits given him rather than to hold public drawings for all holders of $9.60 tickets, as authorized by law. In fact, he had already collected a good deal of money from would-be braceros. The *síndico*, however, who is also a member of the town council, and who this year was an unusually fair-minded person, felt this unethical behavior so violently that he reported it to Morelia, and an official came who supervised a legal drawing, much to the mayor's discomfort. Later the síndico said to the official, "Look, how about giving each of the members of the town council a permit, so that we can use it or give it to a relative?" This small degree of benefit from public office seemed to him to be quite natural, and he was somewhat surprised when the Morelia official said no, that nobody would receive a permit other than by the legal draw.

Jaime Pelón owns a busy and relatively profitable store. What taxes does he pay? For a liquor license, $125 annually; to the State Receptor of Rents, $44 monthly; and to the municipio treasury, $75 annually. These are the legal small town fees, he says, and all stores of similar size pay the same. This year, fortunately, he once said, he didn't have to pay the local treasury fee since he was town councilman. This struck him as a perfectly natural fringe benefit for a politician, a minor advantage that no one could complain about. Once a year a state inspector comes from Morelia and finds all kinds of infractions in the way Jaime conducts his business. This year he paid $140 in "fines" directly to the inspector, who gave him a receipt. He is sure that the inspector simply pockets the money, but he is not particularly exercised by this rather modest cost of doing business. He sees the inspector as having a favorable position, and as long as he exploits it in such a restrained fashion he can hardly be criticized.

One day I asked Valentín Rivera the size of his plots on Carichuato Hill. He had seven, one of which he had drawn at the time the Indigenous Community bought the hill, and divided it into fields, and the remainder he had purchased from other men who had decided not to farm. They were surveyed at 75 meters by 25 meters, said Valentín. Then a pause. "But mine are larger." Why? He grinned. It turned out that no other plots are immediately adjacent to his, so each year he cuts a bit of brush and plows a few extra furrows around the edges. Others see what he is doing, but the amount each year is slight, and, following the rule of avoiding trouble, no one wishes to make an issue of the matter. Valentín and the síndico have an unusually strong sense of right and wrong; there are no people in the village in whom I have more implicit trust. Yet Valentín saw nothing wrong in utilizing the happy circumstance of a bit of fallow land around his property to better his agricultural potential.

112

Perhaps it is the relative lack of objective and absolute standards that facilitate rumor, and make it difficult for people to evaluate evidence, and stories, as to credibility and lack of credibility. We are continually astonished at some new belief or assumption that is contrary to everything people have experienced in their lives. So and so has gotten married. She was married years ago, but her husband disappeared and has not been seen since. Has she been divorced? Micaela guesses that a person is automatically divorced if he or she has not seen a spouse in seven years.

On one occasion I was copying birth records in the town hall. Salomón Villagomez, mayor that year, and one of the most intelligent and traveled of Tzintzuntzeños, saw what I was doing, and asked if it were true that in China nearly every birth was of twins, and that lots of mothers had many more children at each parturition. I said no, that twins were quite rare, and that quintuplets was the maximum I had heard about. Adolfo Delgado, town secretary, looked up from his books. He, too, is young and intelligent, and went part way through grade school in Texas speaking an English much of which he has now forgotten. Perhaps I was mistaken, he diplomatically ventured. He had been a bracero in Texas a couple of years earlier, and the wife of a man he knew personally had given birth to twelve children simultaneously, all of whom died. The husband was upset, he said, not because the children died but because the American Government took the wife away. Why should the Government do such a thing, he wanted to know? I expressed skepticism that the woman had had twelve children, but no logic I could adduce shook his firm conviction. After all, he had been there and I had not. Moreover, a woman in Morelia recently had given birth to twelve children — Salomón substantiated this — and since her husband was eligible for Social Security benefits, an ambulance took the children to the hospital. The governor became interested in the case and sent twelve incubators. Were the children still alive, I wondered? Neither man knew, but they had no doubts about the veracity of the story.

This inability to evaluate evidence critically is, of course, one of the major problems in village development. The members of a scientifically oriented society, without always recognizing it, have a mental orientation which permits them to separate the probable and the possible from the impossible and the ludicrous. They have a reasonably accurate critical facility which serves them in good stead when they are faced with the problem of evaluating a new situation, in deciding upon a course of action, and in taking actual steps. Accepting a fundamental orderliness in reality provides them with a framework within which they can judge and appraise, evaluate and measure. Their acceptance of underlying pattern and regularity sets the limits of possibility, and makes possible a critical sense. But, as will be pointed out, the Tzintzuntzeño does not see the universe as ruled by grand laws and regularities; there is no "system" a man can learn which provides him with the guidelines he needs to develop the ability to distinguish between the true and the patently untrue, the logical and the illogical. In evaluating evidence and new phenomena the same ad hoc approach that determines action in all situations must be one's only guide and this, in today's world, is inadequate.

RELATIVE ABSENCE OF FORESIGHT

Tzintzuntzeños are interested in, and concerned about, the future, but they take relatively few steps that can be thought of as influencing the future. Foresight is shown primarily in traditional activities alone. A farmer takes pains to have his equipment ready for plowing and planting when the rains come, and a fisherman tends his nets and boats carefully. But beyond these precautions planning and foresight take forms quite different from those of people raised in a different tradition. Particularly, planning the future use of money seems difficult. A bracero, setting out for the United States, will light a candle to the Virgin, and perhaps promise a distant saint to make a pilgrimage to give thanks should he return safely. But few if any braceros set aside $500 or $1,000 upon returning from El Norte so that they would have the wherewithal for the following year's trip. Consequently, with each year's announcement of bracero permits, aspirants always had to appeal

114

to friends and relatives in order to borrow enough money to meet the costs of the trip.

When people have money, they spend it; when they have nothing, they hope to borrow. The idea of estimating expenses over future time, appraising resources, calculating probable income, and planning accordingly is foreign to all. One year I found Ernesto Reyes and Ambrosio Zaldívar collecting money to lay a mosaic tile floor in La Soledad church. Ernesto showed me his record book which listed collections of a bit over $600. How much would he have to have? Ernesto hadn't the slightest idea. Two kinds of tile, he knew, cost $12 per square meter, and the other two designs cost $15 per square meter. Requests for donations were made for buying one or more square meters of flooring, and consequently contributions listed after names tended to be multiples of the per meter cost. Ernesto told me the church needed 345 square meters of tile, but he had never stopped to figure out — in fact, he couldn't have done it had his life depended on it — what the total cost would be. I asked Ernesto to let me add the contributions listed after each name, which totaled $1,230. Ernesto was delighted, and astonished, to find he had twice as much money as he had assumed. Ernesto can just barely write names; Ambrosio is entirely illiterate. Neither can add. Yet the two men were charged with collecting and disbursing $4,500. It seemed hard to believe that much could come of efforts apparently so blindly pushed forward. And yet, the following year, the floor of La Soledad was beautifully tiled! With a thousand pesos tiles were bought and laid, then a few hundred more pesos were collected, more tile was laid, and so, little by little the work advanced, until the last few meters having been counted, a final push finished the task.

The relative absence of planning and foresight are certainly due in part to the fact that people who normally live a hand-to-mouth existence have little opportunity to develop such skills. Yet this character trait also reflects a deep-seated feeling that the world about one is so capricious and uncertain that to plan ahead is to be presumptuous, and very likely to contravene divine will. The saying "Man proposes, but God disposes," which all villagers quote from time to time, describes the general attitude. Life can be lived with a minimum of foresight, and since the best laid plans are apt to come to naught, this quality seems of slight value to people. Fate and chance are seen as much more significant factors determining what happens to one. Time after time we see laundry hung on the line, and become nearly dry. Then it clouds up and rain obviously is but a few minutes away. But no thought is given to taking in the near-dry clothing and rehanging it if necessary. At best a mad rush occurs when the first drops fall, but more often the laundry is allowed to get drenched, hang all night, and start to dry the next morning. Sometimes the cycle is repeated during a second twenty-four hours, before clothing is finally removed from the line.

Most marriages follow a pattern of elopement, with a token show of stealing the girl. Girls ordinarily go willingly. Nevertheless, stories are told of girls who hoped to marry other men, but were carried away by their present husbands, and since fate willed it that way, they could hardly resist. Raquel Noriega was one such girl. Moicés Marcos, a tough young man, took her, and although she wasn't much interested in him, and had rather hoped to marry another, the story is told as if she really had no choice other than to accompany him; this was her fate. One day I asked Micaela why she had given up her egg business and now had a few hogs. The inevitability of things explained it. She had sold her hens, which had ceased to lay, and was about to buy more when Professor Baity of Montana State University gave her a pregnant sow, which quickly had a dozen piglets that occupied her attention and interest. Then a second sow she had gave birth to piglets, and presently the money she had obtained from the sale of the chickens was all going into hog feed. More hogs, more feed, the chicken house occupied by pigs, no money for hens — in this accidental, unplanned, but inevitable fashion, hogs replaced hens at this stage of her life.

Lack of thought about the future is also seen in attitudes toward medicine and dentistry. People simply complain about aching teeth, but even those who have the money rarely go to a dentist when they note the first sharp pains, and it does not occur to them that fixing a tooth immediately will be less expensive and much less painful in the long run. The only dental planning is that which precedes the decision to acquire a gold tooth, an act based on aesthetics rather than dental hygiene. By the same token, it seems to occur to no one that consulting a physician at the first symptoms of illness may in the long run prove much less expensive, and favor quicker recovery, than waiting until an illness is far advanced. There is an inevitability about what is going to happen to one, and active intervention is not yet generally seen as influencing the outcome.

People believe that individual and group welfare depend, by and large, on conditions beyond one's control. Good luck, in the form of a fine harvest, freedom from robbery or sickness, finding buried treasure, or acquiring a helpful patron, is the principal hope for improvement in position and, conversely, bad luck explains failure. What happens depends on the wish — but not on the grand design — of God. People rarely speak in the future tense without qualifying proposed or hoped-for action with *Si Diós me da licencia*, if God gives me permission. And when I thoughtlessly remark on something I expect to happen in the future, without nodding in the direction of the divinity, villagers will quietly add, *Si Diós nos deja llegar*, if God permits us to arrive [to that point in the future]. Divine providence, above all, is the good fortune that spells human well-being.

But accepting divine providence does not imply belief in a grand design, a pattern and system, which rules the universe. Rather, the universe about one is marked by absence of law and order: it, and God's plans as well, are capricious and unpredictable, quixotic and surprising. Something happens, not because of preordained regularities in the universe and in the world, but because God — or whoever the ultimate authority in the particular instance may be — has willed it. A child dies: it was part of God's plan. The highway comes to town: General Lázaro Cárdenas willed it. Since chance and accident are the mainsprings of the universe, systematic expectations and consistent behavior are seen as valueless. Western-style foresight is a positive value only within a predictable system.

Volition, rather than the dynamics of property, form, and relationships is seen as prevailing in the universe. That is, volition is an essential element in causality. And volition is not limited to divinities and humans alone, but extends to the inanimate world as well. A farmer struggles to remove a boulder from a field: *la piedra no quiere moverse*, the stone doesn't wish to move. The next boulder, of the same size and weight, is easily lifted from its resting place. Why is one stone obstinate, and the other compliant? Volition, not natural law, is what the villagers see as an explanation. The Pátzcuaro train arrives late: *Es muy mentiroso el tren*, says Virginia to explain the event: "The train is very untruthful, it lies." Its volition underlies this unpredictable behavior: one day it arrives late, and the next on time. The fields are dry, the thunderclouds pile high in the sky, but no rain falls. *No quiere llover*, say the farmers, "The rain doesn't wish to come." A knife cut bleeds badly: "the blood doesn't wish to stop flowing." The kitchen fire is slow in burning: "it doesn't wish to heat itself up" (I see green wood as the cause).

To speak of volition, and the quixotic character of the universe, does not imply that events have no cause. Quite the contrary, *everything* has a cause and explanation. It is just that a particular cause does not necessarily produce the same consequence time after time, nor the same event have an identical cause. This essential untidiness in causality seems to place people under compulsion to discover a cause, whatever it may be, for every happening. An event left unexplained is a source of discomfort; a happening to which a cause may be assigned is placed in a satisfying context. One morning I complained of a headache; the wheels in Micaela's head began to spin, and she recalled the day before I had emerged from the hot shower without muffling my head in a towel. Obviously I had been struck by an "air" which caused my head to ache. Another day we were awakened at dawn by the prolonged squealing of a dying hog. Melecio and his compadre Primo Calderón were slaughtering the animal to have food to feed well-wishers who would come at 4 o'clock the following morning to sing *Las Mañanitas* in honor of Mary's saint's day, August 15, The Assumption. "I felt very badly to hear the poor animal scream," said Mary after we had risen. "Of course," said Micaela, heaving a sigh of relief, glad to know why the animal had lingered longer than usual. "When a person or animal is dying, you should never feel sorry," she continued. "It makes it hard for them to die."

Fate and inevitability also account for a person's occupation. When asked what work he does a man will reply that his *destino*, his "destiny," is fishing or farming or whatever it may be. An occupation-as-destiny carries the idea that God wishes it to be thus, that in the case of each individual it is a part of God's plan for him. "It's a providential thing, a person's occupation," is the way people describe their work. A "destiny," a trade, can be changed by learning another; it is not an absolute and immutable commitment. But the change is not lightly undertaken. Destiny, too, is invoked by some people to explain their reluctance to share trade secrets with others. By influencing the occupation, or mode of working, of another, they are intervening in that person's destiny, an act not to be undertaken without considering the implications of meddling with a divine plan.

Human character, too, is thought to be something determined by the same inevitability that rules all other aspects of life. A person is felt to have little control over his character, and no particular responsibility to improve himself, or to give up bad habits. Male drunkenness is common, although less so than twenty years ago. "Juan is a drunk; it's his vice." The vice of drunkenness is a fact of life which explains and simultaneously excuses behavior. A person can't be held responsible for his vices any more than for his physical characteristics, nor is there much feeling that through moral courage and willpower vices can or should be cured or controlled. A villager is killed in a drunken fight. The event is unsettling, since it disturbs the even tenor of life. But a drunken person under the influence of his vice is not held responsible. Some kind of restitution must be made to the bereaved family, but punishment, in the sense of an abstract and appropriate justice, is not seen as part of the settlement. *La debilidad de la mujer es la curiosidad*, says Micaela, crediting all females with her overwhelming passion: "The weakness of woman is curiosity." Whatever the character of a person, it is due to forces outside his being: fate and chance, not environment and training, are responsible.

Yet, and paradoxically, in many families there is a strong sense of responsibility in forming the character of children, and a person of bad habits, who is lacking in courtesy, is seen as an indictment of his parents, who should be more sensitive to "what people will say." In these families children are constantly corrected, taught courtesy, acquainted with the fact that canons of courtesy and proper behavior set them off from others in the village. Character can be instilled in the young by telling them constantly; it can be made to stick only by frequent beatings, for blows, or the threat of blows, are felt to be indispensable in getting ideas through thick skulls. As a consequence, nearly everyone feels his childhood was a period of intense suffering, of blows and beatings which had the same capricious quality as do events in adult life.

There is little idea that character is a basic quality that transcends time. People are judged by what they do and are thought to be as of a particular period. Yesterday's murderer is today happily married to his victim's niece, and the mother-in-law — the murdered man's sister — feels she is lucky to have such a fine son-in-law. People tend to be judged on what they do in the present, and not on the basis of previous behavior. This militates against special respect for the aged. Rudolfo Pelón was a respected potter and trader; today he is old and feeble, respectfully treated, but considered a nobody. Pascual Corral, on the other hand, although past seventy, still actively participates in community activities. He is viewed with great respect, not because he has played a major role in village affairs for many years in the past, but because at the present time he still does so.

The behavior traits mentioned in this chapter — loyalty to friends, sense of humor, a feeling for the worthwhileness of living, suspicion of the motives of others, timidity, a liking for gossip, a belief in fate — can be observed in the overt behavior of people, and inferred from their conversation. The interpretations that can be placed on their behavior depend at least in part on the interpreter's point of view. North Americans, who like to think of themselves as relatively lacking in some of these traits, may see such behavior as regrettable or unattractive. But the Tzintzuntzeño does not see a description such as that given as an uncharitable appraisal; these are the forms of behavior that spell personal security, and which bring happiness and satisfaction in living. To be suspicious is to be cautious, alert, and prepared for sudden attacks. Gossip is fun, and it is the device whereby people are kept in line; it is a basic mechanism whereby people are persuaded to conform to the traditional village norms that are felt to spell safety for all. Timidity and fear do not indicate lack of moral or personal courage; they again reflect an awareness of reality, and a readiness to protect one's self against the dangers that fill the world. To believe in fate is simply to recognize the world for what it is, the first essential assumption in learning the business of living.

To understand in depth more of the logic that underlies these behavior traits we must now turn to a level of interpretation which reveals character traits to be a function of assumptions about the villagers' several universes, the natural and predictable consequences of a particular view of the rules governing the game of life.

CHAPTER SIX

The
Image of
Limited Good

USING A MODEL

In the preceding chapter we described a number of behavior traits, or overt actions, which are common to Tzintzuntzeños. The problem now is to isolate the broad patterns to which this behavior conforms, and to analyze these patterns as they reflect the villager's cognitive orientation. It will be recalled that the assumptions, the implicit premises that express a cognitive orientation are, for the most part, subconscious; the members of a group are not aware that they view their several universes in a particular way, nor that their behavior is calculated to maximize opportunities — as culturally defined — offered by these universes.

In treating of the way in which people look at the world, two levels of analysis are involved. On the one hand we are concerned with *description,* for by observing how people act a cognitive orientation can be learned, just as all other cultural forms can be learned. On the other hand we are concerned with the problem of an economical *representation* of this cognitive orientation by means of models or other devices which account for observed behavior and which permit prediction of behavior as yet unnoted or unperformed. A model is an inferential construct, an analytic abstraction derived from observed behavior, but it is not the cognitive orientation itself, nor is it concerned with describing the view of the world of a group of people. Its function is to subsume and explain concisely — to represent — the infinite forms and relationships of behavior that can be observed, and to state principles to which this behavior conforms, thereby making possible prediction. It does not summarize the behavior as such. By definition a model is an ideal type. In Tzintzuntzan real behavior probably more nearly coincided with this ideal type fifty years ago than it does now. But the model of the traditional community is in no way jeopardized by current changes stemming from the influence of modern Mexico, and of the United States. Quite the contrary, if the model is sound it will enable us to better understand contemporary change processes and modifications in traditional behavior and attitudes.

THE LIMITED GOOD MODEL AND ITS COROLLARY

The model of cognitive orientation described in this chapter, and touched upon briefly in the first chapter, accounts for a very wide spectrum of behavior in Tzintzuntzan, and relates basic values and attitudes to such seemingly diverse institutions as politics and law, religion, economic activities, medical beliefs, and even folklore. This model I call the *Image of Limited Good*. By *Image of Limited Good* I mean that behavior in these and other broad areas is patterned in such fashion as to suggest that Tzintzuntzeños see their social, economic, and natural universes — their total environment — as one in which almost all desired things in life such as land, other forms of wealth, health, friendship, love, manliness, honor, respect, power, influence, security, and safety *exist in absolute quantities insufficient to fill even minimal needs of villagers*. Not only do "good things" exist in strictly limited quantities, but in addition *there is no way directly within the Tzintzuntzeño's power to increase the available supplies.* It is as if the obvious fact of land shortage in the municipio applied to all other desired things: not enough to go around. "Good," like land, is seen as something inherent in nature, there to be divided and redivided if necessary, to be passed around, but not to be augmented. This view, it may be noted parenthetically, seems to me to characterize peasants in general, and it is found in other societies as well.

At this stage of analysis it is methodologically helpful to make a contrary-to-fact assumption: that Tzintzuntzan is a closed system whose dynamics apply only to the local area. In so doing we are momentarily accepting the Tzintzuntzeño view: except in a special sense that will be mentioned later, he feels that existence is determined and limited by the natural and social resources of his community and its immediate hinterland. Consequently, there is a primary corollary to the Image of Limited Good: if Good exists in finite quantities, and if the system is closed, it follows that *an individual or a family can improve its position only at the expense of others.* Hence, an apparent improvement in someone's position with respect to good — and especially economic good — is viewed as a threat to the entire community. Since only so much of the Good is available, someone is being despoiled, whether he sees it or not. And since there may be doubt as to who is losing — it may be ego — any significant improvement is perceived not as a threat to an individual or a family alone, but as a threat to *all* individuals and families. That someone's advantage implies someone else's disadvantage seems to me to be the key to understanding the Image of Limited Good.

The aptness of this model may be tested in several ways. First, we can adduce a number of examples of behavior to see if they substantiate the argument. This is done in the pages that follow immediately. Next the implications of the model may be considered with respect to social and cultural forms and institutions to see if these conform to types that might logically be predicted. This is done in Chapters Seven through Eleven. The structural dimensions of the model are seen in these two bodies of data. Finally, the dynamic features of the model can be examined, as is done in Chapters Twelve through Eighteen. If we find that the processes of social and cultural change occurring in the village today can be explained by, or found to conform to, the model, then we know we have a conceptual tool of the highest utility. Our argument is strengthened, moreover, when we remember that Tzintzuntzan in broad outline conforms to a peasant typology; consequently, if behavior and institutions in other peasant communities also substantiate a limited good model, then we can be fairly sure our approach is sound.

LIMITED GOOD IN ECONOMIC BEHAVIOR

When the Tzintzuntzeño views his traditional economic world as one in which Limited Good prevails, in which he can progress only at the expense of others, he is very near the truth. Land, as previously pointed out, is in particularly short supply, because of Lake Pátzcuaro on one side and Tariaqueri and Yaguarato hills on the other, which restrict fields to a narrow band of rich alluvial lakeshore milpas, and the stony and thin soils of the hillsides themselves. An individual can obtain more land only by purchase (which means exchanging one good for another), by inheritance (which means the land is already in the family), or by chicanery. Unlike the situation in sparsely settled areas, such as that described for Chan Kom (Redfield and Villa, 1934; Redfield, 1950), land-hungry men cannot simply go farther into the bush and hack out new milpas, for people in other villages adjacent to Tzintzuntzan have long since laid claim to such land, and they, too, feel the pinch. Not only is land sharply limited, but over the years hard use without fertilizers, plus constant erosion, have reduced its productivity. Old people say that today crops average less than in their youth.

Tzintzuntzan's productive techniques have changed little since the Conquest, when Spanish implements, domestic animals, and crops undoubtedly increased the potential of the land. Given poor and limited soils, and an oxen-cum-wooden plow technology, no amount of extra hard work will significantly improve a harvest. The lack of the right amount of rainfall, and freedom from insect plagues, rather than work beyond the prevailing norms of good practice, is what determines a good harvest. Pottery and fishing techniques also have changed very little during the post-Conquest era, so that neither can production be significantly increased in these fields.

In fact, it seems accurate to say that the average Tzintzuntzeño sees little or no relationship between work and production techniques on the one hand, and wealth on the other. Wealth, rather, like land, is seen to exist in finite quantity, circumscribed by absolute limits, and no amount of hard work will increase the quantity. Engaging in certain enterprises does not produce wealth; rather, the person fortunate enough to have wealth can engage in enterprises denied others. Most people see the possession of a store in this light. A person lucky enough to acquire money can permit himself the luxury of opening a store, if he so desires, but he does not open a store to amass wealth. As applied to material well-being we may say that an image of a static economy is the pertinent subprinciple of the model of Limited Good. Wealth, like all other forms of Good, is something that does not grow and cannot be made to expand. Within the village time and tradition have determined the shares each family holds; these shares are not static, since obviously they do shift. But the relative position of each villager is known at any given time, and a sudden change calls for explanation.

Specific instances of behavior reveal the view of economic good here described. In the early days of the CREFAL program Gabriel Ospina persuaded Micaela to head an embroidery "cooperative." She was already an excellent seamstress, and knew the traditional cross-stitch patterns of the Pátzcuaro area. Gabriel taught her new designs, and also the types and sizes of tablecloths, place mats, and rebozos that would sell best to tourists. She assumes the responsibility for obtaining cloth and thread, and under her direction from eight to a dozen village girls and young married women make the embroideries, working at standard piece rates. Micaela sells the finished products, and the small spread between labor and material costs and the selling price is her profit.

Pierre Lisse, popular arts professor at CREFAL, would like her to work with him. He thinks he could help her in marketing and with new designs, and that in return she should help instruct embroiderers in other lake villages. But why should she do this, she asks me. Not everyone knows her fine stitches. If they become common property other people, under the stress of competition, will set lower prices and undersell her, and her small profit will shrink to nothing. She thinks it foolish to let a good thing get away from her. A market for embroideries is not infinite; there is only so much demand.

In 1964 Faustino Peña was sent by CREFAL to the Tepic Normal School, three hundred miles away, to give a six-week course in pottery making to school teachers attending a special session. The pay was good, and Faustino enjoyed the feeling of prestige that came with being a teacher, for potters in Mexico usually are looked down upon by others. Still, he doesn't really like to teach pottery, he admits. "I didn't mind teaching the maestros — it takes perhaps four years to become a skilled potter, and teaching them an hour a day for six weeks isn't much — but when the professional potters in Tepic asked me to show them how we use our glaze-binder, I wouldn't do it." The Tepic potters doubtless see Faustino as egoísta; he selfishly refuses to help them. He sees his behavior as prudent. There is only a limited demand for pottery, and if others learn the secrets of his superior wares they will undercut his prices. The teachers, obviously, are not threats; they will not compete with him, so they can safely be shown everything, just as can the anthropologist.

Farmers are also reluctant to share a good thing. Some years ago Ladislao Alonso acquired a very good maize called pipitilla which has a long, narrow cob and big kernels. Other farmers asked him for a little seed, but he refused them. Eucario Cabeza, always alert to new things, was also refused. He asked his young wife Cora and her sister, Pabla, to glean Ladislao's field. Pabla tells the story as if permission were asked and granted, which seems highly unlikely. In any event, the girls gathered some of the fallen grains, Eucario planted them, and thus got the new maize. Today most farmers have managed to acquire the seed.

Friendship and love are also seen as existing in limited amounts, as something that must be hoarded and not shared with others. Adolescent and postadolescent boys, and to a lesser extent girls, form strong "best friend" attachments, dyadic in nature. They exchange gifts with each other, and confide their innermost thoughts to an extent they will never equal in later life. But these friendships usually are brittle; the pals are enormously jealous of each other, fearful they will be abandoned for another, believing that any interest shown in other age mates by their partner must correspondingly reduce the amount of affection they can expect from him.

Potential and real patrons are zealously guarded and cultivated, and every effort is made to reserve the attention of powerful individuals to a single person or family; it is assumed that the bounty of a generous patron is easily spread thin. On one occasion Melecio Hernández was working as a bracero near Berkeley, and we arranged one Sunday to bring him to our home for dinner. Once safely away from camp he remarked that he had a brother there (whom we did not know since he lived in another Michoacán village) who had asked to be brought along. We expressed regret that Melecio had not done so, but he replied, in effect, that we were a Good he highly valued, and that he didn't want to dilute his pleasure by sharing us with another.

Early in our stay with Micaela it became clear she was greatly worried lest someone offer us a more comfortable place in which to stay, and thus lure us away from her. Continually over the first years of renewed field work we had to reassure her that we were delighted to be in her home and that we had no intention of seeking other quarters. Still, she finds it hard to believe that when we visit other friends we are not threatening her with a lesser quantity of our friendship.

That love and affection are limited goods is suggested by the folk etiology of the disease of infancy known as *chipil*. When a mother again becomes pregnant and weans her nursing child, it often fusses, cries, clings to her skirts, and is inconsolable; in extreme cases it may show symptoms of kwashiorkor,* for the loss of protein and other nutritional elements which usually follow weaning is, along with sibling rivalry, the scientific explanation of the illness. But the chípil child is said to be jealous of its unborn sibling whose presence it recognizes and whom it perceives as a threat, already depriving it of maternal love and affection. A mother's love, like all other forms of Good, is limited; she must reduce the amount she gives to one child in order to show love to another.

LIMITED GOOD IN HEALTH BELIEFS

Health is also seen as a Limited Good although, in contrast to the instances described, one person's good health is not necessarily at the expense of others. Good health comes from the innate *esfuerzo* or vitality which one acquires at birth. This is limited and one must, in effect, decide how it is to be disbursed. Natividad Peña says that a person goes through three "ages" in a lifetime. The first, from birth to puberty, is one of gradually increasing body heat — which spells health — and vigor. The second, from puberty to about 30 years of age, is that of maximum strength and vitality. After 30 a person gradually loses his esfuerzo as his body grows old and cold. The outcome is inevitable, but within limits, one can do something about it. The prudent person who conserves his vitality in youth and in the prime of life, who doesn't expend it in frivolities, in late hours, in drinking bouts and other wasteful activities, will have more vitality upon which to draw as he grows old. What one hoards in early life is a bank from which withdrawals can be made in later life.

Long hair on women is greatly admired, but this is seen as a costly use of one's vitality. Our neighbor, Lupe Estrada, has the longest hair in town, reaching to her knees. One day when she appeared at her door to dry her hair after washing it — and doubtless to be admired by passersby — I remarked to Micaela how extraordinary it was. "Yes," replied Micaela, "but notice

* A protein-calorie deficiency disease of early childhood, often triggered by loss of protein upon weaning.

how thin Lupe is," and she named several other women with long hair, all of whom also are thin. Women who choose to enjoy the luxury of long hair must pay a penalty in general health; they cannot hope to have sufficient vitality for a well-fleshed body and unbounded energy. Lola Pichu cut her hair some years ago because of frequent headaches; she hoped that eliminating this drain on her vitality would improve her health. Bacilisa Cornelio cut her hair for similar reasons: a bad pain in her side which came after a bad fright was interpreted as due to the drain on her strength occasioned by her long hair.

Blood is recognized as essential to good health; a person with strong, rich blood enjoys great vigor, whereas a person with thin, poor blood is unhealthy. In a number of Latin American communities blood is seen quite specifically as a limited Good, as a nonrenewable substance which, once lost, can never through normal means be restored. Tzintzuntzeños deny that they feel this way about blood, although it is said drinking deer blood strengthens the heart, and that drinking cow blood is good to strengthen the body in general. At the same time the attitude toward blood transfusions may reflect an old idea now mostly subconscious: to give one's blood to another is a frightening thought. To give a blood transfusion is seen as a foolhardy, debilitating act, and the thought of a professional donor who sells blood is quite beyond credulity. To allow blood to be withdrawn voluntarily from one's body seems almost like permitting an amputation; the step is final, irreversible. One person's fortune in finding blood for a transfusion is another person's — the donor's — misfortune.

LIMITED GOOD AND MACHISMO

Manliness, authority, respect, and honor are seen as existing in limited quantities. To the extent that someone has an excess of these desirable attributes, others must be deprived. Bracero friends often ask me, "In the United States it's the wife who commands, no?" They see domestic authority as limited in quantity, so that if one partner exercises it the other is deprived of it. They find it difficult to believe that a husband and wife can share domestic responsibility and decision making, without the husband being deprived of his machismo, his masculinity. Many believe a wife, however good, must be beaten from time to time, simply so she will not lose sight of a God-decreed familial hierarchy. They are astonished and shocked to learn that an American wifebeater can be jailed; this seems like an unwarranted intrusion of the State into the family as created by God. The very rare woman in Tzintzuntzan who complains to the authorities that her husband beats her is usually told to run along, that she doubtless deserves it for not doing what she is told to do.

Although a majority of men give all or most of their earnings to their wives, and wives are generally keepers of family purses, they — men — say they would not like their wives "to work," i.e., take employment outside of the home. This is a hypothetical situation, of course, since possibilities within the village are limited. The few women who work in the two tortilla bakeries are the only ones who may be said to "work" outside their homes, and these are really family situations. Rather, in expressing these ideas men are thinking of what they have seen in shops and offices in the United States. They feel that when women earn their own money, as do those who sell in the Pátzcuaro market, they get ideas of independence, they want to have authority in the family, and thus they threaten to deprive men of their masculinity, which depends on their unquestioned authority. This is the fix we North Americans have gotten ourselves into, they say; we have surrendered control to our working wives.

Tzintzuntzeños are generally not a belligerent people, and the homicide rate is far lower than that prevailing in many Mexican villages. In general they seem less concerned with the masculinity syndrome, with machismo, than are men in many other parts of the country. But the feeling of the importance of machismo is not absent. The essence of this quality, as seen in Tzintzuntzan, is valor, and un hombre muy valiente, a valiant man, is one who is strong and tough, who is able to defend himself and his family, who doesn't seek quarrels but who doesn't dodge them if forced upon him. Sexual exploits seem to contribute very little to one's machismo. On the other hand, it is admitted rather grudgingly that a killer is probably macho. People are reluctant to name machos. In response to direct questions they usually reply. "Now there are no longer machos; we are all the same." Yet a discussion of various men always reveals that some, much more than others, have the qualities that are recognized as constituting masculinity. It is obvious that when two men fight, the winner emerges as the more macho; he has taken something from the loser, just as a commanding wife takes masculinity from her husband.

Women, too, can have the quality of machismo. One who shows traits of valor and fearlessness is *una gallona*, a "female cock," or *una mujer gallona*, a cocklike woman. At a distance such a woman may be admired. La Adelita, of revolutionary fame, was *una mujer gallona*, who displayed the qualities of fearlessness and valor in a way that makes Mexicans proud of their country. But a man does not want these qualities in a wife; there they are a liability, a constant threat and a source of domestic conflict.

Concern with face and dignity, and sensitivity to public opinion, appear to be a part of the machismo complex, devices whereby an individual attempts to maintain an image of a serious, alert, strong character who is able to protect himself in the face of all attacks. Any action, verbal or otherwise, which is seen as an attack on one's dignity, which causes a person to lose face, is therefore much resented. One tries to avoid situations that encourage such aggression, and if it occurs, it is necessary to strike back with whatever resources are at hand. Almost any person-to-person contest with two protagonists represents this kind of undesirable situation. An election, a lawsuit — even a game — is disturbing because the winner takes something from the loser; he acquires more of the quality of machismo at the expense of his opponent. Hence, as we will see (Chapter Eight), community decisions are made on the basis of consensus, so that no one will have to stand up and be counted. Lawsuits really have no winners, since the aggrieved party's goal is merely to restore the status quo, to recover what has been lost. Even among children there is a predilection for group games rather than for tests of skill or endurance between two opponents.

132

Tzintzuntzeños read contest, with consequent loss and humiliation for one of the two parties, into situations in which the principals probably had little or no sense of struggle. One day Micaela told how a new veterinary doctor had recently started practice in Pátzcuaro, where previously only an untitled veterinarian had practiced. Completely overlooking the fact that there was more than enough business to keep both men busy, she said of the older man, *le machucó*, the young doctor had pulverized and ground him up by virtue of his degree. To her it was not just a question of a better prepared man skimming the cream off the trade; he had, in effect, utterly destroyed the older man because of his superior armament.

BEHAVIOR DEMANDED BY A LIMITED GOOD OUTLOOK

If it is accepted that Tzintzuntzeños see their universe as one in which the Good in life is limited and unexpandable, and hence personal gain is at the expense of others, it logically follows that preferred behavior is that seen by people as maximizing their security by preserving their relative position in the traditional order of things. Two theoretical avenues of action are open to people who see themselves in threatened circumstances, which the Image of Limited Good implies. They may exhibit cooperation, to as pronounced a degree as communism, burying personal differences and placing sanctions against individualism, or they may follow the opposite road of unbridled individualism, in which everyone is on his own.

Tzintzuntzeños, like other peasants, have chosen — or had forced upon them — the second alternative. The reasons are not entirely clear, but two factors seem significant. Cooperation requires leadership. This may be delegated democratically by the members of the group itself; it may be assumed by a strong man from within the group; or it may be imposed by outside force. Peasants, for reasons that should become clear in our subsequent analysis, see the democratic delegation of authority within their community as a threat to their interests, and usually they refuse to submit voluntarily to strong local leadership. Arbitrary assumption of power by a local strong man sometimes produces *caciques*

133

or petty *jefes políticos* in Mexico, but this type of power also has unavoidable limits: the truncated nature of peasant political forms, with real power lying at a higher governmental level, usually effectively discourages local assumption and exercise of power, except as an authorized or tolerated agent of these outside forces. Local development of good leadership which might make possible cooperation is discouraged by the rulers of the political units of which peasant communities are components, because they see such action as a potential threat to their interest. In Mexico the municipio in theory is "free and independent," but no one, and least of all the villagers, is fooled by these words. Among Mexicans with a genuine interest in democratic processes there is a continuing dialogue on what can be done to strengthen municipio self-government without at the same time running the risk of hindering the developmental activities which are felt to be the responsibility of the central government.

Again, economic activities in peasant societies require relatively limited cooperation. In Tzintzuntzan, for example, most families can produce their own food, or produce the handicrafts whose sale makes it possible to buy supplies. They can carry their produce to market without the aid of others, and they need no cooperatives to sell it. Farming can be done without the aid of others, and in a pinch a family could build a fairly presentable house. Tzintzuntzeños do not in fact live with the full degree of independence theoretically possible, but they know they can meet their needs with remarkably little cooperation from others.

LIFE: A PERPETUAL STRUGGLE

Whatever the explanation, Tzintzuntzeños are remarkably individualistic in attitudes and behavior. Every person sees himself in a perpetual and unrelenting struggle with his fellows and the world at large for possession of or control over what he considers to be his share of scarce values. Everyone sees himself, almost from birth to death, facing a hostile world in which access to the few good things in life to which one has a right is constantly threatened by hunger, illness, death, abuse by neighbors, and spoliation by powerful people outside the community. Only within the nuclear family is it felt there is some degree of mutual support and aid, of pooling of interests, of ability to trust.

Since life is a struggle, *una lucha*, one must use whatever resources he has to "defend" himself. When asked how things are going, a man may reply, *Pues me defiendo*, that is "I'm managing to defend myself," to make both ends meet. Or, in a near-hopeless situation, he may ask, perhaps a bit belligerently, *Con qué me defiendo?*, i.e., "With what do you think I can defend myself?"

To defend one's self, in the narrow economic sense, means to be able to take care of one's self and family, to have enough to house, clothe, and feed a wife and children. But in a wider sense it means the ability to face up to all the natural and super-natural threats that fill a peasant's world, to have effective means to counterattack in the face of danger. To be able to defend one's self, then, means to have the wit, knowledge, and resources to take the right step at the right time, to remain on top of the situation. A modest degree of machismo, under such circum-stances, is a desirable quality. A man who is valiant, who doesn't look for trouble but who doesn't dodge a fight, is obviously a poor target for unscrupulous people who may wish to take what is not rightfully theirs. Machismo is a highly useful protective pose, an advertisement to the world not to abuse or presume.

Since man sees himself as always on the defensive, extreme caution and reserve, and a reluctance to reveal true position and possession, are also protective qualities. Trust is something that can be exercised only with the greatest care, since to trust is to let down one's own defenses by letting another know their true nature. Under conditions in which men feel they are subject to surprise and attack, the intense suspicion that has been described for Tzintzuntzeños becomes intelligible. It pays to listen with the senses as well as the ears, to search for all clues that may reveal true intentions. Since everyone else is also engaged in a life struggle, it is only prudent to assume his first interest is himself, and if this means disregard for others, it is only what is to be expected. A doctor, unless closely watched, may short-cut an operation; no one will know the difference unless a family member is there to keep tabs on him. A CREFAL student will short-weigh eggs, hoping to pocket the difference; naturally he wants to look to his interests. The CREFAL pottery professor obviously didn't want to help people since — as in Faustino Peña's case — he would only be aiding potential competitors.

INABILITY TO COOPERATE

The reason for the inability to associate in major communal efforts now becomes more clear: since more Good than already exists cannot be produced, cooperation is a pointless activity, the whim of outsiders who doubtless have some ulterior motive. The ideal man who, in a cooperative undertaking, takes nothing from his neighbors, can gain nothing, but he risks, through participation, exploitation on the part of associates who may be less scrupulous than he. The typical Tzintzuntzeño, like most other peasants, sees major cooperative efforts as personal threats, and not as devices to improve community life. Consequently, reluctance to cooperate is, with a Limited Good view of the world, highly rational behavior, just as the other characteristics that have been described also make sense when seen as reflecting the belief that everybody is in direct competition with everybody else, and where advance on the part of one is thought to be at the expense of others.

EQUILIBRIUM: THE KEY
TO A HEALTHY SOCIETY

In Tzintzuntzan the healthy social organism is perceived as one in which essential equality with respect to access to Good prevails. The good society, as we have noted, therefore conforms to an equilibrium model; security and safety are achieved within the village by maintaining the status quo, by permitting no significant changes in the traditional allocations of Good. Behavior that upsets these traditional allocations, or that merely suggests the possibility of an upset, is viewed as threatening to the community at large. It is for this reason that Tzintzuntzeños attempt to maintain the fiction that "Here we are all equal."

136

Everyone knows that Eucario Cabeza, Pánfilo Castellanos, Isaac Enríquez, and a few others are, by prevailing standards, well off. Informants will admit that these men are *más acomodados* ("more accommodated") than others, but to say they are *más ricos* is disturbing, for it reminds one that perhaps the social organism is not quite in proper balance. The same is said, it will be recalled, of machismo; people feel better if equality for all characterizes this personal quality.

The use of the euphemism "more accommodated" in place of "rich" indicates how sensitive this area of thought is. To think of rich families in the village is to be reminded of the threat they constitute to social stability. The thought of wealth differences, which everyone knows exist, is therefore made less unpalatable by a more neutral expression that lacks most of the strong emotional overtones of the precise word. The parallel to the United States is striking: the euphemism "well-to-do" to describe families that have far more wealth than most can safely be used when to say "rich" would be thought vulgar. When it is essential to use a euphemism we can be sure we have struck a point at which the members of society feel apprehension or discomfort, that we are in a "sensitive" area of great significance to the analysis of our data.

Since an equilibrium of — to use Eric Wolf's apt expression — "shared poverty" spells a healthy social organism, individuals or families acquiring more than their share of a Good, and especially an economic good, are viewed as a threat which requires corrective action. This kind of progress, since it violates preferred norms of behavior, stimulates cultural and social mechanisms intended to redress the imbalance. Individuals or families who lose something, who fall behind their accustomed place, are also viewed as a threat, although in a different fashion: their envy, jealousy, or anger may result in overt or hidden aggression toward more fortunate people. This kind of change in position, although less disturbing than an advance, also stimulates social mechanisms in some situations which are intended, at least symbolically, to correct the imbalance.

The self-correcting mechanisms that promote community equilibrium conform to three general types: (1) the steps taken by *individuals* and *families* to maintain their position in the system, and the ways in which they try to avoid both sanctions and exploitation by fellow villagers and others; (2) informal and usually unorganized group behavior, i.e., the sanctions invoked by the community, when it is felt someone is violating the behavior norms that spell security for all; and (3) institutionalized behavior, the formal and major community activities which neutralize achieved imbalance. Each of these forms will be examined in turn.

On the level of individual and family behavior, two rules or guides are followed although, of course, they are rarely, if ever, consciously formulated: (1) do not reveal evidence of material or other improvement in your relative position, lest you arouse envy and invite sanctions; and should you be forced to display improvement, or be unable to conceal it, take the action that neutralizes the consequences and eliminates the danger of sanctions; (2) do not allow yourself to fall behind your rightful place, lest you and your family suffer.

A family deals with the threats presented by suspected or actual improvement in its relative position by a combination of two devices. Its first — and continuing — effort is directed toward concealing or camouflaging the evidence that might lead to this conclusion. People wear less good clothing than they can afford, they are reluctant to reveal well-being by improving their homes, they try to eat unobserved so the quality and quantity of their food will go unnoticed, and they build high walls around their patios so envious neighbors cannot see in.

In the second instance, when a family quite obviously has improved its position, its traditional step is to meet the situation head on, to admit an improvement in relative position, but to show that it has no intention of using this position to the detriment of the community by neutralizing it through costly ritual expenditures. Until very recent years, and even at present as far as most people are concerned, Tzintzuntzeños, like other peasants, have not competed for prestige with material symbols such as dress, housing, food, and gadgets, nor have they competed for authority by seeking leadership. Most people indicate a strong desire to look and act like everyone else, to be inconspicuous in position and behavior. And by seeking, or even accepting, an authority position, the ideal man ceases to be ideal. The power he now has will inevitably invoke sanctions, however unmerited; it will be assumed he will use his position to further his own interests, which will assuredly be to the detriment of the community at large. A "good" man, therefore, usually shuns community responsibilities other than those of a ritual nature, for by so doing he protects his reputation and avoids trouble. Needless to say, this behavior heavily penalizes Tzintzuntzan today by depriving it of the leadership which is now essential to its development.

The mechanism invoked to minimize the danger of loss of relative position centers, as has already been made clear, on the machismo complex. A valiant individual automatically commands the "respect" about which people in Tzintzuntzan are so touchy, and he can strive toward the goal, however illusory, of being able to live *sin compromisos*, free of obligations toward others.

These are the basic steps taken by, and the principal forms of behavior shown by individuals and families, in order to live peacefully with their neighbors, and to avoid the sanctions that they know will come if they significantly violate these norms. But no one can really avoid these sanctions: informal and unorganized group behavior keeps constant pressure on even the most ideal characters. In Tzintzuntzan most of these sanctions are informal, taking the form of criticism, gossip, backbiting, and slander. These add up to public opinion, and it will be recalled that Tzintzuntzeños are almost morbidly sensitive to "what people will say" should they violate customary norms in work, dress, or other behavior forms. Although informal, these sanctions are obviously powerful.

In other peasant communities in Mexico one occasionally reads of a wealthy man being killed; presumably he had pushed his luck too far. The relatively few murders that occur in Tzintzuntzan do not conform to the sanction pattern; perhaps villagers feel no one is so wealthy that his threat can be countered only by his elimination. More common in Mexico than murder is witchcraft or the threat of witchcraft, to discourage people from antisocial behavior (as well as, naturally, for personal grudges). Most Tzintzuntzeños today profess to be unworried about witchcraft; they believe the Tarascans both practice and fear it, but say that it is hardly an element in social control within the village. Yet the lurking fear of this kind of attack is probably more widespread, particularly among the illiterate population, than people like to admit. The story of Jesús Peña, who freely tells how he was bewitched when he was mayor, shows how the fear of this activity produces action which others are believed to desire. And if we recall the significance of euphemisms as indicators of sensitive areas of culture, it is clear that fear of witchcraft is more important than informants' statements indicate. The common Spanish words for witchcraft — *hechicería* and *brujería* — are never used in everyday speech. The euphemisms *la mala enfermedad* ("the bad illness") or *el daño* ("the damage") are always substituted, and a person who is suspected of having been bewitched is said to have had his blood "irritated." Thus, fear of witchcraft seems to be one of the negative sanctions that help to keep people in line.

Real or imagined changes in the status quo are denied or discouraged by the mechanisms just described, which operate on an individual and family level, and on the informal community level represented by fear of public opinion and other, harsher sanctions. The third of the self-correcting mechanisms, that of institutionalized behavior, swings into operation to meet achieved superiority. It acts to neutralize the threat to the community by restoring the balance felt to be essential to a sound society. As in other Latin American peasant communities the Tzintzuntzeño who improves his economic-power position is encouraged — and sometimes forced — to restore the status quo by serving as a mayordomo for a fiesta. The great expenses and conspicuous consumption which are the lot of the mayordomo reassure others that the advantage he has achieved is being thoroughly dissipated. The mayordomo's reward is prestige, which he receives in return for wealth. Prestige, in fact, is the only Good that is not strictly limited; any number of men can achieve it by fulfilling village ritual obligations, and the only practical limit to the amount will be the number of men who can accept a costly sponsorship. By accepting harmless prestige in return for dangerous wealth, a mayordomo is disarmed, shorn of his weapons, and rendered impotent.

There is good reason why, in Tzintzuntzan, the fiestas consume so much wealth in the form of fireworks, musical bands, food and drink, and Masses. These are redistributive mechanisms which permit a family that potentially threatens community stability to restore the status quo gracefully, thereby returning itself to respectability accompanied by a new prestige. Wolf, speaking specifically of the "closed" Indian peasant communities of Mexico, as they emerged following the Conquest, puts it thus: "The system takes from those who have, in order to make all men have-nots. By liquidating the surpluses, it makes all men rich in sacred experience but poor in earthly good. Since it levels differences of wealth, it also inhibits the growth of class distinctions based on wealth" (1959:216).

The traditional Tzintzuntzan fiesta cycle conforms to this model of a mechanism to keep a system in balance. In its elaborateness it provided opportunity for everyone to obtain some degree of prestige, women as well as men, and in its costliness it successfully drained off incipient accumulations of wealth that would have produced functional class distinctions and other social tensions that would have threatened the viability of the community. This system is described in greater detail in Chapter Ten. Here it is sufficient to note that the religious fiesta system is completely congruent with the Limited Good model; it, or some equivalent device whereby great amounts of wealth are consumed, *must* exist as an ecological safety valve to reduce pressures which constantly build up and which, if allowed to go unchecked, would turn the community from one type of organization into another.

A picture of the ideal traditional Tzintzunzeño begins to emerge: a man who works to feed and clothe his family, who fulfills his community ceremonial obligations, who minds his own business and who does not try to take advantage of others, who does not seek to be outstanding, but who knows how to protect his rights. The ideal man must also avoid the appearance of presumption, lest this be interpreted as trying to take something that belongs to another. In tracing the diffusion of new pottery-making techniques that have appeared in recent years I found that no one would admit he had learned anything from a neighbor. The inevitable reply to my question about where something had been learned was *Me puse a pensar*, "I thought of it all by myself," accompanied by a knowing look and a tapping of the temple with the forefinger. At first I assumed this reluctance to give credit to others was due to egoísmo, the selfishness villagers constantly attribute to each other. Yet if egoísmo, as exemplified by unwillingness to admit profiting by a neighbor's new pottery knowledge, is seen as a function of an Image of Limited Good, it is clear that a potter *must* deny that the idea is other than his own. To confess that he "borrowed" an idea is to confess that he has taken something not rightfully his, that he has presumed and knowingly upset the equilibrium and the self-image he tries so hard to maintain.

Similarly, in trying to determine how godparenthood ties are initiated, I found few informants who would admit that they had asked friends or relatives to allow them to be compadres; most informants insisted they were asked by someone else. Obviously, someone has to ask. But informants appear to fear that admission of asking may be interpreted as showing a tendency to presume, to impose on others, trying to get something to which they may not be entitled.

The ideal Tzintzuntzeño spends his life walking a psychological tightrope, on which a single misstep, to right or left, will spell disaster. On the one side lie the ever-present dangers of gossip, criticism, character assassination, and perhaps witchcraft and physical attack. Too much ambition, too much aggressive action, too much improvement in one's way of living, or even no reason at all, will invoke them. But on the other side lie the even more frightening dangers that threaten the person who is not able to defend himself, who is not sufficiently macho to avoid being a target of others, who falls behind his rightful place in the order of things. The only safety lies in holding to a straight and very narrow path.

That people are continually preoccupied with — in an almost literal sense — keeping to this path is revealed in dreams. Laura Prieto "dreams only pure tragedies, like my life." She finds herself unclothed in public, with only a rag of rebozo to cover her nakedness, but lest she presume, she is afraid to ask friends she sees in the crowd for something with which to cover herself. She tries to move her legs, but they are like lead, and she can hardly crawl. In other dreams people are breaking into her house to steal. But in her most frequently recurring dream she is walking along a knife-edge ridge which falls away steeply to deep ravines on each side. A misstep, and she is lost. She knows she can't go on without falling, so she sits and weeps.

In Manuel Herrera's most frequent dreams he is walking on the edge of a cliff, terrified for fear he will be tripped by an unsuspected root, and thus catapulted over the brink; or he is walking over a very narrow bridge suspended high above a rushing stream, where the danger of falling is very great. Macaria Gómez frequently dreams she is walking along a narrow ridge of land with deep water on both sides; she feels she is about to fall, and only awakening from the dream saves her.

Preoccupation with conformity is indicated by the reaction of people to psychological tests. In the fall of 1964 Dr. Michael Maccoby administered Rorschach tests to a series of respondents. After completing the test almost all showed great anxiety over whether they had given the same answers as those who had preceded them. Their apprehensions were eased when they were assured that other people had also seen a bat, a rabbit, or a burro on one or another of the cards, just as they had.

I have said that in a society which is ruled by the Image of Limited Good, and which is viewed as a closed system, there is no way save at the expense of others whereby an individual can acquire more Good. But at another level peasant societies are, by definition, parts of an open system: they interact with town and city, and with the supernatural and magical worlds. Thus, an individual can acquire Good — money, a powerful patron — by tapping sources that are recognized as lying beyond the village system. Such success, although envied, is not perceived as a direct threat to community stability, for no one within the town has lost anything. Still, such success must be explained. In modern Tzintzuntzan, emigration for wage labor is the most common way in which to tap more distant sources of wealth. A number of people have moved to Mexico City and other, lesser cities, but the two hundred men who have gone one or more times to the United States as braceros best typify this phenomenon. Returned braceros generally are not criticized or attacked for having acquired their wealth, for it is clear that their good fortune is at the expense of the village only to the extent that their obtaining a work permit may have deprived another of the opportunity of going. Braceros, therefore, can safely spend when they return — on improved houses, on clothing, on radios, on trucks — because the source of their improved well-being is known. The considerable improvement in standards of comfort in Tzintzuntzan houses in recent years is not alone due to the capital braceros bring to the village; it is also due to the fact that braceros don't have to be afraid to spend their money.

Although Tzintzuntzeños are less aggressive than many Mexican villagers in finding wealthy and powerful patrons, they are not reluctant to form such ties when opportunity presents itself. Since such patrons reside beyond the village, they are not part of the local closed system. Consequently, their aid and material help, like bracero earnings, though enviable, are not seen as a threat to others, since no one has been deprived of anything. In Tzintzuntzan a villager who is known to have such a patron can freely reveal the forms of Good that may come to him. Not only can he reveal them but, in fact, he is well advised to advertise his luck *and the source thereof*, so there can be no doubt as to his basic morality. This open ostentation — making a point of calling attention to new and valuable possessions — is just the opposite of usual behavior, which is of course to play down or conceal good fortune.

THE EXPLANATORY ROLE OF TREASURE TALES

Obtaining entrance to the United States for work, or acquiring a powerful and helpful patron, are merely special cases of a much more pervasive pattern: the belief that luck and fate — which represent points of contact with an open system — are the only socially acceptable ways in which to acquire more Good, since they are the only ways that do not take from others. In traditional peasant communities an otherwise inexplicable increase in wealth is often seen as due to the discovery of treasure which may be the result of chance, or of such positive action as making a pact with the Devil. In Tzintzuntzan the character of treasure tales, viewed as part of a total cultural pattern, tells us a great deal about how luck, fate, and wealth are viewed.

Here, in the evening, when work is done and family and friends gather to relax, conversation is very likely to turn to how so-and-so, poor as a churchmouse, found a treasure and began to live far above his previous mode of life. In fact, apart from a constant preoccupation with health matters and from discussions as to how the necessary permits can be obtained to enter the United States, no topic arouses such lively interest. No one with whom I talked has actually seen treasure at first hand, but no one doubts that a number of fellow villagers have found it. The stories they tell take particular forms. In contrast to myth, legend, and folktale, which may deal with other worlds, other times, and other beings, treasure stories are all short, "historical" accounts about people still living or recently dead, to whom something happened at places as specifically located as well-known houses, fields, trees, or rocks. One type of story is the well-known pact with the devil in which the protagonist sells his soul in return for great wealth. The other principal type tells of the accidental discovery of treasure consisting of gold ornaments buried by Tarascan kings to hide them from Spanish conquerors; of colonial gold and silver being freighted to Pacific coast ports, hurriedly buried by muleteers fearing attack, and then lost track of; and of silver pesos buried by army generals during the Mexican Revolution. The following summaries illustrate the forms taken by treasure tales in Tzintzuntzan.

1. Salvador Enríquez was a potter, so poor he lacked animals to carry clays. Like other poor potters, he packed his raw materials on his back, "and his tumpline had worn all the hair off his head, he was *that* poor before he began to live well." His daughter, after cutting her bare foot several times on a stone in the yard, lifted the slab out with a hoe, and to her astonishment found a pot containing pure silver. Salvador bought the village's first sewing machine, opened a store, built a fine house, and began to live on a scale previously unknown in Tzintzuntzan.

2. Several boys were playing in the *aljibe*, a vault beneath the cloister adjacent to the church. One of them, Jaime Enríquez, struck an old chest and saw something gleaming behind the rotten wood. He ran to tell his father, Gaudencio, the sacristan, who ejected the boys and locked the room. That night Gaudencio sent his eldest son, Angel, who took his friend Eleno Miranda and the two removed the treasure, which in part consisted of golden sandals, left there by the Tarascan kings. Shortly thereafter Eleno opened a fine store on the plaza "with clothing and everything." Angel "entered commerce," bought a truck to carry a bingo lottery from fiesta to fiesta, and became Tzintzuntzan's richest man.

3. Isaac Enríquez, the second son of Gaudencio, did not share in this wealth, but he had similar good luck. Once while felling a banana tree in his patio he found buried treasure, with which he purchased the fine old house of Salvador Enríquez (who had died), the best lakeside milpa, then a truck, and finally a maize mill.

4. Andrés Huerta, servant to Antonio Fernández, was driving

probably incorrectly thought to be a Titian "Descent from the Cross." But few Tzintzuntzeños believe the painting was burned: it is now exhibited in a famous museum in New York City, they say. On the morning following the fire, attempts were made to pin the blame on someone. The Daughters of Mary accused the members of the Third Order, who in turn accused the Sinarquistas, who in turn indicted the "communists." Then someone remembered that Conrado Cabeza, the poorest of the poor, had returned the day before from Mexico City wearing catrín clothing and "passing out $100 bills." Although he lived close to the church, he did not appear until the following morning when, weeping wildly, he asked the rhetorical question how it was possible that he hadn't heard the warning bells and the din of the attempts to extinguish the flames. The villagers wondered, too. Shortly thereafter Saul Romano, who also had been very poor, opened a store. Then it was recalled that although he was sacristan, he had arrived at the fire without his keys, so no one could enter the burning building until it was too late to save it. Next Eliseo Miranda opened *his* store, and in reconstructing events the villagers decided he hadn't been present the night the church burned. The pieces now fell into place, and the villagers had a cause for something which had not happened in over four hundred years of Church history: the three men were in league, and they had sold out to unknown Americans who wanted the picture, arranging to cover the theft of the Titian by setting fire to the church so people would believe it had been destroyed.

The second, and more recent story, appeared during the summer of 1961. Silverio Caro, a man of forty, was a very poor potter. After his father's death he quarreled with his brother about their inherited house, so his brother bought his share, thus giving him money to acquire a small plot near the highway. He built a modest house, worked hard as a potter, and then opened a pottery stand to sell to passing tourists. Little by little he left pottery making to others and bought his merchandise. Then, in search of expanded markets, he traveled to Mexico City, Cuernavaca, and other tourist centers and established contact with store owners. In short, he became one of the two or three most successful middlemen in town. Early in 1961 he bought a large house on the highway, admitting to a payment of $15,000. Next he reconstructed the house, fitting part of it up as a store, and adding kitchen, dining room, and bedrooms to the pre-existing structure. These costs, to people who know building expenses, obviously represented at least an additional $15,000. What was the explanation? Potters do not accumulate capital sums of this size.

One night while returning from a selling trip to Mexico City, the story goes, Silverio sat next to a wealthy American woman tourist on the battered second class bus in which they were traveling. While she slept he reached into her purse, removed $40,000, got off at the next stop to avoid detection, and continued home on a later bus. This story is universally believed in Tzintzuntzan. Why would a wealthy tourist travel overnight on an uncomfortable second class bus?, I ask. Well, who knows. How is it known that Silverio robbed the woman? Did he confess? No, but she must have come here and complained to the authorities. And of the hundreds of Michoacán villages from which Silverio might have come, how did the tourist know it was Tzintzuntzan? This is hard to explain, *but it is even harder to explain how else Silverio could be spending so much money.*

Silverio knew the story, and he obviously felt vulnerable; he realized that his economic good fortune *was* hard to explain in traditional village ways. Once when talking with me he pled innocence, and pinned the blame for the gossip on the couple who have the pottery stand adjacent to his. They have done less well than he, and he found it perfectly natural that, jealous of his fortune, they should attack him.

In the years following 1961 Silverio continued to prosper. More rooms, including the prestigious second story, were added to his house. He bought a compressor for making *paletas*, the flavored ice-on-a-stick sold in most parts of Mexico, and next he acquired a comfortable house for his daughter and son-in-law. Estimates of his total expenses ranged as high as $70,000. People began to realize that the first story was insufficient in itself to explain his well-being. So, early in 1965 a second story began to circulate. A niece worked in a restaurant, some say in Morelia and others say in Pátzcuaro. Somehow she came by a substantial sum of money illegally. Those who say she worked in Morelia recount that a diner retired to the patio for an afternoon siesta, and that she removed his wallet while he dozed. Those who tell the Pátzcuaro version say the owner of the restaurant died, and that the niece dug in the kitchen and found where he concealed his profits. In both variants of the story she gave the money to her uncle for safekeeping — and he continued to keep, and spend it. One of Silverio's compadres told me Silverio himself admits his niece gave him the money, but that it was a gift. In any event, with two stories, villagers can now explain how Silverio lives so much better than other people.

FATE AND LUCK

Interest in treasure tales is but one expression of a wider view: that any major success is due to fate and luck, or the favor of deities, but not to hard work, energy, and thrift. Luck, by definition, is capricious. There is no system or natural order to which to appeal for an explanation as to why one person has it and another does not, or why good luck turns to bad luck, and vice versa. The economic facts of life as the Tzintzuntzeño sees them fit his wider view of a universe in which everything happens by chance, in which the order and regularities of a grand system are lacking.

These economic attitudes are also congruent with the Image of Limited Good model. For the underlying, fundamental truth is that in an economy like Tzintzuntzan's, hard work and thrift are moral qualities of only the slightest functional value. Because of the limitations on land and technology, additional hard work does not produce a significant increment in income. It is pointless to talk of thrift in a subsistence economy, because usually there is no surplus with which to be thrifty. Foresight, with careful planning for the future, is also a virtue of dubious value in a world in which the best laid plans must rest on a foundation of chance and capriciousness. The life experiences of Tzintzuntzeños, and the nature of the economic world as they see it, simply provide no base on which the concept of planning and foresight can develop.

An individual in Tzintzuntzan who might practice the traditional values inculcated in middle-class North Americans would be seen not only as not praiseworthy, but as a positive fool who would be wasting his time in a hopeless endeavor. The gambler, instead, emerges as more properly laudable, as worthy of emulation and adulation. If fate is the only way in which success can be obtained, the prudent and thoughtful man is the one who seeks ways in which to maximize his luck positions. He looks for the places where good fortune is most apt to strike, and tries to be there. This, I think, explains the interest in lotteries in countries and among classes where economic opportunity is limited. They offer the only way in which the average man can place himself in a luck position, and they offer one of the few ways in which he can make real progress without being viewed as a threat to his fellows. The man who goes without lunch and deprives his family of necessities in order to buy a ticket is perhaps not the ne'er-do-well he appears to be to people who participate in an expanding economy with unlimited opportunity. He is, rather, the bright young man of his society who is taking the steps best calculated to improve his position. A lottery ticket is the only "growth stock" he can buy. The odds are against him, but it is the only way he knows in which to work toward real advancement.

In Tzintzuntzan, buying lottery tickets is not common behavior. Perhaps with greater access to them, and more faith in the honesty of the government, the habit would spread. Nevertheless, Tzintzuntzeños see the lottery as a functional equivalent to buried treasure. Once I remarked to Doña Andrea Medina that buried treasure had not been found for fifteen to twenty years. She agreed, but hastened to call my attention to the lottery; as she saw it, one form of luck opportunity had simply been replaced by another.

When measured against the economic and social conditions that have prevailed in Tzintzuntzan for many generations, behavior based on a firm belief in luck cannot be considered unrealistic or illogical. Rather, such behavior represents an accurate appraisal by villagers of how a person has been able to get ahead. Obviously, there are new opportunities today that did not exist when the cognitive orientation that still produces this behavior was developed, and these will be described in subsequent chapters. Here we are considering the model of a traditional community, which accounts for prevailing values and long-standing behavior forms, and we are not describing changing contemporary attitudes and actions.

CHAPTER SEVEN

The
Fear
of Envy

THE PREVALENCE OF ENVY

In small, poor communities ruled by the Image of Limited Good, where security rests on maintaining the traditional distribution of the good things in life, even minor improvements with respect to these desired things are going to be quickly noted. And although someone's access to Good need not inevitably be attributed to deprivation of another, betterment of position is likely to arouse the envy of those who consider themselves less fortunate. Where people have so little, and where life is so uncertain, the good fortune of fellow villagers seems bound to arouse envy. In Tzintzuntzan, as in the Italy and the India described by Banfield and Dube, envy is a dominant note in people's character. To see others gain an advantage reminds one of his own scant resources, his unfulfilled hopes, or his habitual bad luck. "All of Pascual's children have become school teachers, have they not?" The implied praise in my question is hardly concealed. Ah, yes, but Pascual has been school custodian for twenty-five years; he has been a friend of the inspectors who come from Morelia. He feeds them when they are in the village, and through these friendships he has obtained scholarships for his children. "My children would have made better teachers," says Macaria, "but I didn't have the opportunity Pascual had."

When people envy, it is quite natural for them to fear the consequences of the envy of others. At one level this fear is dealt with in a straightforward and simple fashion: Tzintzuntzeños simply attempt to conceal those things they suspect or know may arouse envy in others. For this reason a good many people, in clothing and home comforts, live well below the level they can afford. By appearing to be no better off than their poorer neighbors, they hope to avoid envy and its consequences. Wigberto Paz, although not a village leader, has a good sense of responsibility — by local standards — and always contributes to community projects. However, he won't go beyond minimum conveniences in fixing up his house, and his clothing is as tattered as that of anyone in town. He has electricity and water, as do half of the village families, but he refuses to lay a cement or tile floor, or cut windows in his rooms to lighten interiors. He is frankly afraid people will envy him, so he tries to protect himself with this age-old peasant device of simulating poverty.

Most new houses have good windows opening onto the street, many with glass. But until very few years ago houses with windows kept shutters closed most of the time; their only apparent function was to permit a quick and furtive glance down the street. Micaela's husband, Melecio, was much opposed to putting glass windows in the first modern room of their house. Fear of robbery was one reason — he felt a tightly closed house was safest — but even more important was his feeling that "without windows, people can't look inside, see what we have, and want it." Glass windows to Melecio were breaches in his personal defenses, and an invitation to envy.

Although some women, and particularly teenage girls, now dress in city clothes for fiestas, to visit friends, or to promenade in the plaza, no woman in workaday garb going about her chores is apt to go outside her house without her rebozo shawl. Often, of course, the rebozo is used for carrying infants, and it can also be used to transport small purchases. It is good protection against the elements as well. It is, in short, a highly utilitarian element of dress. But at least as important as any of these reasons is that it serves to conceal any object a person may be carrying through the street. Purchases made in the Pátzcuaro market or a local store, food gifts coming from or going to the home of a comadre or friend, a garment made in the home of a seamstress — whatever a person carries is best concealed from prying eyes which might, at the sight of the object, be filled with envy. The rebozo, because it offers psychological protection to village women, will continue as a part of costume long after its present utilitarian needs are no longer served.

SYMBOLIC EXPRESSION OF ENVY

Envy is, of course, an emotion found in every society, and since it reflects feelings of hostility, and sometimes is an implicit threat of aggression, it threatens the stability of group life unless it can be controlled. Large, complex societies appear to be able to absorb a good deal more envy than can peasant societies, without endangering themselves, yet they, too, require devices for coping with the ever-present threat of unbridled envy. Much envy in complex societies is controlled by permitting its expression in a particular symbolic form: compliments, and expressions of admiration. Not all compliments reflect envy, of course, but between equals or potential equals the feeling, however subconscious, is present far more often than most people care to admit.

In commercial and industrial societies — but not in peasant societies — to pay a compliment or to express admiration are perhaps the only nondisruptive ways in which these strong and rancorous sentiments can be directed overtly toward someone. The true feelings, when envy actually underlies them, are dressed up and sweetened, but for all the courtesy people are but rarely fooled. At least subconsciously they recognize that compliments may veil envious feelings, and the person complimented suspects he may be vulnerable to some form of aggression, such as unkind gossip behind his back, because he has in effect been told he has something such as a possession, a capability, or a talent, which others would like to have. This is why, I think, in contemporary American society, where the ability to compliment is the mark of a well-bred person, the recipient often experiences some embarrassment and discomfort, floundering in his attempt to respond in just the right manner, and sometimes making the gesture of denying that he really merits praise.

In Tzintzuntzan, unlike the United States, compliments and praise are rarely heard. This behavior pattern is not due to egoísmo, to selfishness, or to bad manners, as I was inclined to believe for a long time. Rather, in the context of the Limited Good model it is apparent that this customary behavior makes complete sense. The person who compliments is, in fact, guilty of aggression; he is saying the other has some trait or quality or possession that he would like himself (thus evoking the spectre of envy), or he is telling the person he compliments that he has risen above his proper level, and that his behavior may trigger sanctions. Behavior thought to merit compliments in some other societies is precisely the behavior the village sees as threatening, and which it wishes to discourage.

If symbolic devices to neutralize the danger presented by envy are essential in large and impersonal societies, they are even more necessary in small, delicately balanced communities like Tzintzuntzan. The overt devices just described, and above all concealment and secrecy, however useful, are not in themselves adequate to protect a person from danger; symbolic acts as well are needed in the armamentarium. Symbolic words and acts that tell a person suspected of harboring envious feelings that he has no reason to be envious, or that he can share in the good fortune, are therefore highly functional. In this fashion the illusion of absolute equilibrium is maintained; with equal access to Good, or with a sharing of available Good, no one need feel envious of another.

An inverse but complementary logic applies in those instances in which individuals or families have suffered a loss. The desired equality has been destroyed, and the afflicted persons become threats because of their envy of others who have not suffered a loss. Symbolic behavior which is seen to neutralize the possible consequences of this envy, by redressing the inequity, is therefore highly valued.

THE REMOJO

In Tzintzuntzan there are various symbolic acts and other forms of customary behavior which seem best explained in the above context: to protect people from the possible consequences of envy directed toward them. These acts are most frequently noted in situations in which people are found to have something new and desirable, in which they have plentiful amounts of things often in short supply, and in which families have suddenly been deprived of some highly valued Good. For example, when friends note that someone has a new possession such as a garment, a kitchen utensil, a household furnishing, or a piglet, they may shout *el remojo, el remojo,* which means "You must give us something to make up for the new possession you have." Usually no return is expected, but the owner is careful to acknowledge the request by saying A *sus órdenes,* thus symbolically placing the object at the disposal of those demanding the remojo, who can now have no reason to be envious. For more striking acquisitions, owners may forestall action by offering something before being asked. When José Calvo enlarged his store and increased his stocks he gave small presents to his best customers, laughingly assuring them it was the remojo due them. Perhaps the occasional housewarming fiesta offered friends may also be thought of as a remojo* to counter possible envy.

On other occasions friends may admire something new without asking for a remojo. The owner characteristically replies with something like V*erdad? Yo lo veo muy feo,* "Really? I think it's very ugly." He thereby suggests that the admirer is mistaken in his appraisal, and that he has no real reason for envy. And, per-

---

* In its common sense the verb "remojar" means "to soak something in water." In a figurative sense it means "to invite friends to drink," to celebrate the debut of a garment, a purchased item, or some other happy event for the host. Cf. English "sop."

haps, the custom of wearing a new garment in public for the first time at a major fiesta, when a great many people will be similarly decked out, is a protective device to dilute the envy of those not fortunate enough to have new clothes.

Domestic animals, especially the larger varieties, represent relatively high values in Tzintzuntzan, and are thus potential objects of envy. Although informants deny that the evil eye can afflict animals, it is considered bad form to express extravagant admiration for an animal, since it is thought this may cause it to fall ill. Some people quickly sell an animal so admired, hoping to recoup their capital before it is lost through possible death.

ENVY AND PREGNANCY

In Tzintzuntzan babies generally are considered highly desirable, at least until the fourth or fifth, so both a new baby and its mother can be objects of conscious and unconscious envy. In a society which places high value on masculinity, the siring of a healthy offspring is the best possible evidence of possessing this quality. But the sickness or death of the child casts doubts on the father's true masculinity, since a weak infant suggests a sire lacking in vigor. For these, as well as other reasons, every care must be taken to save the child from the danger that may result if it is envied by others who resent the "new possession" of the parents. This care takes the form of delaying the time when the cause for envy may be generally known. An expectant mother tries to conceal her condition as long as possible, and speaks of the forthcoming event only when forced to do so. That this is a sensitive area of culture is proven by the use of euphemisms in speaking of pregnancy. Pregnancy is classed as *una enfermedad*, an illness. Thus, when a question is raised about an expectant mother, her condition may be glossed over by saying "she is ill." If questions or comments persist, amplification takes the form of "she is ill *de la cinta.*" The derivation of *cinta* is not entirely clear: in the sense of "band" it may refer to an abdominal sash or belt, or it may come from *cintura*, meaning "waist," or *encinta*, meaning "enceinte." Whatever the origin of the word, the expression is euphemistic, permitting avoidance of the word "pregnant." A woman may also be described as being "in an interesting condition." But to say "I am pregnant" or "She is pregnant" causes much apprehension.

The act of birth itself is also played down by using the euphemism *aliviarse*, "to get well," rather than by other terms which more directly suggest what is happening. A birth itself receives no publicity. New fathers scrupulously avoid mentioning the event, even to friends, and when the news leaks out enquirers are assured that they "have a new servant at your disposal in your house," in effect being told that since the child is also theirs, they have no cause to be envious. Moreover, lest the enquirer envy the father his house, this, too, must be placed at his disposal.

THE BOLO

For baptism the infant must be taken to the church, so there is no way to conceal its existence. A mother, however, never attends the baptism, even though it occasionally is postponed until after the forty-day period of seclusion known as the cuarentena. Perhaps this custom — the mother's absence at baptism — reflects a feeling that it is unwise needlessly to expose her to the view of other women who might be jealous of her good luck, before she has fully recovered her strength. And perhaps the institution of the cuarentena itself, when a new mother at least makes a pretense of not leaving her house, is an expression of her need to be fully recovered before facing the dangers of envy that might be directed toward her.

There is no avoiding exposure of the infant at its baptism, however; it must be carried through the streets done up in special baby clothes, as conspicuous as a person ever is. The possible danger is countered by the old Spanish custom of the bolo. When the godparents emerge from the church after the sacrament they find themselves surrounded by a milling crowd of youngsters who shout *Déme el bolo, déme el bolo*, "Give me the bolo, give me the bolo." The godfather must throw handfuls of small coins into the air for which the children scramble wildly. Thus, symbolically, he gives something to others who have not shared directly in the good fortune of the birth. Thoughtful informants see the bolo as a form of remojo, although the latter term is not used to describe it.

THE EVIL EYE

Payment of the bolo does not provide long-term protection. Most women, and childless women in particular (and men, too, as far as that goes), may envy the good fortune of the new mother. Fear of the consequences of this envy is institutionalized in belief in the *mal de ojo*, the evil eye. Although sophisticated informants insist they really do not believe in *el ojo*, we again are led to suspect this is a sensitive area of culture, by the euphemisms used to refer to it. Only rarely is the expression *mal de ojo* heard; rather, of a child suspected as suffering from the affliction, it is said "his blood has been irritated." In the presence of strangers the mother covers the child so it cannot be seen — the rebozo is ideal for this in the street — or she hangs amulets such as coral beads or the "Deer's eye" seed around its neck, which are thought to divert the envious glance from the child itself. But her friends have the right to see the infant. Even the closest of these, however, may unknowingly "irritate the blood" of the child by admiring it. To counteract this possibility, the thoughtful person after expressing admiration strikes the child a time or two on the rump, an act known as *dar una nalgada*, "to give a blow on the buttocks." If the admirer forgets this courtesy, an apprehensive mother may say *Dáme una nalgada* meaning, of course, a slap on the rump of the child. But why should a person strike something admired, an act usually reserved for something scorned or disliked, or to punish a disobedient child? Symbolically the striker seems to say, "I praised the child, but I didn't really mean it. The child is no good. Do you think I would strike something I really covet and admire?" By this simple act the suspected or implied envy is denied, and the mother is reassured.

Some mothers consciously let their children stay dirty, and clothe them in rags, thus hoping to protect them from possible admiration by making them unattractive. This behavior is even more characteristic of Tarascan mothers in the hamlets adjacent to Tzintzuntzan.

160

THE BRIDE'S FAVORS

A groom who acquires a bride may also be envied by his bachelor friends. By taking a girl from the available pool he has reduced the supply left to the others, and he has acquired access to favors they would all appreciate. This imbalance is symbolically stated, and then remedied. In Tzintzuntzan most marriages begin with elopement. The young man, aided by friends, "robs" the girl, takes her to the home of a relative or friend, has sexual relations with her, and then announces their intention to marry. On the morning following elopement the girl is expected to prepare a big pot of *atole*, a maize beverage much esteemed in Michoacán, and much consumed on ceremonial as well as other occasions. When the groom's friends come to the house where she is lodged she gives them small pottery cups of *atole*. She seems to be saying, symbolically, "You have no reason to envy your friend (the groom-to-be); here, I can give you a favor, too, so you are all equal." On other occasions the atole is served by the girl to the people who have come to make formal peace between the families of the boy and the girl. Informants say the reason is to show that the girl is a good cook and will be able to take care of a new husband. But, in view of the first and major context of the rite, it seems likely that this is a symbolic device whereby many people can share in the new couple's happiness.

FOOD AND ENVY

Eating habits also reflect the feeling of danger from the envy of others. Silence while eating is a primary virtue, instilled in children from an early age. They are told such things as "The guardian angel is at the table," or "Be quiet, for the guardian angel is serving you your food." The training is so successful that even when a hundred or more children gather in a patio for a government-sponsored school breakfast, they eat in near-silence. Husbands also usually insist on silence while they eat, sometimes prohibiting their wives from talking as long as food is laid out.

The more sophisticated villagers who sometimes eat away from home in small restaurants and market stalls also know the wide-

161

spread Mexican (and Spanish-American and Spanish) custom whereby a diner who sees someone enter the room says *Gusta?* (*usted comer*), meaning "Would you care to share my meal?" He who enters replies *Buen provecho,* i.e., "Good appetite, may your food agree with you," thereby telling the diner he has no reason to fear envy and that he may eat in peace. The entrant, of course, would never accept the proffered invitation, and the courtesy appears to have the sole function of recognizing that envy may be present, and at the same time of eliminating the cause.

In a society in which food is a scarce commodity, and in which many people do not have enough, a person who is seen eating may well expect to arouse envy. A diner caught with food feels obligated to ask the intruder to join him and, of course, the offering of food is a major expression of recognizing the ties that bind family members, friends, neighbors, and compadres. Nevertheless, extensive hospitality can be expensive. By maintaining silence a diner is less apt to call attention to his good fortune, and by concentrating on eating rather than conversation, he reduces the period of exposure to sudden visits which may involve him in added costs.

To have it known that one is eating is potentially dangerous, and this threat is reflected in hospitality patterns. Guests are invited formally to meals only on such ritual occasions as a marriage, a baptism, or a saint's day celebration. A very few honored friends and close relatives form the core guest list. Often — with baptismal godparents, for example — the host must go to their home and formally escort them through the streets to his house. Other guests are invited in a casual and informal manner, not to eat, but "to accompany us," so that the words "food" and "meal" and "eat" are not uttered at all. When I am invited to a fiesta the invitation often is a model of studied carelessness; the host wishes it to appear to be a spur-of-the-moment thought he had when he realized he was passing my door, and the occasion for the implied meal is not mentioned at all. Only occasionally have I been asked outright a day or two in advance to come to a particular fiesta.

When guests arrive for a fiesta they find a table set, but planks that can be quickly converted to a table always lie nearby, and almost certainly additional places will have to be improvised. When I have arrived early I have sometimes asked who or how many people are expected, but no one knows the answer, and the prudent family always prepares what seems like sufficient food to feed the entire village. In fact, apart from the core guest list, no one can know who will appear until the last straggler has passed the door. As the host escorts the honored guests to his home, he is highly conspicuous, especially if godparents are carrying the newly baptized infant. Friends and neighbors appear at their doors, and the host feels compelled to invite them to "accompany" him. Some accept, others do not, but no prediction is possible. Chance determines the final guest list at every fiesta.

Informants say the reason one is never sure how many people will come is that the guests of honor have the privilege of inviting *their* friends. There is undoubtedly truth in this statement: assorted friends of guests do turn up. But it seems likely that the host, subconsciously at least, fears that a neighbor who sees him with guests of honor will feel envy, and that possible harmful effects of this envy can be neutralized only by inviting the neighbor to share in the banqueting. The casual and euphemistically phrased invitations seem to reflect a desire to conceal or deny that a real fiesta is to take place, lest the word get around and too many people to be accommodated know of the event.

Once at the table the host apologizes profusely for the poor fare, however elaborate and bountiful it may be. Simultaneously urging guests to eat "with confidence" he reminds them he is a humble man with a poor house, and that they must forgive him his inability to attend to their wants in the style they merit. So strongly is this apology imbedded in hospitality behavior that the narrator who once told me the story of Don Juan Cantimplata felt impelled to have the Devil apologize — not once, but twice — to the trickster boy hero who is being given a guided tour, for the poor shape in which he finds Hell. "You'll have to excuse me for the way things are," says the Devil. "I'm really just beginning to get the place fixed up." A visitor, it is clear, should not even begrudge the Devil his Hell!

Food secrecy is also reflected in the universal custom of carefully covering with a cloth or rebozo any cooked or uncooked food that is taken from one house to another as a part of reciprocal exchange patterns. Some people, when asked, say the reason is to protect the food from dust or germs, but since bacterial contamination is hardly ever given a thought in any other context, it seems more likely that prying eyes are viewed as the greater danger.

WAKES

The instances described are ones in which equilibrium, in which the status quo, is threatened because someone *acquires* or has something others might wish to have, and the behavior appropriate to the occasion symbolically expresses the envy and simultaneously counters the danger. The complementary but inverse situation is when someone *loses* or seems in danger of losing something desirable, upsetting the delicate balance demanded by the dynamics of the system. This form of danger, and its neutralization, is best seen in the custom at wakes whereby every mourner comes with a gift such as a few pesos, a couple of kilos of beans or maize, candles, or some other useful item. Friends, relatives, and neighbors are under strong compulsion to attend wakes; they see it as an important part of the reciprocal pattern that characterizes social relations within the village. With gifts they appear to say to the bereaved family, "You have suffered a loss, which we regret, but you need not feel envious of us, for we bring gifts to make up for the loss of your loved one." In this symbolic fashion the status quo is restored.

SALUD!

The widespread Tzintzuntzan (and Mexican and Spanish) custom of wishing a person good health when he sneezes, also may be explained in this way. To say *salud!* when someone within earshot sneezes is almost a compulsion, and should good health not be wished, the sneezer feels quite uncomfortable. Should someone for any reason fail to say salud! a sneezer may, half humorously and half seriously, remind him of his lack of good manners by saying, "May Jesus accompany me until I find myself with human beings," implying that one's company is less than human. But why should a sneeze be such a sensitive area of culture? Among some tribal peoples in Mexico a sneeze is associated with soul loss, which leads to illness and possible death. This belief is not found in Tzintzuntzan but, says Micaela, speaking for the village, "all illness begins with a cold," the onset of which is frequently signaled by sneezing. A person who sneezes then may be presumed to be in danger of losing his health, making him envious of those who remain well. To say salud! thus becomes an elementary precaution, calling the sneezer's attention to the fact that it is hoped he will remain in good health, that no one wishes him to fall ill. A difference in health between two people puts the better off of the two in a potentially vulnerable position. By the same token, people do not like to be told that they are looking well, since this implies they may be envied. On those rare occasions when a health compliment is uttered, the receiver may remind the speaker that he was at death's door only a week earlier, or otherwise point out that his health is not nearly as good as the remark implied.

THE SECRECY SYNDROME

There appear to be two basic ways in which societies can meet the fear of the consequences of overt or suspected envy: the person or group suspecting envy may hide or deny its advantage, expecting to live primarily on its own immediate resources, or it may share or offer to share it in the most open fashion, confident that the law of averages will return to it an amount equal to that given out. In societies marked by relative equality, both niggardliness and generous hospitality, with its implied return, appear to offer about the same access to the good things in life. For reasons not entirely clear, Tzintzuntzan, like most other peasant societies, has opted for the first alternative. The initial defense of possession is to attempt to hide or deny its existence: birth secrecy, the cuarentena taboo against the mother leaving her house until she is again strong; eating in silence; covering food being taken through the streets; profuse apologies for humble fare at fiesta meals; allowing children to be dirty and unkempt; wearing ragged clothing; the reluctance to improve houses; and the "I think it very ugly" denial that an admired item merits praise.

The second defense is symbolically to offer to share some Good, without expecting acceptance, or to offer some trifling compensation for good fortune or absence of bad fortune: the *Gusta-Buen provecho* invitation and acknowledgment in restaurants; the "it is at your disposal" reply to a remojo request; the "you have a new servant in your house" admission that a baby has been born; the baptismal bolo; the atole served by the bride-to-be; and the gifts taken to wakes.

Only as a last and inevitable resort does a Tzintzuntzeño share or offer to share well-being, with full knowledge that the invitation will certainly or very likely be accepted: inviting people other than honored guests to a fiesta meal and, in the most extravagant of all gestures, sponsoring a major part of a religious fiesta.

As to the reasons why Tzintzuntzan, and most other peasant societies, prefer the first alternative, it is clear that the secrecy syndrome is psychologically more congenial to a Limited Good view of the world than is non-hoarding behavior. Moreover, the physical nature of the village, with stout houses, high walls, and closed doors and windows facilitates secrecy. Up to a point, a good deal of luck can be concealed in a way that is impossible in villages — in much of Africa, for example, where the alternative form of behavior is very common — where thatched-roofed, stick-walled huts are placed close together, where cooking odors waft from one dwelling to another, and where conversation is easily overheard by any neighbor or passerby.

CHAPTER EIGHT

Government,
Decision Making,
and Conflict Resolution

THE EQUILIBRIUM MODEL

The evidence that suggests Tzintzuntzeños have a Limited Good view of the world about them has been presented in the preceding two chapters, and the way in which this view leads to an equilibrium model for the healthy social organism has been described. It is clear that in the villagers' minds the desirable — in fact the only safe — community is one in which all people have, or by a fiction can be assumed to have, about the same access to wealth and other good things in life. Significant inequalities are seen as threatening the community, and behavior which suggests that someone has, or is attempting to obtain, more than his share of some Good, is considered disruptive. By the same token, behavior that clearly maintains the status quo, or which re-establishes a status quo temporarily disturbed, is applauded.

A striving to maintain equilibrium thus emerges as the dominant pattern in Tzintzuntzan culture, a consistent organization of beliefs and actions reiterated in the major institutions of the community. In this and in the following chapter we will examine the ways in which governmental activities, decision making, and conflict resolving mechanisms, and health concepts and behavior conform to the equilibrium model. Then, in the chapter on religious ritual, we shall explain the manner in which these elaborate ceremonies have the latent function of helping maintain basic economic equilibrium. Finally, in discussing the Dyadic Contract we will see how patterns of reciprocity in the primary social relationship — that between two individuals — establish an equilibrium between partners. In these chapters my purpose is not a full ethnographic description of the customs and practices associated with these major cultural categories. Rather, I am concerned with describing and analyzing basic cognitive orientations and behavior forms, bare of as much incidental detail as is possible, so that the structural similarities can be more readily seen.

THE MUNICIPIO AND ITS OFFICIALS

In Mexico local government is based on the municipio, a concept roughly corresponding to the American township. But the implications for local government are quite different, in that few small communities are discrete units. Rather, for administrative purposes, for tax collecting, for voting, and for other activities, all communities within a single municipio are bound together, and bear some organic relationship to all the other units. Tzintzuntzan, for example, is the *cabecera*, or head, of the municipio which bears its name, and which also includes other settlements both Tarascan and mestizo. All these communities participate in electing five *regidores*, or councilmen, who serve for three years, and who each year select one of their number as "municipal president," or mayor, and a second as síndico, an office invested with judicial and investigative functions.

Thus, some of the officials whose decisions affect Tzintzuntzan are not members of the community at all. Although the mayor usually is a Tzintzuntzeño, about once in six years he comes from another settlement in the municipio, and at any given time not more than two councilmen are from the village. The municipal treasurer and its two judges, usually but not always Tzintzuntzeños, are appointed by the mayor, but must be approved by higher authorities in Morelia, capital of Michoacán, whereas the "mayor's secretary," who records vital statistics, and the "judges' secretary," who keeps legal records, are appointed by the mayor alone. They usually serve over a period of years, regardless of changes in their supervisors, since relatively few villagers have the qualifications necessary for this work.

The success of municipio government depends on the treasurer's ability to collect taxes and hold them prior to disbursement. Principal sources of municipio income are fees for registering land and house titles, for selling livestock, for registering livestock brands, for animal-slaughtering licenses, for marriage acts, and for permits to operate retail establishments. During the early 1960's municipio income (which of course includes that from all communities, and not just Tzintzuntzan) averaged $22,000 per year, of which $16,000 went for officials' salaries. These, except for that of the treasurer, are very modest, even by local standards: the mayor and the two secretaries, $6 daily; a "militia" commander, $4; and a policeman-gardener, $3. Councilmen other than the mayor receive nothing. The treasurer, on the other hand, is entitled to 30 per cent of the income he collects, which works out at $300 to $900 a month, depending on the time of year. Since peones earn $5–8 a day, it is clear that town officials must, and are expected to, augment their incomes by various means.

Judges receive gratuities, often from both contending parties, and they may keep a part of the fines they assess. The mayor is entitled to keep marriage fees above $16, and other sources of income accrue to him. During recent years some mayors charged varying amounts for bracero permits. The legal fee was $9.60 for a raffle ticket which determined who the lucky men were to be. A mayor who charged up to about $50 to get a permit for a friend was not felt to be abusing his office; this was seen as a reasonable sum for his efforts, and one of the ways to compensate him for his inability to attend to other personal matters during his mayoralty.

The treasurer has no strong box or safe. He simply puts income in his pockets, carries it home, and keeps it informally until it is paid out. The important thing to note in this financial system is that other than street lighting *no real community services are provided*. Almost all income goes to keep the system running, largely in the form of salaries, and there is virtually no excess for community projects or betterment. Moreover, *there is no provision in the system for the community formally to levy taxes for special projects.*

The municipio government is not seen by villagers as a local self-government device, designed to meet governmental and financial needs of the community through local responsibility. It is a system set up from outside, whose officials, in time of emergency, have the responsibility of appealing to State officials in Morelia for special help. Consequently, when funds for civic projects — the annual fiesta, a new pump for the water system, purchase of communal lands — must be collected, there is no formal way to do so, and to make sure that everyone pays according to his ability. Rather, an ad hoc committee is formed to set a quota, and families must be cajoled, or bludgeoned into paying. Needless to say, any collection, however meritorious its purpose, causes a great deal of bad feeling within the community.

COLLECTING TAXES

A second level of government in the municipio is the office of the *Receptor de Rentas*, the State tax collector. This official, named from Morelia, is always an outsider; it is taken for granted that a local man would be so bound by kin and friendship obligations that he would be seriously handicapped in making his collections. The greatest source of income in this office is property taxes on fields and homes, at the rate of $15 per $1,000 of assessed value. The transfer of title to property is also taxed at the same rate; consequently, much property is registered, and taxes are paid, in the names of people long since dead. Although this delay would seem to be a potent source of litigation, the possible troubles seem not to compensate for the expenses involved, which would amount, in effect, to double taxation the year a transfer is made. Usually the purpose in not registering new owners following a death is to skip an entire generation.

Other sources of income to the State include taxes on stores, nixtamal mills, on cattle, and vehicular license plates. State income is far higher than that of the municipio, averaging nearly $150,000 annually during the early 1960's. This income, like that of the municipio, comes from all communities and all property within the municipio, and not just from Tzintzuntzan, whose share cannot be determined from the records, since local breakdowns are neither required nor kept. On a per capita basis Tzintzuntzan's contribution works out at about $35,000, but if we recall that it has less land than most communities, it is quite possible the figure is only $25,000 to $30,000 annually.

The bulk of these tax monies passes on to the State and National governments. The only local service provided is potable water, for which the monthly charge of $2.40 is insufficient. Thus a part of the pump-tender's salary, and minor repairs are covered from the Receptor's office. But, in case of major expenses, such as a new pump, action must be taken on the same ad hoc basis used to meet all other unusual community needs, since the regular system does not provide for such emergencies. The Receptor of Rents receives as salary 18.75 per cent of his receipts, so he is by far the best paid individual in the village.

It should not be thought that Tzintzuntzan and similar rural communities are milked by a heartless central government, simply because most tax monies leave them. Actually, the village receives far more than it contributes to the national economy. Major constructions, such as the school, a new building for the school breakfast program, and a new health center, are mostly or entirely provided for from State and National funds. Ongoing school expenses alone amount to many times the total tax income in Tzintzuntzan. At the end of 1964, for example, school personnel were being paid a total of $8,800 per month. Thus, in school

171

salaries alone Tzintzuntzan receives more than $100,000 a year, which is three to four times the total amount it pays through the State Receptor of Rents.

The only governmental unit limited exclusively to Tzintzuntzan is the *Comunidad Indígena*, the Indigenous Community, the corporate village structure surviving from colonial times when Indian communities held communally all their lands. Its contemporary functioning is even harder to grasp than those of the other systems, since it has no physical office, and very little formal structure. It is headed by a president, elected in open meeting at which all heads of families, whether natives of Tzintzuntzan or not, may participate. He keeps such records as he deems worthwhile, calls meetings if something requires action, and otherwise "defends" the community interests. His term is for an indefinite period, and when asked people often have to think hard to remember who he is. Still, for some types of action, the community can be mobilized through this mechanism.

It is the Indigenous Community, for example, that is convoked for action on such specific items as repairs to the roof of the monastery (in which the priest lives), or a new pump for the potable water system. So, however informal and often inadequate the system, and however vague its functioning is in the minds of people, it is fairly significant in community life.

DECISION MAKING

Whatever the particular institutional context, an underlying principle in decision making in Tzintzuntzan is not openly to oppose anyone, nor to express fundamental opposition to an idea expressed by another. A direct confrontation in which two candidates are in direct opposition — and hence one must lose — or in which in public discussion one tries to have his ideas take precedence over others, is disturbing to all, since an equilibrium is destroyed, and every effort is made to avoid such situations. Hence, decisions must be based on consensus, gradually achieved, after a thousand slight movements and bits of progress bring the leader of a meeting to the point where he can announce a course of action, reasonably confident no one will disagree. For other than specifically political acts, a community meeting is usually announced by the priest at early Sunday Mass, which most heads of family will be attending. Following Mass interested persons assemble in the churchyard, to listen to the problem and to decide on action.

On one occasion the then priest, Father Huacúz, without specifying the subject, announced a meeting after Mass. Only about twenty-five men first appeared, scattered in small clusters over a wide area; later, more joined them. Ignacio Arriaga, president of the Indigenous Community, began to address the group, haltingly and slowly. For some time it was impossible to tell what the purpose of the meeting was. Little by little it became apparent that the roof of the monastery leaked, and the priest wished it repaired. After fifteen minutes of rambling presentation of the problem, Ignacio asked, "What shall we do?" There was no response. Valentín Patiño, town mayor, also asked the same question. Still no response.

Then someone suggested it might be a good idea to take a look at the roof (no one had thought to do this prior to the meeting) and appraise the magnitude of the problem. Camilo Reina tentatively suggested naming a "commission" — he had picked up the word while living in the United States — but receiving no favorable response he soon became quiet; he is unpopular in town, and his ideas are apt to be ignored, however much merit they may have. Various other suggestions were made, all with much timidity. Someone recommended forced contributions but, remembering earlier similar attempts, this idea was not carried further. Finally it was decided that a group would look at the roof, estimate the need, and set about making a collection. Carried away with enthusiasm, one man offered a hundred roof tiles, another a heavy wooden beam, and still another handed a $50 note to Antonio. A pencil and paper emerged from nowhere, and promises and contributions were written down.

The dynamics of this meeting reflect a great deal about the process of reaching consensus. All suggestions are made with the utmost diffidence, and group reaction is carefully noted by the speaker. No suggestion does more than go slightly beyond previous decisions that have been approved. Thus, failure to back a suggestion is seen as an inconsequential setback, not a threat to the face and dignity of the speaker. As the discussion develops, and the general direction of opinion is noted, people become more confident, even more voluble; now they can speak with greater certainty that they are in the mainstream of opinion. At this stage speakers step forward from their groups, remaining if their point is approved. Others then move forward slowly to join them. Finally, as consensus is neared, the participants have congregated in a tight knot around the leader; physical proximity and solidarity reflect the agreement that has been reached. But no one — not even the leader — feels free to take the major step of saying, in effect, "Here's the problem; what do you think of this solution?" And no listener dares risk suggesting a full solution, whatever ideas he may have. In both cases the danger of a rebuff, of being slapped down, is too great. Such behavior sets the stage for probable direct confrontation with others who hold different ideas, and this must be avoided at all costs.

On another occasion the school director called a meeting of parents to decide on special uniforms for the September 16 Independence Day parade to be held in Morelia. As an outsider, in a position of authority, he took a more positive stand than a villager would have done. He had noted, he said, that during the previous three years the uniforms had been blue, and he wondered if it wouldn't be good this year to have a new color — green, one of the three colors of the Mexican flag. For twenty minutes or more he talked about the importance of a smartly clad group of scholars "to call the attention of officials in Morelia to the school," and about the importance of school in general. Trinidad Rendón, head of the Committee of Fathers, got up and said he thought the idea was very good. Other muffled comments were taken to mean assent, and hearing no conflicting opinions, the director thanked the parents for their attendance and support. "Muchas gracias, Maestro," they replied, and nearly all the men and about half the women filed out.

174

But a small knot of women gathered around the director and discussed the problem for another fifteen animated minutes. If the blouses as well as the skirts and trousers were of the new material, the cost would be excessive. Most children had white shirts or blouses, so why not just make the trousers or skirts of green cloth? The director agreed to this reasonable compromise, which was hammered out of a dozen or more tentative suggestions, much as in the case of the monastery roof. No woman went far out on a limb, and the director was spared the indignity in the full meeting of a contrary opinion of a magnitude which he might feel to be a personal attack. Everyone was satisfied with the final decision, and with the resulting full cooperation of mothers, the uniforms were ready for the parade.

ELECTIONS

The mechanics of local political elections are difficult to understand; for the villagers, even those who participate and are elected to office, there is something of the quality of the unknowable that characterizes the supernatural and the city. This is not altogether surprising, for election rules are set by Mexico's principal party, the PRI (*Partido Revolucionario Institucional*), and at every step a party functionary who is usually a local deputy, a townsman from Morelia or Pátzcuaro, oversees village politics in the area he represents. PRI is opposed, locally and of course nationally, by PAN (*Partido de Acción Nacional*), a conservative group. Major differences of opinion among the real leaders of Mexico are resolved behind the scenes in PRI, and the contending factions of professional politicians, the business community, labor unions, the army, and the agrarian groups, come to compromises much as, in the American South, the real contests normally are within a single party. Few politicians not members of PRI expect success.

This general rule holds for Tzintzuntzan. Although a few men say they belong to PAN, and perhaps occasionally a PAN candidate is named, local officials always are PRI members. In the fall of every third year PRI sends word from Morelia that candidates for regidores, the councilmen, are to be named. Each of the municipio's five sections, which correspond to wards, names one or more candidates, plus an alternate, a *suplente*. PRI always has a full slate of five candidates and five alternates, and PAN is said sometimes to put up a slate. The mechanics of naming these candidates are unclear. Primo Calderón, judge, and one of the most able and well-informed men in town, says that wards away from Tzintzuntzan locally decide on three pairs of candidate-cum-alternate, within each party, whose names are sent to Tzintzuntzan where the mayor decides on a single pair. In Tzintzuntzan itself a meeting is held in Pascual Corral's theatre, and local candidates and alternates are named, thus completing one or more slates (i.e., PRI always, and possibly PAN).

These slates are sent to Morelia — by PRI, Primo thinks — where they may be approved, modified to any degree, or thrown out entirely and new men named. No one knows until word comes from Morelia. On the first Sunday in December elections are held, and the successful candidates are named. On New Year's eve these five men meet and name one among themselves mayor for the coming year, subject to confirmation from Morelia. Since the councilmen serve for three years, three of the five normally can expect to have a term as mayor. The Limited Good inherent in the situation — three places for five contenders — produces a great deal of wheeling and dealing as the councilmen jockey for position and seek support from others. In theory, three men can simply decide to form a bloc and pass the office around, ignoring the minority of two; this sometimes happens. But political alliances are brittle, and firm agreements are broken because of subsequent events and reappraisals of personal advantage, so that it is never possible to predict who, in a future year, will be mayor.

The villagers do not see the system for electing local officers as a device for choosing men in whom they have confidence as leaders. Rather, it is a system within a system, one of the areas in which people move and manipulate, build alliances, seek to obligate, all to the end of maximizing position and security within the village. The dynamics of the system reflect, with the overtones politics brings everywhere, the concepts of interpersonal relations that dominate in the village at large. Elections are not thought of as a means of local self-rule; they are simply another setting within which contenders seek to "defend" their interests, with the community usually seen as the loser. Benigno Zúñiga, an active politician, thinks the American system would be better, and he uses the analogy of two fighting cocks competing in a free election, in which one emerges as out-and-out victor. I think he is wrong; at the present stage of political development in Tzintzuntzan an electoral system in which one man's victory must shame the loser — must kill him, to use Benigno's fighting cock analogy — would bring even more dissension in the village than the present system.

Elections in Tzintzuntzan should not be viewed as a contest between more or less equally matched opponents, American style, any more than a bull fight should be thought of as a contest between equally matched contenders. Both election and bullfight are elaborate dramas, which go according to highly stylized rules of the theater, rather than of sports. Elections here are, above all, a device to permit people to participate in a patriotic manifestation, to declare their loyalty to Mexico and to their community, and to express their pride in being Mexican. In a developing country such as Mexico this type of expression of national solidarity is highly important in the nation's progress, and must be balanced against the imperfections of the electoral system, as evidenced in Tzintzuntzan.

VILLAGE VIEWS ON SOLVING CONFLICTS

In a community where another's success is seen as a threat to one's welfare, and where everyone struggles to defend his interests, conflicts of varying intensities are inevitable. Most dissension in Tzintzuntzan is relatively minor, often representing real or imagined infringement on property rights. The basic timidity of villagers is reflected in a low incidence of homicide: during the past generation there have been only about 15 murders, most perpetrated under the influence of alcohol. For a Mexican village that has grown from 1,000 to 2,000 people during this period, this is a very low rate.

Prevailing concepts about how to settle conflict are quite

distinct from those of the United States, but they conform well to the realities of life in the village, and in many respects they are highly humane. The basic principle of conflict resolution reflects the principle of equilibrium which underlies all feeling about the healthy social organism: maintain the status quo at all costs, don't humble or shame others, but protect your rights. The concept of justice, as an abstract quality, can hardly be said to exist, nor is the idea of punishing or rehabilitating the offender a part of the view of crime. Rather, *conflict resolution consists in restoring the status quo previously existing,* so that the litigants, regardless of where blame may lie, emerge with essentially what they had to begin with. The idea of damages is lacking. Complainants want to recover what they have lost, but normally they seek nothing beyond this as compensation for the attack, for hurt feelings, or even for court costs. The goal in a legal dispute is to find a modus vivendi so that the disputants can continue to live, if not in harmony, at least in the absence of open conflict.

In all interpersonal relations a person who takes or obtains something not rightfully his from a second party feels himself to be in an uncomfortable position; the anger of the wronged individual is a constant threat. People feel they can live in peace with their neighbors only if these neighbors have no claims on them beyond the normal reciprocal obligations all recognize. If a complainant obtained damages, he would have something the village would see as belonging to the defendant, however serious the latter's original aggressive act. Should the defendant, as a consequence, attack the complainant, the latter would receive little sympathy. When a settlement is reached, it is important that neither side feel it has gained or lost; however bitter the feeling, both parties live in a tiny community, they must pass each other a dozen times a day, and they must be able at least superficially to live together amicably. No one must emerge as a victor who has shamed or humbled the other.

ABSENCE OF GROUP RESPONSIBILITY

The general patterns of interpersonal relationships previously described for Tzintzuntzan are reflected in other ways in the

178

feel that being deprived of liberty is the worst thing that can happen to them; in a way, it is even more grave than being murdered. Consequently, there is no crime, however heinous, not atoned for by a few years in jail. The Caryl Chessman murder case aroused wide interest in Tzintzuntzan, anu he was the object of much sympathy. His life was dramatized in Mexico on a radio soap opera, and during the summer of 1960 his name was on the lips of almost everyone. One man even christened his battered pickup truck "Chessman." We were often asked how American legal processes could be so unjust as to torment Caryl Chessman; he had already been in prison for twelve years, and now it looked as if he would be executed. We tried to explain Chessman's crime, as determined by a jury: assault and rape, one victim in a mental hospital from which she would probably never emerge, and we emphasized how American justice has almost unlimited checks and balances, with all kinds of opportunity for appeal, to minimize the possibility of a miscarriage of justice. Chessman, we pointed out, had been able to utilize all these appeals, which takes time, so he had had to spend a long time behind bars. But our arguments meant nothing to local people. First of all, in a community in which nearly all girls are "robbed" — the fine line between forcible rape and accepting fate is not clearly drawn — Chessman's crime did not seem too great. Not a few local women had had experiences which seemed little removed from those of Chessman's victims, and they simply married their attacker. Moreover, even if Chessman was guilty as American courts had decided, he had already served twelve years in prison. This, by local standards, atones for *any* crime. He therefore should have been set free rather than faced with execution. A crime of passion can't be helped, and taking a life in cold blood, which *can* be helped, seems a far more terrible thing.

Most people feel that a fundamental responsibility of local legal officers is to try to prevent cases from reaching Pátzcuaro, where matters are then out of village hands, and where final judgments — which will always be costly — will not be designed to heal village wounds. "The law is for those who don't know how to defend themselves," says Bernardo Zaldívar, by which he means there is a double standard. An army general murders someone and goes free, but if a poor Tzintzuntzeño is unlucky enough to fall into a full-dress trial, he can be sure of jail. In criminal matters, as in most other things, city ways are quixotic and unpredictable, and it is felt best to avoid being drawn into this web.

SOME SPECIFIC CASES

Attitudes toward and practices in solving conflicts can be illustrated by several cases. On one occasion Micaela discovered that Eucario Cabeza was quietly lifting stones from a half-finished wall on one side of her milpa to complete a wall around his milpa, which was adjacent to hers. Micaela's decision to bring suit was based not so much on the justice of her claim as the fact that Eucario is highly unpopular in town, and she felt sympathy would be on her side. Moreover, she knew she had the right personal relationships: Primo Calderón, the judge, is the father of her stepdaughter's husband, and José Calvo, síndico, is a firm friend. In the public hearing Eucario denied guilt, but when the site was visited and the stones observed, he confessed to the charge but said he had taken the stones because they weren't really being used.

Micaela asked that her wall be restored to its original half-finished condition. She wouldn't insist on the original stones, since her field was not cultivated at the time, and Eucario's was. If he would restore her wall after the harvest, when he would have more time, she would ask for nothing more. In addition, her husband, Melecio, would work with Eucario in rebuilding the wall. This offer was accepted as the verdict. José, in private, mildly criticized Micaela for leaving a half-finished wall; it was an invitation for someone to steal, for if the wall had been completed, Eucario probably wouldn't have taken the stones. José said he thought he would impose a small fine on Eucario as his — José's — compensation for lost time, but otherwise Eucario would not be punished. He had taken a gamble, had lost, and was very mildly punished. Micaela, for her part, was satisfied. Eucario is a man with a violent temper whose wrath she doesn't want to incur by pressing her case as far as possible. Melecio felt the quarrel was not his concern. The property will go to Micaela's daughters, and not to his children, and being a mild man in all things, he probably would not even have brought suit. But he did agree to help rebuild the wall.

Another case was a senseless near-tragedy. Ambrosio Horta, for no apparent reason, suddenly shot and seriously injured his friend Gregorio Fernández with a .22 calibre pistol. Gregorio had entered a bar to buy cigarettes and had been invited by Ambrosio and Raul Marcos to have a drink, which he accepted. Suddenly, several drinks later, Gregorio heard a loud report and felt himself wounded in the neck. Raul grabbed the pistol and shot at Ambrosio, slightly wounding him in the buttocks. Lola Pichu, síndico, had the responsibility of determining the circumstances of the case. She took depositions from all parties and sent them to Pátzcuaro to the office which would take charge should Gregorio die or the dispute not be resolved locally. It became apparent there was no previous bad blood between Ambrosio and Gregorio; it was just Gregorio's bad luck to be in the way when Ambrosio — who is "very scandalous" in his behavior — decided to *tirar balazos*, to shoot his pistol for the sheer joy of hearing the reports.

While Gregorio was in a Pátzcuaro hospital his two uncles (his father is dead) met with Maximino, the father of Ambrosio, and Julián Horta, his brother. The uncles said they would ask only that Ambrosio's family pay medical costs to cure Gregorio; that although he lived by his work and had no other means of support, they would not ask for extra money to support his family until he could work. Maximino recognized the justice of this demand, but he is not wealthy, and he felt he had to "defend" himself as far as possible. "I'm the meat and you are the knives," he said, meaning he was at the mercy of the uncles, in spite of which he suggested he pay only half the medical bills, which the physician had said would be about $1,500. The uncles refused this offer, so next he said, "Of the three parts, I'll pay two," or $1,000. This offer was also rejected. So he sighed, and agreed to pay all medical expenses.

The síndico then asked them to sign a document setting forth the terms of the agreement, and also stating that the matter was terminated and that henceforth there would be no hard feelings between the families. Initially fines for Raul and the barkeeper, who had a bad reputation for serving drunks, were discussed, and the latter was actually jailed overnight. But with the major settlement accomplished, further penalties seemed to contribute nothing to community stability, and the matter was dropped.

In 1962, during "The Function," the Fiesta of the Señor del Rescate, Donato Estrada, about eighty, had a temporary pottery stand next to that of Priciliano Molinero, a man half his age. The latter noted that Donato had had good sales, and when he went to the hills to bring down his livestock, Priciliano followed him, struck him with a rock, and robbed him. Donato lingered a week and then died. Priciliano's crime was witnessed by a youth who told Pátzcuaro authorities, who upon investigating discovered a blood-covered serape in Priciliano's house. Priciliano served about eight months in the Pátzcuaro jail, returned to Tzintzuntzan to collect his belongings, and went off to the tierra caliente, where he is now said to live. In spite of the unusual premeditated nature of the assassination, Donato's family planned no vengeance. Priciliano had been punished, however mildly, he was out of the village, Donato had been an old man near death anyway, and it was deemed best to let matters stand as they were.

CHAPTER NINE

Health
and Equilibrium

THE THEORY OF HEALTH

In Tzintzuntzan the healthy social organism and the healthy human organism are seen as conforming to a common equilibrium model. The healthy society is one in which there is an even distribution of wealth and other forms of Good; the healthy body is one in which there is an even distribution of heat. Wealth and other forms of Good therefore bear the same relationship to the healthy society as does heat to the healthy body. The social organism is threatened when the equilibrium that spells health is upset through excessive concentration of Good in one part of the society, i.e, in the hands of a few people. It is also threatened by excessive loss of Good, as when a family loses one of its members through death. The human organism is threatened when the equilibrium that spells health is upset by excessive concentration of heat in one part of the body (often through *calor subido*, "risen heat," in which heat is compressed into the head and upper body), and it is threatened by loss of heat, when a part of the body is invaded by cold.

The steps man takes to restore the equilibrium in a "sick" society and a sick body are similar: drain off the excess of wealth and other Good, or the excess of heat, as the case may be; or add wealth, or heat, or otherwise remedy the imbalance that produces the unhealthy condition. The mechanisms whereby this is done in society have been described, and those used in the practice of curing and maintaining health will now be examined.

ORIGINS OF THE THEORY

The principal system to which health and medical ideas and practices in Tzintzuntzan conform is a folk variant of Greek humoral pathology, based on the Hippocratic doctrine of the four humors, elaborated by the Roman physician Galen, further developed in the Arab world by such men as Rhazes (c. 850–925) and Avicenna (980–1037), and transmitted to Spain when that country was dominated by the Moslems. According to this system each of the four humors had its "complexion," consisting of pairs of qualities. Blood was hot and moist; phlegm, cold and moist; black bile, cold and dry; and yellow bile, hot and dry. Moreover, since the three most important organs of the body — the heart, brain, and liver — were thought to be respectively dry and hot, wet and cold, and wet and hot, the normal healthy body had a complexion preponderantly hot and moist. But this balance varied with individuals, and a person's complexion might be hot, humid, cold, or dry. Natural history classification was rooted in the concept that, in addition to people, medicines, foods, and most natural objects also had complexions, based on pairs of the qualities of temperature and degree of moistness. Illness was thought to be caused by an upset in the normal equilibrium of a person's complexion, due to increases or decreases in his humors, or to other causes. Thus, medical practice consisted mostly in knowing the patient's natural complexion, determining the complexion of the illness, or its causes, and restoring the fundamental equilibrium that had been upset. This was accomplished by such devices as diet, internal medicines, purging, vomiting, bleeding, and cupping. For example, broth from chick peas, thought to be hot and moist, would be prescribed for epilepsy, thought to be caused by an excess of black bile, which was cold and dry. Barley, cold and dry, would be used for fever, caused by an excess of blood, hot and moist.

At the time of the Conquest of America an extremely complex humoral pathology constituted the theoretical framework for scientific (but not popular) Spanish medicine. The system had been carried to the point where complexions were not only marked by pairs of qualities, but — as pointed out in Chapter One — the qualities were graded in intensity on a scale of from one to four. The conceptual framework of humoral pathology for medicine, and the complexions of plants and animals, was brought to America at the time of the Conquest, and American plants heretofore unknown in Europe were quickly classified.

In time humoral pathology in America filtered down to the folk level, losing on its way the qualities of dryness and moistness, but maintaining the hot-cold dichotomy, minus formal degrees of intensity of temperature. At least in Spanish America, modified humoral pathology continues to be the dominant nonscientific conceptual framework within which health and illness are understood by the "folk," and within which curing practices are carried out. In Tzintzuntzan today foods, beverages, herbs, medicines, animals, and humans are characterized by a quality of "heat" (n. *calor*; adj. *caliente*, "hot," and *irritante*, "irritating") and "cold" (n. *frío*; adj. *frío*, and *fresco*, "fresh"). Sometimes actual temperatures are involved, as when a person becomes overheated by the sun, or chilled by contact with cold water. More often the putative degrees of hot or cold are innate characteristics, or properties, of substances, much as in the United States carbonated beverages without alcohol are "soft," whereas distilled liquors are "hard." Although formal degrees of temperature are lacking, some substances are thought to be especially hot or cold. Thus, wheat, *cherimoyas*,* coconut meat, the castor bean plant, and capulín

---

* Also *chirimoya*, the custard apple, *Annona cherimola*.

cherries are "very hot," but pears and watermelon are "very cold."
A few substances, such as the papaya and the "manzana" banana,
are neutral, or "cordial."

The following examples of foods, beverages, and herbs, about
which there is general village agreement as to qualities, illustrates
this dichotomy:

Hot items	Cold items
Beef	Rabbit
Pork	Pork lard
Goat	Pigeon
Hen	Chicken other than hen
Oil	Duck
Distilled drinks	Beer
Ice	Milk
Honey	Eggs
Mineral lime (for tortillas)	Salt
Wheat	Maize
Beans	Rice
Squash seeds	Squash
Melon seeds	Melon
Peanuts	Barley
Garlic	Celery
Avocado	Tomato
Coffee	Coconuts
Chocolate	Pineapple
Most chiles	Potatoes
Tobacco	Cucumbers
Cherimoya	Lime (fruit)
Figs	Pears
Orange blossoms	Oranges
Epazote (herb)	Mallow
Rue	Coriander
Basil	Artemisa

An analysis of more than two hundred items reveals certain
patterns. From the standpoint of curing, the most interesting
is that the hot herbs are more than twice as common as the cold
herbs. Garden vegetables are overwhelmingly cold, in spite of
common exceptions such as garlic and onions. Indigenous Mexican fruits tend to be hot, while European fruits tend to be cold.
Seeming contradictions abound: pork is hot but its lard is cold;
melon and squash seeds are hot but the flesh is cold; often the

187

leaves or blossoms of a tree have one quality, and the fruit has another.

CAUSES OF ILLNESS

Just as the idea of qualities of foods, beverages, and herbs follows the doctrine of humoral pathology in Tzintzuntzan, so does the concept of health. The healthy body is thought to be marked by a preponderance of heat over cold, just as in classical times. The heat is relatively mild; perhaps warmth would be a better word, for a strong heat represents real or potential illness. It is essential that healthy heat be *evenly* distributed over the body: head, chest, stomach, legs, and feet must all be in balance. The body is seen as a self-correcting organism which strives to maintain its even heat, an endeavor usually successful unless the body is attacked from outside sources of heat or cold of an intensity which it is unable to resist.

Heat may attack the body following exposure to high temperatures such as the rays of the midday sun, a hot bath, and radiation from a cooking fire or pottery kiln. "Heat" may also attack the body as a consequence of strong emotional experiences such as anger, fright, envy, or joy (which are classified as "hot" experiences), from injudicious ingestion of hot foods and drinks, and from the emanations believed to be given off by a corpse.

Cold attacks and enters the body in the form of air (*aire*) which strikes the head and upper torso, from exposure to cold water, or from stepping barefoot on a cold floor, from contact with iron or steel (both of which are classified as cold substances), and from careless use of cold foods and drinks. Since the normal state of the body is warm, Tzintzuntzeños believe that extreme cold is more threatening than extreme heat; it can produce a greater disequilibrium. The significance of the preponderance of hot over cold herbs becomes apparent in this context: more weapons are needed to fight cold than to fight heat.

In the condition called calor subido ("risen heat"), which is a body state producing illness, but not an illness itself, both hot and cold elements are involved. Calor subido results when a person steps barefoot on a cold tile or cement floor, or gets his feet wet in a rainstorm. One morning I talked with Natividad Peña while she worked at pottery, her two small granddaughters playing happily about. It began to rain and Margarita, the elder, started to take off her shoes to go wading. Nati shouted in some alarm for Margarita not to take off her shoes "so the heat won't rise on you." Some people profess reluctance to install hard floors in their bedrooms because of the health hazard. However cold enters the feet, it compresses the heat normally there into the already warm upper part of the body, producing excess heat, much as the plunger of a piston compresses and heats air. This excess heat in the head and upper torso breaks forth as any of a number of illnesses.

The body, it is clear, is continually bombarded by heat and cold: a housewife must cook before an open fire, her husband fires their kiln, drafts of air are everywhere, people attend wakes, and wet feet are a common experience. Why is it that only relatively rarely does a person succumb to these threats? The answer can be given with no more certainty than can modern science explain why, continually exposed to germs and viruses, a person only occasionally falls ill. Tzintzuntzeños believe, however, that the state of the body varies, and that its ability to resist the attacks of cold or heat depends at least in part on the state in which it finds itself. It is most secure when characterized by the normal, evenly distributed heat which has been described. However, there are certain activities, or states, which raise this heat to higher levels. The most common causes of greater-than-normal heat are sleeping, eating, working with the hands or with the eyes (reading and needlework make the eyes hot), baptism, extreme unction (both presumably because the holy oils used in the rites are hot), and exposure to real heat such as the sun, a cooking fire or lighted kiln, ironing, making tortillas, or bathing in hot water. Making candles also raises body heat, since beeswax is hot. The menstrual period, pregnancy, childbirth, and the postpartum period are also times of above-normal heat.

In all these situations no remedial action is necessary, since with the passage of time the body automatically re-establishes its equilibrium. But while more than ordinary heat prevails, a person is particularly susceptible to illness caused by the intrusion of cold and, to a lesser extent, by the intrusion of heat. Thus, many precautions must be observed. A person who awakes from a sound sleep should not eat cold food for half an hour or so. A man who returns home with dirty hands, "hot" from recent work, will not wash them until some time has passed. During pregnancy a woman approaches cold foods with greater-than-normal caution, and during the postpartum period it is thought best that she not sew, knit, or otherwise touch iron or steel lest she suffer hand cramps.

CURING TECHNIQUES

For people in a state of temporary excess heat, health measures are primarily preventive. For illness caused by the invasion of the body by abnormal amounts of heat or cold, remedial action must be taken. To illustrate, if *deposiciones*, a medium-serious diarrhea, is diagnosed as caused by cold, the patient may be given a tea made of the hot herbs *cinco llagas* and *cenicilla*. If it is thought to be due to heat it can be treated with a drink made of tomato skins, a pinch of ashes, granulated sugar, and other cold substances.

Common hot poultices believed useful in extracting excess cold are made of chopped onion mixed with alcohol, of chocolate, of commercial *elemento* oil, and of a wide variety of hot herbs. Cupping (*la ventosa*) is functionally a hot poultice, since it is applied to extract cold. Common poultices to draw heat include cold herbs and, rarely, the *pichón partido*, a treatment for typhoid and other fevers in which a live dove is split in halves and stuck to the chest and back of the patient. The dove is cold, and thus draws out the fever, which is said to "cook" the bird in half an hour or less. A hen's egg (cold) is rubbed over the body of a child suffering from the evil eye (hot), drawing out the heat in the same manner as a cold poultice. An enema of cold herbs in water used to treat fever and hot constipations also conforms to this pattern. *Chiquiadores*, or *parches*, usually in the form of leaves placed on the temples for headache, are tiny poultices. If the ache is believed to be due to heat, a leaf of the ash or lemon tree, or of a rose vine (all cold) is used. Turpentine on paper makes a hot chiquiador to be used if the ache is thought to be due to cold.

Calor subido, although triggered by cold entering the lower part

190

of the body, is best considered as a hot cause of illness, since it is the concentration of heat in the head and upper torso that does the damage. Calor subido breaks out in the form of headache, earache, sties, fever sores, tonsillitis, strep throat, and bronchial ailments ranging in severity from slight colds to pneumonia. Following the theory of opposites attracting each other, the cure for these illnesses is to apply heat to the feet. Hot poultices of chopped onion mixed with alcohol, or of chocolate, are placed on the soles, or the feet may be placed in hot water. Since the purpose of the treatment is to draw heat from the upper part of the body, at first glance this looks like a violation of the basic principle. What is seen as happening, however, is quite consistent. The cold that has driven the heat upward must be withdrawn; this is accomplished with the hot poultice or hot water. This then leaves a temperature vacuum which is filled when the displaced heat flows back to its proper place. Simultaneously, and to hasten the cure, some of the excess heat concentrated in the upper regions of the body may be drawn off. For headache this is done with hot chiquiadores. For pneumonia due to calor subido, a poultice of roses, pork lard, and the tepusa herb, all cold, slightly tempered with the hot tequistique herb, is applied to the chest, in addition to the hot foot poultices.

Most informants believe that all strong emotional experiences, such as fright, jealousy, envy, anger, pleasure, embarrassment, and grief are hot, and can cause illness. The principal named diseases believed caused by emotional experiences are bilis, tiricia, muina, chipil, and mal de ojo (evil eye). The first four strike the person who experiences the emotion; in the last a child is the victim of the envy of some other person. Bilis is probably the most common of these ailments. Informants say that any of the above-mentioned emotional experiences, with the possible exception of envy and jealousy, cause the bile (la hiel) to overflow from the gall bladder (vesícula biliar), falling into the blood, which is thereby caused to "boil." Various herbal concoctions, which are preponderantly cold, are used to treat these ailments, except for the evil eye which, as previously pointed out, is cured by rubbing the hot body of the child with a cold egg.

Several points about the hot-cold dichotomy are noteworthy. One is the amazing, continuing vigor of this ancient system of medical beliefs and practices; this is due, certainly in part, to its flexibility, and the ease with which it adapts itself to new situations. Although after the Conquest humoral pathology lost its properties of moisture and dryness, it gained new vigor by incorporating indigenous medical beliefs into the simplified Spanish system. Fright, for example, a widespread native American explanation for some illnesses, was easily incorporated into this conceptual framework by being assigned a hot quality. The other emotionally derived conditions previously described also appear to be entirely or principally American rather than European in origin, and they, too, have been adapted to this same framework.

The process of accommodation continues, and today many patented and proprietary medicines, and some medical treatment by physicians, are interpreted in the same way. Vicks VapoRub and aspirin, for example, are classified as hot, but Milk of Magnesia is cold. When María Matos was given vitamin shots the doctor told her to bathe at least every third day, justifying this modest bit of badly needed health education by telling her it was "to reduce the irritation" (irritación is synonymous with caliente and calor) of the vitamins. From these instructions, however, María deduces that vitamin shots must be hot, since they need cooling water to neutralize them.

Micaela's elder daughter, Lola, was taught by doctors during the antimalarial campaign to draw a drop of blood and to prepare a slide to be sent to Morelia for laboratory analysis. A villager suspecting malaria could present himself to Lola, who would take a tiny blood sample and give him three pills the doctor had left her for such cases. The pills, says Micaela, are to prevent *aire* from entering the body via the tiny aperture left by the needle-prick.

The reader may wonder, as did the anthropologist, how many different qualities can be remembered by Tzintzuntzeños. The answer is, of course, that different people recall different numbers. But no one can simply recite a full list of hot and cold substances.

Everyone commits to memory a longer or shorter list, but beyond this limit doubtful items are classified by inverse logic: the informant considers the way in which a particular food or herb is commonly used in treatment, recalls the quality of the illness or its cause, and concludes that the item must be hot or cold, as the evidence indicates. "What is the quality of beeswax?" I ask Virginia Pichu. She can't answer right off, but reasons, "It's good for rheumatism, which comes from cold, and in making candles one's hands get hot and must be kept out of water, so it must be hot." Other informants reasoned that burro milk must be cold since it is used to cure whooping cough from calor subido, beef tallow is hot since a person who uses it to treat rheumatism must be especially careful to avoid water, and oppossum meat is cold because it is given to a person whose blood is "irritated," i.e., hot.

How is the cause of illness determined, and a hot or cold classification decided upon? The procedure is a little like that of assigning the quality of a doubtful remedy. When someone falls ill he and others think back, looking for the most likely kind of occurrence that might have caused the trouble. This event is then seized upon as evidence of the legitimacy of the ailment, and cures are prescribed that are harmonious with the diagnosis. A person with a headache considers both the possibility of having been struck by air, and calor subido. If he remembers that on the previous day he got his feet wet, the latter explanation is decided upon. If the feet were kept dry and warm, and the sufferer has no recollection of stepping barefoot on a cold floor, he will probably have no difficulty in recalling a draught of air which must have struck him as he came out of his house into the cool night air. A person with diarrhea or stomachache tries to think what he has eaten. If more hot than cold foods come to mind, heat is the villain; if more cold than hot foods, cold is responsible.

A few folk illnesses, such as the widespread Mexican fallen fontanelle (caída de la mollera), fallen womb (caída de la matriz), and strains, sprains, and dislocations (lastimaduras) are not explained according to the hot-cold dichotomy. But they, too, conform to the equilibrium model that underlies health views, since in all cases the cure consists of restoring the displaced organ to its normal position, i.e., to achieve the pre-existing steady state.

193

CHAPTER TEN

*Religious
Ritual: Its
Latent Functions*

THE CEREMONIAL SYSTEM

In few peasant communities does one find a more elaborate and colorful religious life than in Tzintzuntzan. From the simple dramatization of the visit of the Three Kings to the Christ Child on Epiphany, through the elaborate *Judea* passion play of Easter Week, to the folk manifestations of the classic Spanish Corpus Christi, and the midnight cemetery vigil of All Soul's Day, culminating in the Christmas piñata-breaking parties* and nativity scenes and Masses, there are few days of the year when the visitor does not find some religious act of interest to him. For most Tzintzuntzeños religion is a vital force which permeates almost

* Traditionally, a piñata is a pot decorated with colored paper, filled with fruits and candies, and suspended so that it can be swung about. Blindfolded children strike at it in turn with a stick the size of a broom handle, until a lucky blow shatters it. As the contents fall to the ground, all the children scramble to pick up their share.

every aspect of living. The early Franciscan friars did their task well, and for over four hundred years Tzintzuntzan has been intensely Catholic. No one is a Protestant, and no one is a nonbeliever. Religion is the ultimate validation of life, and of the values to which people consciously adhere.

But my purpose in this chapter is not to describe in detail the varied activities that testify to the importance of religion to the villagers: this already has been done in *Empire's Children*, and although there have been some changes, the picture is still very much as recounted nearly twenty years ago. Rather, I am here concerned with describing and analyzing the traditional yearly fiesta cycle — now badly decayed — as it functioned to help maintain the economic equilibrium which the villagers see as essential to the social health of the community. This cycle, in Mexico usually called the *mayordomía* system, involves the ceremonial sponsorship by a person or small group of people of an image or a church building or chapel, usually for one year. Prayers are said periodically, candles are burned, Masses are paid for, food is served on ritual occasions, and images are carried in procession. In Tzintzuntzan a sponsor is called a *carguero*, rather than a *mayordomo* (the more common term in Mexico), because he assumes the *cargo*, the charge or responsibility, as defined by custom.

The cargo system is now almost a thing of the past in Tzintzuntzan. It flourished until the beginning of the Mexican Revolution (1911), and as late as the 1920's it was still quite vigorous. Since that time, for a variety of reasons, it has eroded away, little by little, until today the modern survivals merely hint at the complexity of the traditional yearly round. Yet because to know the system, in full flower, is essential to understand the model of a traditional peasant community, I attempt to describe the mayordomías as they functioned until the periods indicated.

In Tzintzuntzan the system presumably began with the first Franciscans or, more likely, with Don Vasco de Quiroga who, shortly after his arrival in Michoacán, established "hospitals" in the principal Tarascan villages. Although little is known about the actual history of these utopian communities, it is evident that the basic Spanish system of sponsoring sacred images and buildings, and a yearly cycle of feast-day celebrations, was an essential part of this idealistic system in which religious and civil activities were thoroughly integrated. These continued, in the mayordomía pattern, long after the communal plan, if it ever was achieved, broke down.

The hospital building proper, in Tzintzuntzan and other lake villages, was called in Tarascan the *kenguería*, after the *kenguí*, the chief steward of the building. It was also sometimes called the *güatapera* (as in many modern Tarascan communities), although this word seems more properly to have applied to the kitchen of the building. To judge by the organization that survived until recent years, the principal mayordomías were organized around the kenguería in such a fashion that the church feast days all had groups which assumed primary responsibility for them.

Tzintzuntzan was (and is) well provided with churches to support an elaborate ritual system. The oldest buildings are the sixteenth-century Franciscan convent and adjacent chapel, which is now the parish church, and which was entirely rebuilt in the early 1950's following its destruction by fire in 1944. La Soledad chapel is a full-sized church completed in 1631. Technically the property of the Indigenous Community rather than the parish, it is the site of the principal Easter Week activities, as well as occasional Masses during the remainder of the year. Adjacent to it is the beautiful "open chapel" called La Concepción, under the roof of which was an altar where the priest said Mass while the parishioners stood or knelt outside. This chapel, dated 1619, was one of the last of its type to be built in Mexico. Many years ago it fell into disuse, and although reconstructed in 1962, it has not been reconsecrated. In addition to these structures, the chapel of the Virgin of Guadalupe in Ojo de Agua is important in the ceremonial life of the community.

THE MAYORDOMÍAS

In the late nineteenth and early twentieth centuries there were seven mayordomías integrated around the kenguería, and making use of the first three churches, and one other mayordomía which, although outside the kenguería complex, was very important.

Moreover, several minor mayordomías also existed in the first half of the present century. The seven kenguería groups were divided into two sections: four *cargos chicos* (small mayordomías) and three *cargos principales* (principal mayordomías) named as follows:

Cargos Chicos:
  (1) Cargueros de Nuestra Señora del Rosario
  (2) Cargueros Mandones
  (3) Capitanes de Barrios
  (4) Cargueros de la Judea

Cargos Principales:
  (5) *Cargueros de la Cruz*
  (6) *Cargueros de la Soledad*
  (7) *Cargueros de la Kenguería*

The extra major mayordomía:
  Cargueros de la Capilla de la Virgen *de Guadalupe*, in Ojo de Agua.

Ignoring for the moment this last-named group, the most important thing about the system was its hierarchic nature; the seven basic groups were graded in importance. The four "small" cargos may at one time have been ordered, perhaps in the sequence here given. However, present-day informants say all were equal at the earliest times they can remember, but inferior in rank to the three "principal" cargos which were stratified in the sequence given, with the Kenguería at the top.

At least in part the plan followed what has been called the "ladder system" in describing the indigenous communities of Guatemala and Chiapas. According to this system an aspiring young man began community service at the bottom of the "ladder" whose two sides corresponded to the religious and civil hierarchies of his community. First he served a lowly religious (or civil) function, and then a correspondingly lowly civil (or religious) function. Next he advanced a step up the ladder, in turn filling slightly higher religious and civil positions until, little by little, skipping back and forth from one hierarchy to the other, he reached the top and became a principal, a respected village elder. In the modern villages where this pattern still prevails, civil and religious functions are thoroughly integrated, as in the hospitals of Don Vasco's day.

In Tzintzuntzan during the period in question, the civil hierarchy had been very poorly developed, and progress up the ladder is described solely in religious terms. Nevertheless, many of the ritual activities required the presence of the *juez*, or judge, to legitimize them, and he was a man who had fulfilled important religious cargos. It is not clear, however, whether he was eligible to be judge only after completing all seven cargos, or whether he took time out as he rose to serve a period as a civil authority. Those men who completed service as cargueros of the kenguería were known as *principales*, or *alcaldes* (literally, "mayors"). They had fulfilled all formal religious obligations to their community, and now functioned as a council of elders, somewhat political in nature, in that it was their responsibility to represent the village in "facing" the outside world.

The following summary account of the carguero system is reconstructed up to the first quarter of the twentieth century, when Tzintzuntzan still had relatively little contact with the outside world, and when its traditional cultural forms appear to have represented the end period of three relatively static centuries. My intention is not to describe in full detail all activities of cargueros, but rather to give a general idea of the kinds of things that were expected of them, the amounts of time they invested in their activities, and to the extent possible, to determine the financial implications of sponsorship of an image or building.

THE "SMALL" CARGOS

As previously pointed out, the "ladder" of rank and prestige applied to the first four "small" cargos only in the sense that a young man must serve in each before he could aspire to serve at a higher level: within themselves, they were ungraded, and there seems to have been no advantage in starting with any one as against the others.

Cargueros de Nuestra Señora del Rosario. The image of Our Lady of the Rosary was kept in the La Concepción open chapel, tended by three cargueros named *mayordomo* (steward), *capitán* (captain), and *fiscal* (roughly, "treasurer"). Every Saturday morning they, like all other cargueros in the kenguería complex, gathered at the kenguería for the prayer known as the *kénikua*, after which each group carried (or had carried for it) the image in its charge in a procession around the churchyard.

In addition to these continuing duties, the Rosario cargueros functioned during Corpus Christi. The captain selected a girl seven or eight years old who, wearing a flower crown, danced to the music of guitar and violin during the Thursday, Friday, and Saturday of Corpus festivities. Natividad Peña remembers that when she was this age (i.e., about 1911) and her parents were captains, just beginning their climb up the ladder, she was a dancing girl. On Thursday of Corpus the mayordomo paid for the music and prepared food to feed the kenguería cargueros and other important people in the system; on Friday the captain did the same, and on Saturday, the fiscal.

Cargueros Mandones. These cargueros, who had no specific individual names, were associated with the old barrio system. Their principal obligations came during carnival when they gathered together several dozen chickens and in turn visited the homes of the village elders who had completed their climb to the top of the ceremonial ladder. In front of each house they suspended a chicken by its feet, for the *descabezando*, or "beheading" dance. Each elder danced with a carguero beneath the chicken, and then reached up and grabbed the unfortunate fowl, which was his to keep. Doña Andrea says the dancer simply touched the chicken, while Micaela says he pulled the head off. From the name of the act, the latter explanation seems more likely.

On Sunday and Monday before carnival one carguero dressed as a woman, as *la mariguía* ("the one who is a Mary"), a second wore a tule reed bull over his head, and the others dressed in "any kind of crazy costume." They danced through the streets, each in turn with *la mariguía*, to the tunes of the orchestra they had hired, stopping in front of all houses to collect money to be used in defraying the costs of the fireworks which they had to furnish later in the year for the fiesta of San Francisco.

Capitanes de Barrios. Originally each of the barrios of Tzintzuntzan had a *cabeza*, or head, who held office during his lifetime, and who kept in his home an image of the saint after whom the barrio was named. In addition, each barrio had a ceremonial captain, a carguero, who held office for one year. These cargueros participated in the Saturday morning kénikua prayer and procession. On the eve of The Conception each offered a small fiesta for the people of his barrio, with pozole, atole (a maize gruel drink), and a *mollete*, a crown-shaped piece of bread. On the floor, on a new tule reed mat, there was placed — "begging your pardon," says Doña Andrea — a chamber pot in which each male guest dropped a *real* coin and each female guest a half *real*. A "complete orchestra" of several musicians with stringed instruments played for the procession in which the mat with its chamber pot filled with coins was carried to the kenguería. There the participants were met by the *kenguí* and his associates who were sponsors of this fiesta in honor of the Virgin.

On Candlemas the barrio captains also co-sponsored with the kenguería cargueros a fiesta known as *la chapeadera*, at which a number of cargueros were elected. After the principals — who were entitled to attend all ceremonial gatherings — were quite drunk the cargueros smeared their faces and fingernails with red paint, to the great amusement of the other participants.

Cargueros de la Judea. These five cargueros, the only ones of the ancient system who still functioned in 1965, are named captain, mayordomo, *sargento* (sergeant), *centurión*, and *alfárez* (ensign). Vulgarly they are called "broad bean cargueros" because on each Friday of Lent, when meat is forbidden, they offer in turn pozole with this meat substitute. Each carries a candle in the Lenten Friday evening Via Crucis processions. On Friday *de Dolores*, immediately preceding Easter Week, the centurion dresses a boy in white tunic while the mayordomo and captain dress two more young boys as "Jews." Armed with machete swords, they escort the mock centurion, who is mounted on a white horse, to the rosary. On Maundy Thursday, the mock centurion stands behind the apostles as they eat the Last Supper in the passion play, and then he accompanies them to the lavatory footwashing in the church. On Good Friday he changes to black clothing after the Santo Entierro image of Christ is raised on the cross, and after it is lowered he stands watch all night. New cargueros are elected in the house of the outgoing centurion on Easter evening, after which they take office. The election I attended in 1945 was gay and hilarious, and it was clear that, because of the very heavy expenses involved, a basic part of the technique in persuading a man to serve as carguero is to get him thoroughly drunk, so that his resistance will be low when the honor is thrust upon him.

THE "PRINCIPAL" CARGOS

After a man had served in each of the four "small" cargoes, he could aspire to the last three. These steps, as previously pointed out, allowed no deviation from the prescribed sequence, which was that in which they are here described.

Cargueros de la Cruz. These three cargueros — the captain, sergeant, and alférez — had duties on Holy Cross Day and on San Francisco's fiesta on October 4. For the former they paid for Mass, for music, and, aided by the women of each barrio, they decorated the street crosses. On the latter occasion their biggest expense and chore was to rent costumes from owners on Janitzio for three *Moro* dancers. These costumes were elaborate black velvet affairs decorated with silver fishes, which cost $50 each year, in earlier days a large sum of money. The Moors danced on October 4, 5, and 6, and on each day in turn a carguero paid for the music and provided elaborate food for the village elders. They also helped the cargueros of the Rosario with the fiesta of Corpus Christi.

Cargueros de la Soledad. These four, a mayordomo, fiscal, *diputado* (deputy), and *escribano* (scribe), functioned until 1942 when the priest, unsympathetic to the mayordomía system, forbade them to continue. They were collectively in charge of La Soledad chapel and, in addition, each had a special charge: the mayordomo the Santo Entierro image of Christ, the diputado a small Santo Entierro also called Niño Jesús, the scribe a cross, and the fiscal a bell. Each cared for the chapel for a month, three times in all during the year, burning copal incense morning and evening before all images in the chapel, and ringing the bells Thursday afternoons to summon the other cargueros and their wives to clean the building. Friday evenings all gathered to pray, and on Sundays they took the Niño Jesús image to Mass in the parish church.

All four participated in most major town fiestas throughout the year. They arranged for the dramatization of Christ's ascension on Ascension Thursday, and on Corpus Christi they took the big image of the Santo Entierro to Mass in the parish church, after which they joined with the cargueros of San Isidro in throwing fruit, corn, wheat tortillas, and other foods from the church steps. During All Souls' night they visited houses where an ex-carguero of La Soledad had died, praying for souls, and later they went to the church to stand guard over the catafalque.

On December 16 they placed the Niño Jesús image in the parish church, and after dark carried it to the home of a carguero of the Virgin of Guadalupe in Ojo de Agua where it was placed on a small altar. On Christmas Eve they returned to this home, were given *pontedura* (toasted maize with brown-sugar syrup), and then they returned the image to the parish church, arriving just in time to place it in the *nacimiento* (nativity scene) for the midnight Misa del Gallo. For carnival each carguero made a sugarcane fence in a corner of La Soledad behind which he piled seasonal fruits. The fiscal, with a reed mat bull on his head, was baited by and attacked the other cargueros and, after more horseplay, on Ash Wednesday, the cargueros gave away the fruit and sugarcane after their blessing by the priest.

During the passion play the Soledad cargueros removed the Santo Entierro from its coffin, placed it on the cross, then lowered it, and stretched it on its bier. On Easter Saturday they attended a big meal known as the *pinole* fiesta, and on Easter Sunday, new cargueros took over. This cargo, because of its many obligations, was considered the most onerous and expensive of all.

Cargueros de la Kenguería. These four cargueros were called kenguí, *prioste* (steward), escribano, and fiscal. The first two were of higher rank, and a man had to serve as one or the other before achieving the status of principal. That is, the kenguería cargo was itself graded, requiring two services of each carguero. Before acting as kenguí or prioste a man first served as escribano or fiscal. The kenguí himself moved with his family to the kenguería where he lived for the entire year, caring for the building and its images, and serving as host for all the ritual activities carried out during the year. But apart from this very considerable interruption in the daily life of the kenguí, the expenses and duties of these cargueros were less than those of several of lower rank. They cared for the image of La Purísima Concepción, patroness of La Concepción chapel, and paid for the Mass in her honor on December 8, after which they offered pozole, atole, and brandy at the kenguería, to which as many as five musical bands are said to have come to compete with each other, as is still done in the Tarascan area on festive days.

On Candlemas, as mentioned, they were co-hosts with the barrio captains at the chapeadera fiesta, and on Maundy Thursday they offered candied *chilacayote* squash and bread to kenguería visitors. When a carguero or former carguero in any of the mayordomías died they attended the wake, taking candles and offerings of food and money. After completing their year in office, the kenguí and the prioste ceremonially washed their hands, symbolizing the fact that they had served at all levels, thus completing all community ritual obligations. Henceforth they would be known as principales or alcaldes, village elders entitled to attend all fiestas, to be fed and given drink, to be shown extraordinary respect in all ways, and to serve as members of a powerful if informal village council to make decisions on all basic matters.

Cargueros de la Capilla de la Vírgen de Guadalupe. When Doña Andrea Medina came to Tzintzuntzan from Quiroga as a bride in 1903, these cargueros were very important, which suggests that this cult is fairly old. At that time there were three cargueros; subsequently, in the early 1940's, the number was increased to the present twelve. These cargueros sponsor the fiesta on December 12 in honor of the Virgin of Guadalupe, and during the remainder of the year each man cares for the chapel for a month, and pays for the Mass said on the twelfth day.

"SERVING THE COMMUNITY"

Turning from description to analysis, we ask this question: why did men undertake a costly series of obligations which would leave them in straitened circumstances during their most productive years? Doña Andrea who, with her husband, José María Peña,

203

went through all steps of the system, and who would have lived in the kenguería had the custom not broken down just as they arrived, continually refers to "serving the community." She quotes Don José as saying, "Look, we have children, boys, and tomorrow or the day after they are going to want to enter houses where fiestas are being given, and the first thing they will hear is, 'Well, these *metiches*, these nosy ones, what do you think of that?' " and they would be challenged as to their right to be present: "Your father, what did he ever do to serve the community?" So that their children might not appear presumptuous, Doña Andrea and her husband felt it necessary to assume cargos. Mindful of their humble origins, they felt that in this way they and their children would achieve respectability. A man of fifty, whatever his origin, who had "served the community" through all the principal mayordomías, had achieved the status and prestige he needed to take his place among the other honored elders, and to give his children a good start in life.

It is clear, too, that the social activities in which cargueros participated were a source of great enjoyment. Doña Andrea lovingly describes the preparation of each kind of food for each event, and the ritual — and frequently the horseplay — that was a prescribed part of every activity. In villages lacking other forms of entertainment — even lacking games for adults — the cargos added spice to the yearly round, providing diversion and excitement in what was otherwise an unending cycle of drudgery. And in a society in which the bonds between people are usually weak, the mayordomías offered opportunities for feeling, through group participation in the same rites and acts, at one with the community. More so than in any other settings, the mayordomías provided voluntary associations for participants. Beyond the desire to achieve prestige, then, people went through the system because they had fun, and they had enjoyable and meaningful contacts with friends and neighbors.

CARGUEROS AND PRESTIGE

The mayordomía system must also be examined at another level: that of its structural significance with respect to the villagers' view of a world marked by Limited Good. Eric Wolf, speaking generally of the traditional Indian communities of Middle America, has hit upon the essence of this significance. The accumulation and reinvestment of wealth by one man, he argues, threatens to take from others the instruments of their livelihood, and it leads to power which, unchecked, corrupts. Therefore the community must abolish wealth and redistribute power continually to maintain the social and economic equality that spells security and constitutes a defense against the outside world. Wolf correctly sees a tour of religious duty as leaving a man for the time being impoverished, yet wealthier in prestige. Thus, the religious system in these communities "became the chief mechanism through which the people gained prestige, as well as the balance wheel of communal economics. . . . Like the thermostat activated by an increase in heat to shut off the furnace, expenditure in religious worship returns the distribution of wealth to a state of balance, wiping out an accumulation of wealth that might upset the existing equilibrium. In engineering parlance, it acts as a feedback, returning a system that is beginning to oscillate to its original course" (1959:216).

Although the Tzintzuntzeños would not themselves understand this logic, it is clear that their carguero system served the same purpose. It was the visible evidence that "here we are all equal," that no one, for long, had more than his share of limited economic good. Prestige and status were the only commodities the community could permit a man to accumulate in large amounts, and these could be acquired only through what, in Western society, is known as conspicuous consumption. A man, therefore (and always with the aid of his wife), could direct his ambition only in one direction: achieving the status of principal, at the cost of repeated cycles of hard work, each of which could end only in near-bankruptcy.

The size of a mayordomía system presumably adjusts itself to the thermostatic needs of a community: enough openings are provided so that the village can be kept in balance, so that all threatening excess wealth can be drained off. In Tzintzuntzan, in any one year, there were twenty to thirty "small" cargo openings available, the exact number depending on the barrios recognized in fact or theory. Since a young man had to serve in all four small mayor-domías there would be, of course, fewer entering doors than the number of annual vacancies. Since many men would find themselves unable to afford to rise higher on the ladder, eight or ten was perhaps the usual number of entries each year, and in a community that averaged about a thousand people, this presumably was adequate. The system was flexible, and if there were not sufficient new candidates in any year, a man could be asked to repeat an office, even against his will, as the price of continuing to higher levels. Thus, Doña Andrea's husband, José María, served as captain in the Rosario mayordomía, as barrio captain, as a mandón, and as centurion in the Judea, in that order. Then he repeated the Rosario cargo, presumably because a younger candidate was lacking. And in 1945 I saw José Reyes practically forced to repeat as Judea fiscal, after completing a year as captain.

Among the principal cargos there appears to be a flaw in the scheme: there are three cargueros for the first de la Cruz mayor-domía, four for the second Soledad, and two per year for the final kenguería step (since a carguero had first to serve as escribano or fiscal before he could be kenguí or prioste). How did three de la Cruz cargueros fill four Soledad positions? I don't know. Perhaps a Soledad carguero, as in the small mayordomías, could be asked to repeat a year. The only thing that seems sure is that only two men, of all those in the village, could be admitted each year to the rank of village elder. If the estimate of eight to ten entries a year is correct, the "dropout" rate, to use a modern expression, was 75 to 80 per cent.

THE ROLE OF ELECTION

In other words, only a very few men had the productive capacity to constitute a threat to the delicate economic balance of the community, *or were perceived by the community as having this capacity*. For, although many men certainly chose the hard path of a life of sponsorship, the community could not afford to depend on voluntary, laissez-faire mechanisms alone. Too much was at stake. It had to be able to coerce any individual who was deemed

206

a threat into divesting himself of a large part of his wealth. He had to be respectable, whether he wished to be or not. This is clearly seen in the election procedure. Depending on the mayordomía in question, a retiring carguero, a judge, or some other umpire would ask el público, all the assembled adult males of the community, if so-and-so suited them for a particular cargo. The shouted approbation or objections determined whether the individual took the cargo or not. Thus, individuals of whom it was felt the time had come to divest themselves, could be named and elected without their raising a hand, and even over their objections. And once named, it was impossible to refuse office, however reluctant the person might be.

The elective mechanism, therefore, was essential to the functioning of the system. Voluntary assumption of a cargo, with the prestige reward dangling before the candidate, was not enough. Only in mayordomías outside the kenguería complex could this latitude be allowed. This is, for example, the mode of assuming a cargo in the Virgin of Guadalupe mayordomía. Here assumption is consequent upon a manda, a vow to the Virgin, and the candidate's serving is dependent upon the priest's confirmation. Although the Guadalupe mayordomía is an avenue to prestige — particularly today in the absence of most of the other mayordomías — historically and functionally it is basically different in that it serves personal, and not community ends. An individual undertakes the chore because of some specific thing he wants or needs; he works for himself, and not for the community. Thus, although both kenguería and Guadalupe mayordomías are similar in outward appearance, their basic functions are quite distinct.

THE NATURE OF PRESTIGE

Another question remains to be answered. Why does caring for images, going through ritual duties, and spending money on food, candles, Masses, fireworks — in short, conspicuous consumption — constitute "serving the community?" Why does this lead to prestige? And why is prestige, unlike other forms of good, not seen as a threat to the community? On a superficial level, providing food and entertainment for the villagers, and keeping their relationships with the supernatural, on which they are all equally dependent, in good order, was certainly "service." But this explanation, correct as far as it goes, suggests that conspicuous-consumption-to-gain-prestige is the same behavior trait as that found in Western societies, that spending buys or equals prestige. This, I think, is not true.

I suggest that prestige is the consequence of ability or willingness to symbolize a society's concept of its "ideal man." In societies which stress production and the acquisition of material wealth and power, the ideal man is the shrewd and hardworking soul who achieves these goals. And the achievement of these goals is indicated by the open squandering of what underlies them; an individual who has been so successful in doing what his society expects of him that he can maintain his position on a fraction of what he has is indeed secure. Viewed in this way, conspicuous consumption as a device to validate "ideal man" status functions in a particular way in an acquisitive society. But, and this is often overlooked, it can function quite differently in other types of society; the same outward form conceals different ends.

In Tzintzuntzan, and in other peasant societies, the conspicuous consumption that underlies the mayordomía system leads to prestige, not because it calls attention to productive or acquisitive capacity, but because, in a different way, it permits a man to show visibly that he conforms to the ideal type of his society. It permits him to emphasize his commitment to the equality principle which means a healthy community. He, more than anyone else, is "equal," and because of his dedication to the ideal that is seen as spelling social stability, his society not only can afford to extend to him prestige, *but it must do so.* The equality of shared poverty rests on one pan of the Roman balance, and prestige rests on the other. The stronger the commitment to shared poverty, as shown through carguero activities, the greater the prestige load to keep the scale in balance. Prestige is not, therefore, a gift of a grateful community to those who feed and entertain; rather, it is something the community *must* concede to keep the scale in balance.

For, without the compensation of prestige, the dedicated carguero is in danger of falling below the average and this, as we have seen, is also viewed by the community as a threat to its stability and equilibrium. Only by offering prestige is the community able to prevent a carguero from turning from one type of threat — a has — to another — a has not.

Did the system, in fact, work as the model requires? In part, yes, and in part, no. Contemporary cargueros of Guadalupe have individual expenses as high as $1,000 a year — three months' work for a potter family — and total expenses to maintain the cult for a year are divided among twelve families. In earlier days, with more elaborate activities and fewer cargueros in each mayordomía, proportionate expenses were far greater. Doña Andrea is proud that she and Don José were able to do their part *a punta de nuestras canillas*, from sheer elbow grease, the profits from sale of pottery made during extra long working days. Other families were not so fortunate. They sold their lands (mostly to the less carguero-minded farmers of the hamlets of La Vuelta), "annihilating" themselves — the expression is Doña Andrea's — in order to keep up with ritual obligations. The evidence suggests that Tzintzuntzeños were so industrious in keeping their ceremonial system going that they did irreparable damage to their economic system. For during the last years of the nineteenth and the first years of the twentieth centuries, the Tarascans gradually settled Ichupio and then moved in on Tzintzuntzan, until their fields now come to the western edge of town. Moreover, the Ojo de Agua, until about 1900 a nearly deserted area with only the chapel, has gradually built up as a Tarascan settlement of 170 people, apparently as lands became available from sale because of Tzintzuntzan cargueros' needs for cash to support their ritual activities.

It should be clear that, once a carguero system is established, the lure of prestige keeps it going. Only occasionally, I suspect, did a villager have to be drafted for service. And only a minority of those who did climb the rungs of the ladder probably represented a real threat to economic equilibrium within the community. Most cargueros undoubtedly were like Doña Andrea and her husband José María: hardworking couples with a high sense of responsibility toward their children, achievement oriented, who followed the only course permitted by their culture in which to exercise this personality trait.

That the pattern is basically Middle American Indian is suggested by those families which supported the system, and those which did not. When asked about the families that provided cargueros, informants mention the Cuiríz, the Calvos, the Huipes, the Tzintzúns, the Zaldívars, the Felices, the Reyes, the Guilléns, the Zacapus, the Rendóns, and the Estradas. All these are "original inhabitants," whose immediate ancestors were Tarascan-speaking and who, as far as is known, have always been associated with Tzintzuntzan. The Tarascan families such as the Aparicios, Cornelios, and Pichus, who came to Tzintzuntzan several generations ago from other lake villages have also supported the carguero system. The families that have had the means but have not supported the system tend to be mestizos who, within the past two or three generations, have come from *los ranchos*, small non-Indian settlements to the east of the lake: the Servíns from Los Corrales, the Barrigas and Zavalas from Santa Cruz, the Calderóns from Urundaneo, the Villagómez from Quiroga, and the Corrals, Campusanos, Fuentes, and Rangels, all from similar communities.

This leaves a number of families traditionally of Tzintzuntzan who took much-reduced parts in carguero activities. The smug descendants of those families which did participate will, when questioned, indicate that families like these "never amounted to anything" or "were always very poor." Apparently the community recognized, subconsciously at least, that many people, because of continual low incomes, were not a threat to village stability, and they were allowed to eke out a marginal existence in peace. Perhaps the mestizo families began to come at a time when the system was already losing vitality, so their presence no longer constituted a threat; or perhaps their refusal to play the game hastened the demise of the cargueros. The system can tolerate very few if any holdouts if it is to remain vigorous. It is noteworthy that today members of the mestizo families that did not participate tend to be well above average in education and wealth, and they have provided more than their share of the village's innovative personalities, as will be shown in Chapter Sixteen. Perhaps the same ability that has led them to this position enabled them to recognize the futility of the traditional carguero activities. Certainly, the end of the system was due in significant part to increasing numbers of people who felt the rewards did not justify the expenses.

CHAPTER ELEVEN

The
Dyadic
Contract

RECIPROCITY: THE BASIS OF SOCIAL RELATIONSHIPS

We have now seen, in such major institutions as religion, health, conflict resolving mechanisms, and in views about wealth, how cultural forms and behavior combine to maintain a basic equilibrium state. A satisfactory condition is one in which there is an even balance between opposing forces and people, in which Good is evenly distributed, and in which no one takes unjustly from another. The same view of equilibrium helps us to understand the basic principle that underlies social relationships. This principle, as will shortly be pointed out, is one of reciprocity between partners, of an even exchange whereby an individual acquires the support he needs in ordinary and special times, without running the risk of being accused of taking something from others.

Before explaining the system of reciprocity that underlies social relationships in Tzintzuntzan, it may be helpful to remind the reader again that the villagers, like other peasants, feel they have no real knowledge of, and consequently no significant control over, natural and supernatural forces, and over the wider social and economic systems — including those of cities and the national government — in which they live. These are areas in which direct intervention is felt to be useless. Yet Tzintzuntzeños, like all other men, believe that to live they must have mastery over some significant part of their environment. Since only the local village world, and the people and beings with whom they have continuing contact, are seen as really knowable, *in Tzintzuntzan concern with social relationships and manipulation of the social environment takes precedence over concern with manipulation of nature and of extra-village systems in general.* Tzintzuntzeños are enormously preoccupied with their relationships with each other, within the formal structures of family, and compadrazgo, and within the informal structures of friendship and "neighborhoodship." They are also interested in their ties with outsiders with whom they have or may have significant contact, and — at another level — with Christ, the Virgin Mary, and the saints. Some personal security in a generally unpredictable world can be achieved, it is felt, only through the ability to exploit all these relationships to best advantage.

Every Tzintzuntzeño's primary concern is to be able to "defend" himself in the *lucha*, the struggle he conceives life to be. In this struggle he knows he is basically on his own, and that it is up to him, with his scant resources, to defend himself and his family against the dangers of the world. On a formal and institutional level, an individual expects to receive a good deal of help from members of his family, and from favorite compadres. These are legitimate forms of support, appropriate to an honorable man because their reciprocal quality is recognized. Beyond these obvious ties, the ideal of successful defense in life is to be able to live *sin compromisos*, without obligations, without entangling alliances, to be strong, masculine, independent, able to meet life's continuing challenges with a minimum of help from others. Bernardo Zaldívar, in the early days of CREFAL, accepted technical and financial aid in the chicken ranching project, but he quickly decided this was not for him. Unlike some of the others who accepted similar aid, he repaid in its entirety his $1,000 loan. When asked to accept a much larger loan to improve his pottery workshop, he refused. *Quiero vivir sin compromisos*, he said to me in discussing these events. "I want to live without being obligated to others." He spoke for most Tzintzuntzeños.

THE IMPORTANCE OF OBLIGATIONS

Yet, paradoxically, strength and relative independence can be achieved only by saddling oneself with a wide variety of *compromisos*. One's ability to defend himself stems from the number and quality of the obligations he recognizes toward others for, of course, each obligation is coupled with an expectation of a particular kind of support at the appropriate time. Hence, no one loses sight of the necessity for continually manipulating and exploiting the institutional and other ties that exist or can be created which will minimize life's dangers and maximize its opportunities.

Some of the ways in which obligations are incurred, and commitments from others obtained, have been examined in previous chapters within the formal frameworks of marriage, the family, and the compadrazgo. Yet the most important thing of all in the social structure of Tzintzuntzan is an informal, unnamed principle of reciprocity that underlies all formal ties, cross-cutting them at every point, serving as the glue that holds society together and the grease that smooths its running. This principle of reciprocity, which I call the "dyadic contract," can be thought of as a sociological model which reconciles the institutional roles already described with the real behavior that can be observed. Its particular utility as a model lies in the fact that it explains the behavior of people in all the situations in which they find themselves: between those of the same socio-economic status, between people of different statuses, between fellow villagers, between villagers and outsiders, and between man and the beings of the supernatural world.

THE DYADIC CONTRACT MODEL

The dyadic contract model postulates an informal structure in which most of the really significant ties within all institutions are

214

achieved (hence selective) rather than ascribed (hence non-selective). The formal social institutions of Tzintzuntzan present each individual with a near-infinite number of people with whom he has culturally defined bonds implying mutual obligations and expectations. But no individual could possibly fulfill all the roles imposed upon him by the statuses he occupies in his village's institutions; he is forced to pick and choose, to concentrate on relatively few. In other words, the formal institutions of society provide everyone with a panel of candidates with whom to interact; the individual, by means of the dyadic contract mechanism, selects (and is selected by) relatively few with whom significant working relationships are developed.

In Tzintzuntzan everyone, from an early age, begins to organize his societal contacts outside the nuclear family, and even to some extent within it, by means of a special form of contractual relationships, and as he approaches and reaches adulthood, these relationships grow in importance until they dominate all other types of ties. These contracts are informal, or implicit, since they lack ritual or legal validation. They are based on no idea of law, and they are unenforceable through any type of authority, even one as diffuse as public opinion. They exist only at the pleasure of the participants. They are noncorporate, since social units such as extended families, barrios, or villages are never bound. Even nuclear families cannot truly be said to enter into contractual relationships of this type with other families.

These contracts are essentially dyadic: they bind *pairs* of contractants, rather than groups. That this distinction is important becomes clear when we remember that in Tzintzuntzan there are no vigorous voluntary associations or institutions in which an individual recognizes identical or comparable obligations to two or more people (always excepting the basketball team). Each person is the center of his private and unique network of contractual ties, a network whose overlap with other networks has little or no functional significance. That is, A's tie to B in no way binds him to B's partner, C. A may also have a contractual relationship with C as well, but the fact that all three recognize comparable bonds gives rise to no feeling of group association. An individual conceptualizes his relationships with others as a focal point at which he stands, from which radiate a multiplicity of two-way streets, at the end of each of which is a single partner, completely separate from all the others.

The kinds of people (or beings) with whom a villager forms these ties include persons of comparable socio-economic position both within and without the community, people of superior power and influence, and supernatural beings such as Christ, the Virgin Mary, and the saints. Contracts develop between members of a family as close as siblings; they bind compadres beyond the formally defined limits of the institution; and they unite friends and neighbors in close union.

Since there are no ritual or legal forms to validate dyadic contracts, what is the evidence that justifies the model? And how can a villager himself be sure he is in fact closely tied to someone else, who also recognizes their special relationship? An outsider in Tzintzuntzan quickly learns of an elaborate reciprocity pattern, occurring almost entirely between pairs of individuals, in which goods and services are continually exchanged. Some of the exchanges are easily visible, as when plates of steaming food are carried by children from one house to another. Other manifestations of the exchange pattern are not so readily seen, as when a compadre or friend speaks for another in a ceremonial act. But in its totality the reciprocity system validates, maintains, and gives substance to the implicit contractual networks. The symbolic meaning of these exchanges (as contrasted to purely economic activities) is accepted without question by all villagers. They know that as long as a person continues to give to and receive from a partner, he rests assured that that relationship is in good order. When an exchange relationship between two people terminates, it is overt evidence to both that the contract is dead, regardless of the formal institutional ties or the religious validation which may continue to bind the participants. During the life of a contract, each partner expects to receive something he wants or needs from the other partner, at times, in ways, and in forms that are clearly understood by both. Each partner, in turn, acknowledges his obligation to give something to the other,

216

again at times, in ways, and in forms that are a function of the type of relationship involved.

TYPES OF DYADIC TIES

Two basic types of contractual ties may be recognized, depending on the relative statuses of the partners. "Colleague" contracts — the expression is mine, and not the villagers' — tie people of equal or approximately equal socio-economic position, who exchange the same kinds of goods and services. These contracts are phrased horizontally, and they can be thought of as symmetrical, since each partner, in position and obligations, mirrors the other. Colleague contracts operate primarily within Tzintzuntzan, but they also tie villagers to individuals in adjacent peasant communities.

"Patron-client" contracts — again the expression is mine — tie people (or people to beings) of significantly different socioeconomic statuses (or orders of power), who exchange different kinds of goods and services. Patron-client contracts are thus phrased vertically, and they can be thought of as asymmetrical, since each partner is quite different from the other in position and obligations. Patron-client contracts operate almost exclusively between villagers and non-villagers (including supernatural beings), since socio-economic differences in Tzintzuntzan are seen as so slight as to preclude the role of patron.

In addition to these informal, implicit contracts, villagers of course also recognize formal and explicit contracts, represented by such acts as marriage, establishing compadrazgo ties, and buying and selling property. These contracts rest on governmental and religious law, are legally or ritually validated through specific acts, are usually registered in writing, and most are enforceable through the authority of the particular system that brings them into being. They often are dyadic, but they may also bind several people, as when the baptism of an infant brings two parents, two godparents, and a godchild together. These formal contracts may be but are not necessarily congruent with the informal dyadic contracts, since the latter cut across all formal institutional boundaries and permeate all aspects of society. For example, two

217

compadres are bound by formal ties validated in a ritual ceremony. This tie may be reinforced and made more functional by an implicit dyadic contract, making the two relationships congruent. Or two people may sign a paper authorizing one to sharecrop a field of the other; this formal relationship may be underlain as well by the general exchange pattern that spells a dyadic contract between the two signers.

COLLEAGUE TIES

With these preliminary remarks in mind we can turn to examine in more detail how this contractual system functions, first considering ties between colleagues and second those between patrons and clients. Between colleagues, reciprocity is expressed in *continuing* exchanges of goods and services. The goods and services are tangibles; incorporeal values play little part in the system. For example, a partner whose special knowledge about a glazing process is a trade secret is not likely to instruct a dyadic partner, just because they exchange many other things. Over the long term the reciprocity is complementary, because each partner owes the other the same kinds and quantities of things. Over the short term the exchanges are not necessarily complementary, because a material item or service offered to partner A by partner B does not require subsequent return of the same thing to cancel the obligation (and it may in fact require something different, as pointed out in the following paragraph). Rather, it is a question of long-range equivalence of value, not formally calculated yet somehow weighed so that in the end both partners balance contributions and receipts. In the usual situation each member of the dyad simultaneously counts a number of credits and debits which are kept in approximate balance.

Within the long-term complementary pattern, there are short-term exchanges, often noncomplementary, in which a particular act elicits a particular return. For example, a friend fixes a bride's hair for the wedding; the friend must be invited to the wedding feast, or if for any reason she cannot come, food must be sent to her from the scene of the dining. One compadre organizes a saint's day mañanitas pre-dawn serenade for another compadre, providing guitar players, a chorus, and a tray, or "crown" of fruit and flowers. The honored compadre reciprocates by inviting the serenaders in for drinks and the hominy-like pork pozole expected at many ceremonial meals. But these specific, non-complementary exchanges are merely minor oscillations within the long-term, major dyadic patterns which bind partners over years and decades. The non-complementary saint's day exchange probably will be made complementary later in the year, when the second compadre returns the favor.

A very important functional requirement of the system is that *an exactly even balance between two partners never be struck.* This would jeopardize the whole relationship since, if all credits and debits somehow could be balanced off at one time, the contract would cease to exist. At the very least a new contract would have to be gotten under way, and this would involve uncertainty and possibly distress if one partner seemed reluctant to continue. The dyadic contract is effective precisely because partners are never quite sure of their relative positions at a given moment. As long as they know that goods and services are flowing both ways in essentially equal amounts as time passes they know their relationship is solidly based.

TYPES OF EXCHANGES

The forms of exchanges can be examined in terms of services and goods offered and reciprocated in ritual and non-ritual settings. These lines are not hard and fast in the minds of Tzintzuntzeños, however, and a material return in a non-ritual setting may help counterbalance a service previously offered in a ritual setting, and so on around the circle of logical possibilities.

Services lent in a ritual context usually are associated with life crises such as baptism, confirmation, marriage, and death. They include a compadre's go-between services to make peace after an elopement, making funeral arrangements for a godchild who dies a "little angel," help and comfort extended on the occasion of a death, such as sitting up all night at the wake with a bereaved husband or wife, and the like. Goods offered in a ritual context include the financial responsibilities of marriage godparents, the expenses incurred by a baptismal godfather when his godchild dies young, aid to a father with the costs of his son's marriage, and particularly the help given partners when they are faced with major fiesta expenses. When a man is a carguero he visits the homes of relatives, compadres, and friends with whom dyadic contracts are recognized, asking them to "accompany" him, that is, to contribute foodstuffs and money. Emphasizing the ritual character of this transaction is the fact that raw foodstuffs equal to about half that given are returned following the fiesta.

At ceremonial meals, such as a saint's day fiesta, a wedding, a baptism, or a funeral, guests bring pots into which they pour surplus food from the heaping dishes served them. This is taken home to be eaten the following day. At any festive meal some people invited are unable to come, and others not specifically invited must be remembered. After the guests have been served, children are sent to the homes of those who have not come with plates of hot food, so they, too, can share in the festivities.

Something of the magnitude of help obtained on such occasions can be seen in the contributions made to Guillermo Morales when his son Miguel was married. The siblings of his wife, Carmen Peña — Wenceslado, Natividad, Jesús, and Faustino — gave respectively one *fanega* of maize worth $50; a hen, a case of beer, and $10; a kilo of red chiles; and $30 in cash. Carmen's married nieces and nephews Esperanza, Celia, Melania, and Adolfo, all Peñas, gave respectively a turkey, 10 kilos of rice, $20 in cash, and $5 in cash. Alfonso Rendón, Guillermo's first cousin, gave $15. Maximiano Guillén, his second cousin, contributed substantially to the costs of music. Bulmaro Molinero, to whom Guillermo is marriage godfather, gave two turkeys, and Jesús Jiménez, Carmen's baptismal godfather, paid the $40 that the church service cost. Lucas Morales, José Calvo, Felix Lara, Ernesto Reyes, Severiano Urbano, and José Cortés, all compadres of one type or another, gave money averaging $10 each. Altogether the aid totalled well over $600 and without it, it would have been impossible for Guillermo to stage the fiesta.

Services in a non-ritual context take an unlimited number of forms. One helps nurse a sick friend or relative, gives a hypodermic injection without the usual small charge, purchases something on request in Pátzcuaro, loans a stud boar without asking the *maquila* fee, sews a dress or makes a picture frame free of charge. San Judas Tadeo and San Anacasio are very helpful in the return of lost or stolen objects. People who have pictures of these saints on their family altars sometimes will loan them to others to help recover a lost item. The picture of San Anacasio of the late Tiburcio Peréz and his wife María Morales is considered "miraculous," since it has helped in recovering so many things. As a part of their exchange obligations Tiburcio and María permitted neighbors and friends to burn vigil lights on their altar, beneath San Anacasio's picture, as they implored him to lend them help. Any one of a thousand helpful acts is considered, and remembered, as a service incurring some form of reciprocal obligation.

In a non-ritual context goods are exchanged when neighbors drop in to borrow an egg, a few chiles, or some other food or household item immediately needed. When men went to the United States as braceros they always borrowed money from friends and relatives, returning the money upon completing their contracts and adding as well some item such as a pair of nylon stockings or a sports shirt which served to keep alive the exchange relationship. A person with heavy medical expenses expects to receive money as an outright gift and as a loan, thus simultaneously being repaid for earlier transactions and incurring new obligations.

THE ROLE OF FOOD AND DRINK

The continuing informal exchange of food and drink is particularly important in maintaining the dyadic contract. Except on ceremonial occasions invitations to meals almost never occur. But when someone — a relative, a neighbor, a compadre, or a friend — with whom the exchange pattern is fully developed drops in, he or she usually is not allowed to leave without being offered whatever food is available: a tortilla, perhaps with a fried egg or beans, a bit of candied sweet potato, a glass of milk, a cup of coffee, or fresh fruit. The nature of the food or drink is not important, but if they are offered they *must* be accepted. Failure

221

to accept proffered food or drink seriously jeopardizes an exchange relationship, since it appears to represent a denial of mutual understanding, and friendly feelings, which are basic to the dyadic contract.

Since men do not cook, they are denied the opportunity to express affection and friendship to partners by offering them food. But they *can* offer drinks, which represent the same symbolic values. This is certainly a major reason why men drinking in a store feel compelled to invite any friend who enters to drink with them, and why they become so angry and belligerent on the rare occasions when their invitation is refused; symbolically, their proffered friendship is being rejected. Undoubtedly many Tzintzuntzan men drink more than they really want to simply because they are caught in a trap in which only through offering and accepting liquor can they maintain important social relations.

Temporary hostility between people normally on good terms is sometimes expressed by refusing to accept food and should someone, simply because of lack of appetite, not eat, the cook begins to speculate as to the cause of what she interprets to be anger directed toward her. Children, irritated with their mothers, will often suffer hunger pains rather than make the gesture that will heal the breach, and few filial acts are more distressing to mothers than a child's refusal to eat. Micaela recalls how her first husband, Pedro, when angry with her, would punish her "by not eating for three days," and she would not eat either "from mortification." No one should refuse food (or drink) by saying he is not hungry (or thirsty), since he knows his motives are immediately suspect. Only by appealing to an upset stomach, or better yet medical treatment that forbids certain items, can proffered food or drink be gracefully refused.

To be able to offer food to those one loves and respects, and whose friendship is valued, is highly prized. When Natividad Peña's younger daughter Chelo eloped without warning she found consolation in the fact that, unlike her elder daughter Teresa who lives a day's trip away, Chelo would be nearby and she could take food to her whenever she wished. She recalled how, when she and Vicente lived in El Rincón, next door to her brother Faustino and his wife Pachita, she would often send them something as simple as a tortilla filled with beans, simply to express her happiness in being near them. Especially if there is a delicacy in the house it is nice to be able to send some to people closely tied to one. Nati's greatest sorrow in Teresa's marrying out of the village is that it is so hard to send food to her. Once when she and Vicente killed a hog and made *chicharrones* (cracklings) she sent her son Gaudencio on the long bus and train trip to deliver some to his sister.

The food and drink exchange, important in all institutions, seems especially so between friends and neighbors. Because the ties to these people are unstructured, in a formal sense, in contrast to those of the family and the compadrazgo, even greater attention to constantly reaffirming the relationship is deemed desirable. The offering of food and drink is the quintessence of this reaffirmation, and if someone professes friendship but fails in this informal exchange, he is said to be a "friend with his lips on the outside," that is, not a genuine friend.

Food exchanges tell us something else about dyadic contracts: they are not all of equal intensity. The situation is similar to that of American friendship patterns in which we see, visit, and interact more with some friends than with others, but the friends we see less often are still qualitatively different from mere acquaintances or professional associates, since we do recognize social and other obligations toward them. High-intensity contracts can be distinguished from low-intensity contracts by the way in which food is handled. If we see some people almost always being offered food when they come to a house, we may be sure that a high-intensity dyadic contract is operating. If continuing exchanges of various types with other people are noted, but less thought is given to informal offerings of food, then we know the contract is of lesser intensity.

LINGUISTIC EXPRESSIONS OF RELATIONSHIPS

In colleague contracts, as has been pointed out, a functional imperative of the system is that an even balance in exchanges never be struck, since only when partners simultaneously recognize both obligations and expectations as being outstanding do they feel a relationship is in good order. Conceptually, a precise balancing of debits with credits is tantamount to terminating a contract. Consequently, behavior that suggests the striking of an even balance, or the desire to strike an even balance, is interpreted as unfriendly, and normally to be avoided — unless, of course, an individual does in fact wish to terminate a relationship. To put the matter in a slightly different way, behavior forms between partners that confirm or reaffirm recognition of a contract are highly valued, whereas behavior forms which do not reaffirm recognition of a contract, or which may suggest the speaker or actor feels the contract is no longer very important, are seen as threatening and hostile. Once the importance of this point is grasped, certain aspects of behavior in Tzintzuntzan which at first seem puzzling and incomprehensible fall nicely into place.

When I first began to take presents to people in Tzintzuntzan I was much disturbed when they were accepted with what seemed to me a distressing lack of enthusiasm, bordering on ungraciousness. At most a perfunctory *gracias* would be mumbled, and often nothing at all would be said. I feared I was not pleasing, or that more had been expected of me. Then I realized that this was standard behavior between the villagers themselves. When a tray of uncooked food, covered by a cloth, would be sent as a contribution to a carguero's fiesta expenses his wife would accept it unceremoniously at the door, carry it without looking under the cloth to the kitchen, unload the tray, and return it and the cloth to the donor with no more comment than normal passing of the time of day.

This "lack of courtesy" among a normally courteous and ceremony minded people puzzled me until I realized that the objects offered were viewed, not as gifts, but rather as one among many items forming the exchange system existing between partners, an item for which repayment would be made in another way at a later date. Tzintzuntzeños recognize — realistically, I think — that in their society there can be such a thing as a "gift" given apart from an existing or a potential exchange pattern between people only in a very special sense. Any favor, whatever its form, is part of a quid pro quo negotiation, the terms of which are recognized and accepted by the participants.

Both linguistic and other behavior forms show why the word "gift" is inappropriate to describe the goods and services that are exchanged in Tzintzuntzan. In American society a gift is thought of as something transferred from one person to another without measurable compensation. That it may, in fact, be part of a continuing exchange pattern is beside the point. A gift is accepted with enthusiasm and with thanks, verbally expressed, which symbolize something more than the courtesy thanks that accompany commercial transactions, since the words are recognized, subconsciously at least, as striking a conceptual balance with the donor's thoughtfulness.

In Spanish thanks are expressed in two distinct linguistic forms: *gracias* (literally the plural form of "grace"), usually translated into English as "thank you," and *Diós se lo pague*, meaning "May God (re)pay you for it." The first form serves for casual, informal interchanges of no moment between persons of equal status, or equal status at least as far as the occasion that calls forth the word is concerned. But *Diós se lo pague* is used in an entirely different sense, in which the thanker acknowledges the great difference in position and the fact that the object or service can never be reciprocated. Beggars, for example, acknowledge alms with this expression. Only by asking God's favor for the donor can the beggar in any way repay the giver; neither expects any other balance. An item acknowledged with *Diós se lo pague*, then, can properly be considered a gift in the American sense. An item or act acknowledged by *gracias* is something else, for the form is a courtesy and nothing more.

In Tzintzuntzan both forms are used. I hear *Diós se lo pague* when I give something considered by the recipient to be far outside the normal patterns of friendship exchange, such as a substantial monetary contribution to help with unusual medical expenses. When I give lesser items, such as a cut of cloth for a skirt or dress — something within the normal range of exchanges — I may hear *gracias*, or perhaps nothing at all. The recipient and I know the item given will be reciprocated with pottery, a tule-reed figure, fish, or something else commanded by the recipient; the cut of cloth is not a gift, nor are the pottery, the figure, or the fish.

The usual absence of verbal thanks and visible enthusiasm accompanying exchanges does not mean, of course, that the transactions are cold, calculated, and emotionless. People enjoy these transactions enormously; it is gratifying to know one is living up to his obligations, and that one's partners continue to value the association. Some of the fundamental values of the culture are expressed in the exchange acts themselves, and people sense and appreciate this fact, even though they would have trouble verbalizing it.

Another form of linguistic behavior which at first thought seems contrary to reason can be explained by the feeling that behavior suggesting a desire to terminate a contract is threatening, while behavior reaffirming the desire to continue a contract is reassuring. In Tzintzuntzan an individual often greets an acquaintance, or acknowledges the presence of a stranger on a trail, with *Adiós*, the common Spanish form of "goodbye," and more literally, "[I commend you] to God." Conversely, he very rarely says *Adiós* when taking leave of a friend, preferring some such form as *Hasta luego, Ándale* ("Run along"), *Nos vemos* (We'll be seeing each other"), or — perhaps most frequently — *No nos despedimos* ("We won't say goodbye"). I think it is clear that for a partner to say *Adiós* is potentially dangerous, for it can be interpreted to mean that he does not expect to see his partner for a long time, that he is perhaps tired of him and does not really want to continue the relationship implied in the contract. Or it may imply that the speaker is unwilling or unable to honor his obligations. The expression *Adiós* is therefore conceptually equivalent to *Diós se lo pague* in giving thanks for a gift; it is perceived as balancing the equation of obligations and terminating the relationship. Partners thus prefer to take leave of each other with a verbal expression that emphasizes the continuity of their relationship by expressing the belief, and hope, that they will soon again be together.

But why *greet* a stranger or an acquaintance by saying "Goodbye" to him? The use of *Adiós* in this context is consistent with the perception of interpersonal relationships described earlier in this chapter. An individual cannot be a partner to all the world, and many of the people he sees, and with whom he has some contact, cannot be his partners, and should not be mistaken in assuming that, for a particular act, he wishes to initiate a contract. *Adiós*, then, is both an expression of social distance, and a device to maintain it, a way to recognize that a contractual tie is absent. It is courteous and respectful, but not at all intimate. It says, in effect, "I see you, I greet you, I wish God to go with you, I respect you — but I must remind you that we have no claims on each other."

There are still other symbolic ways in which a contract can be denied, temporarily because of momentary anger, or permanently. Macaria Gómez' stepdaughter Melania receives a multiplicity of goods and services from her, and from her daughters Laura and Victoria: food, clothing, sewing of dresses for her children, money, and many other things. Macaria, in return, receives primarily the satisfaction of having grandchildren around her (her own daughters are unmarried), and Melania also from time to time gives small presents or other material tokens of affection. On one occasion Macaria's daughters were sewing uniforms for Melania's two oldest daughters for the school Independence Day parade. For some obscure reason Melania became angry, lost her temper, shouted and screamed, and as a crowning insult, insisted on paying for the sewing of the uniform, something she had never done before, and which left Laura and Victoria thunderstruck. Melania's payment was seen as a hostile act, as indeed it was intended to be, in which she was saying "Since I am paying for this service I am not indebted to you for anything, and you have no future claim on me." The fact that normal relations were restored later in the day in no way affects the symbolism of the act.

PATRON-CLIENT TIES

With patron-client contracts, in contrast to colleague contracts, one of the two partners is always of significantly higher position, from which stems the power which permits him to be a "patron" to the other. The Spanish word *patrón* has several related meanings: an employer of workers, a ceremonial sponsor, a skipper of a small boat, the protecting saint of a village or parish, the protecting saint to all people who bear his (or her) name. All these definitions are correct for Tzintzuntzan. A patron, it is clear, is someone who combines status, power, influence, authority — attributes useful to anyone — in "defending" himself or in helping someone else to defend himself. But a person, however powerful and influential, is a patron only in relation to someone of lesser position — a client whom, under specific circumstances, he is willing to help. Tzintzuntzeños all look up to a number of patrons. Each recognizes the saint whose name he bears as *mi santo patrón*, and everyone knows San Francisco is patron of the village. All accept the Virgin of Guadalupe as patron of America and Mexico, and consequently as their patron as well. In addition, a few adults refer to people in Pátzcuaro, Morelia, and other towns as *mi patrón*, because of relationships in which they assume the position of subordinate partner. Tzintzuntzeños have no corresponding word for themselves as clients. Since they represent near-bottom in the Mexican socio-economic hierarchy, they do not look down upon others from the lofty position of patron, and they do not think of the relationship as one in which a person may be either patron or client, depending on relative position and power.

Analytically, two basic types of patrons may be distinguished in Tzintzuntzan: (1) human beings, and (2) supernatural beings. The former include politicians, government employees, town and city friends, godparents or compadres of superior status, influence, or special abilities, and Church personnel, especially the local priest. The latter — the supernatural patrons — are God, Christ, the Virgin Mary, and the saints, the last three in any of their geographical or advocational manifestations. Even the devil is a potential patron since, as we have seen (page 147), he can bring one great wealth. All human patrons, except the local priest, are from outside Tzintzuntzan, since the status differences that are essential for a patron-client relationship are lacking within the

228

community. Supernatural patrons are those associated with the local churches or with family altars, as well as those found in more distant communities.

As is true of colleague contracts, the partners' recognition of mutual obligations underlies and validates the patron-client system. There are, however, two important differences in exchange patterns. First, the patron and client exchange different kinds of goods and services, and second, *whereas all colleague contracts are continuing, a significant part of patron-client exchanges are non-continuing, or short-term.* That is, a particular good or service offered by a prospective client requires an immediate and specific return from the potential patron. If the offer is reciprocated, the patron-client contract is established, but the act of reciprocation either simultaneously terminates the contract or establishes conditions for termination in the near future. To be more specific, patron-client relationships involving human beings are like colleague contracts, in that goods and services are exchanged as time passes, with no attempt to strike a balance, since this would cancel the contract. In some instances in which the patron is supernatural, the relationship continues for a long period, with no attempt to strike an exact balance. But in many other instances, and particularly those in which a supplicant asks for help in time of sickness or other crisis, it is expected that the granting of the request is cancelled out, or balanced off, by the supplicant's compliance with his vow. Hence, no contract exists until the request is granted, and no contract exists after the supplicant complies. This type of patron-client contract is terminated by striking what is recognized as an even bargain between the contractants, the very act that is zealously avoided by colleague contractants so that their relationship *will not* be terminated.

Tzintzuntzeños, recognizing their humble position and lack of power and influence, are continually alert to the possibility of obligating a person of superior wealth, position, or influence, thereby initiating a patron-client relationship which, if matters go well, will buttress the villagers' security in a variety of life crises that are only too certain: illness, the sudden need for cash, help in legal disputes, protection against various forms of possible exploitation, and advice on the wisdom of contemplated moves.

Exploiting the compadrazgo system, as we have already seen, is one of the most obvious ways of gaining a patron, and wealthy city relatives, local ranchers (of whom there are only a few), and storekeepers in nearby Pátzcuaro with whom one may have commercial relations are common targets. When Pánfilo Castellanos' son Lucio was married, his wife's nephew, who had become a successful Pátzcuaro doctor, agreed to be marriage godfather. A pre-existing family tie was thereby strengthened, and the new godfather was under strong obligation to help with free medical attention, possible loans, and advice that the greater experience of a town dweller makes possible. Pánfilo and his wife, in return, expect to take presents from time to time to their nephew, to invite him to family fiestas and meals in Tzintzuntzan, and perhaps to drum up trade among ill villagers. Macaria Gómez persuaded a distant bachelor cousin, Isaac Martín, whose mother controls one of the few remaining haciendas in the Pátzcuaro area, to be baptismal godfather to her eldest daughter, Laura. Isaac, in addition to the general prestige he sheds on Macaria, has loaned her money to help with her chicken ranching, and he gave her a fairly large sum when she underwent a major operation. His return is less clear. When he visits Tzintzuntzan, on rare occasions, he is fawned on and made over in extravagant fashion, and perhaps in a land where large landowners are not popular, it is good to have villagers who speak well of one.

Patron-client compadrazgo relationships, although formally identical to those binding socio-economic equals, are in fact recognized as quite distinct by all participants. This is especially apparent in linguistic usage. Compadres of the same status, as has been pointed out, usually are extremely formal with each other, in theory at least dropping the familiar second person singular personal pronoun "tú" in favor of the formal "usted." Client compadres, of course, are extremely formal with their patron compadres, as with all other human patrons, but patron

230

compadres, almost without exception, address their village compadres with the familiar "tú," so that the relative status of the two partners is never in doubt. Isaac Martín, for example, is considerably younger than Macaria Gómez; yet, because of his superior status, it is taken for granted by both that he will address her as "tú" and she will address him as "usted."

Although the compadrazgo institution is an excellent way to establish a patron-client contract, less formal acts also work well. One day while I sat with Silverio Caro in his roadside pottery stand, a small car drove up with three people. Silverio greeted the driver, *Buenos días, doctor,* in such a way that it was clear that they had had previous contact. After buying several pieces of pottery the doctor and his friends left. Silverio then explained that this was a relatively new doctor in Pátzcuaro whom he had consulted professionally, and it became clear to me that he was carefully building a relationship with him. The regular price of the merchandise selected was $16.50, but Silverio had charged only $13.00. If, on future visits to Pátzcuaro, the doctor were to show a bit more consideration than usual, or go out of his way to show friendship in some other way, Silverio would take presents of pottery and feel that his relationship with the doctor was good health insurance.

On another occasion Silverio invited me, in a rather vague way, to come to his house and look at his storeroom of pottery. Since I had done this many times previously, the reason was obscure. After inspecting and praising the quality of the ware, and accepting a small ashtray as a gift, I was about to leave when Josefa, his wife, invited me to sit down on a chair. Presently the design came out: would I not, she wondered, bring a used television set the next time I drove from the United States to Mexico, which they would buy from me at cost? I explained that, as a tourist, I could not bring merchandise other than personal effects into Mexico, and that customs officials are best not deceived. Silverio and Josefa accepted this with good grace, and it was clear that the ploy had been attempted in a "nothing ventured, nothing gained" mood. They were not upset, nor did our friendship suffer.

The establishment of the UNESCO CREFAL community development training center in Pátzcuaro in 1952, and the subsequent attention given Tzintzuntzan for several years, multiplied village contacts with people of superior power, and nearly every faculty member and student who visited the village became patron to a number of people. The patrons received presents of pottery, fish, eggs, and chickens, and free meals on occasion, and in return they offered medical help, tools, and a variety of technical and personal services.

Within Tzintzuntzan, although there are wealth differences, there are no social distinctions sufficiently great to justify using the patron-client concept to describe personal relationships, the priest being the single exception. The three priests who have served in recent years have been reluctant to accept compadrazgo ties, although they have done so on rare occasions, thereby establishing patron-client bonds. But other less specific ties exist. The priests need helpers to maintain Church ritual, to arrange flowers and candles on altars, to clean the buildings, and as sources for some of their food. They, in turn, can confer extra spiritual blessings on their supporters, and they can, because of their education and knowledge of the world, give temporal advice as well. So, it seems to me, it is proper to think of the priests as participating in exchange relationships with the villagers, in which they are patrons and the villagers are clients.

In these patron-client relationships between human beings, one sees both similarities to and differences from the colleague contracts. As with the latter, the relationships are continuing, and neither patron nor client attempts to strike an immediate balance, which both recognize would terminate the contract. But unlike the colleague contracts, the partners are not equals, and make no real pretense to equality. It is, in fact, this asymmetry, and particularly the ability to offer one's partner something distinct from that which he offers, and to receive something one's fellows do not have at their disposal, which makes the system worthwhile. Within the village, local colleague ties provide a man with all he needs, at peak periods of demand, of the kinds of goods and services to which he himself also has access. The

232

patron's utility lies in the fact that he can provide things not normally available in the village, things that at times are badly needed.

At first glance the patron-client compadrazgo, which is formally as well as informally contractual, appears to contradict the dyadic principle: in its important forms it binds a minimum of five and a maximum of eight people (e.g., for baptism, the child, parents, and godparents; for marriage, the godparents, the couple, and the parents of both bride and groom). The contradiction, however, is more apparent than real, since the *meaningful exchange-based* ties which underlie the system's formalities seem normally to involve dyads only. Above all, the patron is always an individual. For example, Isaac Martín, godfather to Laura Prieto, is patron both to her and her mother, by means of two distinct ties. The basic, implicit, informal contracts bind two people, and though they may appear to "blanket in" others, there are no doubts in the participants' minds as to the nature of the relationship.

SUPERNATURAL BEINGS AS PATRONS

Just as individuals cast about among human beings for patrons, so do they turn to the saints, and to the various manifestations of Christ and the Virgin, testing their willingness to enter contractual relationships with them (i.e., by helping, by responding to overtures). Some of the resulting dyadic contracts are, like all those previously described, continuing, in that an even balance is never struck. Other contracts are rather different, in that they are called into being for a specific crisis, in response to the supplications of a human being. If the contract is made, i.e., if the supernatural being grants the request of the supplicant, the latter is obligated, at his earliest convenience, to fulfill his part of the bargain, to strike the balance by complying with his offer. This terminates the contract. An individual may try to renew the contract at a later time for a new crisis but, as will be seen, he often will attempt a contract with a different patron on each new occasion.

Continuing patron-client contracts with supernatural beings are best seen in the daily prayers and lighting of candles practiced by most villagers. Every home has one or more simple altars, usually a shelf with a few wilted or artificial flowers and guttered candles beneath several pictures of Christ, the Virgin, and an assortment of saints. This low-pitched daily homage is believed to gain the protection of the beings invoked, not for specific crises, but against the thousand and one unthought dangers that lie in wait for the unwary. In the room in which Laura Prieto sleeps and sews, the wall altar holds pictures of the Virgin of Guadalupe, as well as several other virgins and saints. When she sits down to sew, or at other times when she "just feels like it," she lights a vigil light "to all of them." She is paying her respects, asking them to continue to watch over her in return for this attention. Her mother pays little attention to this altar, but she prays to the Virgin of Guadalupe before arising in the morning, and Divine Providence is the object of a credo before she goes to sleep. In return, the mother hopes to receive her "daily necessities." Laura's stepfather is addicted to Souls in Purgatory and Our Lady of Perpetual Help, to both of whom he prays daily. In other homes the pattern is similar.

A noteworthy point in this pattern is that altars are not really centers of family rites, even though several members may light candles. Each member of the family has his special responsibility toward the patrons he has selected, who he feels favor him. No one, except upon special request, is responsible for acts of deference and respect for other family members. If Laura is away for a day or two on a pilgrimage, her mother feels no compulsion to light candles to Laura's patrons, although she will certainly ask her own patrons to care for her daughter. In the continuing type of relationship with supernatural patrons, the dyadic pattern that characterizes other village relationships is the rule.

Apart from what may be called "obligatory" patrons — Christ and the Virgin, shared by all villagers — how does one select continuing patrons? There is no rule; one simply follows hunches or whims, as in the case of Laura, who decided to add San Martín de Porres to her altar after hearing about him in a radio *novela*. Manuel Herrera, with impeccable logic, says he supposes the Virgin is really the most powerful. After all, *Ella tiene más parentesco con el Mero Jefe,* "She's the most closely related to the Big Boss."

Other patrons who logically fall in the "continuing" category are relatively unimportant. San Francisco, patron of Tzintzuntzan, is, as we have seen, not highly regarded for his miraculous qualities, and his fiesta is perfunctory. A person's name saint likewise receives little attention, although his day itself is often marked by the equivalent of an American birthday party. Occupational patrons — San Isidro for farmers, for example — also receive short shrift in Tzintzuntzan. The devil as patron is more theoretical than real; no one, of course, admits to this relationship. Yet stories are told, usually about people in nearby villages, in which a petitioner becomes wealthy by selling his soul to the devil, thereby establishing a relationship which endures not only through life but through all eternity.

THE VOW

Non-continuing or short-term contracts with supernatural patrons are best seen in the practice of votive offerings. When an individual faces a crisis, such as illness, accident, or an unusual need for money, he (or she) makes a *manda* or *promesa,* a vow or solemn promise to a saint or one or another of the many images or manifestations of Christ or the Virgin, to do some pious act known to be pleasing to the patron. In the simplest pious acts, for rather minor crises, the petitioner lights a candle and prays, or hangs a silver *milagro* at the altar of the patron invoked. The silver (sometimes base metal) votive offerings are small representations of parts of the body such as an arm, a leg, eyes, breasts, or even an entire body in kneeling posture, or of pigs, goats, sheep, horses, or cattle. The one selected depends, of course, on the nature of the supplication: a pig for a lost or sick sow, and an arm for a sore arm.

In more serious crises the client promises the patron to wear a *hábito,* a plain religious garment, for a number of months, and to refrain from all kinds of public entertainment and amusements if the request is granted. Women who suffer from headaches or who are otherwise sickly, and who may believe their long hair

235

is an excessive drain on their systems, occasionally cut off their braids and hang them at the altar of the Virgin, pleading for relief. Guadalupe Huipe recently offered her braids to the *Imaculada* image of the Virgin, and to comply with her promise painstakingly glued each hair to a skullcap to be worn by the Virgin. Ofelia Zamora did the same thing 20 years ago, but with the passage of the years the hairs fell out and the Virgin became a bit bald, so Guadalupe had the opportunity to do something she felt would be particularly welcome to the Virgin.

When a person finds himself in sudden, grave peril, he commends himself to one of the advocations of Christ or the Virgin, and if he is saved, he orders a *retablo,* in classic form a painted metal sheet which graphically portrays the danger, shows the patron floating in the sky, and at the bottom has a line or two describing the miracle. For other grave crises, or in the hope of very special favors, a supplicant promises the Santo Entierro advocation of Christ to assume the role of penitent during one or more Good Fridays, either hobbling about with leg shackles or carrying a wooden cross along a prescribed route through the village. In other cases — usually illness — one appeals to a "miraculous" saint or image of Christ or the Virgin in another town, promising to go on a religious pilgrimage to fulfill the vow if the request is granted.

Several examples will show how the system works.

Valentín Rivera on two occasions has taken silver votive oxen to the church of San Antonio in Morelia, for aid in finding lost animals. San Antonio is patron of animals, and he is also very skilled in helping people find things such as, for farmers, lost animals, and — for young maidens — husbands. Benigno Zúñiga has taken silver eyes and a silver leg to the altar of Nuestro Señor del Rescate, both times for personal illness. Few if any adults have not, at some time or other, made use of ex-votos.

Laura Prieto was afflicted with giant urticaria which caused her great suffering. She visited a Pátzcuaro doctor, who prescribed medicine, and then she appealed to the Virgin of Health ("the most miraculous Virgin in Pátzcuaro"), promising to wear the Virgin's "habit" for six months if she were relieved. Within a week she was much improved, so Laura bought the costly, heavy, scratchy wool, made the dress, wore it six months, and faithfully abstained from all public recreation. The doctor received no credit for her recovery.

Most painted retablos in Tzintzuntzan are dedicated to the "miraculous" Señor del Rescate, whose extraordinary powers were noted sixty years ago when he was credited with saving the village from decimation by smallpox. A few are also placed on lateral altars dedicated to the Virgin of Guadalupe and Our Lady of the Sacred Heart. One, showing a painting of Christ on the Cross, with a woman kneeling below, bears the legend, "I give thanks to the very miraculous Señor del Rescate for having saved my life in a very dangerous operation April 10, 1950, from which I nearly died. I offer myself with all my heart to El Señor. Glafira Ceja who resides in Ciudad Juárez, Chihuahua." A second, large, framed, hand-lettered script without picture says simply, "A miracle which the Señor del Rescate did for me. I give my most sincere thanks to our Señor del Rescate for having saved my life when I was a prisoner in the Pátzcuaro jail in 1919. Eligio Carrillo." A third, modern retablo consists of three framed postcard-size photographs, the first of which shows a man about to descend from a roof on a ladder, the second the man sprawled on the ground, and the third the victim being swathed in bandages. The caption reads "Estanislado Alvarado. I give thanks to Christ Crucified for saving me from this horrible fall. Zamora, July, 1961."

Of the nineteen retablos hanging in 1961, twelve were related to health, and seven dealt with personal problems such as finding a lost animal, delivery from prison, drunkenness, avoiding military service, and the sparing of animals from the hoof and mouth disease. All but one were placed by the individual who was in danger or great need; the exception was a man who gave thanks for his wife's restored health. Curiously, only one of the retablos was hung by a Tzintzuntzeño: a widow who thanks Our Lady of the Sacred Heart for the "miracle" of making it possible for her to have a house. Why this discrimination by local people? As far as El Señor del Rescate is concerned, Benigno Zúñiga probably

237

speaks for the village when he says this Christ *es casi de la familia,* is almost a member of the family, and can be approached successfully in a number of simpler ways, such as vigil lights and silver votive offerings. It looks as if it is a case of distant fields looking greener. San Juan de las Colchas, and San Juan de los Lagos, says Micaela, are where Tzintzuntzeños like to hang retablos.

Although a person usually vows to be a penitent in time of serious illness, other grave matters may also be resolved in this fashion. When Bartolo Zúñiga bought a used truck with his bracero earnings he did not know how to drive, and he greatly feared wrecking it. He promised the Santo Entierro that he would be a penitent for two Easters, wearing leg shackles, if the patron would help him learn to drive, "putting skill in my hands." The truck was spared, and Bartolo complied with his vow.

Illustrating the pilgrimage pattern, Manuel Herrera, while working as a bracero in California, fell ill, not gravely, but enough so he feared he would lose work time, a critical matter for a man on a short-term contract. He promised the Virgin of the Rosary in Coeneo, about fifty miles from Tzintzuntzan, that if she cured him quickly he would make a pilgrimage to her church to light a 5-peso candle in her honor. He recovered without lost time, and shortly after his return to Mexico he visited Coeneo as promised.

Although acceptance of most religious cargos in the old mayordomía system was associated with the prestige quest, a man undertook to be carguero for the Virgin of Guadalupe, in Ojo de Agua, in response to a vow made in time of need or trouble. And Tzintzuntzan's biggest modern fiesta, the "function" in honor of Nuestro Señor del Rescate, began as the consequence of a vow. Guadalupe Estrada, sacristan in 1900 during a terrible smallpox epidemic, remembered an old painting of Christ half hidden behind an altar and, casting about for help in the eclectic fashion of the villagers, he turned to it and cried out, *Ay, Señor, porque no rescates a tu pueblo,* "why don't you rescue your people?" And then he quickly added, "If you do I promise to establish a cult in your honor." The epidemic quickly died down, the painting came to be called *del Rescate* because it saved the village,

238

Guadalupe served as carguero until the fiesta was well established, and San Francisco, the official patron, slipped into near-obscurity, since he had done nothing for his clients.

The way in which non-continuing, short-term contracts with supernatural patrons differ from continuing contracts should be apparent from the examples given above. Except for offerings of ex-votos and candles and prayers, *the vow or promise is conditional upon the patron granting the request.* The offering of the would-be client, the promise of a pious act, must be carried through only if the patron in fact fulfills his (or her) part of the bargain, which is the act that brings the contract into being. Laura would not have worn her habit if she had not greatly improved; the retablos would not have been hung if the favors requested had not been granted; Manuel would not have gone to Coeneo if he had become seriously ill; and Bartolo would not have worn leg shackles as a penitent if he had had an accident in learning to drive, since no contract would have been established. "Thus we really lose nothing," says Laura's very practical mother, in explaining how the system works. Neither patron nor client is under continuing obligation to his partner as a consequence of a successful exchange. The relationship is a one-time, one-subject affair, and with an exact balance of obligation struck, both partners are free to go their own ways, perhaps but not necessarily coming together at a future time.

Although Christ and the Virgin may be appealed to in a general sense, and in any specific manifestation, and any saint may be approached, some are recognized as especially powerful or "miraculous" (like the Virgin of Health in Pátzcuaro); others are particularly efficacious for certain things. San Judas Tadeo, as previously mentioned, helps people find lost objects. If he is appealed to, and fails to help, his picture is turned to the wall or placed face down on a chair as punishment, in spite of the fact that the priest inveighs against this impious act.

In general, though, an eclectic approach is utilized in seeking special aid. When Macaria Gómez feared a gall-bladder operation, her daughter Victoria promised to wear the habit of the Virgin of Health for three months if the operation were not necessary; her daughter Laura promised to make a pilgrimage the four hundred miles to the famous Virgin of San Juan de los Lagos (two neighbors had told her this virgin was "especially miraculous"); one friend promised the Virgin of Counsel in Santa Clara del Cobre to bring Macaria with her on pilgrimage; another friend promised the Virgin of the Rosary in Coeneo to bring Macaria with her; whereas her stepdaughter simply vowed alms to El Señor del Rescate. Macaria avoided the operation, but is in some doubt as to who receives credit. Her husband, Manuel, in addition to the Virgin of the Rosary in Coeneo, has at some time appealed to El Señor de la Exaltación in Santa Fe, to the Holy Virgin in the abstract, and to most of the saints and pictures of Christ and the Virgin in the Tzintzuntzan churches.

Several points in the manda complex require further discussion. Can a well-wisher make a vow that implicates another person, so that person must comply? At first glance it looks as if Macaria was implicated by her friends. However, if the person implicated refuses to comply, the responsibility bounces back to the one who made the vow, and he must extract himself from the predicament as best he can. It is hard to tell how often this kind of manda is made; not often, probably, because the priests say that it is wrong to make a manda in the name of another person.

Actually, except for major vows, supernatural patrons seem not to be choosy about who completes a manda; the important thing is that it be completed. If, for example, one makes a minor manda to El Señor del Rescate to light a candle and it isn't convenient for the petitioner to comply, he or she gives the candle to a child, with the promised alms, and sends the little messenger along to do the job. Manuel once bought a house that turned out to be haunted. Twice he wrestled with the ghost before he realized it was a soul in purgatory; then he asked it what it wanted and was told it had died before lighting a fifty-centavo candle to the Virgin of Light in San José Church in Morelia. Manuel promised to light the candle, which he did, and the ghost departed in peace, his contract fulfilled.

Can a person make a vow or promise to more than one potential patron for a single reason? Some informants say no. When

I asked Laura Prieto she mumbled "yes," looked embarrassed, and acted as if maybe it was really cheating a bit to do so. In fact, there seems to be a number one object of the request, but, following the usual pattern of trying to get the most potential help possible in every situation, a number of people make secondary requests, hoping that these acts will slide by unnoticed by the major object of attention.

Do two or more people jointly petition a single patron? For example, might two daughters say to the Virgin of Health in Pátz-cuaro, "We promise to wear your habit if our mother is restored to health?" All the evidence I have indicates that this is not done. No informant ever used a plural personal pronoun in describing a petition; no informant ever suggested that his responsibility was shared with another; and no informant ever said that anyone else was equally implicated with him. In all nineteen retablos, the petitioner who fulfills his vow is a single person. Several people may take action in the face of a single calamity threatening a family, but each action is dyadic, independent of the others, involving a single petitioner and a single patron. Patron-client relationships are enormously personal, and the benefits that accrue from a successful contract are not willingly shared by a client. It rather seems as if the bounty of a supernatural patron, like all other good things in life, is looked upon as a Limited Good, and to the extent one shares it with others, so in that degree is one's portion reduced. Two petitions to a single patron will not produce twice the bounty; they will simply dilute and divide a finite quantity. Where this point of view prevails, it is clear that several people individually appealing to several patrons is a more logical policy, offering greater potential help, than the same people appealing collectively to a single patron.

THE PALANCA

To understand fully patron-client relationships, both between human beings alone, and with the supernatural, the concept of *palanca*, or "lever" must be recognized. Broadly speaking, the palanca is *a way of access to a patron*, a device to reach someone with "leverage." "For example," Micaela once said to me with disarming candor, "I want something from you, but I don't want to ask you directly, so I ask Mariquita (Mary Foster) to approach you. She is my palanca." And again, "When I ask a friend to help, I say *Que me hagas una palanca,* you be my lever." A palanca, it is clear, is a go-between, someone to whom ego feels reasonably close, who can be helpful in getting to the real patron. A palanca is, perhaps, a semi-patron as well as a patron. He can help in himself, but his real value resides in his ability to influence favorably the ultimate source of power.

As previously mentioned, priests are reluctant to accept compadrazgo ties with villagers. Consequently their nieces or sisters who keep house for them are deluged with requests to be godmothers, and they often accept. These women are looked upon as palancas. The relationship with them is not particularly valued in itself, but it is assumed that via them the client can more easily gain the ear of the priest in time of need; they are the lever, the device to achieve the desired end. This rather cynical view of the approach to a priest is seen in the saying *Por el santo se besa la piaña,* which means that in order to reach the saint who may help one, the supplicant must be prepared to kiss the pedestal on which the saint's image stands.

Although the word "palanca" is used only for human beings, it is clear that this concept is equally applicable to the supernatural. In trying to work out the pattern, I commented to Micaela that the person who wants to get ahead looks for palancas, tries to get them in debt by offering a meal or doing some other favor, but one is merely trying, and until the potential palanca comes through, one doesn't know. Nevertheless, a person keeps searching for the best palancas. *Es la misma cosa con los santos,* said Micaela with considerable feeling, "it's the same thing with the saints." One continually tries different saints, shopping around, hoping to find the most influential ones, or the ones that can help the petitioner most. When I suggested to other informants that saints were really palancas, most were shocked; but a few, not too upset to speculate, said in effect, "Yes, that's really the way it is."

The concept of the palanca also helps us in understanding the real nature of the patron-client relationship with saints. The saints,

242

and the Virgin Mary as well, in one sense are patrons in that the contract is made with them, but ultimately they are only palancas, or go-betweens. *Cuando Diós no quiere, los santos no pueden,* the saying goes. "When God doesn't wish it, the saints can't do it." The saints and the Virgin are, then, advocates, special pleaders, whom one can approach more readily than God. They will handle your case when presented with it, but only if God wishes it can they be successful, and must the fee be paid, in the form of the petitioner complying with his vow.

Doña Andrea Medina, a woman of strong character, repository of much of the information in this book dealing with earlier years in the village.

Doña Natividad Peña and her husband, Don Vicente Rendón, in the patio of their house. Through the open door the lake may be seen.

A part of the plaza as seen from the highway.

CHAPTER TWELVE

Change: Culture, Personality, and Infrastructure

RURAL AND URBAN MEXICO

Tzintzuntzan, it should be clear from the preceding chapters, has a strong penchant for the status quo. Perhaps in no other type of society do cultural forms, social structure, and personality so combine and mutually reinforce each other in maintaining a resistance to new ways. When, therefore, we returned to the village in 1958 after being absent twelve years, we were not really surprised that visible signs of change were so few. Those which did strike us seemed relatively superficial in comparison to the signs of stability. Few women still wore the traditional heavy wool skirts of red or black felted cloth which had been common at the earlier period, and the white pajamalike *calzoncillos* of the men were now replaced by blue jeans. More patios than formerly were enclosed by high walls, and here and there new doorways appeared, showing that the settled area was increasingly densely populated. But the external boundaries of the village had not extended outward, and from the pyramids to the east the view seemed identical to that of 1940, when we had first passed through Tzintzuntzan.

The cultural stability of Tzintzuntzan was in striking contrast to developments in much of the rest of Mexico, for the immediate postwar years were a time of unparalleled economic growth for the country at large. Major cities underwent such transformations in this period that they were hardly recognizable to visitors of earlier times. Mexico City more than doubled in population, and its tallest buildings soared from a mere dozen to nearly fifty stories. Guadalajara had become a modern urban center, although still beautiful in spite of such intrusions as Woolworth and Sears, Roebuck stores facing each other across the principal downtown intersection. Even Morelia, though maintaining its colonial charm, had been forced to cope with motor traffic by installing traffic lights and cutting down the fine row of palms that had graced its principal avenue.

Although it might seem that a village that changes very slowly would be a poor candidate for a restudy, the very contrast between the two postwar Mexicos explains why the opposite is true. On the one hand Mexico has experienced a notable industrial, business, commercial farming, and urban social development probably unequalled in the Free World among countries starting at a similar level of development. On the other hand, thousands of villages like Tzintzuntzan have shared only modestly in this progress, so that the gap between traditional villages and modern urban areas is greater than before the war. That the Mexican government is vitally concerned by this inequality is amply demonstrated by the new schools, potable water systems, health centers, and new roads now increasingly visible, even in remote areas of the country. Yet in spite of the magnitude of this effort, it is clear that much is still unknown about the processes and problems of modernization in traditional peasant areas, not only in Mexico but also in most of the rest of the world.

The questions of practical concern to all newly developing countries where populations and expectations tend to outrun the marshalling of resources to support them include such points as: the

248

potential for and limits to social and economic change in peasant villages; the kinds of extra-village influences that facilitate change; the types of social and economic developmental projects that best aid villagers to achieve higher standards of living and well-being; the nature and relationships of the economic, technological, social, and organizational factors which govern village development, and which must be consciously manipulated in technical aid programs; and the new forms of behavior peasants will have to accept if they are to benefit from the changing conditions which increasingly rule their environments.

For various reasons Tzintzuntzan proved to be a good laboratory in which to search for some of the factors implied in these, and similar, questions. Fourteen years had elapsed since the initial field work was undertaken, and more than twenty years were to elapse before the second major phase of the continuing Tzintzuntzan research was terminated. Although two decades is a short time in an absolute sense, in anthropological research it represents a relatively long time span. During these years it has been possible to build on the initial base line, to date — often to the year — the appearance of new material items and technological practices, and to learn a great deal about the individuals, their personalities, and the kinds of families from which they come, who were instrumental in the innovative process. Finally, the vital statistics records in Tzintzuntzan are perhaps the best of any peasant community thus far studied.

APPROACHES TO CHANGE

In considering the changes that have come about in Tzintzuntzan during the past twenty years, and how these changes can contribute to an understanding of the rural modernization process in general, it is well to remember that the nature and extent of any significant change in a community results from the complex interplay of two types of phenomena. First, there is the personality of individuals, their view of the conditions that govern life, the ways in which they respond to stimuli, the social forms that structure their relationships among themselves and with the representatives of the wider world, and the basic cultural forms that set the values to which people subscribe. These are psychological, social, and cultural factors. And opposing these there is the ecological environment of the community, the productive methods at its disposal, and the basic support and opportunity provided by such aspects of the national infrastructure as transportation, technical services, credit facilities, schooling, medical facilities, and the like. These are economic and technological factors.

To state the matter in a slightly different way, there are two principal approaches to the study of social and economic change. One is through the individual. It stresses the importance of identifying the innovator, who first begins to do something new, and it follows the spread of innovations from the originators through the community at large. The study of the personal qualities of people, such as ambition, and the need to achieve, is a part of this approach. Degrees of innovation and the urge to achieve are both closely bound to the social forms and values of the people they characterize, and to the cognitive orientation of the members of the group.

The other approach to the study of social and economic change is through national culture. It stresses basic economic and demographic processes, the problems of capital accumulation, industrialization, public administration, and education and social welfare services, all of which impinge on every community. Both approaches must be considered in order to understand how change comes about in peasant villages.

Tzintzuntzeños probably are among the least change-prone people to be found in a country as modern as Mexico. A large part of this inability and reluctance to change is due, as we have seen, to personality and social factors: village culture and society, reflecting a cognitive orientation that views all good things in life as finite, have conspired to produce a personality type which ensured the traditional community's viability. This personality is passive rather than active. The ideal man strives to be like his fellows, to stand out from them in no way, live at their level, share their poverty, avoid accumulating wealth for personal ends, eschew leadership, refuse to actively participate in communal activities other than those associated with ritual.

This personality is ill-adapted to the problems of the modern world which now surround Tzintzuntzan. Yet community life still discourages the development of precisely the type of people who can adjust to and benefit from contemporary conditions. The word "ambition" implies opprobrium, and the individual who exhibits it can expect to be criticized. Those who now accumulate such wealth, as resources and new circumstances permit, continue to be suspect, and they are damned for being egoísta and stingy when they no longer support the mayordomía system. The community still makes it very difficult for a person to be different, to take forward steps, to show foresight, to think and act openly in his own interests. People know that the conditions of life have changed drastically in recent years, yet their traditional mentality and world view forces most of them to try to cope with these new conditions with the behavior forms they know spelled security in earlier generations. Personality, we know from many acculturation studies, is usually the last element in culture to change; that which was a protective mechanism and worked well under static conditions of life becomes a drag and a handicap when adhered to under the new rules.

Yet the reason for Tzintzuntzan's slowness to change cannot be explained solely by the prevailing personality type and traditional social forms. For there are people who are innovation-prone (and they will be discussed in Chapter Fifteen), who like to experiment, to try new ways, who have ideas, and who are anxious to break the shackles of the past. Sometimes the local social factors just mentioned prevent these exceptional people from doing what they would like to do. More often, perhaps, they are unable to realize their innovative potential because of extra-village circumstances, and particularly because there is no fully developed infrastructure to train them and support them in their efforts. Without innovative mentalities, without people with curiosity and a desire to try new ways, change cannot come about. But an innovative personality, to produce change, must be supported by a cultural environment that nurtures its creativity. Without this supporting infrastructure an individual innovative drive is only a potential, as yet unrealized.

251

The way in which the two types of factors — infrastructure and innovation, and creativity and personality — work is illustrated by the two following accounts, one detailing a minor but pleasing success, the other a sad failure. The first deals with nothing more important than cooking a few sweet potatoes. Once I gave Micaela an electric hot plate, thinking it might sometimes be useful when she wanted to cook a single dish. One evening she placed a small pile of sweet potatoes on the kitchen table. "I wonder if they would cook in an enamel pan on the hot plate?" she mused. "The heat ought to rise rapidly through the metal walls of the kettle." Since the traditional way to cook sweet potatoes is in a clay pot over a slow wood fire, this idea represented quite a break with custom. Melecio, her husband, scoffed. "What a caprice! It's clear the air will strike the enamel pan so the heat won't rise, and the potatoes on top will not cook."

"Well, we'll try it simply as an experiment," rejoined Micaela. Then Lola entered the kitchen and, though usually willing to try new ways, she joined her stepfather in his doubts. Micaela looked uncertain, but determinedly continued, "We'll make the experiment!" Then Virginia entered the room and she too joined the scoffers: the air would strike the edges of the pan, the steam would not rise, the potatoes on top would be raw while those on the bottom would stick and burn. In short, it was a hopelessly foolish idea. But Micaela had made up her mind and no amount of opposition would discourage her. And to her delight (and mine, too), the potatoes cooked in much less time than usual, and her family pronounced them perfect. A creative personality had triumphed over the negativism of the tradition-minded.

In the other story an inventor, a near-genius, was denied success because a supporting infrastructure was lacking. Julio Calderón, as a truck driver, learned about mechanics and the operation of diesel engines. Then, as the consequence of an accident, he lost his driver's license. At home, and at loose ends, he began to think of how kerosene might be used to fire pottery kilns. At first he thought of a huge wick, similar to those in kerosene stoves, but this idea he quickly discarded as impractical. Then, thinking of how fuel is vaporized in diesel engines, he hit upon the idea of introducing kerosene into a chamber externally heated, where it would be converted into gas which could be burned in a pipe grid with dozens of tiny holes. By placing the vaporizing chamber beneath the grid, once the burner was going the fuel would automatically vaporize.

By trial and error Julio determined the size of chamber necessary to supply enough gas for a burner in a standard Tzintzuntzan kiln, and similarly, he worked out the size of the jet that gave the best heat. The process of constructing prototypes was long and painful, for he lacked tools and basic materials. He had to use galvanized water pipe, and iron valves, since·heat-resisting materials to handle gases were not available. No small drill would pierce the pipe, so each 1/16 inch jet was improvised by drilling a larger hole, then filing a "v"-shaped notch in one side of a nail, cutting the nail in short lengths, and driving the pieces into the larger holes. To weld and reweld the sections of the burner as the experiment progressed required repeated bus trips to Pátzcuaro. Julio was also faced with the opposition of village potters. Instead of supporting him they criticized him, and tried to have him thrown out of the now abandoned pottery workshop, on the grounds that he had not cooperated in building it. They could see a successful oil burner as benefiting only Julio, and not themselves. Fortunately, however, the National Indian Institute held title to the workshop, and it gave Julio permission to continue his experiments.

The burner worked amazingly well on a kiln-load of bricks the first time it was tried. But defects in design and construction were apparent from this trial. Once ignited, the minimum heat that would keep the burner going was in excess of the very low initial kiln temperature required in firing pottery (as contrasted to bricks, where an initial hot fire is acceptable). This shortcoming could be overcome by using a small wood fire until the pots were warmed to the point where they could take a hotter fire. More serious was the fact that pipes and valves designed for water were not vaportight, and could not stand the high firing temperatures. Joints leaked gas, which ignited, and with each firing flakes of iron broke

253

off inside the pipes of the burner, and little by little the jets became clogged, so that just at the point where the highest temperature was needed, the burner was no longer able to produce it.

Because of friendship obligations toward me, several potters rather reluctantly agreed to help in the delicate task of loading the kiln, and to advise on the technical problems of heat control throughout firing. On one occasion the burner worked almost perfectly, and a number of glazed vessels resulted that were clean, brilliant in color, and tougher (because of higher than normal temperatures) than those which could be produced by wood firing. Moreover, we estimated that the combination of wood for the initial low heat, and kerosene for the major part of the firing, represented about 60 per cent of the fuel cost of wood alone.

Yet Julio, a real inventor, was licked by the lack of a cultural infrastructure that would have permitted him to eliminate the bugs in his invention. I often thought, as I worked with him, how different the outcome would have been had he lived where he could have had access to the knowledge and equipment of an industrialized, urban center. Here he would have had proper tools, places to buy heat-resisting materials, and access to mechanical and engineering advice that would have solved the relatively minor design problems that remained in the apparatus. An innovative mentality of the first order was defeated because it was not supported by the infrastructure we, in industrialized countries, take for granted.

These two stories reveal what I believe to be the key to understanding cultural change, and especially to the strategy of planning change in traditional communities: innovative personalities — like Micaela and Julio — must be identified, aided, and educated, and they must be provided with an environment in which their ambition and desire for change can flourish. It is pointless to try to create ambition in people, an achievement drive, if they cannot simultaneously be provided with the new services and supports their awakened interests demand. But it is equally pointless to try to create a modern infrastructure, with the social, medical, educational, and communication services that make it up, without devoting great attention to the traditional conditions of life, and

254

without trying to help people understand how these conditions have changed, and what their new opportunities are. Creating a modern infrastructure is, above all, a matter of economics and technology. The opening of peoples' minds is, on the other hand, an exercise in applied behavioral science, which requires the best practice in such related fields as community development, social welfare, agricultural extension, public health, and education. Both are essential in a developing nation; neither makes much sense without the other.

CHANGES THAT MUST COME

The developing Mexican infrastructure has very strongly affected Tzintzuntzan during the past twenty years. It can be thought of as the "profile" of new economic, social, and communication influences which increasingly impinge upon the village. To describe it means to list and appraise such factors as school, health services, the Church, the highway, radio, the experience of braceros, and CREFAL's program. These influences, generally good as far as they go, are as yet not sufficient to complete the task of helping change a statically oriented to a dynamically oriented community. Mexico, as a nation, and through its government, must educate the Tzintzuntzeños more effectively than it has done to date, and find ways of giving them access to the knowledge necessary to change their out-of-date view of the world. The terrible intellectual isolation, and the lack of effective two-way communication with what most people still feel to be an unknowable outside world, is only partially solved by the local school, and by the other resources that little by little are coming to the community.

But the responsibility is not all that of a distant government. In the face of the present and future Mexican infrastructure, Tzintzuntzan must produce modified personality types who can see and take advantage of the changed conditions of life, and it must accept extensive reworkings of both its social structure and the system of values that has prevailed for generations. For example, with an emphasis on an individual getting ahead, and no longer feeling that he must divest himself of any economic surplus, social and economic differences will be accentuated. This

255

will be reflected in a new prestige system. Economically successful people may compete with each other with the status symbols
of the city, and the prestige that accrues from participating in
ritual events will come to have only minor significance. In a previously classless society, it is certain that classes will emerge.

Again, with closer ties to the larger national world, opportunity
will be seen in a much wider universe than previously. The most
able people will not try to solve their problems within the village;
they will, most of them, migrate to the cities, thus repeating a
process that has characterized all industrializing countries.

Those who remain behind will have to learn many new things.
They will be forced to learn that capital accumulation, however
modest the scale, and economic foresight, are essential for the
person who wishes to enjoy a higher standard of living; they will
have to accept the fact that the hand-to-mouth approach to life,
without foresight and future planning, which in the past has characterized even those families in which it is not necessary, will not
work. Parents will have to insist on their children's education, in
a way most now do not do. A sense of community responsibility,
and a willingness to stick one's nose into village affairs, and to
assume obligations, must be developed, and people will have to
demand a more competent administration. They must be willing
to do more than criticize when an official abuses his position, or
runs off with the contents of the treasury. They must come to see
that outside change agents with no personal axe to grind are a part
of the modern world, and that their advice and help are essential
in their progress. In a multitude of ways, traditional behavior and
social forms must alter.

With these preliminary remarks we can turn to consider in more
detail the processes of change in Tzintzuntzan, particularly as
exemplified by specific occurrences during the past twenty years.
Our procedure is first to examine the profile of influences which
impinge on the village, and which bring change. Then, in subsequent chapters, we shall consider demographic and economic developments, the structural and ideational modifications in the
prestige system as revealed in religious and social practices, and the
innovative process and the nature of innovators. And finally we

256

shall ask, and speculatively answer, this question: Where does Tzintzuntzan go from here?

Although there are no hard and fast lines, in a general way we can say that two basic kinds of influences impinge upon Tzintzuntzan: formal and informal. By formal influences I mean those which result from government or other institutional planning, and which are directed specifically at the village in one way or another. By informal influences I have in mind a series of phenomena such as radios, tourists, seasonal and permanent migration (i.e., braceros, and urban emigrants), movies, and the like. Most of the latter can be lumped into the category of communication, which by bringing increased contact with the wider world has expanded economic opportunities.

CHURCH AND SCHOOL

The formal influences are relatively few, and not all are recent. The Church, of course, brought about the first major village changes in modern history, when the Tarascan Indians who formed the original population of the village were converted to Christianity. Although for generations the Church has hardly been a force for change, and although it still sees its primary purpose to be the villagers' spiritual welfare, there are signs that it, under the local guidance of a new and vigorous generation of priests, will again take an active part in the community's social and economic development. Father Fuentes provides a new type of model, as compared to the priests of earlier generations. By raising hogs for sale, he exhibits an entrepreneurial spirit quite new in the community. He has organized a savings club among village children, into which they put small sums each week. Thus they are learning thrift habits, and the importance of planning for the future. Catalina Calderón, age nine, now has $30 deposited; she plans to use this money to help finance her university training to become a dentist!

The school, too, has existed for a long time in Tzintzuntzan. Prior to the Revolution it produced, at least among the mestizos, a number of people educated well beyond what one might expect from a three-year curriculum. The literate elderly people of today,

257

and their parents, are the ones whose names appear as registered in school during the last two decades of the nineteenth century. Although school continued in a desultory fashion during the Revolution, the records suggest severe deterioration in the quality of teaching — and, certainly, in the penmanship of the teachers whose records, at one time kept in meticulous and beautiful scripts, become almost illegible in recent years.

But the school, in spite of its limitations, over the years has stimulated at least a few people to think. One evening Micaela asked me if my government sent me to Mexico, as well as other similar people to all parts of the world. When I asked why she thought this might be true, she told how when she was in the third grade — her last year of school — she and several other girls had arrived early, and were studying the map of Mexico which hung on the wall. How did mapmakers know the Gulf of Mexico was where it was shown? The Pacific Ocean? The Rio Grande and the United States? Who, in short, "invented" what is on maps? When the teacher arrived they asked him, and he said *El Gobierno* sends people all over the world. In fact, it has four men. One starts to the north, another to the east, the third to the south, and the last to the west. These men go in a straight line, on trains, on horseback, on foot, and in boats, looking to both sides, taking photographs, writing down notes on what they see, where towns, rivers, and mountains are, and finally they return to Mexico City where they put their information together and then draw maps. Micaela thought perhaps my mission — with notebooks, cameras, and a plethora of questions — was similar.

Until the early 1930's, education was segregated. By 1935 the school had become the "Official Mixed School Eréndira," indicating that coeducation had been achieved. Since the fine school *Dos de Octubre* was inaugurated in 1939, coeducation has always been the rule. In 1945, when the building was still new, I was favorably impressed with the six-year curriculum that prevailed, and the quality of the teachers. When I first revisited it in 1959, the situation was shocking. Over the years the building had been stripped of its equipment: the carpentry and forge tools were gone, desks and benches were broken, window panes were lacking — even the

258

electric light fixtures had been stolen. The flush toilets and showers had long since ceased to function, and falling roof tiles endangered the children's lives. The director of the school was apathetic, obviously thinking only about how to get away from Tzintzuntzan. Children ran wild during classes, and teachers showed little desire to control or educate them. Enrollment had grown only from about 175 to 200 since 1945, in spite of a 50 per cent increase in village population.

The following year a new principal, Don Alejandro Pérez Salas, a mature and dedicated man, was placed in charge. Director Pérez accomplished a great deal, in spite of parental apathy, lack of funds, and a devastated school plant. By 1964 registration rose to 377 (out of 512 children of school age, as determined by a school census), and daily attendance averaged 330, divided between 177 boys and 153 girls. Obviously an able and dedicated teacher can accomplish a great deal, but limitations in budget and plant equipment, and bureaucratic red tape severely handicap even the exceptional man. Nevertheless, it is clear that, of the formal influences in Tzintzuntzan, emphasis on good schools and teaching can and should be by all odds the most important.

HEALTH SERVICES

In the field of health the Mexican Government has taken important steps in recent years. CREFAL introduced a health center in the mid-1950's, which was taken over by the Ministry of Health in 1957. An auxiliary nurse trained to give inoculations, dress wounds and infections, and to keep pre- and postnatal and well-baby clinic records of the physician who came two afternoons a week from Pátzcuaro was placed in charge. At the same time the Ministry vigorously pursued a campaign of building latrines and laying concrete floors, agreeing to match the home owners' financial contributions. About fifty people participated in the latrine program, and a smaller number took advantage of the help with floors. Public baths and washtubs, with hot and cold running water, were installed at about the same time. These services, coupled with the potable water system of the late 1930's, and the relatively easy access to private physicians (for those able to afford

259

them) following completion of the highway, have all been significant in reducing the death rate and in promoting a higher level of general health.

Health services were further implemented in 1963 with the opening of a modern steel-frame prefabricated health center, with a resident trained midwife and assistant to care for a variety of health problems. The Ministry agreed to erect and maintain a five-room building to include hospital beds, delivery room, and consultation rooms, if the village would contribute the land, 2,000 big bricks, two tons of cement, five of lime, six loads of sand, six of gravel, and $5,000. Although there was some opposition to the suggested site, at the back of the main plaza (where villagers had envisioned a modern town hall), most people agreed the Ministry was offering them a bargain, and they made good on their pledge. A minimum quota of $15 was set for each family, and a new trick was tried, which had a good effect: names were posted in the plaza, with amounts of contributions, so everyone could see who was doing his fair share. Some men contributed from $100 to $200, the latter the largest contribution.

Although basic services continue to be pre- and postnatal, and the well-baby clinic, conducted by a physician from Pátzcuaro, the nurse-midwife actually runs the center like a general clinic, sewing up wounds, dressing infections, giving injections, and delivering babies. A year after the center was opened an average of over 300 hypodermic injections a month was being given, nearly a hundred "cures" of all types were administered, and a dozen or more new prenatal cases were registered. In one remarkable two-day period the nurse inoculated more than 600 children against whooping cough, and later she gave several hundred doses of oral polio vaccine — three drops on the tongue, without benefit of sugar lump.

In 1963, a school breakfast was inaugurated to ensure, as much as possible, that children would have at least one nourishing meal a day. The government provides powdered milk, beans, and flour to bake bread, and each child is required to pay ten centavos, a token fee which, however, has the highly important function of placing value on the breakfast.

Although designed for the poorest children in town, the school breakfasts, which are served in a new prefabricated dining room adjacent to the school, has met its greatest opposition among the members of this class. Some children, tasting powdered milk for the first time, spat it out and refused to return. Others of the poorest parents, suspecting some government plot, refused to send their children. So the program is only partially successful among the classes for whom it was designed. On the other hand, more enlightened parents recognize a good thing when they see it, and their already well-fed children are among the most regular in attendance. Director Pérez thinks from 5 to 10 per cent of the children arrive at school each morning on an empty stomach.

OTHER INFLUENCES

From 1953 to about 1958 CREFAL had a significant effect on Tzintzuntzan. Because of its planned scope, because it represents a type of community development approach widespread (and subject to both praise and criticism) in much of the world, and because of the important lessons that can be learned from the experiment, this influence is discussed in a separate chapter (Seventeen). Other "formal" influences are less important than those just discussed. Perhaps increasing attention from politicians in Morelia can be considered as constituting formal influence. Certainly, Tzintzuntzeños must learn that a political franchise should be a basic element in improving their community, even if it can be exercised only on a local scale. The future of political activity in Tzintzuntzan will depend, of course, on extra-village events. The National Indian Institute, by encouraging popular arts and crafts, and the National Museum of Popular Arts, by loans of money and the purchase for sale of merchandise of high quality, have also had some effect on the village, particularly in fomenting pride in local production, and in helping people realize the new economic possibilities in catering to a national and foreign tourist market.

Two types of badly needed formal influence are conspicuous by their absence: the agricultural extension agent, and the *promoter cultural*, the rural social welfare and cultural activities extension agent. The need for the former is especially great. Farmers know that there are now seeds, fertilizers, insecticides, and cultivation techniques that greatly increase production. But they don't know how to acquire the necessary information. About 1935 an extension agent came to Tzintzuntzan. He taught Primo Calderón to compost the manure of his cattle, which Primo has done ever since, to the benefit of his fields. He appears to have been the only agricultural specialist who has ever stopped in town. Primo, Ignacio Estrada, and Gildardo Zaldívar know that there is a Ministry of Agriculture office in Morelia, and that a farmer may be told helpful things if he goes there. Several years ago when his fields were threatened by an unusual insect plague, Gildardo took samples of the bugs to this office, where he was given a sack of insecticide and told where he could buy more. The insecticide was successful but, unfortunately, it turned out to be a bad year for worms, too, so the crop did poorly. About 1935, Gildardo's father bought a bag of chemical fertilizer, and Gildardo thinks it improved crops where applied. However, his father never repeated the experiment.

Ignacio Estrada began using chemical fertilizers on a small scale about 1955. He (and other villagers) learned about it from friends in Santa Cruz, a small mestizo village in the municipio, agriculturally more advanced than Tzintzuntzan. The first year he mixed the fertilizer with earth before applying it, fearing it would burn the plants if applied directly. This so diluted the nutrients that they had little effect. Only subsequently did he learn that it came in the proper strength, and should be applied directly, but there was still uncertainty about the dosage. Then again, he says, he knows that for some conditions insecticides should be combined with the fertilizers, but he doesn't know how to do this. Other farmers have made tentative attempts to use fertilizers, insecticides, and even hybrid seed. But for lack of help, these attempts have been almost entirely unsuccessful. A formal agricultural extension project in Tzintzuntzan would certainly first meet a good deal of apathy among the farmers; still, of all the things to be done at present, this promises most in meeting a basic need of the village.

The informal influences impinging upon Tzintzuntzan fall into a general category of improved communication. The highway in the late 1930's, with frequent bus service, was the first of these influences in recent years, and it is difficult to overestimate the importance of the new mobility for Tzintzuntzeños. Electricity, which came at about the same time, brought the first radios. Until cheap transistor models became available, at first brought by returning braceros but now available everywhere in Mexico, radios were of course limited to houses with electricity. In 1945 that meant 14 per cent or fewer of the homes, the percentage of houses with current. By 1960, 50 per cent of the houses had electricity, and 38 per cent had radios. By 1965, after the flood of transistors, the number of radios had probably doubled. Radios are the principal source of information — and misinformation — about what goes on in the world; they blare forth almost continuously. For potter families that spend a large part of their time working quietly in their patios they are a godsend, since they break the monotony of the work and provide topics of conversation.

The printed word, by contrast, is still a negligible influence on opinion. No one subscribes to a newspaper or a magazine, and the idea of reading for pleasure is almost entirely limited to comic books. In 1964 Benjamín Huetzen began to distribute a few copies each day of "The Voice of Michoacán," the local Morelia newspaper which, with improved roads, has aggressively sought to build circulation, and which sends trucks branching out of the state capital to drop off bundles of papers in each village where there is an agent.

Tzintzuntzan, obviously, has not been neglected by the Mexican Government, nor has it lain beyond the reach of informal influences. As compared to other Mexican peasant communities, it has fared much better than average. A village with a paved road, frequent bus service, potable water, electricity, a telephone, a full primary school, and a health center is not physically isolated from the rest of the country, nor is it without essential elements in an infrastructure that will be very important in its development. Yet in spite of these relatively favorable circumstances, change is a slow and halting phenomenon. The reasons for this apparent paradox will be considered in the following chapters.

CHAPTER THIRTEEN

A Population
Explosion: Causes
and Consequences

BIRTH AND DEATH RATE CHANGES

During the four centuries following Don Vasco de Quiroga's departure, Tzintzuntzan's population was stable, fluctuating around
1,000. A high birth rate was counterbalanced by a high death rate,
and small-scale local immigration seems to have just about balanced emigration. Resources, although limited, were adequate to
meet the simple needs of people who knew no other way of life.
Then, in the mid-1940's, the picture began to change. Slowly at
first, and then faster and faster, the population crept upward. The
1,077 people of 1940 became 1,336 in 1950, and 1,840 in 1960.
Five years later the population was at least 2,200.

In the few years I have studied it — less than a generation —
Tzintzuntzan has doubled in size. This is a frightening fact. There
is one very simple explanation for the recent population explosion: increasingly effective environmental sanitation and medical

services have drastically reduced the death rate, while the birth rate remains very high. Emigration and immigration have had very little effect on population growth during these years. The magnitude of the problem is shown in the following table, based on births and deaths in official records for the five years preceding and following each of the government censuses in 1940, 1950, and 1960:

Decade centered on:	1940	1950	1960
Birth rate per 1000	46.8	50.7	44.1
Death rate per 1000	29.8	16.8	8.7
Net increase per 1000	17.0	33.9	35.4

In other words, because of a drastically reduced death rate the population of Tzintzuntzan is now increasing, through natural increment, more than twice as rapidly as twenty years earlier. The explanation for the mid-point rise in the birth-rate curve is not clear. It is possible that traditional prenatal care, which included abdominal massaging — not to say pummeling — and which produced frequent spontaneous abortions and stillbirths, had by then changed sufficiently to influence the birth rate. Birth records of the 1930's repeatedly show such entries as "born dead, a product of the masculine [feminine] sex." These entries for the most part cease in the early 1940's, about the time the birth rate appears to have begun its rise.

Whatever the uncertainty about the rise in the birth rate around 1950, the reasons for the significant drop during the most recent decade are clear. These years cover the period during which large numbers of men who worked as braceros in the United States were absent. They also cover a period when, thanks to an increase in the use of electricity, people began to stay up later than formerly and when, also, they have had more diversions in the form of radio and once or twice weekly local movies. Contraceptive measures, on the other hand, caused no part of this modest drop. Although one hears occasionally of herbs that produce abortions, their use, if known at all, is certainly rare. It is clear that the teachings of the Church, plus lack of access to knowledge and equipment, have prevented the dissemination of contraceptive practices. Friends often remark how strange it is that in the United States, where people are so wealthy, families are small whereas in Mexico, where people are poor, they are large. A few men have hinted that they know or suspect something about contraceptive devices, but the subject is highly sensitive and little discussed. All married women desire children, but now that most children live to grow up, mothers tell us that they think three or four babies are enough.

A puzzling characteristic of Tzintzuntzan's birth statistics, for which I can offer no explanation, is the long-range numerical superiority of live female over male births. From 1931, the first full year of locally kept statistics, through 1963, a total of 1,112 female and 1,034 male births were recorded, giving a ratio of 107.5 female births to 100 male births. This is just the opposite of the United States, where among the white population male births exceed female births in the approximate ratio of 106 to 100.

PROBLEMS IN MEDICAL TREATMENT

The dramatic drop in Tzintzuntzan's death rate is, as previously pointed out, a consequence of government public health measures, particularly in environmental sanitation and infant immunization, and of much greater use of private medical facilities. Each of these factors works in a way somewhat different from the others: curative services are particularly responsible for the drop in the adult death rate, whereas immunization explains a major part of the drop in the infant and childhood death rates. Both groups benefit about equally from environmental sanitation. The end of World War II brought frequent bus service on hard-surfaced roads, new doctors in Quiroga and Pátzcuaro, more money (mostly from bracero earnings) for medical care, and the first generation of antibiotics, all of which meant means were at hand to save lives formerly lost. Prior to 1945 almost no one consulted a physician. By 1965 many people consulted physicians *if* they felt they could afford it. Medical care was, and is, very expensive for Tzintzuntzan incomes. This means infants and small children have not benefited from the physician's attention as much as adults. A married couple with half a dozen children often will risk large sums of money to save a parent, but to take a newborn child to a doctor usually represents an expense they feel they cannot justify. Hence, the decision to seek medical aid is not lightly made, and it involves economic and social factors foreign to many Americans.

The following example illustrates some of these problems. In August, 1959, Filomena Villalba was delivered of a healthy baby girl, attended by her mother, one of the village's three midwives. Filomena had had no scientific prenatal care, but since this was her sixth child she had not felt the need to consult the public health physician who occasionally visited Tzintzuntzan, and both she and the baby suffered no complications. But two weeks later the baby — Eloísa — awakened with bad diarrhea. Since she had not been baptized, this rite received first attention. Finding godparents, and locating the priest, and then the ceremony itself, took most of the day. By then it was too late to take the baby to Pátzcuaro, and the parents hoped it might be better the next morning. It was worse, obviously very ill. Natalia Paz, its aunt, described it as nearly dead: eyes sunk in, no color, the skull apparently split under the skin. "Never in my life have I seen such a thing," she said. "It looks like it had been dropped on its head, but Filomena says no." Natalia thought the baby was as good as dead, and gave up plans to fire her kiln, so she could attend the wake.

Filomena's husband Francisco, accompanied by his mother, decided to take the baby to a Pátzcuaro doctor, who hospitalized it and ordered plasma injected. But the injection was poorly handled, the needle slipped out of the vein, and the plasma produced a blister under the skin. Since no one except Francisco and his mother were present, the error was not caught until the nursing sister dropped in by chance. She chastised the father for having allowed it to happen. When the doctor returned he reinjected plasma, this time in the baby's foot, and this seemed to work. But in the night the baby cried continually, and at midnight a nursing sister ordered Francisco to take the baby away because it was disturbing the other patients. His protest was to no avail, and he was forced to pay $15 for a taxi ride home at 1 o'clock in the morning.

Next morning he returned to the hospital with the baby, and

was immediately bawled out by the doctor for having left without authorization. By now Francisco was beginning to wonder if he were not in the middle of some horrible nightmare. The doctor gave him medicine to be injected, and told him to return the following day. But by now he was facing opposition from his mother. She felt that the tiny infant had been stuck so many times with hypodermic needles that the cruelest thing in the world was to continue treatment. She also objected to the doctor's instructions to give the baby lots of water, since that treatment went directly against usual village practice. Natalia likewise felt it terribly cruel to stick so many needles in a defenseless baby, and she, too, objected to water. I urged that the doctor's instructions be followed, and she finally agreed that perhaps boiled water would be all right, but not "uncooked" water. Next day the baby was a bit better. But by now the house was without wood for cooking, so Francisco spent the morning gathering wood, rather than keeping his appointment with the doctor. Fortunately this did not slow recovery, and after a couple of more visits, Eloísa was well on the road to recovery. Treatment had cost about $300.

The story illustrates some of the imponderables in medical decision making. When Eloísa fell ill, the family knew if she were taken to Pátzcuaro to a doctor, unknown but obviously significant medical expenses would be involved. The parents and their five older children live on about a hundred pesos a week, from the sale of pottery. This barely suffices for current expenses. If medical costs ran high, the narrow economic security of the family would be seriously threatened. Was it fair to jeopardize the livelihood of the family on the off chance that this new infant, hardly yet a member of the family, might be saved? A great many parents are forced to conclude that it is not fair. Not all Tzintzuntzeños experience the same unpleasant treatment as did Francisco in the hospitals to which they go; many praise the attentions they receive. But this is not an isolated case, and fear of possible humiliation and thoughtless treatment makes some people reluctant to commit themselves to city medical care. And even the person who is most firmly convinced of the ability of doctors finds it disturbing when prescribed treatment diametrically opposes traditional home care. Everything considered, Eloísa's survival was something of a miracle. The family, not surprisingly, gives God the credit.

INCREASING ACCEPTANCE OF SURGERY

In addition to the use of injections and internal medicine prescribed by physicians, a growing number of Tzintzuntzeños now accept surgery. Before about 1950, nobody, or almost nobody, had undergone surgery. Beginning then several people were operated on in Pátzcuaro, and most did not survive, probably because their cases were far advanced and nearly hopeless before they were willing to go to such desperate lengths. In spite of this inauspicious start, during the past fifteen years from forty to fifty Tzintzuntzeños have undergone major surgery, and most have survived. Some surgeons refuse to accept advanced cases which they consider to be almost hopeless, feeling that the probable deaths will adversely affect their reputations as doctors. Although this may look like a heartless attitude not in keeping with the Hippocratic oath, it is likely that in the long run the results will be beneficial, since people will be forced to bring patients to doctors before illnesses reach terminal stages, and while there is still a good chance of successful treatment.

Although some people say they would prefer to die rather than undergo "the knife," it is lack of money rather than lack of confidence that prevents more surgery. Since operations cost from $1,000 to $5,000, including the doctor's fee, hospitalization, and expensive drugs — a year or more of income for most families — it is clear that relatively few people can afford them.

Because patients usually wait a long time before consulting physicians, the average length of hospitalization is much greater than in the United States. Few appendectomies have required less than two weeks of hospitalization, and some have necessitated stays of as much as a month. Thus, long hospitalization and the drastic use of costly drugs raises surgical costs well above what they might be, if people delayed less long in seeking the physician's help. When Virginia Pichu was operated on for a ruptured appendix in 1960 she spent eighteen days in the hospital, and had a bill of about $4,000. These expenses were met by the sale of a cow, a young bull, and three large hogs. Loans from friends aided substantially, and 21 friends and relatives gave gifts totaling $325. Six months later she still had outstanding debts of $800. Had Virginia undergone surgery before her appendix ruptured, it is likely her costs would have been only about half as great.

Physicians and surgeons are not without their rivals, who make use of some of the same remedies they do. Many Tzintzuntzeños consult a Pátzcuaro pharmacist who listens to their recital of symptoms and then prescribes one or another of his medicines. The fact that he charges nothing for his diagnosis is commented upon favorably, in contrast to the costs of visits to doctors. Still other people simply buy penicillin on their own account, which is administered in pharmacies, or injected by any of the several village women who have learned to give hypodermic injections. Often villagers bring antibiotics and other medicines prescribed by physicians to be administered by these women, who thus play an informal but highly important role as medical auxiliaries. Although the relative lack of control over the sale of ethical drugs in Mexico appears lax by United States standards, it must be remembered that there are not yet enough physicians in rural Mexico to meet needs, and that the growing facilities of the Ministries of Health and Social Welfare are not normally available to village people. In spite of abuses, easy access to antibiotics and other modern drugs unquestionably has resulted in a significant saving of life as compared to earlier years. Medical standards are not absolutes; they are a function of the level of development of a particular society.

The folk medical curers — the *curandero* and *curandera* — are not competitors to medical doctors. Of the several practitioners, none is even remotely a full-time specialist, so the economic threat to vested interests sometimes cited as a hurdle in introducing modern medical practices in underdeveloped areas is absent. Curanderos treat people who cannot afford doctors, and they treat children and adults diagnosed as suffering from such things as the evil eye, bilis, dislocations, and emotionally based disorders which medical doctors are thought not to understand. Folk medical practices handicap the physician chiefly in that they often delay the patient's arrival at the hospital until he is critically ill. As a health problem they present a moderately important but rapidly diminishing barrier. Far more people today fail to consult physicians because of economic reasons than because of traditional health beliefs and practices. With rising incomes, with state-subsidized medical services, and with more knowledge about the costs of treatment (generally extremely modest by United States standards), increasing numbers of Tzintzuntzeños will avail themselves of scientific treatment.

IMMUNIZATION GAINS

In contrast to the role of the physician and surgeon in reducing adult deaths, the great improvement in health in infancy and early childhood is due to the immunization against smallpox, whooping cough, diphtheria, scarlet fever, and now polio, that has become a routine government service. The following table shows the numbers of deaths caused by selected diseases reported in each of the three decades we are studying. Since the 1960 population is nearly double that of 1940, the drop is even more dramatic than it appears.

Disease	1940	1950	1960
Gastroenteritis	65	57	27
Bronchial ills	48	39	32
Fevers, all kinds	45	20	6
Whooping cough	16	9	2
Bilis	45	23	13
Agotamiento	36	28	24
Heart	0	4	9
All other causes	66	45	38
Totals	321	225	151

Since only three or four death registrations were accompanied by a medical certificate, the causes given must be interpreted with a good deal of caution. *Agotamiento*, for example, means that the patient, usually but not always 45 years of age or over, wastes away, becoming thinner and thinner, eating less and less, and finally dying. Obviously a great many medical explanations are possible for these deaths. Bilis, though it refers especially to liver and kidney ailments, also includes other glandular and organic malfunctionings. On the other hand, bronchial and gastroenteritic deaths are not hard to identify, whooping cough is obvious, and fevers, although representing different illnesses such as typhoid and general infections, form a not illogical folk category.

With these reservations in mind, several conclusions can be reached. Immunization has eliminated whooping cough completely: the last recorded death was in 1959. No smallpox deaths have occurred for a generation. The great reduction in fevers presumably reflects increased availability of curative medical services and antibiotics. The fact that gastroenteritic illnesses drop relatively little until the last decade indicates that a great reduction in fly population is principally responsible. An increase in the number of latrines in the 1950's is partially responsible for this drop. Another factor appears to be semi-annual DDT antimalarial spraying carried out in the late 1950's and early 1960's by the World Health Organization and the Government of Mexico. Since malaria formerly was present, but was never a great killer here, it looks as if the major benefit of the antimalarial campaign has been not so much the elimination of malaria as the vast reduction in gastroenteritic deaths. A corollary conclusion is that, with the end of this campaign, and without continuing measures to control flies, gastroenteritic deaths will again increase. Fly control through spraying will also be more difficult in the future because new strains more resistant to insecticides have already appeared.

Bronchial deaths, including pneumonia, have dropped relatively less than the others, reflecting the fact that for most such ailments there is no single act, such as immunization or fly control, that can dramatically reduce rates. Health education is of paramount importance here. If all people could be persuaded to sleep on raised beds instead of cold, drafty, dirt floors, a major improvement would follow. Warmer winter clothing, and better care of initial bronchial symptoms would also raise health levels. Considering the elements of nature and custom that conspire against the sufferer from the common cold, the wonder is not that so many people die from its complications, but that so many recover.

The saving of life in infancy and early childhood is producing an increasingly young population. In 1945 only 51 per cent of the population was twenty years of age or less; in 1960 the figure had risen to 63 per cent. Thus, great as the rate of population growth has been during the past twenty years, it may prove small compared to that of the next decade, as this great wave of youth enters the child-bearing years. The present youthful population also explains the phenomenally low current death rate of 8.7 per thousand. Because of the sudden drop in infant and childhood deaths in recent years, people who would previously have been included in current death figures have postponed their appearance until a later date. The mortality curve is thus temporarily distorted, and it will remain so until larger numbers of people who previously died young have reached the advanced ages where medical science is of little avail. We can therefore expect that, in spite of further improvements in health and medical services, the death rate will rise somewhat in future years.

EMIGRATION AND IMMIGRATION

Population movement has had a much smaller effect on the size of Tzintzuntzan than has natural increase through births. Of the 1,231 people reported in the 1945 census, 845, or 70 per cent were still in the village in 1960. In addition, 880 children born since 1945 were counted in 1960, as well as 152 people who had moved to the community from outside. Of the 386 people counted in 1945 who were not present in 1960, 194 had died, and 192 had moved away. With a net loss through emigration of only 40 during this fifteen-year period — the difference between the 192 who moved away and the 152 who moved in — it is apparent that Tzintzuntzan has not yet begun to feel a major pull from urban centers. Nevertheless, although percentages are still small, increasing numbers of emigrants move to cities, and particularly Mexico City (which accounts for 33 of the 192 emigrants), bypassing Pátzcuaro and Morelia on their way.

That is, the familiar "two-step" urbanization pattern reported in much of Latin America, whereby the route is from village to provincial town to national capital, appears poorly developed in Tzin-

273

tzuntzan. Moreover, as compared to urbanizing Africa, India, and perhaps parts of South America, the population flow back and forth between village and city seems relatively slight. When people leave Tzintzuntzan for a town or big city, they usually leave for good, returning, if at all, for short visits at long intervals. Still, these *emigres* do provide an avenue of new information for those who remain at home. When Tzintzuntzeños visit Mexico City they usually stay with city relatives, and the things they bring back — ideas and material items — are those they learn about from these more sophisticated former villagers.

There is some tendency for Tzintzuntzan to lose its most desirable and its least desirable people. Thus, women who have illegitimate children or who take up with men without benefit of clergy frequently leave town, as do murderers and other lesser criminals, such as Gregorio Méndez, who left town with his large family when irregularities were encountered in his records as municipio treasurer. On the other hand, young people who finish all six years of school are much more likely, with or without additional secondary schooling, to seek their fortunes away from the village than are those who have had less schooling. Since 1942, the first year of a graduating class, almost exactly half of these have left Tzintzuntzan. As the quality of primary schooling improves, and as more and more children are able to find places in secondary schools, and thus to prepare themselves better for competition in wider areas, increasing numbers of these very desirable young people will undoubtedly leave town. I suspect that the major reason for the relatively small emigration from Tzintzuntzan to date is that people are so woefully equipped for another life, and understand so little of the wider world, that they simply cannot compete with other Mexicans.

Tzintzuntzan's problems will not be eased by the loss of its best-educated people. On the other hand, local opportunities are so few that it is unreasonable to expect them to remain behind. There are many other places where, with a good education, they can better serve themselves, and the needs of Mexico itself. As yet, the best-educated youngsters have little idea about how they can enter the professional and commercial world which they know exists

274

around them. About the only clear opportunity for advancement lies in attending a State normal school and then going into teaching in rural schools. One of the major challenges facing the Mexican nation is to provide more and better advanced education for its rural peoples, combined with vocational guidance that will enable the brightest young people to make realistic and intelligent choices in their future education.

THE BRACERO EXPERIENCE

More important than urban migration, as an influence for change and economic improvement, has been the temporary migration of braceros to the United States, and especially to California and Texas. Although two men went to *El Norte* shortly before World War I, and about a dozen went in the early 1920's, the major movements to the United States have been in response to a series of Mexican-American treaties, beginning early in World War II, and terminating at the end of 1964, whereby Mexican farm laborers, mostly from central Mexican states classed as "distress" areas because of lack of employment opportunities, were contracted to do field labor. The plan of the bracero program was simple. Each Mexican state government with distressed areas received a number of permits, the total determined by American estimates of its agricultural needs in each year. These were then distributed to the mayors of municipios in the distressed areas. Any farmer could, on payment of $9.60, register himself on the list from which lots were drawn. If he was unlucky, he stood to lose only the registration fee; if lucky, he was supposed to receive the necessary papers permitting him to work in the United States.

Because of higher wages and better working conditions than elsewhere, California was the most popular destination. Lucky permit holders for that state traveled by train or bus to Empalme, near Guaymas, where they waited from a few days to several weeks for processing. When contracted they were taken in buses directly to the farm area where they were to work. In California, during the program's last years, braceros reported hourly wages in the 1.00–1.10 dollar range, from which 1.75 or 2.00 dollars was deducted daily for room and board in dormitory-style accommoda-

275

tions. Men were paid only for the hours worked, and depending on work available these fluctuated rather widely from day to day. Nevertheless, in the two to six months that the average stay lasted, men normally earned far more than they could have earned at home, and this accounts for the extremes to which they were willing to go in order to be contracted. One of my most difficult problems, in the years I have known Tzintzuntzan, has been to convince friends that I do not have the power to obtain bracero or other immigration permits for them. Many, I am sure, feel that I am welching on friendship obligations.

Responsible braceros sent dollar checks to their families to support them during their absence, and to build up capital used to improve houses or buy land. Other braceros seemed to forget their families, and there were cases in which mother and children suffered because of this neglect. Still, and on the whole, wives were pleased when their husbands went to the United States, because of the economic improvement it meant to them. Returning braceros brought from 100 to 300 dollars worth of presents to their families, in the form of clothing, transistor radios, and mechanical gadgets. Including the value of presents, checks sent home by mail, and cash brought at the end of the trip, a man lucky enough to work steadily for six months might clear from 10,000 to 15,000 pesos. Counting those whose contracts were much shorter — forty days was the legal minimum — average earnings were considerably less, perhaps in the 2,000 to 7,000 peso range.

Economic gain was the major factor in wanting to be a bracero, but, especially among the younger men, the opportunity to see the world was also an important motivation. In a rural society that lacks government and private scholarships for foreign travel and study, being a bracero was the only way open to young men to travel far from home and see how life is in another country. Consequently, the hardships and sometimes unfair treatment braceros experienced were usually looked upon as a part of the game. If Tzintzuntzan is a fair sample, the accounts in the United States of bracero abuse and exploitation are greatly exaggerated. Of the scores of returned braceros with whom I have talked, not one has said he would not like to return.

276

The magnitude of this movement is seen in the 1960 census which showed that almost exactly 200 Tzintzuntzan men — 50 per cent of the adult male population — had been in the United States, many of them ten times or more. Adding the years through 1964, when the program was terminated unilaterally by the United States, the figure would be considerably higher. During the 1950's from 50 to 150 men seem to have gone each year. The economic and social consequences of this mass migration are discussed in later chapters.

CHAPTER FOURTEEN

*Economic
Development
Problems*

FACTORS PROMOTING ECONOMIC IMPROVEMENT

Although at first glance Tzintzuntzan appears to have changed little, it is now a much more attractive place in which to live than it was in 1945. Not everyone has improved his position, and in the next chapter we will see that a fourth or more of the people have remained over the years of the study at a bare subsistence level. But apart from this problem group, most people eat better food and wear better clothing than formerly, live in more comfortable and hygienic houses, and purchase luxuries as well as necessities. They spend more on amusements and medical care, they are healthier, live longer, and travel more widely. A much higher percentage of school-age children attend class, and more children complete the full six-year primary course, and go on to secondary school in the neighboring towns. Drinking has declined appreciably, and people express increasing interest in national and international events.

In this chapter we shall examine some of the factors that have brought about these improvements, and particularly how much potential they have to accelerate the tempo of betterment in Tzintzuntzan. That is, has a sound foundation been established which will permit a healthy growth of levels of living in the community, or is the present improvement due to temporary circumstances which will not project into the future? Before attempting to answer this question, we must consider the ways in which higher levels of living can come to a community. They are, of course, varied, and seldom exist in isolation.

In the long run, progress cannot be divorced from increasingly efficient productive techniques, whatever the products may be. But, although economic systems of peasant villages like Tzintzuntzan may look simple, they are in fact rather complex, and there are always additional factors that influence standards of living. New forms of employment, for example, and new occupations may bring added income to the community. A greater demand for village products will raise prices and hence total income, even if productive processes remain unchanged. A stable income in the face of falling prices for purchased commodities also produces the same favorable effect. And, in peasant villages around the world, outside infusions of money and services are becoming increasingly significant in development.

But before examining the ways in which these factors bear upon development in Tzintzuntzan, I wish to emphasize that the economic processes of the village can be understood only as a part of a national and an international system. The model of the "dual economy," in which it is postulated that in developing countries self-contained village economic systems flourish side by side with national economic systems, with few points of contact, does not explain the processes of production, distribution, selling, and buying in Tzintzuntzan. At every point Tzintzuntzan is tied to national, and even international, forces. The value of money, the nature of markets, the prices which villagers pay for manufactured articles, and which they receive for their own products, are determined by extra-local, national circumstances. In economic matters, as in so many other aspects of life, Tzintzuntzeños exercise remarkably little control.

Turning now to specific changes during the past twenty years, the first striking fact is that the basic processes which account for agricultural, fishing, and pottery production have changed remarkably little. Descriptions of how things were done in 1945 fit very well in 1966. In agriculture the steel moldboard plow is now widely used when root-embedded fields must be broken; this is faster and more efficient for this task than the old wooden plow (which continues to be favored for planting and cultivation), and represents some improvement. An extremely limited use of fertilizers and insecticides, the rare hiring of a tractor or a threshing machine, and other tentative experiments such as hybrid maize, probably have affected village production little. Farming methods in general continue to be traditional, and it is hard to see how agricultural production can have increased other than by incorporating a little additional — and very marginal — land on Carichuato Hill, purchased some years ago by the Indigenous Community. In other words, because of population growth, Tzintzuntzan's agricultural position is relatively less good than in earlier times.

The story is the same with fishing. The traditional dugout canoe and chinchorro seines of past generations account for the bulk of production. A few fishermen have learned to jig for black bass using artificial lures; this is an innovation of unknown origin. Yet, if anything, total fish production has fallen rather than risen.

For most potters, the only improvement in productive techniques consists in buying the glaze in pulverized rather than lump form. In the average pottery-making cycle, this represents a saving of half a day of backbreaking work for the wife, but when it is considered as but one of many steps in pottery production, the overall gain in efficiency is slight. It is possible that an increasing market demand for special wares will lead some potters into a more rational productive process, but to date only a few halting steps have been taken in this direction. Traditionally, it will be recalled, potter families engage in *all* productive steps, from gathering clays and firewood to selling the finished pieces. This system precludes specialization, other than that within the family itself: the husband to obtain the clay and wood, the wife to grind glazes on the metate, and to mix the paste, the husband to fire the kiln, and so forth. A few potters now are beginning to buy firewood from woodcutters, finding that it is more profitable to make more vessels than to wander the hills in search of scarce wood. Bernardo Zaldívar has gone an important step further: he limits his pottery activities to painting and glazing, and to firing his kiln. His wife, Concha, is unable to keep up with his need for plates and bowls, so he buys a large part of his produce, in the form of unfired greenware made to his specifications, from several widows and elderly people who are unable to fire alone. Although all his methods are orthodox, this division of labor enables him to produce considerably more fine pottery than would otherwise be possible, and consequently he enjoys a greater income than most other potters. With steady demand for good ware, it is not unlikely that these rationalizing steps will be adopted by other makers of specialty pieces.

It is, however, only in merchandising that we find appreciable gains in efficiency in the pottery industry. The muleteer who in 1945 was still a basic cog in the distribution process disappeared completely during the period 1950–1955, displaced by improved roads with greatly increased truck and bus traffic. Fewer potters than formerly now go to the Friday market in Pátzcuaro and the Sunday market in Quiroga with the sale of their wares as the primary objective. Perhaps as many people make the trip as ever, but purchase of staples at lower prices than those which prevail in the village is now the principal excuse for the outing. To dispose of their wares increasing numbers of potters prefer to sell directly to full-time middlemen in other towns who come with trucks, or to one or more of the fifteen local owners of pottery stands on the highway. This slightly increased division of labor, which leaves the potter with more time to make pots, and which utilizes inherently more economical transportation means, represents the most important improvement in productive efficiency in Tzintzuntzan during the years we are considering. In the overall picture, however, it is a very modest factor.

Nor have new sources of livelihood significantly increased the villager's well-being. Most people continue to earn their livings at the same occupations as in 1945. At that time 13 per cent of the villagers were farmers and 7 per cent were fishermen; in 1960 the percentages were identical. Potters in 1960 represented a percentage point or two less than in 1945, whereas day laborers had increased by the same amount, from 7 per cent to 9 per cent of the family heads. Muleteers, who constituted 5 per cent of family heads in the earlier year, represent the only occupation that has disappeared. In a functional sense these men have been partially replaced by the owners of pottery stands on the highway, and by the few men who deliver pottery and other local arts and crafts by bus and truck to curio stores in tourist centers.

By 1965 there were fifteen of these individuals, all of whom had sales stands, and some of whom also traveled to sell, leaving wives or teenage children in charge when away. In line with the economic independence often accorded women, a third of the stands were owned and managed by wives. This new occupation is the consequence of a growing flood of Mexican and foreign (primarily American) tourists, coupled with a rapidly developing appreciation of the esthetic values of Mexican popular arts. Beginning in 1953, CREFAL teachers brought new paints, glazes, and binders, and began to instruct interested potters in new methods. The immediate influence was slight, and few glazes and designs of that epoch survived. But a number of potters were imbued with the idea of experimenting, and these men learned that it was not necessary to stick to what parents and grandparents had always done. A few of the boldest and most artistic began to make new forms such as fish flower vases, tripod fruit bowls, and large, red-burnished platters.

Then, in 1955, Consuelo Zaldívar set up the first stand on the highway, laying out a few of these new objects on the ground. When tourists stopped to buy, her younger brother Teófilo set up a table, and a few months later Salvador Cuiríz recognized the opportunities in this new mode of merchandising. Presently there were a dozen or more stands, by now simple wooden constructions with shake roofs. An important immediate significance of the stands was that they provided a quick market test for new ware. A potter who developed something a bit different could tell, within a few days, whether it was worth his while to pursue his efforts. Also, the potters quickly learned that people would pay higher prices for unusual pieces that pleased them. As sales grew, and as new local pottery and tule reed products attracted the attention of tourists, stand owners began to go farther afield in search of merchandise, buying in Capula, Santa Fe, Patamban, and other popular arts villages.

Unfortunately, although a number of people have profited significantly, maximum success in exploiting this new occupation is inhibited by lack of knowledge of the ways of the wider world, and by victimization by unscrupulous buyers in the big cities. Salvador Cuiríz receives requests from the United States, from shop owners who as tourists have passed through Tzintzuntzan. He knows how to pack pottery so that it will travel safely, and he knows how to ship it by rail. But he knows nothing about customs brokers, nor how to find their names, nor of routes to the United States, nor of business ethics. Could he trust a broker if he knew one? He wishes he could be sure. So for lack of knowledge, a profitable outlet for Tzintzuntzan pottery is lost.

Adolfo Delgado established contact with a store owner in Mexico City, and made several deliveries, always going personally with his ware. So when, on one occasion, the shopowner pled temporary lack of cash to pay for a large order Adolfo was apprehensive, but not really upset. His "friend," the shopowner, promised to send him a money order in several days. When the money failed to arrive, Adolfo wrote, but received no answer. On his next trip to Mexico City he went to the store, found it was vacant, the owner gone, and no one knew where. Adolfo lost more than $1,500.

STOREKEEPING

As buyers, rather than sellers, no marketing innovations have occurred to favor local people. Local stores continue to sell at somewhat higher prices than the same commodities cost in stores in

Pátzcuaro and Morelia, and the Pátzcuaro public market on Fridays, and to a lesser extent on Sundays and Tuesdays, functions very much as it did in 1945. Tzintzuntzan consumers, like those in other Mexican villages, suffer from the absence of a system of wholesale grocers which would enable small store owners to compete on something like equality with town and city stores. The major grocery and hardware stores in market towns such as Pátzcuaro are both wholesale and retail in nature. That is, they sell across the counter to local customers, and to customers who come to town from surrounding villages. And they also sell in wholesale amounts, at a 10 per cent discount, to the small, capital-shy storekeepers of villages. These, to cover costs of transportation, to pay for their stores (usually a room in their house that opens to the street), and for their profits, must mark up prices 10 to 20 per cent above those of the firms from which they buy. Consequently, villagers put off such purchases as they can until they have occasion to visit Pátzcuaro, to the detriment of the local economy.

Storekeeping in Tzintzuntzan is, at best, only a moderately profitable occupation. The high costs of merchandise, the small quantities in which products are sold, the need to give extensive credit, and the failure of many customers to pay up, makes it a risky business. At most only two or three stores, and possibly only one — information on the subject is very difficult to obtain — can be called successful. The risks in storekeeping are illustrated by the high mortality of selling ventures. Of sixteen stores and bars, large and small, that existed in 1945, only two were still functioning in 1960 under the same ownership. In 1965 there were four stores that could be called good-sized by local standards; four more stores were rather small, and an additional five were *tendejones,* very small operations. All sold alcoholic drinks as well as groceries and some general merchandise.

In addition to these basic emporia, Tzintzuntzan in 1965 boasted four nixtamal mills, two tortilla bakeries, three other bakeries, three butcher shops (none of which sold meat every day), two soft drink and beer stands in the plaza, and a billiard parlor. The major conclusion to be drawn from studying the history of commercial enterprises is that a majority are pretty ephemeral. A person acquires a bit of capital, perhaps as a bracero, decides to try his luck, buys his stock, sells a little, but is unlikely to succeed. Except for the two stores that have been in the same hands over some years, the history of most commercial enterprises bears out the widespread feeling that wealth is not produced by a store, but that, rather, wealth permits someone to afford the luxury of a store. Significantly, and unlike other occupations, storekeeping does not run in families. None of today's storekeepers has inherited a business from his father.

Changes in average price levels, for articles and commodities produced for sale, and for those purchased by villagers for local consumption, tell us something about economic processes, and about changes in standards of living. During the interval between 1945 and 1960–1965 (during the latter years prices were very nearly stable), prices for most locally produced commodities and merchandise rose on the average between 300 per cent and 400 per cent. For example, utilitarian pottery sold wholesale by the unit known as the peso rose from $24 to $80–85. Fish prices climbed relatively more than most other prices, averaging a 400 to 500 per cent increase. A growing population around the lake, increasing Mexican demand for lake fish, and a non-expandable supply account for this gain. Curiously, net and canoe costs only doubled during this period, so that at least in theory, fishermen would appear to have profited by these price rises. Many say, however, that total production has fallen off so they appear to be just about holding their own with respect to total purchasing power.

Since prices of agricultural commodities fluctuate a good deal throughout the year, from a low point just after harvest to a high point just preceding it, it is difficult to compare accurately prices today with those of 1945. For example, in 1961 maize fluctuated from $1.80 to $3.00 per four liters, and beans from $1.50 to $2.50 per liter. Average prices of these crops, plus that of the third staple, wheat, appear to have increased only about 300 per cent in these years. The economics of this increase are not clear. Although domestic animals used in agriculture have risen in price an average of only 200 per cent to 300 per cent, the best lake shore milpas have risen 500 per cent, from $3,000 a hectare in 1945 to $15,000 for the same plot in 1965.

On the average, it seems, price rises for locally produced commodities such as food, housing materials, and the like have neither favored nor prejudiced Tzintzuntzeños. Their increased buying costs are just about offset by increased sales prices. On prices of many commercially manufactured items, however, Tzintzuntzeños have benefited considerably. An increasingly efficient and broad-based national industry, and improved transportation, are producing merchandise whose prices have risen somewhat less rapidly than prices for which the villagers sell their pottery, fish, and tule reed objects. Most clothing costs have risen about 200 to 250 per cent, and necessities such as sugar, light bulbs, metal pails, razor blades, and kerosene have risen only about 200 per cent. Obviously the people of Tzintzuntzan, and those like them in other traditional villages, have profited from Mexican industrialization.

OUTSIDE SOURCES OF AID

In order, however, to account fully for the improvement in living standards in Tzintzuntzan, it is essential to realize the role of outside sources of aid, for in total effect, this category far exceeds all the other factors combined. This aid takes two principal forms: constantly improving Mexican Government services, and bracero earnings. The former are permanent, and constitute the local manifestation of the developing Mexican infrastructure on which national progress is dependent. These services include such things as the paved highway, potable water, electricity, the school, school teachers, the school breakfast plan, the public baths and washtubs, and the new health center with its nurse-midwife and visiting physician. This is an impressive list, a tribute to the growing strength of the Mexican economy.

Bracero earnings, on the other hand, in some ways are more spectacular as a source of improvement in living levels, but they are also an ephemeral source. In 1960 I listed all the new or significantly improved houses of the preceding several years: of a total of forty-two all save one had been paid for out of bracero savings.

In large measure, too, improvements in clothing (as well as changing styles) are a consequence of the bracero program, for personal clothing, and clothing as gifts to friends and relatives, represent by far the largest item in the list of objects brought back. Only one of the village's several trucks and pickups was not acquired by a bracero. A high proportion of radios were brought by braceros, and four or five television sets have been imported in recent years. To have from $5,000 to $15,000 in hand at one time presents even the most progressive Tzintzuntzeños with a dilemma. The large amounts of money brought by braceros would, in other commercially and industrially oriented societies, represent risk capital, to be invested in productive activities. But in Tzintzuntzan, there is only one traditional form of investment: land. Consequently, with very limited land, and intense competition for it, prices are driven to astronomical heights. And most bracero earnings not invested in land are used, as indicated, to build or improve homes, for clothing or radios, and for other consumer goods. Only in the case of the few trucks have bracero earnings been invested in capital goods which themselves contribute to production. This seems to me to be a major tragedy. For lack of knowledge most bracero earnings have contributed little or nothing to the long-term good of the community, simply because there are no productive enterprises about which people know. The process has been a little like that of keeping a sick person looking relatively well by repeated blood transfusions. Once the transfusions cease, the real condition becomes apparent.

Tzintzuntzan's economic transfusions ceased December 31, 1964, when the bracero program was terminated. The immediate effect in 1965 was less than for most other Mexican villages, since Tzintzuntzan was one of the few communities permitted to send workers to California under a special dispensation, because of a critical shortage of harvest hands for certain crops. But in the near future the end of the bracero program is almost certain to cause a major economic (and perhaps social) crisis in Tzintzuntzan, and in the thousands of similar Mexican villages which, over a twenty-year period, have grown accustomed to this outside source of aid. Standards of living will fall, people will eat less well, new clothing will appear more rarely, and home necessities and luxuries will become scarce. Market towns such as Pátzcuaro will suffer as well, since villagers will no longer have the same amounts of cash to spend. Whatever the American justification for ending the program, the consequences will be serious for Tzintzuntzan and other comparable Mexican villages, until the Mexican Government and Mexican industry can take up the slack.

ATTITUDES ON ECONOMIC PROCESSES

It is perhaps worthwhile to examine the extent to which people understand economic processes, as well as the ways in which their attitudes have changed in recent years. As with other aspects of culture, the range of understanding and opinion is greater today than it was twenty years ago. There are those, like Melecio, who still believe poverty reflects the will of God and that, far from resenting his condition, the poor man should accept it happily. One evening the conversation turned to the relative merits of wealth versus poverty. The rich man, said Melecio, can't eat because of his stomach. He told a story of a poor muleteer who entered a country inn, wolfed down a plate of tripe, and then asked for a second. A rich hacienda owner watched him with envy, bemoaning the fact that he could eat only oranges, bananas, and other fruits; the good, simple things in life were denied him. Micaela, the protagonist of progress, said she thinks it's nicer to have money than not to have it.

Melecio then talked of how as a young man he needed only a blanket and the ground for a bed. "I lived for eight years on Mount Zirate," he said, "sleeping under the trees at night." "Huh," replied Micaela, "for that you have your rheumatism you're always complaining about." This stumped Melecio for a moment, but he was not convinced. The rich can't sleep at night, he felt, since they have to lie awake for fear someone will come to rob or to kill them. Melecio, since he has nothing, feared nothing, he insisted, not even death. Micaela was unmoved. "The minute you have a pain you start taking pills of all kinds, looking for remedies," she said. Melecio was nonplused, but not for long. "Well, one has to make the fight," he replied, and everyone laughed.

288

The good old days of real silver money represent for Melecio a time of lost opportunity. "Why then a good meal cost only six centavos, and with a peso or so one had enough to buy anything he wanted." "But how much did you earn in those days?" asked Bernardo Zaldívar. "*Pues*, 25 centavos a day," replied Melecio. "And now you earn 10 pesos a day," said Bernardo. "I tell you, it comes out just the same. I used to get 5 pesos for a kiln load of pottery, with which I bought a fanega of maize, glaze for the next batch of pottery, and food for a week or two. Now I get 100 pesos, and I buy the maize, the glaze, and the food. It comes out just the same." Melecio was unconvinced. The important thing to him was that things used to be very inexpensive, and now they are expensive. The argument reminded me, in reverse, of Sir Boss, in *A Connecticut Yankee in King Arthur's Court*, as he tries to explain to Dowley that a 100 per cent rise in wages is no improvement if prices go up as much or more. For the untutored the relationship between shifting income and expenses is one of the most difficult to learn of all economic lessons.

Bernardo, in fact, thinks that it is perhaps just as well that very little silver finds its way into today's peso coins. "When I used to get 100 pesos in silver, I put it in my piggy bank; I didn't want to use it for anything. Now I say to myself, 'It's only paper, it's not really worth anything,' and I buy beams for the house or spend it in some other way, so I think maybe we live better than we used to." The conversation turned to banks. Melecio, and his neighbor Juan Guillén, expressed the belief that no smart person would put money in a bank, that banks cheated and robbed depositors. Bernardo disagreed. They used to be that way, he said, but today it is different; the Government sees to it that banks are safe, and all employees have to put up a big bond. Still, while standing up for banks, Bernardo says that if he had a thousand pesos or so, why put it in a bank? Why not fix up the house or spend it for something useful? Even Bernardo has only a rudimentary notion of saving in this way for a rainy day.

Grasping what for people in more complex societies seems elemental economics is for village people often difficult. Micaela is one of the most progressive of villagers, but she feels the way the

289

water system is handled and the prices charged are immoral. In 1960 the main pump burned out, because the villager placed in charge of it had not the slightest idea of how to run and service it. For a long time people hauled water themselves, or bought it for $2 a burro load, at a cost of $4 to $8 a week. Even then, of course, a home was on very short rations, and most laundry had to be carried to the springs in Ojo de Agua. Lacking formal authority to assess villagers, town authorities tried (and ultimately succeeded, after some months) to collect on a voluntary basis the $3,000 necessary for repairs. I suggested that it might be better to charge an extra peso a month, on top of the usual $2.40 bill, and thus painlessly collect the amount, rather than causing village strife by the voluntary approach. Micaela was aghast. She, like nearly everyone else in town, would openly oppose any increase in water rates, whatever the prospects of better service. Gildardo Zaldívar, on the other hand, understood the economics very clearly. In Pátzcuaro, he pointed out, water costs $5 a month, but there is almost always water. Much better, he said, for Tzintzuntzeños to pay $5 a month to accumulate repair funds, so that they wouldn't be faced with long dry periods. All the time Micaela was arguing against this logic, she was paying up to $10 a week for a few cans of water. Yet Micaela realizes that under certain conditions time may be money. Most nixtamal mills charge $.25 a *cuarterón* of four liters, but one in the center of town, because of its favorable location, charges $.30. Because of this higher price it is less crowded, and one's wait is shorter. Micaela, when in a hurry, goes there, rather than to her neighborhood mill.

But the time-is-money formula cannot always be worked out in Tzintzuntzan in the same way as in a more complex society. In 1959 Vicente Rendón made use of a threshing machine for the first time; early rains had caught him short, and the ground was too muddy to thresh in the usual fashion, by trampling wheat under the hooves of horses. In an hour and a half the machine, which came to Vicente's door and shot the chaff through the window into an empty bedroom, threshed four loads of wheat of 160 kilos each, for a total cost of $48. I asked how this compared with traditional threshing costs. According to Vicente, at the very least two long days would be needed. Four horses at $3 each a day, two assistants at $5, and their food, for a total of about $50, plus the owner's time, is the way formal cost calculations worked out.

In spite of the obvious cost advantage of the machine, when it is calculated in this way, Vicente did not use it in the following years. He owns two horses, which would probably stand idle if not used, and his son helped him with the threshing at no additional cost. Moreover, he prefers threshing to pottery making, his alternate work. Calculated in this way, the machine is considerably more expensive than the traditional method. Vicente recognizes, however, that for a really big farmer the machine has become essential.

The traditional economy of Tzintzuntzan, like that of all peasant societies, is based on the philosophy of small unit sales, slow turnover, and high markup. Most people still see merchandising in this way. But a few pottery merchants are beginning to appreciate mass merchandising. Alfonso Delgado tells how it finally dawned on him that selling a lot for a small profit is more advantageous than selling a little at higher unit prices. One day he pointed out a tule angel of a size he buys at $.50 to $.60 and for which, in common with the other highway vendors, he asks $1.00. If a person wants only one, or even half a dozen figures, he is reluctant to lower this price. But if a retailer wants two hundred or more, he is glad to supply them at only $.75 each.

Large-scale selling, however, presents the added problem of greater capital needs. The several thousand pesos of capital a merchant requires to buy and deliver merchandise in Mexico, to cover the time until payment is received, and to cover bad debts, is extremely difficult to come by. There is no well-defined source of capital in the village. Unlike peasant communities in India and many other parts of the world, there are no professional money lenders, and since interest is not charged, loans from friends and compadres represent the only possibility of borrowing. But, although friends feel compelled to help in time of sickness or other crises, they do not usually see the obligation as extending to financing commercial enterprises. To use Sol Tax' apt phrase, this is an economy of "Penny Capitalism."

Pottery merchandising is clearly an enterprise in which capital can be profitably invested. It is, in fact, one of very few investment opportunities in Tzintzuntzan. But Tzintzuntzeños do not understand the principle of capital and its uses, and almost no returned braceros, many of whom had the means to start out in pottery merchandising, have set up a pottery stand or a store. People are capitalistically minded, in their approach to solving individual problems, but lacking an understanding of what capital is, how it can be used, and how it builds returns, they spend much money beyond that needed for basic necessities in a haphazard, nonproductive fashion. Cash tends to burn holes in their pockets, and if a door-to-door vendor comes with an attractive gadget when there is a bit of spare cash on hand, many villagers are easy marks. Economic attitudes, and an understanding of economic processes, have changed even less than have economic practices.

We can now approach the question raised at the beginning of this chapter: has a sound foundation been established which will permit a healthy economic growth in the community, permitting continued rises in standards of living? It is clear that a considerable part of present changes is the consequence of bracero earnings, and until a substitute can be found for this lost source of income, the village will suffer. An increasingly affluent national economy, based on efficient industry and rational agriculture in other places, will permit the Mexican Government to step up its support for traditional villages, including Tzintzuntzan. But local resources and local practices cannot themselves significantly increase the level of well-being of the villagers. The ways in which outside and local resources together might be brought to bear on the problem of Tzintzuntzan's development are discussed in Chapter Eighteen.

CHAPTER FIFTEEN

Innovators
and Innovation

IDENTIFYING INNOVATORS

In the final analysis, cultural change, whatever the gross indices used to measure it, consists of the cumulative changes in behavior of the members of a social group. Somebody adopts a new material item, tries a new medical treatment or agricultural practice, or changes a traditional attitude. Others follow, and presently a new cultural fôrm characterizes the community. Innovators, i.e., the first to try new ways in their communities, are therefore a basic key to understanding change. In Tzintzuntzan, as in all other communities, a small percentage of people can be called innovators. Exactly how many cannot be said, for innovators do not form a sharply defined class. Rather, as in the definition of social classes, it is a question of a continuum from one pole to another — in this case, the pole of conservatism to the pole of progressivism — and the precise point at which dividing lines are drawn depends on many factors. With this qualification I suggest that about 5 per cent, or at most 10 per cent, of Tzintzuntzeños can be thought of as innovators.

After the innovators have demonstrated the merit of a new way, however "merit" is seen, as economic advantage, prestige, or some other desired thing, much of the rest of the population then usually follows along, depending, of course, on resources as well as will. Much innovation costs money, and not all families can innovate as much as they would like. This great middle section, neither the leaders, nor the last to change, constitutes perhaps 60 to 70 per cent of the population. Finally, there is a group that appears, over the years, to have changed very little at all. Because of poverty, lack of education, or lack of curiosity and drive, this group seems apathetic toward possible improvements in its way of life. About this group, which constitutes a fourth or somewhat more of the population, I know least of all from first-hand experience. Its members usually make poor informants, they are less receptive than others to an anthropologist's intrusions, and they are less interesting to be with. Nevertheless, as will be seen in the following pages, census and other quantitative data tell us a great deal about the people in this bottom quarter.

In this chapter I am concerned with the differential behavior with respect to change demonstrated by Tzintzuntzeños, and particularly with the characteristics of those who are innovators. Two disparate bodies of data form the principal sources from which generalizations are drawn: (1) my 1960 census, with data on houses and furnishings, occupations, travel experience, literacy, formal education, voting habits, and the like (only heads of families were considered in analyzing these data); (2) an empirically derived list of "innovators." Over the years I have tried to keep track of the first people who have "done anything new." "Anything new" I consider to indicate an innovative spirit.

The kinds of things I have used as indicators include sending a child away to secondary or commercial school, acquiring a sewing machine, a radio, a steel plow, a truck, a nixtamal mill, using chemical fertilizers, insecticides, hybrid seed, a toothbrush, renting a tractor or a threshing machine, developing new pottery tech-

294

niques and styles, and many more. Each time I have learned of an innovation I have filled out an "innovator's" card for the person in question, and as more is learned about his (or her) history, other pertinent data are added. The list currently runs to fifty-four persons; it includes men and women, who are not family heads, and even some who have been dead a good many years. The sample is by no means complete; some people on it probably should not be there, and others who properly belong are certainly missing. Still, the sample is sufficiently large and sufficiently random to tell a good deal about who innovators are, and about some of the characteristics they have in common. It should be noticed that not all people on the list are equally innovative: some show only one or two innovative attempts, and others show half a dozen or more.

CHARACTERISTICS OF INNOVATORS

The first thing that strikes one about this list is that seven of the fifty-four people are not natives of Tzintzuntzan, and an additional twenty-one are members of families whose parents or grandparents came from other communities, i.e., who are not "old" Tzintzuntzan families. By contrast, only twenty-six innovators are from "old" families, and a number of these are innovators only in a rather limited sense. In other words, a bit more than half of the innovators are persons, or members of families, who have moved around, and who are less rooted in a single community than those who, as far back as we can see, have always stayed put. A goodly proportion of innovation in Tzintzuntzan is the result of families who have moved in, bringing new ideas and material items with them, and even more important, the will to change. A person who himself comes from another community — even if it is as close as La Vuelta and the mestizo ranchos of the municipio — or whose immediate ancestors were immigrants, is more apt to innovate than if his ancestors have always been Tzintzuntzeños. Geographical mobility seems to correlate with innovation, a fact that is supported by census data to be given a little later.

The second thing that is noteworthy is the relative infrequency with which potters appear on this list. Only fifteen, or 28 per cent are potters, compared to 55 per cent (of family heads) in the community at large who are potters. Potters, by this measure, are only half as likely to innovate as non-potters. This indication of general potter conservatism is again strikingly borne out by census data.

A third general trend indicated by the list of innovators, for which, however, the quantitative data are not adequate to be expressed as a percentage, is the tendency for the innovative spirit to run in families. Julio Calderón, born in Chucándaro about 1885, was one of the first two men to go to the United States, shortly before World War I, where he remained several years and learned to speak passable English. Upon his return he opened a bakery, and was a successful farmer as well. His son Primo also spent time in the United States, and he has been a progressive farmer showing initiative in various ways, such as composting manure. His wife, Mariquita Servín, is from a progressive family, all members except her leaving the village for wider opportunities. She early acquired a nixtamal mill (her father had the first one in town, about 1926), and she has been among the first to have such home improvements as a kerosene stove, and then a gas stove. Two of their three sons are innovators. Julio showed real genius in developing a gas burner for firing pottery and bricks, and Jesús became a master weaver in the CREFAL cooperative.

Pascual Corral, born in Coenembo, former mayor and for long the school custodian, has always been a leader. His five children all became school teachers, and have otherwise shown unusual characteristics. José Guadalupe Estrada was a leader in his day, and his sons, now past middle age, have all shown exceptional (for Tzintzuntzan) innovative capacities. Micaela, who shows one of the strongest innovative drives in town, is the daughter of an unusual mother, an early sewing machine owner, and a firm believer in literacy and education. In turn, Micaela's daughters show similar interests in new and different ways and things.

Obviously, by no means all innovators come from innovative families, and not all innovative parents have innovative children. But the tendency is marked and, once families with innovative histories are isolated, it is possible to identify quickly a majority of town innovators.

Five Tarascans appear on the list of innovators. Although the number is small, it shows that 9 per cent of the innovators are Tarascans, which is quite close to their 11 per cent of the population. The sample is very small; adding my impressionistic estimates, Tarascans appear on the average to approximate the mestizo population in tendency to innovate. Some of the most noteworthy innovators are Tarascans, on the one hand, and on the other, some of the very poor Tarascans seem to be the least progressive of all villagers.

OCCUPATIONAL DIFFERENCES IN INNOVATIVE TENDENCIES

Turning now to analyze census data, we find that family heads representing the principal occupational groups within the village show significant differences in such things as literacy, schooling, voting habits, quality of homes, and travel patterns. The following table reduces these differences to a percentage or point scale:

Occupation	Averaged rank	Literate	Schooled (percentages)	Voted	Homes	Travel (point scale)
Merchants	1	83	74	83	15.7	1.9
Farmers	2	66	49	75	10.6	1.6
Day laborers	3	68	62	68	6.8	1.6
Fishermen	4	56	44	72	5.9	1.7
Potters	5	53	45	60	7.0	1.0

Each column will be discussed briefly. The average literacy rate for village family heads is 60 per cent. Counting women and children, the literacy figure for the village would be appreciably lower. The meaning of "literacy" is not easily defined in communities like Tzintzuntzan, and the word of each informant as to whether he was literate was taken at face value. True competence ranges from real reading and writing ability to laboriously scratching out a signature. The column headed "Schooled" records the family heads who indicated any formal schooling whatsoever, a crude index, since the possibilities range from one year to a maximum of six years (without going outside of Tzintzuntzan to secondary school, a practice of very recent years only). Literacy is largely but not entirely the product of schooling, as indicated by the literacy percentages, all of which are somewhat higher than schooling percentages. The column headed "Voted" is based on the census question, "Did you vote in the 1958 presidential election?" which took place eighteen months earlier. The columns headed "Homes" and "Travel" are based on a point scale and show degrees of differences and rank order but not percentages. I have previously mentioned the twenty-point scale devised to rank homes on the basis of presence or absence of electricity, water, latrine, raised hearth, raised bed, tile or cement floor, kerosene stove, glass window, painted exterior, radio, sewing machine, electric iron, watch or clock, and a storebought mattress. The figures in the "Homes" column simply show the average number of points for each occupation group out of the total possible of 20. For example, the homes of merchants average 15.7 points, or more than three-fourths of the total possible, whereas those of potters average 7 points, or only a third of the total possible. "Travel" points are based on the question "Have you ever been to Guadalajara?" (220 miles), "Mexico City?" (230 miles), and "United States?" (1,000 to 2,000 miles, depending on destination). By assigning each destination a value of one, any individual may rate from 0 to 3, depending on whether he has visited none or all of the places indicated. Potters, as we see, average visits to only one place, whereas merchants average visits to almost two. Or, stated in another way, merchants travel 90 per cent more than potters, farmers 60 per cent more, day laborers 60 per cent more, and· fishermen 70 per cent more.

If we assume that being literate, being schooled, and having voted, having travelled, and having comfortable homes indicates progressiveness over being illiterate, unschooled, not voting, not travelling, and having minimal homes — and I think this is a reasonable assumption — then it is clear that the members of some occupations show more evidence of general progressiveness than do the members of others, in the rank order in which they are given in the table. Traders and storekeepers are at the top in all five categories, and usually by substantial margins. Farmers are in second place twice and third place three times (counting a tie with day laborers), for an average second place. Day laborers are also in second place twice, but fall to third place overall because in voting habits and home comforts they are in fourth place. Fishermen are in second, third, and fourth places once each, and in last place twice, for an overall rank of fourth. Potters fall in third and fourth places once each, and in fifth place three times, which places them at the bottom of the list, the same rank as that shown by the list of innovators.

Since so much stress is placed on literacy in village developmental programs, it is worth noting that in Tzintzuntzan literacy correlates positively with a series of criteria suggestive of progressive personalities. Not surprisingly, literacy and comfortable homes go together. If homes are divided into five categories ranging from poorest (with no improvements whatsoever) to best, we find that only 31 per cent of family heads in the former category are literate, whereas 95 per cent in the latter category are literate. From half to two-thirds of family heads are literate in the intermediate category.

The story is the same in travel habits. Of the men who have been to all three of the destinations mentioned, 80 per cent are literate, whereas of those who have been to none, only 39 per cent are literate. Those who have been to any two destinations average 65 per cent literate. Another calculation reveals that literate family heads have visited an average of 1.6 places, but illiterate family heads have visited less than .80.

Literate family heads are also much more likely to exercise their franchise. In the 1958 presidential election 72 per cent of them voted, in comparison to only 50 per cent of illiterate heads.

In drawing conclusions from these facts, we are faced with the chicken-or-egg-first puzzle. Does the ability to read and write provide the confidence and knowledge that leads people to vote, to travel, to enter more profitable lines of work, and to live in more comfortable homes? Or, do the personal qualities that drive people to these achievements also explain their literacy? Thirty-four family heads, including some of the most able and interesting men in town, are literate, in spite of lack of formal schooling. Some kind of personal drive led them to master this skill. Other "literates" are in fact functionally illiterate, in spite of schooling, and their education appears to have helped them very little. In general there is no doubt in my mind but that literate family heads on the average are more useful citizens than illiterate heads, and that universal literacy in Tzintzuntzan is a, and probably the, primary need of the village. Thanks to an increasingly good school, this goal appears to be steadily drawing nearer. Of family heads 34 years of age and under, more than two-thirds (69 per cent) are literate, whereas of those fifty years of age and over, only one-third (33 per cent) are literate. Of family heads in the 35–49 years age bracket, 45 per cent are literate. From these figures it is tempting to assume that in less than a generation illiteracy among all except the elderly will be as good as unknown. Unfortunately this will not prove true, and it is likely that literacy may not rise above about 75 per cent for the foreseeable future. In 1964 only 377 out of 512 school-age children were actually registered in school, and daily attendance averaged only 330. In other words, from a fourth to a third of Tzintzuntzan's children are receiving no schooling at all, or at best irregular schooling. Possible reasons for this situation will be discussed later in this chapter.

WHY ARE POTTERS SO CONSERVATIVE?

I wish now to return to what is in many ways the most puzzling thing to emerge from this analysis of innovation: the differential receptivity of the members of the several occupation categories in the village, and particularly the position of potters.

If potters are, in fact, the least progressive people in Tzintzuntzan, can anything beyond a rather low income be adduced to explain it? I think in large measure the answer lies in the nature of the productive process itself, which tends to encourage a cautious personality, one not given to approaching change lightly. The potter, to ensure his narrow economic margin of security, needs to have as high a percentage of sound vessels from each firing of his kiln as is possible. This — producing successful batches of pottery, kiln-load after kiln-load — requires the most meticulous attention to detail, and to tried and proven procedures. At a hundred points in the productive process error or carelessness can lead to disaster. Failure to balance the two clays that go into pottery paste, failure to carefully grind, sift, and thoroughly mix the clays, carelessness in drying green ware, variations from normal firing temperatures, poorly prepared glaze, careless loading of the kiln — at all these points, and at many more, a potter can go astray. But if a potter rigorously follows the techniques that have worked in the past, and if he avoids the temptation to deviate from his usual methods, he can be reasonably sure that his kiln-load of pots will turn out well. Attention to detail, and refusing to vary tested ways, are the best insurance the potter has against a kiln-load of worthless ware. The cautiousness that spells security in pottery making seems to me to reinforce the essential conservatism characterizing villagers at large, making of potters the most reluctant of all people to try new ways and things.

The potter's potential certainty, if he just does things correctly, characterizes no other productive process in the village. The farmer may be just as careful as the potter in sticking to proven traditional methods, but there may be too much or too little rain, worms, other insect plagues, drying winds, or hail. The best farmer in Tzintzuntzan has only a modest control over the success of any harvest; he is at the mercy of forces beyond his control. The same is true of the fisherman. Like the good farmer, the good fisherman is, on the average, the most successful. But the fish come, and the fish go; the lake rises, and the lake falls. Winds may make it unsafe to fish, and other factors beyond the fisherman's control disrupt his most careful plans. Lacking the certainty that is the potter's, it seems likely that farmers and fishermen are forced to be more philosophical in their outlooks on life, and that this philosophical outlook is reflected in less rigid and more innovative personalities.

THE SUBMERGED QUARTER

In the beginning of this chapter it was stated that perhaps a fourth of the population of Tzintzuntzan showed little evidence of ability or willingness to change. This statement was primarily based on the statistical material that has just been presented, but also on impressionistic data. Whatever the measure that is examined, there seems always to be a significant residue of people who do not travel, do not vote, are not literate, and who live in very poor houses. Although the correlation is far from perfect, these people tend to be the same ones on each scale. It is legitimate to speculate as to whether this condition might be relatively temporary, i.e., if with a special outside push, in the form of unusual aid to help them, might they be brought much nearer the level of the other villagers? Or are there more fundamental factors that make it unlikely that the formal and informal influences now at work on the village will have much effect on them? That is, with our present knowledge about how to motivate people, and with presently available Mexican and international resources (as, for example, CREFAL), can these people be helped on other than a near-charity basis?

An absolute answer cannot be given to this question. But evidence suggests that the response of the members of this group to new opportunity, in all its forms, is qualitatively different and quantitatively less than that of the remaining villagers. Let us look at the following five comparisons between home facilities in 1945 and in 1960:

Item	Percentage of homes having it	
	1945	1960
Raised hearth	60 (estimate)	74
Raised bed	58	64
Water tap	21	48
Latrine	19	42
Electricity	14	50

The 74 per cent of homes with a raised hearth is the highest proportion of all items measured, and the 64 per cent of homes with a raised bed is the next highest. Since of all home improvements these are the least expensive, this is not surprising. What is surprising is that, in a fifteen year period when costly items such as electricity, water, hard floors, sewing machines, watches, and radios were coming into general use, and significantly increasing their percentages over 1945, the percentage increase of these two top-ranking items has been very modest. Why have only an additional 6 per cent of home owners adopted the raised bed which, in its simplest form, costs almost nothing? And why has the estimated percentage rise in raised hearths been relatively low? Why aren't the 1960 figures 100 per cent in both cases?

It looks as if there is some kind of psychological or social barrier that makes the bottom fourth of the population relatively immune to the arguments for change that stimulate the other villagers. The innovators, and the followers — nearly three-fourths of the population — will, it can be assumed, adopt new home furnishings and appurtenances (and doubtless new habits, too, in health, agriculture, and thought) as they have the means to do so, and as they acquire the wish to do so. But beyond these three-fourths, change will be extremely slow; there appears to be an imposing threshold of resistance, and the way to aid this bottom fourth to pass over it is not readily apparent. It is because of this group of people that I suspect Tzintzuntzan is still far from the goal of 100 per cent literacy. These are the people, above all, who do not enroll their children in school, or who keep them out to help with home and pottery-making chores. These children will not enjoy the relative advantages experienced by those of more progressive parents.

In a community in which shared poverty is the goal, and in which those who do well divest themselves of their surpluses, the presence of a bottom fourth is hidden, since absolute differences are relatively small. The members of the bottom group do not, presumably, sponsor fiestas and otherwise take an active role in community affairs, but their difference in spirit is not otherwise particularly visible. But when the mayordomía system begins to disappear, when successful families accumulate surpluses, and start to buy prestige objects, significant socio-economic differences evolve. Not only is the range of extremes much greater than formerly, but the differences are now increasingly visible. It becomes more and more difficult to maintain the fiction that "Here we are all equal," when obviously "we" are not. In 1965·most people still repeated the phrase, as if they felt saying it would make it so, but they spoke without real conviction. Formerly people felt bound in some degree to all other villagers, because of

303

their relative, and apparent, homogeneity with respect to wealth and social position. This tie now necessarily weakens, but it is still too early to tell what the implications will be for the structural realignments that inevitably will follow.

PSYCHOLOGICAL STIMULI TO INNOVATION

In studying innovation and culture change, it is important to identify innovators and followers, and to learn something about their characteristics and their behavior in general. It is equally important to know *why* individuals are stimulated to innovation, and to isolate the circumstances, and the motivations, that drive people to try things not previously done or known. The evidence in Tzintzuntzan (and from other peasant communities in general) suggest two primary and related motivations which stimulate people to new ways, and which underlie and cut across all areas of endeavor. These are the desire for economic profit, and the desire to achieve new forms of prestige and status. Other motivations can also be noticed, of which one is particularly important in programs of planned change in which outside change agents must work with villagers: this is the feeling of obligation people hold toward their friends, their belief that they must work with and aid those persons who have shown similar behavior toward them. The "play" motivation, based on simple curiosity, is also important.

With respect to the economic motivation, it is clear that there are few Tzintzuntzeños who, seeing a new opportunity to make money, and knowing how to go about it, will not attempt to change their traditional behavior to reach this goal. The innovative impulse of the profit motivation is particularly well seen in the appearance of new pottery forms, and in the development of a class of middlemen with their highway stands. The proliferation of tule reed figures likewise testifies to the strength of this motivation, as did the ill-fated venture of Lucas Arias (page 352) in acquiring a bus. The profit motivation also explains the eagerness of male villagers to go to the United States as braceros, and it was this urge that overcame their early fear that the program was a device to lure unwary men into American Army trenches. The

304

profit motivation also underlies the emigration of most villagers who go to Mexico City, and less often, to other Mexican urban centers. It explains why Baldomero Zaldívar saved his bracero earnings for several years to acquire a truck to carry his bingo game from fiesta to fiesta, and it explains why other village men bought trucks for local freighting.

Even potters are not immune to the attraction of more income, and most (but not all) productive and artistic innovations of the past generation have been brought about by an increasing tourist demand for interesting pieces. Not only is the tourist market contributing significantly to the innovative process in pottery in Tzintzuntzan, but it is also bringing in its wake major social and economic changes. In 1945 most potters made the same kinds of ware. Some families, of course, specialized in *comal* tortilla griddles, others in the largest sizes of pots and casseroles, and still others in the red-slipped burnished *tinaja* ware, and Natividad Peña made her lovely white glazed table pottery. Yet there were no trade secrets, and everyone knew the basic techniques, and was able to make anything he felt inclined to. Most of the ware was made for domestic consumption in the lake area, and along trade routes into the tierra caliente.

Then the combination of new ideas introduced by CREFAL, and the roadside stands to sell directly to tourists, triggered the feverish experimentation which has now been going on for more than a decade. The first changes were simply in shapes. But in 1957 Teófilo Zaldívar hit upon the most important innovation to date: he suddenly began to produce an unglazed black ware reminiscent of Oaxaca pottery, buying red-slipped burnished ware and blackening it himself. By 1958 four or five potters knew how to make black ware, but the secret was jealously guarded. In 1959 Juan Aparicio proudly showed me his black ware, but refused to tell how it was done. When I asked about oxygen-reduced techniques he looked startled, but insisted he used a mysterious liquid.

The next year the secret was out, and he invited me to see his work. Fired red burnished ware was reheated until translucent, removed from the kiln, and quickly buried in a mixture of saw-

305

dust and horse dung piled beside the kiln. The resulting reduction of oxygen turned the red ware a lustrous black. Although he denies it, most potters believe that Teófilo, on his trading trips to Mexico City, encountered Oaxaca potters with their black ware, and that they explained to him how they did it. Since in their villages (such as Coyotepec, near Oaxaca City) everybody makes this kind of ware, they would not have felt they were divulging a trade secret.

Meanwhile Bernardo Zaldívar began to experiment with a black glaze upon which designs are painted in white. Originally there was no market for this new ware, and Bernardo wondered if it was worthwhile to continue. Then by good fortune the anthropologists Alfonso Caso and Daniel Rubín de la Borbolla, directors of the Mexican Folk Art Museum (also a retail store), visited town, saw Bernardo's work, recognized its artistic merit, and placed an order. This encouraged Bernardo to continue, and over the years he has developed a famous ware, most of which continues to be sold in Mexico City.

When owners of roadside stands brought green glaze ware from Santa Fe, and from Patamban in the Tarascan sierra, local potters quickly noticed its popularity with tourists. With this stimulation Faustino Peña and his nephew Adolfo Peña, and two or three others, began to experiment with copper (which previously they had used in small amounts in the traditional black glaze), to duplicate the Santa Fe and Patamban vessels. Good quality green ware is now produced in Tzintzuntzan, but it still lacks the brilliance of the products of the other villages that have made it for a much longer time. Profit — and not artistic motivations — explain these important innovative steps in Tzintzuntzan pottery styles.

INNOVATION IN CLOTHING

The second primary motivation to change — the desire for prestige — can be seen at work particularly well in the processes whereby traditional clothing forms have been replaced by more modern ones. In men's dress the desire for prestige, or at least the wish not to appear old-fashioned, has led to new garments which are much

one was under 45 years of age. Still, they were not the poorest people, nor the least important ones. They were middle-class men without pretensions, hard-working and responsible, respected by the community, and not mocked for their old-fashioned ways.

Perhaps they are smarter than most, for adopting modern costume entails a good-sized economic sacrifice. Jeans cost $30, and a turndown collar shirt $10 to $15, or around $40 to $45 for the two pieces. Calzones and collarless shirt, on the other hand, can still be had for about $12 each, or $24 for the combination.

In contrast, the shift in women's clothing finds economics abetting style. The traditional costume consisted for generations of a heavy wraparound skirt of hand-loomed black wool many yards long, Subsequently this skirt was supplemented by a lighter machine-woven fulled black wool cloth, and later a tubular red wool skirt called *bayeta* or, if crossed with black stripes, *zagalejo*, became common among mestizo women. In 1945 the latter two constituted "traditional" women's costume. This was an expensive outfit, costing at least $40 a skirt. With petticoats, belt, blouse, and apron, a minimum costume cost at least $60. Mostly because of this cost a great many women had already switched to cotton dresses by 1945. Of a sample of 545 women, 132 wore only dresses, along with shoes. Another 124 wore dresses, but customarily went barefoot. Thus, some of the poorest women in town were partially modern in dress. Another 215 women owned traditional costume and frequently wore it, but only 40 to the exclusion of dresses.

The switch that was well under way in 1945 continues until today, and now no mestiza and only a handful of Tarascan women in the village itself ever appear in indigenous skirts (but many Tarascans in La Vuelta still favor the older garment). Natividad Peña switched about 1952. She says both the expense, and also *la moda* — she was beginning to feel pretty old-fashioned — were responsible. At first she felt practically unclothed, cold, and not properly wrapped in lightweight cotton dresses. But soon she accustomed herself to the new garment, and now she says she wonders how she ever stood the heavy and hot wool skirt. So change in women's clothing, unlike men's, has been toward function and economy, away from expense and discomfort. In

1945, when traditional costume cost about $60, a dress with its accompanying garments cost only about $30. Today the costs are even more favorable to the cotton dress.

In recent years bracero-brought clothing as well as the development of inexpensive Mexican-manufactured garments, available in Pátzcuaro, has further stimulated prestige buying by both men and women. Many local girls, on festive occasions, are attractively clothed in what, if not the last word from Paris, is a far cry indeed from what their mothers wore twenty years ago. Combined with permanent waves and elaborate bouffant hairdos, the contrast is even more startling. Few men yet wear neckties, but a number now own suits which are worn on festive days, and when their owners travel to large cities. Attitudes toward prestige, and the desire not to be classed as old-fashioned will be increasingly effective in bringing about culture change in Tzintzuntzan.

FRIENDSHIP AND CURIOSITY

A third factor which, under certain circumstances, favors change, is the feeling that friendship incurs mutual obligations, so that one favor must be repaid with another. The working of this motivation may be seen particularly clearly in the initial CREFAL program. While Gabriel Ospina had worked as an anthropologist in the village he had made many friends and had done uncounted favors. As a CREFAL professor he was again in a position to aid his friends. Consequently, when he proposed a series of developmental activities early in the CREFAL endeavor, a great many people supported him, not because they were entirely convinced of the value of the programs, but because *Don Gabriel* had asked their support, and they felt obligated to stand by a good friend. Other popular CREFAL professors also were aided in their work by the feelings of obligation to work with friends which they developed among villagers in the early months of their activities.

The feeling of friendship obligations is a motivation that exists in a much narrower range of situations that those of the desire for prestige and economic gain. At the same time, precisely because it acts in such specific situations — for example, when an outside change agent makes friends with local people — if carefully used it can be one of the most useful of devices in the strategy of planning and carrying out developmental programs. If an innovation such as a latrine, a bed, or a hard floor, or the composting of manure has merit, the particular event that first leads an individual to adopt it is of slight significance. Once adopted, and merit perceived, its use is likely to continue. So, whether the initial impulse is the desire for prestige, the perception of monetary gain, or the compulsion to honor friendship obligations, seems of slight importance.

Still another factor promoting change is simple curiosity, the play motivation. Although Tzintzuntzan lacks an inventive tradition, in which this impetus is so important, nonetheless there are people who try new things and new ways simply because they wonder what will happen, or are curious to know if they can achieve a goal they set for themselves. Julio Calderón's experiments with the oil-fired kiln fall in this category: he was not thinking of economic gain, prestige, or obliging his potter friends. He has an inventive frame of mind, and he was working purely to satisfy himself. Micaela's experience in boiling sweet potatoes in an enamel pan over an electric hot plate falls in the same category. When Eusebio Campos tried a hybrid maize in 1964 he was not overlooking the possible economic benefits, but I think even more important as an explanation of his behavior was his insatiable curiosity about new things. He owned the first truck in town many years ago (which he kept only until he tired of it), and he has been the first, or among the first, to try chemical fertilizers, insecticides, to plow with a rented tractor, and to hire a machine to thresh his wheat. He is a person who, like Micaela, "wonders what would happen." The play motivation, though less effective in bringing about change than those previously mentioned, should not be underestimated, and with future better schooling, and wider exposure to new and stimulating ideas, it is logical to expect that increasing numbers of people will try new ways, out of simple curiosity.

310

CHAPTER SIXTEEN

Society
and Religion:
The Changing
Prestige System

CHANGE AS SHIFTING VALUES

Socio-cultural change can be thought of as representing two levels of phenomena. On the one hand, it is exemplified by the abandonment of old and the adoption of new customs, institutions, rituals, and other behavioral forms. These are specific, often concrete traits, which can be seen, heard, or otherwise easily sensed. They can be documented, counted, described, and entered on slips of paper in an ethnographer's note file. At a deeper level, change represents progressive modifications in basic values and in cognitive orientation, and an understanding of the rules and limiting conditions of life that prevail in one's universe. The specific items which an ethnographer notes, therefore, are simply exemplifications of underlying values and processes which, once identified, lead one to recognize the relationships between what at first glance may seem like discrete happenings. Economic, political, religious, social, and other changes should ultimately be seen as conforming to, or expressing, these fundamental processes. These primary values and unities are what we are interested in, for a catalogue of specific changes is in itself meaningful only as it aids us to discover this deeper level of cultural integration.

In Tzintzuntzan the relationship between changes in specific customs and practices, and the underlying shifts in values and cognitive orientation, is nowhere more clearly seen than in society and religion. For here we see most plainly revealed how the old system of values, centering around religious beliefs and practices designed to maintain a feeling of essential equality and community equilibrium, is giving way to a new system of values, mostly secular, which follows that of all urban and industrializing societies, and which inevitably brings in its wake major social changes. Specifically, the new forms relate to the ways in which Tzintzuntzeños view prestige and its acquisition. Since the old prestige system was the keystone that kept the other parts of the peasant community tightly welded together, it is apparent that understanding the changes that are occurring in this system is a major key to comprehending the new Tzintzuntzan. The destruction of the traditional prestige system, whether viewed as cause or consequence of other changes, represents the destruction of the traditional peasant community. It is an essential preliminary to the creation of a new value system and a new cognitive orientation which must develop if Tzintzuntzeños are to make a reasonably effective transition to the modern world.

It will be recalled that in a stable peasant community the accumulation and reinvestment of wealth by one or a few people is viewed as taking from the others their instruments of livelihood, and the shares of Good that are properly theirs. Through the mayordomía system those people who were potential threats were permitted — even forced — periodically to distribute their wealth, in ways which were enjoyed by the entire community, in return for which great prestige was conferred upon them. Obviously, achieving prestige became an end in itself, and people who by no stretch of the imagination were community threats

312

because of accumulated wealth struggled and impoverished themselves in order to be among the elect few. The pursuit of prestige, on the part of people who felt they had the means to achieve it, has always been an important force underlying major areas of behavior. Under the old system, prestige meant, above all, respectability, the right to hold one's head high, to be heard in village meetings, and to give one's children an honorable place in their society.

Until the 1920's there was only the one major way for an individual (and with him, his family) to acquire prestige: spending large sums of money in ritual fashion for "community service." The back of the mayordomía system was broken, apparently rather quickly, toward the end of the third decade of the present century. Of the kenguería complex of seven sets of cargueros, five disappeared at this time. The cargueros of La Soledad were abolished in 1942, through the priest's action, and in 1945, when I first saw the ceremonial system in action, only the cargueros of La Judea functioned full-blown.

NEW PRESTIGE SYMBOLS

Today prestige is beginning to accrue to those people who have the wealth necessary, and the will to use it, to acquire the material symbols that village people believe characterize city people. Although a majority of families still eschew major display, in the fashion dictated by the traditional personality, increasing numbers derive satisfaction from feeling that they are the first, or among the first, to possess new material items, and fear in displaying these items is decreasing.

A few families are frankly competing with each other in acquiring these visible symbols of material welfare, and by showing their familiarity with city ways, and the acquisition of something new by one induces a restlessness in the others not relieved until they, too, possess the desired object. The symbols have to do with houses rather more than with clothing and personal adornment, although the latter are also represented in the list of new items. A radio was the first of these symbols, but this is now so common that it has lost its prestige value, except in portable transistor

313

form. Ten years ago kerosene stoves first appeared, to reign supreme until the first gas stove was installed in 1959. About 1956 the first blenders reached Tzintzuntzan, and they still have enormous prestige value. Miguel Márquez achieved a coup when, returning from the United States in 1964, he brought his wife a new model with a handle. In the twinkling of an eye all older models were rendered obsolete. Shower baths, first stimulated by CREFAL, have some value, although since they are less visible than other symbols, they have been installed in fewer homes than one might expect. Beginning in about 1960 several families built elaborate tombstones in the cemetery, to replace the usual wooden cross; this has become an important form of display, and husbands and fathers dead twenty years or more now suddenly find themselves encased in concrete. Christmas nativity scenes have acquired status as competitive devices, especially attractive since they are encouraged by the priest. With this cachet, few people fear the possible consequences of ostentatious behavior, and families not otherwise engaged in open rivalry have taken to setting up elaborate nacimientos. Initially they seemed inexpensive, but now, with colored lights, expensive figures, and other trimmings, they have become rather costly endeavors. Houses with a second story seem likely to be the next major step in village competition. Because of the cost, real economic superiority is established by this act, and to date, only three families have achieved this goal. In 1963 Glafira Urbina and Antonio Huipe sent out the first New Year's greeting cards, thereby asserting a degree of sophistication in the ways of the city that lies beyond the ken of most villagers.

SACRED TO SECULAR PRESTIGE SYSTEMS

The mayordomía system appears not to have been dealt its death blow by the competition of secular status symbols. Rather, there is a gap of about twenty years between the time when the mayordomías ceased to offer the means to achieve real position, and the time when the new system began to take hold. The contemporary form of the prestige quest, therefore, should be thought of as having come to fill the gap left by the earlier system's disappearance but not as a cause of that disappearance. Since the new standards are based on attitudes and behavior that run in diametrically opposite directions from the old — ostentatiously displaying scarce and expensive items, rather than concealing and deprecating them — it was probably to be expected that it would take twenty years for the first bold souls to screw up their courage to the point of taking the plunge.

Why did the mayordomías collapse at a time when traditional attitudes and values appear to have continued strong? In part the reason seems to have been Church opposition. Informants say earlier priests often failed to cooperate, and sometimes flatly told cargueros that they could not do certain things. This suggests that the priests of forty years ago recognized the economic penalties the old system exacted. It is probable, too, that the dislocations stemming from the Mexican Revolution, and the period of religious oppression in the late 1920's, also played their parts. When a system is under stress, once a basic act is omitted, it is with difficulty that it is reinstated.

The new, secular prestige value system was almost certainly urged along by the first wave of returned braceros, during the period 1945-1950, just about twenty years after most of the kenguería complex collapsed. These men brought back with them wealth which — since it represented the tapping of sources outside the village universe — was not suspect. It was recognized as not having been acquired at the expense of others. It was therefore "safe" wealth. Moreover, it existed in quantities never before paralleled by other forms of safe wealth — buried treasure or gifts from patrons — and its possessors had been tempted, while in the United States, by a variety of material items whose presence they had previously scarcely dreamed of. The material gifts returned braceros brought with them — radios, wristwatches, clothing, and household items — could therefore be displayed with what, in an earlier period, would have seemed reckless abandon. And once displayed, the race had begun. With the traditional shackles removed from the recognition of envy, increasing numbers of people no longer hesitated to acquire those symbols, as much as their means permitted.

315

The shift from one system to another has not been rapid and is, of course, still going on. Or perhaps we should say that the two are partially being reconciled and merged. For ritual expenses now are becoming a device for conspicuous consumption, within the new framework of trying to outdo neighbors, and some people attempt to validate their status by participating in both systems. Other families, however, with the means to do so, are reluctant to acquire or display the available range of prestige items, because of fears, however latent, of the old sanctions. To spend on today's limited mayordomías is their only avenue to modest status. And, last, there are still a good many people who have a strong feeling for the meaning of the old ritual system, and who regret its disappearance. Although they are not willing to support a full-blown mayordomía system, they take pleasure in participating in less costly religious activities. So it seems likely that the conflict in the minds of many people will remain for some years, and a prestige system based only on pure and unbridled competition for material symbols may be a long time in developing.

Paradoxically, it is even possible that modern manifestations of the old system will take on increased importance, although this will be within the framework of new belief patterns. Two reasons lead me to advance this suggestion. First, with the bracero program terminated, Tzintzuntzeños will not have the easy wealth of recent years; it will be much harder for them to acquire material items. Second, village nationalism and a Church policy of creating strong feelings of unity by sharing a common religion and participating in common rituals, may support the continuation of a prestige-through-ritual expenditure pattern. The Church encouragement of nativity scenes in homes, and its giving of prizes for the most elaborate ones, is a straw in the wind.

THE VIRGIN OF GUADALUPE EXAMPLE

The most important manifestation of a continuing village feeling that participating in religious ritual brings prestige is found in the shift in the reasons for assuming a cargueroship in the Chapel of the Virgin of Guadalupe, and the tendency for people who in earlier generations would have been in the kenguería system, to take an active part. It will be remembered that originally men assumed the role of cargueros of the Virgin of Guadalupe in response to a vow, made in time of trial and tribulation (page 207). That is, the carguero asked for a contract with the Virgin: if she would grant his request, he would make great expenditures for her, as proof of his faith and devotion. This act was not looked upon as "service to the community" but simply as the fulfillment of a personal obligation, in the same fashion that undertaking a pilgrimage or lighting candles before a holy image is looked upon as fulfilling a personal obligation not involving or affecting the community at large. A carguero of the Virgin of Guadalupe who craved real prestige had also to divest himself of money by taking an active part in the kenguería system. Thus, the rationale of the two sets of obligations was quite distinct, even though the outward forms — the care of churches and images, and the sponsorship of fiestas — were the same.

The changes in form and function of the cargueros of the Virgin of Guadalupe began early in the 1940's when, presumably because of expenses, the number was increased from three to twelve, with one to be in charge of the chapel for a month each year. Since the Tarascan community of Ojo de Agua had grown up around the chapel during the preceding forty years, it was assumed to be right for the head carguero, the mayordomo, to be a Tarascan, and for several of the cargueros to be from Ojo de Agua.

Some men continue to assume the responsibility of being a carguero in response to a vow, but increasingly they do not do so. Faustino Peña was a carguero in 1957. How did he happen to do so? For many years he had had the custom, as a muleteer, of bringing back fruit from the tierra caliente, just before the fiesta, and selling it on the highway just outside the chapel door. Even after he ceased to be a muleteer he usually made a train and bus trip to buy produce, since it gave him a good excuse to break the rhythm of pottery making. This year he was seated beside his stand when several friends came by and said, "Faustino, we invite you to join us as a carguero — we're still one short." On the spur of the moment, and with no more thought than that, he accepted. "I have a hard time saying no to things like that," he said, by way of justifying his action.

Faustino was in charge of the chapel during February. He paid a local woman to open and close it each day, and to place the candles and copal incense that were required. On the last day of the month he paid $35 for a Mass, and prepared a daylong fiesta with breakfast and dinner for the eleven other cargueros, and their families and friends. Altogether his expenses for this month were $650 — six weeks to two months of income. About three months before the December 12 fiesta the cargueros met to draw up their *miyukwa*, their budget, which they did in traditional fashion by laying out grains of maize as counters. With a band, reed flute *chirimía* players, Mass, decorations, rockets, and food, this came to about $2,000, of which Faustino shouldered a proportionate share. Thus, his expenses for the year exceeded $800. In this he was aided in the customary fashion by relatives, friends, and compadres. Major contributions came from two of his sisters' husbands, his brother, his wife's father, and from two compadres. Smaller contributions came from many others.

More insight into the changing role of this mayordomía can be obtained by considering the twelve cargueros of 1964, their position in the community, and their probable reasons for shouldering the responsibility. The first thing to be noticed is that, although five cargueros either are Tarascan, or offspring of Tarascans but no longer speak the language, or have Tarascan wives, all are from Tzintzuntzan and none is from Ojo de Agua. The Chapel, formerly somewhat peripheral to Tzintzuntzan's religious life, has been drawn into a major role in the community. Four of the twelve cargueros represent the nouveaux riches or newly successful; they come from families without a tradition of supporting the mayordomía system, families which, in their childhood, were lower middle class. Two of these four have become successful pottery merchants, live in very comfortable houses, and are blatant competitors in the race to acquire a maximum of material symbols of city prestige. To them participation as cargueros appears to serve two purposes: they advertise to the world their ability to buy what

318

they need, and still have money left over for a mayordomía; but by spending money on a cargo, they remind more tradition-minded people of their respect for the old system. Thus, within both prestige systems they stand to gain.

A third of these four learned carpentry in the CREFAL cooperative and has become the village's leading cabinet, door, and window maker. Although his skills, and consequently his income, are based on new village developments, he has elected to validate his status in traditional forms. His home is modest, falling in the lower half in comfort and convenience. The fourth is the son of an innovator who has been financially successful with a truck and with farming. The family formerly lived modestly; now it has one of the best homes in town.

A fifth carguero is a young man from one of the families originally from another mestizo community, which never had a tradition of supporting the carguero system. As a bracero and pottery merchant he has done rather well, and in spite of absence of family tradition, he appears to be validating his status, and expressing his personal commitment to village values, in traditional fashion.

Four cargueros come from families which have long histories of supporting the mayordomía system. They appear to accept as natural this form of establishing their place in the community. The tenth carguero is a status seeker, and a pathetic one at that. Illegitimate, from a lower middle-class potter family, he has been to the United States as a bracero, but continues to be in financial straits. He is making a desperate bid for respectability, a bid he can ill afford. For the final two cargueros, there is no immediately apparent reason for their participation.

Examination of lists of cargueros for other recent years shows similar patterns. People who come from families with no tradition of assuming cargos, but who have achieved some material well-being, very often serve the Virgin of Guadalupe. For some this is doubtless a fairly cynical act; it is a relatively inexpensive way to express a nominal commitment to a system of values to which they do not really subscribe, but which they are not prepared totally to disregard. For others, to be a carguero is simply one more conspicuous expense, like a gas stove or a second story on a house, an additional brick in a new status structure. For other newly successful men the act probably reflects a failure to break away from traditional attitudes; ritual obligations are undertaken at the expense of material acquisitions.

MORE EXAMPLES OF RECONCILIATION

Commitment to traditional values, mixed with an appreciation of *la moda* in the prestige quest, is also reflected in the rapidly increasing number of penitents who carry crosses on Good Friday (page 236). Formerly La Soledad Church had but one cross, which sufficed for all penitents, who carried it in turn. Today the number of penitents has increased to the point where three crosses are necessary to meet the demand. Although in theory penitents conceal their identity, in fact today they are generally known. In 1965 one mother, walking arm in arm with an adult son the following morning, proudly described to me how bruised his shoulder had been when he completed the prescribed course. Utilizing religion as a device to compete for prestige within the new framework of values is also shown by the appearance of more and more tombstones in the cemetery and this, in turn, emphasizes the graveyard not only as a focal point for expressing ancient values, but as a potential device for the community to compete with other communities, and particularly with Janitzio.

For many years the candlelight cemetery vigil of All Soul's Night on Janitzio island has been the most famous in all Mexico, drawing tourists in large numbers. The custom, however, is common to the Tarascan region, including Tzintzuntzan. As a consequence of several historical accidents, Tzintzuntzan now finds itself rivalling Janitzio, and it is not at all displeased with this development. During the early 1930's the churchyard was abandoned as a burial ground, on the orders of General Cárdenas, then governor of Michoacán, and the ground was smoothed and planted in grass, so most burial sites were obliterated. A new cemetery was laid out a couple of hundred yards to the southeast, but this was soon bisected by the new paved highway. Moreover, the priest of that period discouraged the candlelight vigil. The combination of obliterated old graves, few new tombs, and clerical opposition had reduced the practice to a low ebb when I first saw it in 1945. With subsequent clerical approval, and with the accumulation of several hundred graves in the new cemetery, there is again impetus for the former custom. When I first again was in Tzintzuntzan on this date, in 1961, after being away sixteen years, I was astonished to see hundreds of people and thousands of candles, and activity in the cemetery from midnight until well after sunrise. The emotional experience of the vigil, in all its details, and the opportunity to express the ties of friendship by food exchange, fills such an important need in the villagers' lives that it seems likely this custom will continue for a long time. Beyond this, tourists are now beginning to come, just as they do to Janitzio, and the favorable remarks they make about the beauty of the scene are very gratifying to most Tzintzuntzeños.

Since 1945 the rituals associated with Christmas, and especially Epiphany, which center around nativity scenes, have increased in importance, primarily because of Father Huacúz, who encouraged the nacimiento custom, plus the prestige which accrues to those who take part.

The growth in importance of these activities seems due to several interlocking factors. For one thing, the rites bring much pleasure and satisfaction to people; it is a happy occasion, lacking the intense emotional overtones, and consequent strain, of Easter. In the home fiestas I have attended on these dates I have been impressed by the feeling of people that things should be done together, that in these simple rites the cohesiveness of the family and friendship circle, and to a lesser extent of the immediate neighborhood (through piñata breaking) are expressed. Again, there is a good deal of artistic creativity in Tzintzuntzan, and the infinite possibilities in nacimientos are a challenge to show what can be done. Selecting the human figures, the animals, the trip to La Vuelta to gather Spanish moss without which no nativity scene is felt to be complete, all provide creative and pleasurable activities. With the decline in some of the other religious activities, the growing importance of Christmas and Epiphany seem to fill the gap that might otherwise be more pronounced.

The competitive aspect of nacimientos is an important motivation for some people, and families that seek to outdo each other in home furnishings and equipment are the ones that have the most elaborate installations. In a society traditionally non-competitive (except in the specialized form of mayordomía sponsorship), an important transitional point has been reached when people will strive openly to win a prize, and the recognition of position that comes with it. Nativity scenes therefore are a significant indicator of changing village attitudes.

Since 1945 one new, important religious observance has developed, that of Christ the King (Cristo Rey), at the end of October. The growing importance of this day is not due to village factors, but rather to its place in the Catholic calendar in Mexico, visibly represented by the new basilica of Cristo Rey on the Hill of Cubilete, in Guanajuato State. The Tzintzuntzan fiesta takes the form of a Corpus Christi procession, from the chapel of the Virgin of Guadalupe to the parish church, in which representatives of the occupational groups, the municipal authorities, and the religious associations march with banners and with huge flower wreaths. In spite of the effort that goes into preparations, and its relative elaborateness, this fiesta seems to me to lack the spontaneity and the organic function of All Soul's Day observances, and the other, older religious activities of the village.

One important new saint has also become familiar to Tzintzuntzeños: the Dominican, San Martín de Porres, who lived in Lima. San Martín's popularity is a testimonial to the power of commercial radio in shaping culture. In the late 1950's he was the subject of a soap opera, and the villagers followed the unfolding of his life with rapt attention. He is the patron of poverty, they learned, and "very miraculous." "He's black," says Doña Andrea Medina, "but not as black as San Benito," the most famous of Negro saints. Today there are few homes without their picture of San Martín, which shows a tall, dark (but not Negroid) saint, with a cat and a mouse peacefully feeding from the same bowl of milk at his feet, a dove and a dog on the floor in front of him, and hospital sick beds in the background. Except for the program based on the life of the condemned murderer Caryl Chessman, no soap opera has attracted as much favorable attention as the history of San Martín.

DEVELOPING CLASS DIFFERENCES

Visible changes in social structure and behavior are less marked than in religious forms. Baptismal, marriage, and funeral rites continue much as they did twenty years earlier. The compadrazgo remains very strong. Nevertheless I have speculated that, as social and economic conditions in Tzintzuntzan become more fluid, and as people have to adjust themselves to new situations more rapidly than formerly, there may be an increasing tendency to rely on informal dyadic ties, to the detriment of compadrazgo relationships. Dyadic ties have, in changing circumstances, advantages not possessed by the compadrazgo. They need no ritual validation to call them into being and, even more important, they can be terminated if they no longer have a role to play. Their flexibility means that two potential partners can test the attractiveness of a relationship, without committing themselves irrevocably, as with the compadrazgo. If the ties prove mutually satisfying, it is quite likely they will be cemented with the compadrazgo. But they may also continue strong without this ritual validation. Over a longer period of time, and with wider and more diverse interests in the village, it seems likely that the compadrazgo will undergo changes, probably in the direction of greater utilization of family members than at present.

The most significant change in village social structure — as yet incipient — is the beginning emergence of feelings of class differences, and the appropriateness of differential behavior depending on one's perception of position within the system. In one sense there have always been class differences. No one has really believed that "Here we are all equal," any more than the American really believes that "We are all middle class." But these traditional differences were hard to spot. I have found one of the most significant indicators to be the fact that some families recognize what may be called a sense of standards, of a right and a wrong way to do things, of behavior that is appropriate and behavior that is inappropriate, whereas other families seem to lack this preoccupation almost entirely. In the former group of families a child found begging for coins from a visitor would have its ears boxed; in the latter families, it would be encouraged to test its luck. Yet these feelings of social superiority held by some people seem not to have determined great differences in most overt behavior, nor were dividing lines in any way sharp. Children from one group married spouses from the other without unusual parental opposition, and courteous and friendly behavior was manifest across these vague, scarcely defined boundaries. The bottom one-fourth was well camouflaged by the strictures on everyone against ostentatious display, so the fiction of equality was not hard to maintain. Moreover, the village did not possess the means to make possible frequent and important changes in relative economic positions.

Today, because of bracero earnings and the development of pottery middlemen, changes in economic position are much more common than they were twenty years ago. Men who in more complex societies would be called lower middle class in origin now find themselves economically at the top. They build good houses, install gas stoves, and buy beds with innerspring mattresses. But against this new background, behavior forms that went unnoticed in their old homes now appear marked by crudities just as surely as the American nouveaux riches betray their backgrounds, however successful they are in acquiring the material symbols of their economic position. Consciousness of economic position, and the need to validate this position by attitudes and behavior, marks these people, but they are uncertain as to what the behavior is that will give them the respectability they crave.

One of the forms their searching takes is a growing feeling about "eligibility" of suitors for daughters. Formerly it was felt that a son-in-law was the result of chance, of forces over which a man had no control. Today some fathers newly entered into the upper economic ranks show anger if they suspect their daughters are interested in poor boys. Silverio Caro was very upset when his daughter eloped with Roberto Herrera, even though Roberto is a temperate, hard-working young man from a solid and scandal-free family. At first he said he would not bless his daughter, and would have nothing to do with the wedding. Subsequently he acquiesced, but he is a man on the way up, and to act the part of the injured father seems appropriate behavior to him.

Another case ended less happily. Laura Zúñiga, the youngest daughter of an economically successful family, eloped with Santos Villalba. Santos, in fact, came from a "good" family. His father had been a respected citizen, and his older brother had served as mayor. He was known to be honest, hard-working, and reliable, and most parents would have felt him to be an excellent match. But Laura's father had had more far-reaching ideas. Was he not, after all, compadre to powerful government officials? His daughter was beautiful, and she knew how to dress. She should not waste herself on a village lad, he felt. She might even, he reasoned, marry a man from the United States.

So when Laura was brought back from a distant town, to which she had been taken for several days, her father took the unprecedented step of taking his daughter back, almost by force, and then instituting legal charges against Santos and the two friends who aided him, on the patently false grounds that his daughter had been taken against her will. The charges remained for several years, but although the young men were worried about the danger, ultimately they came to nothing. Five years later Laura was still unmarried, a beautiful, well-dressed girl who sat in the pottery stand of her family, a victim of what the village felt was the folly and false sense of grandeur of her parents.

NAMES AS STATUS SYMBOLS

Selecting baptismal names has taken on new importance in a changing social setting. Formerly a name was simply a device to identify a new member of society, and a child was given that of a grandparent, of a parent, or of a friend, the selection being made from a long but rather standard list known to everyone. Now, and increasingly, the selection of a name is seen as a way to express personality, or awareness of the modern world. Since names carry no monetary value, anyone is free to select the name he likes. So it is *knowing about* names previously unused which has status value. During recent years a dozen or more names not previously known in the village have made their appearance. Their source is principally radio soap operas, and, as the programs run in cycles, so do the names. A number of new names have also been brought back from the United States by returned braceros.

In 1962 René appeared as a "good guy" in a popular soap opera, and within a year, three young René's were baptized. Deborah, by contrast, was a very wicked woman in the same story. Micaela thought it was fine and funny for her new milk cow to be christened Deborah, but no infant girls have been so baptized. The popular radio *cantante* Yolanda del Valle has started a rash of Yolandas in Tzintzuntzan, and an Elizabeth has appeared, presumably named after the radio singer, Elizabeth San Ramón. Olga is another new name from a soap opera. Lionel has become quite popular, but nobody seems to know its origin. Other new names during recent years are Bárbara, Edith, Georgina, María Enoe, Froylán, and especially María Hortensia. The appearance of Eréndira, the name of a Tarascan princess, reflects growing knowledge of and concern with local history. One Eréndira, whose father is a historically minded school teacher, has a brother Cuauhtémoc, named after the last of the Aztec emperors.

The concern with class differences which are just beginning to come out into the open, and which are being used to justify differences in behavior, based on economic position, will increase in the future as wealth inequalities become even more marked, as advanced schooling gives some young people a great educational advantage over others, and as increased mobility widens the world in which villagers live and work. The groundwork has been laid, and the next twenty years will produce changes no villager yet suspects.

CHAPTER SEVENTEEN

An
Experiment
in Development

THE NEED FOR OUTSIDE AID

Peasant communities like Tzintzuntzan usually do not have the resources, in knowledge, wealth, and productive capacity, to adjust to the new world in which they now find themselves. Although informal influences are extremely important in shaping the changes they are undergoing, formal and planned programs must exert a basic influence in their transformation. Poor peasant villages must draw on the ideological, economic, and technical resources of the countries of which they are a part, and their successful adjustment to new world conditions will depend heavily on the extent of, and the ways in which, these national resources — the products of education, of industry, and of large-scale, efficient farming — can be channelled to them.

Except for agricultural extension services, Tzintzuntzan has been a recipient of the usual kinds of help governments try to supply

327

to their rural areas. A full primary school has functioned since 1939, and, in spite of its shortcomings, it is the completion of these six years of study that makes it possible for more and more scholars to continue with secondary, commercial, and other forms of advanced schooling. The Health Center, opened in 1963, was almost immediately a success, in part because the less elaborate CREFAL and Ministry of Health centers that existed for several years previously had conditioned people to accept this kind of service, and in part because of the good quality of the attentions offered, and the effective personalities of the first nurse-midwives. Tzintzuntzan has also been the recipient of a major international community development program, and it is the history of this experiment in planned change that concerns us in this chapter. The analysis showing its successes and failures tells us a great deal about the strategy that should guide directed change programs in peasant villages.

FORM AND PHILOSOPHY OF CREFAL

CREFAL (Centro Regional de Educación Fundamental para la América Latina) was established in 1951 in Pátzcuaro, on the grounds of the Quinta Eréndira, an estate that former President Lázaro Cárdenas donated to the program. CREFAL was (and is) sponsored by the United Nations, through UNESCO, and by the Government of Mexico. As suggested by its title — Regional Center for Fundamental Education in Latin America — CREFAL is designed as an international center to train Latin American personnel to work in national programs of community development. Its philosophy has been similar to that of most other community development programs. Briefly, it is assumed (erroneously, I believe) that rural communities encapsulate the basic morality and fundamental virtues of a society, chief among which is a cooperative basis for village life, which stands in contrast to the competitive and individualistic philosophy of urban dwellers. Unfortunately, it is hypothesized, because these communities have increasingly been left behind by a changing world, as well as having been exploited for generations by city dwellers, this natural

328

cooperative tendency is often inhibited. The way to release this
latent natural force, and to utilize it constructively in improving
community life, is therefore to send skilled change agents — cata-
lysts is the term frequently used — who can stimulate villagers to
identify their "felt needs" and who can aid them in mobilizing
their own resources to work collectively toward fulfilling these
needs. These change agents, usually called by some variant of the
expression "village level worker," from their knowledge of people
and communities will aid in coordinating the other formal programs of government, especially in agriculture, health, and social
welfare. Successful community development work is usually seen
as embracing a combination of "community organization" — building new forms of organizations suited to action, and strengthening
existing organizations — and simultaneously improving production
methods and techniques to raise the general standard of living.

CREFAL, in word and deed, conformed during the period of
the study to this general philosophy. It was planned as a training
center, to prepare skilled personnel to work in this field, and the
development activities undertaken in about twenty villages around
the lake were always seen as a byproduct, albeit an important one,
of the training process. These villages served as field laboratories,
where students gained experience, and where community development methods were tested. The village laboratories presented a
dilemma which was never entirely resolved. Although ostensibly
they were used primarily for training, CREFAL needed "developed" villages as evidence of the validity of its philosophy and
methods, and as showcases to which visitors could be taken. Therefore, several villages received intensive attention that went a good
deal beyond the student training level, in the hope that they would
become models of how traditional peasant life can be transformed.
For various reasons Tzintzuntzan was selected as one of these villages. Since Professor Ospina, one of the original CREFAL staff
members, had lived in the community for over a year, more was
known about its people and culture than about any of the other
villages. Since it lay on the paved highway only twenty minutes
from CREFAL, it was also easy to reach, an advantage both for

329

CREFAL personnel and for taking visitors to a showcase. And because of its former greatness, as capital of the Tarascan Indian Empire, sentimental and nationalistic reasons also drew attention to it. For these, and other reasons, the selection of Tzintzuntzan was eminently logical.

CREFAL BEGINS IN TZINTZUNTZAN

Work began in January, 1953, when Professor Ospina, accompanied by a pottery expert and a popular arts professor, met informally with his old friends. They talked about former times, and then Professor Ospina suggested that perhaps Tzintzuntzeños, aided by CREFAL, might work together to solve some of their social and economic problems. At a general town meeting several days later, Professor Ospina explained the program of CREFAL, and exhorted the villagers to think of what they could do through their cooperative efforts. In the report on the first year's activities in Tzintzuntzan one reads that all the projects were designed "to extirpate, little by little, the individualism [of the villagers], at the same time strengthening the philosophy of cooperative work." Concretely, Professor Ospina suggested that a "Commission of Progress" be organized as the instrument for action, and members were designated to represent the several occupations of the village: farmers, potters, fishermen, artisans, embroiderers, school teachers, the Indigenous Community, and the municipal government. A large and centrally located house was offered by its owner as headquarters, and it was reconditioned by cooperative labor and named Casa de la Cultura ("House of Culture"). At the end of a year, the owner repossessed his house, with all of its improvements, thereby confirming the general view that those who participated in cooperative efforts were likely to benefit others rather than themselves.

In 1953 an agreement was signed with the National Indian Institute to provide money and technical aid in improving traditional arts and crafts and, in fact, the Institute built and paid for the pottery cooperative workshop on the grounds of La Concepción chapel. In the economic field five major areas of endeavor quickly took shape:

330

1. Improvements in pottery techniques, and the introduction of cooperative working methods.

2. The development of a weaving cooperative, using modern hand-operated looms.

3. The establishment of a small factory to make furniture of a type already made and sold in other Michoacán villages.

4. The introduction of chicken ranching.

5. The formalizing of embroidery work, already done by a few village women, in a new embroidery cooperative.

In the cultural field a series of projects were undertaken. The first was an effort to enclose the cemetery, on the south side of the village; this, presumably, was of interest to all villagers, and it coincided nicely with the CREFAL desire to have a physically attractive community. For the same reason the institution of "Clean Saturdays" was introduced. People were asked to clean their patios, and the streets in front of their houses, each Saturday. The Commission worked on this for twenty-five consecutive Saturdays and then, assuming the habit was fixed, stopped. Not surprisingly, most villagers quickly slipped back into their old custom of sweeping when they felt like it.

The Commission also bought whitewash at wholesale prices, and a good many people, particularly those in the center of town, were persuaded to paint their houses. Cobbling the main village streets and building stone sidewalks was also a part of the program, and these improvements turned out to be among the most lasting of this epoch. One of the major initial stimulants for cleaning the village, whitewashing walls, and cobbling streets, was the desire to impress visitors who came for the Señor del Rescate fiesta. The signs one still sees marking street names were also put up at this time.

Other early plans — of CREFAL rather than the village itself — included training local "cultural promoters" (auxiliary village level workers), organizing a community store for the sale of arts and crafts, and to serve as a consumers' cooperative, developing home economics programs, and establishing "Happy Sundays" when the band would play in the plaza and villagers would disport themselves in folk dances and other similarly joyful activities.

These goals were never realized, because after an initial enthusiasm it was very difficult to persuade people to continue to participate. Some members of the Commission resigned, and a small *Junta Directiva*, or Board of Directors, was named to foment action. It is reported that most heads of families and young unmarried men, over three hundred in all, volunteered to contribute three hours of work a week on village projects. These "cultural" projects did not outlast the first year, because they did not, in fact, really reflect village desires, but rather the kind of programs CREFAL personnel felt should characterize a developing village. Subsequently, and realistically, the CREFAL program concentrated on economic activities. Each of these will be described in turn. The accounts are those of the villagers (amplified in some instances by my own observations), and substantiated by such documents as still remained in Tzintzuntzan. I wish especially to emphasize that I am not, in any sense, evaluating the larger CREFAL program which has been much more successful in villages other than Tzintzuntzan. Rather, I am describing the reaction of villagers to a technical program as they themselves have seen and evaluated it, to which I add my own appraisal of the experiment.

THE POTTERY PROJECTS

In the pottery program, work began on the cooperative workshop almost as soon as CREFAL came to Tzintzuntzan. The plan was to build a model workshop where potters, working together, and utilizing machinery, and better glazes, molds, and kilns, would be able to produce a better quality ware than formerly that would command higher prices and reach more distant markets. Potters say they were told they would be able to earn, by working collectively, $30 a day. "I thought to myself," said Bernardo Zaldívar, "that's 180 pesos a week. Of course we wanted to work!" Initially it had been planned to construct the workshop by voluntary contributions of time, but the work went so slowly that it was necessary to pay those who came from $3 to $5 a day. "But who can live on that," added Bernardo, who began to be disillusioned early in the game. In spite of discouraging setbacks, the workshop was completed, chalk molds arrived, kilns of semirefractory brick were built, machines to grind clays were installed, and a truck was rented to haul earth.

By this time a good many potters were participating only in a rather nominal sense, but some stuck it out, and a good deal of experimental work was carried out, some of which showed good results. Nevertheless there were problems, the chief of which seems to have been that the potters didn't really understand how and why things were done. Luciano Villagomez, who kept the records of the members, the amount of time they worked, and the sums they were advanced, says that no one ever understood costs, how the debt was funded, or why certain new materials could be combined and others not. The potters were told to do certain things, he says, but rarely was an explanation adequate for their understanding. After a couple of years it became apparent that the cooperative method was not going to work, and the workshop was abandoned.

The next approach was on an individual basis. Five able potters were asked to accept a credit of $5,000 to $6,000 each to enable them to build good family workshops with semirefractory brick kilns of traditional form, but fired with kerosene burners, to acquire electric wheels which, with a template, would give more uniform vessels (which, however, were to continue to be made in molds), and otherwise to modernize their operations. Luciano Villagomez, Ambrosio Zaldívar, Guillermo Morales, and Eleuterio Melchor accepted. Bernardo Zaldívar refused. "Look, Gabriel," he quotes himself as saying, "I've lost 1,135 pesos on my chicken project. I want to be your friend, so don't ask me to borrow money for the kiln." He had, in fact, tried the chicken ranching scheme, but had lost most of his birds in a very cold winter, and had come to be skeptical of guided change.

The history of the individual operations duplicates that of the cooperative. Luciano says that each time a new piece of equipment arrived at his home he was asked to sign, but he had no idea of true costs, nor of how his debt was mounting. When he expressed uneasiness, he was assured that "once production is under way" his debts could be easily paid off. The four men themselves failed to work well together. Ambrosio and Luciano aided Guillermo in building his new kiln, with the understanding they in return would receive similar help. But then Guillermo lost interest in the others. "But it was useful," says Ambrosio, "since I learned how to do it." Then Ambrosio helped his compadre Luciano build his kiln, but Luciano then refused to help Ambrosio. So Ambrosio ended up building his own kiln, alone. Ambrosio, who is illiterate, repeats Luciano's account of the debt: he was always asked to make a mark when equipment arrived, but he never in the least understood the principle of the credit.

In spite of these problems, the project might have succeeded if the power-driven kerosene burner had worked out. By means of a fan, the fuel was blown into the firebox in tiny droplets, which ignited as an explosive torch. As a consequence, it proved impossible to control the heat and to distribute it evenly in all parts of the kiln. So, on the few occasions the potters tried it, part of their production was overfired, some was smoke-blackened, some was underfired, and only a small portion was satisfactory. Luciano says he fired alone the first time, following instructions he had received, and that only a third of his pottery was salable. The CREFAL instructor came the second time, but this time the grate collapsed and the entire load of pottery, worth about $200, was a total loss. The instructor asked him not to mention this setback to the others, lest they lose their enthusiasm. So Luciano carted off his potsherds, rebuilt his grate — and returned to firing with wood.

Ambrosio says the teacher came only once when he was trying to get his burner to function. The story of inadequate supervision at the critical juncture in the experiment, and a piece of equipment not yet perfected, is the same with the other two potters. After these half-hearted experiments, the potters returned to traditional methods. But by 1957 all four were saddled with individual debts of more than $6,000, and this greatly worried them, since the money represented up to two years of gross income.

Luciano says a man came from Pátzcuaro who represented himself as a "judge" who intended to attach his house for the debt. Fortunately Luciano had never bothered to reregister the house in his own name after his father had died, and he thinks (probably erroneously) that for this reason the "judge" could do him no harm. Still, he was badly frightened. CREFAL personnel also put pressure on him, telling him he had "to struggle" to pay off his debt, and that he was a *sinvergüenza*, a shameless one, because he refused to do so. About 1960 a lawyer came from Morelia to look over his workshop, and again he was terrified. But Luciano quotes the stranger as saying, "Don't be frightened. I haven't come to hurt you. What has happened here is not your fault; it is the fault of the people who wanted to help you but who didn't know how." The lawyer probably was from the Banco Nacional de Fomento Cooperativo that had underwritten the loan, come to see if anything were salvageable.

THE WEAVING AND CARPENTRY COOPERATIVE

Work in the weaving cooperative, in association with the carpentry cooperative, also began in 1953. Six young men picked by Professor Ospina were taught to weave the first year by the CREFAL popular arts professor. Unlike pottery, work in weaving was a great technical success. Within three to six months youths who had never seen a loom had become competent in all aspects of the work save the highly technical counting of warp threads to determine design. This was never really mastered by any weaver. But with the number of design motifs they learned, in many combinations, and in many colors, an almost unlimited number of design possibilities existed. Miguel Márquez became such a skilled weaver that, in 1958, he was sent for six months by the International Labor Organization to San Sebastián, a village of traditional weavers in El Salvador, to try to help the people improve their weaving techniques. He found the people very resistant to change, and felt that it was much easier to teach people a new craft about which they know nothing at all, since they don't have to forget the old ways before beginning with the new.

Not only did the Tzintzuntzan weavers learn quickly but, again unlike the pottery experiment, the work was highly remunerative. Wages were set by the CREFAL professor at $7.50 a meter of wide cloth, and $4 a meter of narrow cloth. Some weavers, under pressure, earned as much as $100 a day! This was not all pure gain, since several payless days were required to set up the loom, but even allowing for this, the income was fantastic by local standards. But this very financial success was a major factor in the project's ultimate failure: Tzintzuntzan cloth was not competitive with similar materials woven in other Mexican centers, including Pátzcuaro and Erongarícuaro. In order to cover costs of production, prices were set at $15 to $25 a meter, about twice that of competitive goods. At first this caused few problems. Once the weaving was successfully under way, CREFAL indeed had a showcase project, and hundreds of visitors and tourists came to Tzintzuntzan. Many bought cloth, willing to pay the high prices because of their interest in the work and the project. During the final seven months of 1957, the high point of the experiment, $26,000 worth of cloth was sold, and the four most active weavers each received from $2,700 to $4,500 for their work. But no provision was made for formally marketing produce. Sales depended on tourists who stopped on their way to Pátzcuaro, and on visitors taken to see the workshop by CREFAL personnel. The very able professor who was responsible for the technical success of the project, and who accounted for most of the sales as well, left at the end of 1957. No one replaced him. Meanwhile, the weavers continued to turn out hundreds of meters of fine cloth, most of which piled up to overflowing in the workshop. The following year, 1958, sales totaled scarcely $5,000, and the next year the work was discontinued, except for an occasional order of white cloth from Micaela González for her embroideries.

The carpentry cooperative, which in fact with the weaving cooperative was a single institution, was, like its partner, a technological success but a financial failure. It began with an initial $1,700 loan from CREFAL, supervised by the same professor who directed the weaving. With these funds, basic tools and a small amount of lumber were purchased. Jesús Huipe was picked to be local supervisor, and he in turn chose five young men, only one of whom knew anything about woodworking. For the first three months all worked without salary, practicing by rebuilding the

House of Culture. Then they obtained an unused motor from the school, and CREFAL provided a circular saw and a lathe. This permitted them to make doors, chairs, and tables for local consumption, and to earn very modest salaries. Later about $7,000 was invested in material and labor to fit out a new workshop. Furniture, some of excellent quality, was now the principal product, but sales were on the same chance basis as characterized the woven goods.

Then in 1956 it was decided to add the woven palm work that characterizes a good deal of popular Mexican furniture, and an outside specialist came to teach the local people. Six youths were hired initially, and when the product sold amazingly well, five more joined in. The next eighteen months represented the high point of the carpentry work: nine woodworkers and eight palm weavers worked long hours, earning the generally good salary of $10 to $15 a day. In the final seven months of 1957, sales totalled $52,000. On one notable day the CREFAL professor brought guests who purchased $5,000 worth of furniture. Then the professor left, and few CREFAL visitors came to buy. Since the local people had been taught nothing about marketing, they had no idea what to do, and since their basic wage rates had been set a little above that of men doing similar work in nearby villages, their product — technically as good as any in the state — was not really competitive with other furniture sold through pre-existing commercial outlets. Furniture piled up and, after credits were exhausted and it was no longer possible to pay salaries, the workers drifted off to other jobs. During the first eight months of 1959, less than $5,000 of merchandise was sold, and subsequent to that year, sales fell to zero.

Meanwhile, by the end of 1958 the debt of the joint cooperative with the Banco Nacional de Fomento Cooperativo had risen to $136,000, at which point, to no one's surprise, all credit was cancelled. Added to the approximately $30,000 owed by the four potters, and the heavy investment of the National Indian Institute in the pottery workshop, the direct expenditures to foment increased production in Tzintzuntzan reached a sizable figure.

The chicken-ranching program, unlike those just described, was financed directly, and at relatively small cost, by CREFAL. Money was loaned for constructing small, simple chicken houses, to provide at cost the chicks that would become laying hens, to buy, mix, and distribute feed, and to vaccinate the birds. CREFAL then collected and marketed the eggs, crediting the sales price against the individual loans, and then paying the balance to the individuals concerned. On the island of La Pacanda a similar program has been highly successful, and has literally revolutionized life (Smith 1961). CREFAL also has had notable success with this scheme in Erongarícuaro, and to a lesser degree in other lake villages.

In Tzintzuntzan, for various reasons, the program was less successful. Six people, including Micaela González, borrowed money for 125-bird projects. At first, there proved to be no serious technical difficulties, and shortly the henhouses were in operation, skillfully supervised by an able teacher. People were delighted with the initial results, and it looked as if chickens and eggs might go far in solving the village's economic problems. But almost from the first the participants compained that the CREFAL students shortweighed the eggs they came to collect, and that it was impossible to draw out their profits from CREFAL, which was holding them to expand the scale of operations. Then during a cold and wet winter many birds died. Bernardo Zaldívar decided not to continue with the operation, and from his pottery sales he repaid his debt. Little by little the other men dropped out, some repaying debts and some not. Reasons for the loss of interest, despite initial good prospects, are not entirely clear. Guillermo Morales and Luciano Villagomez had their hands full with pottery work and henhouses proved, in their case, to be the innovative straw that broke the camel's back. But more than anything, people seemed to resent the patronizing attitude they felt was shown by some CREFAL personnel, and to resent their inability to find out exactly where they stood on debits and credits. Micaela, after learning how to vaccinate, and after learning about commercial suppliers of birds, who also provide feed and purchase eggs, decided to go it alone. She simply pulled out of the program, paid her debts, and for several years ran a small egg business. This independent action caused irritation at CREFAL, and she was branded an ingrate. Part of the resentment, no doubt, stemmed from the fact that she was no longer a successful statistic, to be included in the annual report. It always seemed to me, however, that CREFAL should have been proud of her, rather than angry. She gave them credit for teaching her how to raise chickens, and then showed how well she had learned her lesson by making a success of going it alone. What CREFAL considered to be a failure was, in fact, a fine achievement.

THE EMBROIDERY PROGRAM

For many years Micaela and her daughters, Lola and Virginia, had embroidered tablecloths, place mats, napkins, aprons, and other garments, using a traditional cross stitch and simple designs of colonial origin. Gabriel Ospina, in searching for ways to help women, hit upon the idea of forming a group of embroiderers, to be directed by Micaela. No real formal co-operative was set up, in spite of the name that was attached to the operation. The CREFAL popular arts professor kept records, and signed receipts, and Micaela instructed the participating girls and young married women in the techniques of embroidery. An initial loan of $6,000 came from the National Indian Institute and with this, and other funds that became available, small looms on which rebozos could be woven were introduced, and several girls learned to operate them. Initially, and for several years, as many as twenty-five girls worked at embroidery, many coming each afternoon to Micaela's house but some — the married women — working in spare moments in their own homes.

During the period when the popular arts professor worked in Tzintzuntzan, the work went well, and the production was disposed of to CREFAL students and visitors who came to see CREFAL's Tzintzuntzan program. After the professor left Micaela has continued to operate what is, in fact, a small private enterprise, paying the same wages to the girls who continue to work, and selling

339

production to the passing tourists who learn about her embroideries. In one sense this was the most successful of the CREFAL projects. No major loans remained unpaid, wages and selling prices were competitive with other centers, as many girls could work as wished, and they could work as much or as little as their time permitted. Girls without other ways of earning money now had an opportunity to pick up small sums, and generally there were no complaints about how the project functioned.

RESULTS OF CREFAL'S PROJECTS

It is clear that the CREFAL experiment in community development in Tzintzuntzan has been much less successful than had been hoped. CREFAL itself considers the work a failure, and in Tzintzuntzan CREFAL is criticized a good deal. Yet there is a residue of great value in the experience, and a good many years must elapse — as with the 1931 Cultural Mission — before an objective appraisal can be made of how planned community development affected the village. Except for embroidering, none of the programs continues to date. Yet each left something of value. In pottery a number of men learned that there are new ways of producing vessels, and that there are many ways to combine colors and glazes. With the tourist market's growth, and the demand for interesting pieces, an experimental mood now prevails that, without the CREFAL stimulus, would be lacking. Those who participated in the workshop learned how to mix new colors, to try new combinations of glazes, and to seek new styles. So CREFAL equipped them to cope more successfully with changing circumstances and new opportunities.

Through the weaving and carpentry cooperative, a number of young men learned new trades which are today their sources of livelihood. One young man has the only carpentry and cabinet shop in town, and by local standards he does well. Another, because of the skills he acquired in Tzintzuntzan, has become a successful carpenter in Pátzcuaro. Two more are now government employees on Cultural Missions in Veracruz and Hidalgo states, teaching carpentry. Still other young men continue to ply their trades, although outside of Tzintzuntzan.

340

The early CREFAL efforts in environmental sanitation, in health education, and in setting up the first Health Center, also were important in modifying health attitudes and practices, in the direction of modern ways, and in bringing improved health to the villagers.

Again, a great many villagers enjoyed the personal contacts with teachers and students from the other Latin American countries, and their interests in, and awareness of, the wider world were sharpened. In spite of criticism of the methods of some teachers and students, villagers learned, probably for the first time in their lives, that there are city people who can have a genuine concern for their welfare, unmarred by expectations of personal gain at village expense. People soon learned to turn to these individuals to ask help in solving personal problems, problems often totally unrelated to formal CREFAL programs. Bernardo Zaldívar once remarked that in spite of his reservations about some aspects of the CREFAL programs, he felt he had learned a great deal, "especially things of theory." What did he mean by "theory?" Well, how to deal with the government, how to meet people, what his constitutional rights were — in short, he gained the knowledge and self-confidence which have made him one of very few individuals who have effectively represented the community in its dealings with the state and national governments.

LESSONS LEARNED FROM CREFAL'S PROJECTS

In another sense the CREFAL program has been useful because of the lessons that can be learned from it. It must be remembered that this was one of the first of such projects after the war, and that much less was known about how to carry out a program than is known today. What are these lessons, and what do they mean to the theory and practice of contemporary community development?

Both general and specific points are involved. Perhaps the most important lesson has to do with our understanding of the relationship of an innovating bureaucracy to a client group in a directed culture change program. For the evolution of international community development programs, including CREFAL, parallels that

341

of such fields as public health, agriculture, and education. This evolution has been marked by three clearly delineated phases, of which only the first two are fully recognized. In the first phase it was assumed by program planners and field technicians that aid based on the philosophy, methods, and programs of developed countries would, if offered to people in less developed countries, be eagerly accepted. It was assumed that the merit and advantages of such aid were self-evident. The naiveté of this assumption was rather quickly recognized. It was found that a program evolved according to the needs of a technologically advanced country could not simply be grafted onto the structure of a country whose needs were quite different, and whose social and cultural ways, not to mention its infrastructure, represented vastly different forms.

In the second phase of the evolution of international developmental programs — a phase which continues to the present — it has been assumed that the major problems in local development are rooted in the society and culture of the community itself. Villagers, it has been reasoned, are potentially anxious to join with their fellows in finding answers to their problems which, with a little help, can easily be identified, but often they are inhibited by cultural, social, and psychological barriers which they cannot hurdle without additional help.

Consonant with this point of view, in the best contemporary community development thinking, it is assumed that the first step in carrying out a successful program is to study thoroughly the social and cultural forms of the client group. This reveals the barriers that discourage change, and points the way to the steps that can be taken to overcome them. This analytic approach also is seen as uncovering the local motivations which can be utilized in formulating a strategy for specific projects such as school building or adult literacy classes. When a project does not go according to plan, it is assumed the need is to return to analysis of the community to spot the problem that somehow eluded attention in the first attempt. In other words, the sophisticated point of view characterizing phase two might be phrased as: "In order to work successfully in a community, one must understand thoroughly its social organization, cultural forms, and values."

342

The CREFAL program began at a time when this view represented the most advanced thinking in developmental work. Consequently, the selection of Tzintzuntzan, because it had been thoroughly studied and described by anthropologists, represented wise planning. Moreover, the high personal esteem in which Professor Ospina was held by the villagers, and their obvious willingness to work with him, was another point favoring success.

Yet experience in CREFAL and elsewhere shows that much more than the cultural forms of the recipient group must be known if work is to go well. This is because in all programs of directed culture change at least two socio-cultural systems interact with each other: (1) the client group, the community, and (2) the innovating bureaucracy. For a community development organization, like any bureaucracy, can be looked upon as a society with specific cultural forms, much as a village community consists of a society with its culture. It is composed of persons of both sexes, of different ages, organized into a hierarchy marked by power and authority, with well-defined roles and occupational specializations, with mutually recognized rights, obligations, and expectations. The members of such a bureaucratic "society" share common values, they engage in professional rituals, and they operate on the basis of implicit assumptions about themselves and their goals that normally are not questioned. The cohesive and divisive forces, the stresses and strains, and the rivalries and jealousies found in such a society are similar to those found in village communities and other natural social units.

The barriers to change in village communities are very real, and the search for ways of motivating villagers to action must always be a basic part of the community development method. But barriers are equally characteristic of all bureaucratic organizations, and these barriers, in contemporary developmental work, constitute very grave problems, in part simply because they are not yet fully recognized for what they are. Bureaucracies, like individuals, find it more comfortable to analyze other people's problems, rather than to turn inward and ask how their own shortcomings may adversely affect their performance.

Bureaucratic barriers are partially rooted in the relationships

343

prevailing between members of the group. Differential perception of roles, lack of common understanding of responsibilities, personal antagonisms, weak leadership, and poor teamwork in general all severely handicap an organization's efforts. And some bureaucratic barriers are rooted in the personal psychological problems of the group's members, and in the way these people see themselves vis à vis their fellow workers, and particularly the members of the client group. When, for example, a technical specialist envisages his role as that of a paternalistic figure who must teach children, any who turn out to be "bad children," i.e., who are uncooperative and refuse to do what he asks of them, cause him extreme anguish. He believes he is working in selfless fashion to aid people who need help. In fact, subconsciously at least, he feels that those who do not do what he asks are denying to him the evidence of accomplishment which is his way of gratifying his ego and gaining his professional colleagues' approval. The hostility which may mark his behavior toward members of the client group can be a major barrier to change.

In other words, it is just as crucial to successful directed culture change to understand the cultural forms, the system of social relations, the group and individual values of the bureaucracy's members, and the implicit assumptions that underly their work, as it is to understand the group toward whom a program is directed. In hindsight it is clear that CREFAL personnel were almost entirely unaware of this third stage, insofar as their work in Tzintzuntzan was concerned, and that many difficulties that were encountered stemmed from CREFAL planning and operations, and from the psychological problems of some of the personnel, rather than from deficiencies in the local people themselves. CREFAL personnel generally blamed Tzintzuntzeños for the failure of formal programs, and they were reluctant to consider their own errors in trying to help villagers as a contributing factor. Perhaps the greatest stumbling block of all was the unquestioned acceptance of the community development movement's central dogma: that peasant villagers are, or would be, highly cooperative if only given the chance, and that therefore

344

programs must be cooperative. It will be recalled that the first year's projects were designed "to extirpate . . . the individualism [of the villagers], at the same time strengthening the philosophy of cooperative work." It should be clear, from the evidence presented earlier in this book, that Tzintzuntzeños are anything but cooperative, and that major programs based on this mistaken assumption must be doomed to failure. It is evident that the most promising programs were those in which people could accept or reject participation on an individual basis. To raise chickens required only a single decision, and once committed, a man did not depend on what his colleagues did or did not do. Had the kerosene-fired kiln functioned, this project, too, would have succeeded, because it represented individual effort in which participants were not bound to the efforts — or lack of efforts — of a great many others.

A second major error in the CREFAL experiment, also rooted in CREFAL itself, and not in the village, was the failure to develop a comprehensive, broad plan in which *all* factors that might bear on success or failure were taken into consideration. Rather, development was looked upon as a collection of projects, the precise mixture of which was determined by available personnel. Pottery making, weaving, carpentry, chicken raising, and embroidering were all considered to be more or less separate activities that would aid distinct groups of people. Each was viewed principally as a technical exercise, to teach new methods and to improve old ones. Except for pottery, technical success was achieved in each field. Yet the programs failed because, apparently, no serious thought was given to other critical factors, especially the problems of marketing and cost accounting. The popular arts professor, an able teacher and a humanitarian, felt that the rural wages in Mexico were much too low; he was determined that in Tzintzuntzan skilled artisans should receive living wages. But no individual can make such a decision, because forces that determine wages in a free market economy, like those which determine prices, are impersonal, and normally are beyond individual control. Had Tzintzuntzan weaving and woodworking

345

been priced competitively, and wages set accordingly, and had efforts been made to formalize marketing procedures, the results might have been quite different.

Still another shortcoming in the CREFAL approach, apparently little recognized by teachers and students, stemmed from the villagers' extreme sensitivity to real and imagined slights and insults, which comes from generations of unhappy dealings with city people. Whatever the truth, people in Tzintzuntzan felt that some of the students and teaching personnel were very patronizing in their attitudes, and that they often ordered villagers about in an arbitrary and sometimes humiliating fashion. The teachers and students who were most thoughtful about the feelings of villagers were the most successful in their work.

IMPORTANT INSIGHTS

Several other lessons that can be learned from the CREFAL experience can be summarized briefly:

1. In teaching new techniques, it is often easier to begin with people who know absolutely nothing about the skill involved, rather than to try to change deeply entrenched practices. Weavers and carpenters learned quickly, because they had nothing to forget; potters were much more resistant to improving methods they knew worked.

2. In working with villagers, attempting to teach too many new things simultaneously may be self-defeating. To ask potters to revolutionize their methods, and to expect them simultaneously to master chicken ranching, seems beyond the bounds of the possible. If families of whom nothing else was expected had received help in chicken ranching, the new practice might have persisted, as it did on La Pacanda. And if potters selected for intensive work had not been burdened with the care of and worry about chickens at the same time, they might have been able to make greater progress.

3. To ask people to assume heavy debts, and to experiment with untried and unperfected techniques, is to invite failure. If the oil-fired pottery kiln had been perfected prior to its attempted

346

introduction, and if the professor had been able to demonstrate a satisfactory operation, it is likely that it would have been eagerly accepted.

4. It must not be assumed that a few demonstrations and lectures are sufficient to teach new skills. Constant supervision and attention over a long time are essential. An important factor in the popular arts professor's technical successes lay in the fact that he was in Tzintzuntzan almost every day, all day long, month after month. He was thus present to correct mistakes quickly and to oversee all phases of learning. The pottery professor, on the other hand, spent much less time in Tzintzuntzan, and he was not present on critical occasions such as firing kilns when his guidance was most needed.

If the CREFAL program had been carried out with the wisdom and skill that, on the basis of experience, would now be available, would the outcome have been different? This question of course cannot be answered. It seems likely that some of the projects would have achieved a measure of enduring success; there is no reason why, with markets, a few weavers and furniture makers might not have made a go of it. But it must be remembered that Tzintzuntzan is a particularly conservative community, and the measures that have worked in other, more progressive rural communities, however skillfully introduced, might not have achieved the same success. Some of the blame for the relative failure of CREFAL projects certainly rests on the shoulders of the Tzintzuntzeños, on their unwillingness to believe that teachers and students have no personal axes to grind, on their inability to work together on projects in which all stood to gain, and on their constant readiness to suspect, and to believe, the worst about all others, fellow villagers as well as outsiders.

CHAPTER EIGHTEEN

What Is
the Future?

SOUND PLANNING ESSENTIAL

Each year the mainstreams of Mexican development come closer to Tzintzuntzan and some, like the school and the health center, have established major beachheads within the village. People are beginning to lose some of their fear of the urban world, and they have more confidence in their state and national governments than formerly. Young people set their sights higher than their parents did, and they are demanding, and some of them enjoying, opportunities denied the older generations. Yet most Tzintzuntzeños are still marginal to the remarkable social and economic progress that has marked their country during the past two decades, and it would be unrealistic, in spite of these steps forward, to pretend that Tzintzuntzan, and many other villages like it, do not pose serious problems for the Mexican nation.

Tzintzuntzan is poised on the brink of enormous, far-reaching, and inevitable changes. These changes can lead to a better and happier life for Tzintzuntzeños, in which they will increasingly play a significant role in the modern Mexican nation. But increasing population pressure and rising expectations, in the face of static economic opportunities, can also bring social unrest. The latter alternative need not come to pass. But to make sure that it does not, sound national planning and increased aid and guidance from outside the village are essential. This will require the intelligent utilization of theory and knowledge, not just of the economist and the engineer, but of the behavioral sciences as well. It is necessary to appraise the basic ecological and natural environmental circumstances that limit Tzintzuntzan's growth, and to know its economic and technical potential in relation to Mexico as a whole. It is equally necessary, if we wish to help Tzintzuntzan, to know the ways in which village people understand the universe about them, the manner in which they perceive change, the psychological motivations that stimulate them to take new steps, the barriers that hold them back, and the social and economic relationships that both bind them to and separate them from towns and cities.

FACTORS INFLUENCING DEVELOPMENT

In this final chapter we shall summarize some of these sociocultural and psychological factors that influence development both positively and negatively, and we shall suggest how significant they may be for contemporary social and economic planning. Then we shall review and discuss some of the pitfalls in delivering developmental services. Finally, we shall ask ourselves what kind of economic and social future the community can expect, and offer tentative answers.

The first, and basic, argument advanced in these pages, from which the other arguments follow, is that all normative group behavior — the culture of every society — is a function of a particular understanding of the conditions that delimit and determine life, a correlate of certain implicit assumptions, of which the average person is totally unaware. In Tzintzuntzan (and in other peasant societies) this "particular understanding" can be

349

described by the Image of Limited Good. With this cognitive orientation Tzintzuntzeños, over many generations, developed and maintained a viable community which brought a modicum of economic security, and about the same range of joy and sorrow, satisfaction and disillusionment, and certainty and uncertainty experienced by peoples in very different societies. This traditional world view served Tzintzuntzan because it represented reality with fair accuracy.

Today it is less and less accurate. Tzintzuntzan now is a part of a dramatically expanding national economy, and there are opportunities on a scale undreamed of even a generation ago. The growing Mexican infrastructure impinges upon Tzintzuntzan at new points every year, and at each, villagers are invited, figuratively speaking, to "come into the nation." The infrastructure, with the support, services, and opportunities it offers, cannot yet provide all the cultural stimuli Tzintzuntzan needs — we remember Julio Calderón and his oil fired kiln — but it is growing faster than the traditional cognitive orientation is changing.

Hence, in listing the fundamental factors which hold back the village, and which must be solved if the first of our two alternative futures is to be achieved, we must put at or near the top increasingly outdated assumptions about the conditions that govern life. The ideal man of traditional society is no longer ideal in a changing world. The personality characteristics inculcated in him in childhood and by his experiences, which enabled him to function successfully in a relatively static society, now are an enormous drag, a heavy weight which most people are as yet unable to shed. The ideal man of earlier years, who still is the prevailing type, finds himself bewildered and confused by present conditions; in the new world he is increasingly a misfit.

It would be nice to believe that an outmoded world view is *the* major factor holding back Tzintzuntzan and other peasant villages, for if this were true, rural problems would then be easy to solve. For cognitive orientations change, and an Image of Limited Good sets no absolute limits to a village's advancement. Basic as it is at the present time in preventing villagers from taking advantage of the opportunities that already exist, it is not a perpetual part of life, and as time passes, and especially with sympathetic and understanding outside aid, it will melt away.

But there are at least two other major barriers to smooth and successful change. One of these, like a world view, is not absolute; it can and will change, and in much the same way and under much the same circumstances as world view will change. This barrier is lack of access to knowledge and information about the contemporary world, coupled with continuing exploitation by unscrupulous city people. But, although ultimately this factor will be reduced to manageable size, as has occurred in the economically most advanced countries of the world, for some time in the future Tzintzuntzeños will be severely handicapped because of this ignorance and lack of defense.

The third major barrier, unlike the first two, sets absolute limits to change; it has to do with the village's inherent economic potential, its natural resources, its geographical location, the national and international demand for its present and potential products, and its population growth. This, obviously, is the key factor, and satisfactory answers to the problems it presents are much harder to find than for the first two barriers. Answers cannot be found alone in the immediate, local area. Although a start can and must be made on this level — as CREFAL attempted with pottery, carpentry, and weaving production — local success will depend heavily on circumstances far removed from the village.

PENALTIES OF MARGINALITY

The first of these three barriers — a particular cognitive orientation and its relationship to contemporary conditions — has been the principal theme of this book. It therefore should need no further elucidation. The isolation — perhaps "marginality" is a better word — of Tzintzuntzeños has been touched upon several times, but here it seems desirable to re-emphasize and illustrate the point. In spite of great physical mobility and extensive communication with the wider world, most Tzintzuntzeños are intellectually far removed from the world, and ill-equipped to evaluate and appraise new events and opportunities, still unsure

351

as to where to turn to find answers to the new problems that face them. The extensive physical contact Tzintzuntzeños have with the world has led even CREFAL personnel to assume that the villagers have a much better understanding of new ideas and methods than they really have. Although CREFAL teachers may not have recognized it fully, one of the greatest contributions of some of them was the confidence, as friends, they instilled in villagers, and their ability to give sound advice on many kinds of problems. A continuing service of this type would be of inestimable value in the orderly development of the village. For all too often, in testing new contacts with the world, and without sympathetic and able guidance, the villagers' fingers are burned.

Some years ago Lucas Arias spotted a community need which offered a challenge to his entrepreneurial talents. Buses passing through Tzintzuntzan were so loaded that they failed to stop to pick up local passengers, and people would wait hours for a chance to ride to Pátzcuaro. Lucas felt the amount of local demand would support several round trips daily for a Tzintzuntzan-Pátzcuaro service. Through an acquaintance, an official of one of the franchised bus lines, he acquired a battered vehicle, paying for it, since he had little idea of automotive values, far more than it was worth. But he was happy — for a short time. Then he began to learn the facts of life. A government franchise? The bus line official who sold him the bus fought him on this. The bus drivers syndicate? The organized drivers pointed out clearly that they wanted no local competition. Taxes? Servicing the bus? On every point Lucas encountered insuperable and unexpected odds. With intelligence, a progressive spirit, and the ability to recognize opportunity, he was still defeated, since he had imperfect knowledge of the world he wished to enter, and no way to acquire that knowledge, save through crushing experience. Sadder, if wiser, he sold his bus back to the official who had sold it to him, at a fraction of what he had paid.

Another story ends less sadly, but teaches a similar lesson. Faustino Peña is one of those who has successfully developed new glazes and designs to meet tourist demands. But local supplies of the needed materials often are not available. He remem-

352

bered Juan Pánfilo who, in the mid-1930's, had taught pottery in Tzintzuntzan's short-lived trade school, who now lived in Tlaquepaque, near Guadalajara. Juan had been a friendly person, so Faustino made the two hundred mile trip to search him out and to ask his help in acquiring glazes. He found Juan, who remembered him, and expressed his delight at being able to help his old friend. How much did the glaze cost? Four pesos a kilo, said Juan, and so that Faustino would have time to see the sights, he himself would bring it to his house, and Faustino could return to pick it up in the afternoon. Faustino was overwhelmed by such consideration, and deeply touched. He wandered the streets of Tlaquepaque and by chance passed a store where glazes were sold. Out of curiosity he entered, asked prices, and found that his glaze cost $1.80 a kilo. Fortunately he had advanced nothing to the faithless Juan, so he filled his needs and returned home, with yet another lesson in the perfidy of city people.

The third major barrier to Tzintzuntzan's development — its meager economic potential — is as evident as the ways of overcoming the barrier are obscure. Land is limited and mostly poor; handcrafting of pottery, which attracts tourists, is inefficient as a productive technique, and it can never raise the economic standards of all potter families. For small industry the village offers no attractions. Even modest amounts of industrial wastes would pollute the lake, destroying the livelihood of fishermen in many communities, and threatening the area's scenic beauty. Other than pottery clays, there are no known natural resources. Rail transportation, though only ten miles away, is closer to scores of other communities blessed with more ample sources of water, land, and skilled hands. Meanwhile, the population mounts, pushed by a high birth rate and a low death rate. As Tzintzuntzeños say themselves, the village's principal product is children. The braccro program relieved the worst of the economic pressure for twenty years, but now that it is ended, no full substitute is in view.

There are other barriers to change. Among these is the absence of real cooperative mechanisms, such as voluntary associations dedicated to specific community tasks. This makes it difficult, but not impossible, for the community to take advantage of unusual situations as, for example, the Ministry of Health's offer to build a health center if the village would contribute certain things.

Change in Tzintzuntzan is also complicated by the fact that what to city people seem like simple explanations and instructions, and what must therefore, it is assumed, be equally intelligible to Tzintzuntzeños, are in fact often anything but clear. Rosalía Noriega took her infant son to a Pátzcuaro doctor who prescribed oral medicine. By chance I passed her door the same afternoon and asked about the baby, who had been ailing for some time. Much better, she said, but she was puzzled by the doctor's written instructions, which she showed me. What did "8:00 A.M." and "8:00 P.M." mean, and what was *por una semana?* How often did this mean? I carefully explained that tonight at 8 o'clock she should give the baby a spoonful, tomorrow morning at 8 o'clock another spoonful, tomorrow night at the same hour, and so forth until *desde hoy en ocho días,* until eight days from today, the usual way of saying "week." Rosalía is nominally literate, she runs a little store, and she is perhaps brighter than average. Yet faced with a physician's instructions which to me seemed crystal clear, she couldn't make out what she was to do, and without my chance visit it is hard to say what she would have done.

LACK OF TAXING AUTHORITY

One of the most important secondary barriers to change is the lack of village authority to levy and collect taxes for local works. As has been pointed out, local taxes taken by the municipio are just sufficient to maintain the municipal government; there is no surplus for public improvements. Every village project must therefore be carried out by voluntary or forced special contributions, which inevitably cause friction, and hence discourage authorities from taking badly needed action. The much larger sums collected by the state tax collector leave Tzintzuntzan, returning several times over in the form of regular and exceptional grants for teachers' salaries and occasional capital works

354

such as the health center and the school breakfast building. The only way, then, in which the village can have access to major capital sums is to open the heart of the governor or some other official who, as a special favor to the village, agrees to undertake some enterprise. If a small percentage of state taxes could be left in Tzintzuntzan, to be expended for public works, or if small levies could be set for specific purposes, the community would gradually learn something about local initiative and responsibility, and modest developmental efforts could be placed on a sound financial basis. Such a plan, of course, would require honest accounting by municipio officials, and this in turn would mean competent supervision from the state capital.

The attitude of Tzintzuntzeños toward government and government officials is paradoxical. On the one hand it is assumed that there is no such thing as a disinterested public servant who does a job because he is paid to do so. It is taken for granted that officials and employees at all levels — national, state, and municipio — have an ulterior motive that underlies their interest in what they do. On the other hand, government is seen as the only source of aid and improvement in the village. So the Tzintzuntzeño sees himself inextricably bound to a system which he thoroughly distrusts. Resolving this dilemma is one of the principal tasks that faces the village, for only increased government cooperation can solve many of the problems, such as low agricultural production, which face the community.

Fortunately, people are beginning to modify their opinions of the government. When, in 1963, to counter local village corruption in allocating bracero permits, a state official came from Morelia and conducted an honest and impartial drawing, villagers were favorably impressed. Bernardo Zaldívar, although he still speaks for a minority, believes that government does much more for people than formerly. When he was about seven he had smallpox, and at that time it was assumed everyone would have it, and that a good many children would die. Now children are vaccinated, and smallpox no longer strikes people. Whooping cough, too, Bernardo notes, is a thing of the past. He thanks government for both of these improvements.

355

There are, it is clear, a great many barriers to change in Tzintzuntzan. But the picture is by no means one-sided, for there are positive factors as well which favor change. These are found mainly in the traditional social organization of the community. That is, in one way the atomistic social structure of the villagers, and the attitudes of mutual distrust that accompany it, discourage cooperative efforts. But in another way this same atomism means Tzintzuntzan is less hampered than are many other communities with a more cooperative tradition. In much of the traditional world reciprocal obligations to friends, and especially relatives within the extended family, lineage, or clan, discourage the accumulation of capital. In many African societies these obligations are imperatives, and not optional, so that the potentially exceptional individual is dissuaded because any improvement in his earning power will immediately be dissipated by fulfilling these obligations.

In Tzintzuntzan the equivalent obligation which leveled economic differences was far more institutionalized. An improvement in material position was neutralized by sponsoring a costly mayordomía, in which everyone in the village to some extent shared. This ritual obligation to the community is, as we have seen, no longer significant in preventing the accumulation of capital. Moreover, the informal exchanges associated with the dyadic pattern of ties are not quantitatively crippling; they are important, but they are not a serious handicap for an individual who wishes to accumulate capital. Returned braceros, for example, might bring a couple of hundred dollars worth of presents, but if they had been prudent and had had the luck of a long contract they were still able to set aside four or five times that amount for their own use.

Tzintzuntzan's dyadic pattern of social cohesiveness, and the associated pattern of shifting ties, also has strengths as well as weaknesses. Most important, it inhibits the development of factions which, as in much of India, constitute such a barrier to change. Tzintzuntzeños ally themselves with those people whom they like, and with whom they feel association is mutually satisfying. If subsequent reappraisal convinces them that they were wrong, or that conditions have changed, they drop their obligations, to form new ones. To the best of my knowledge no man has refused to take part in a project because of his father's enmity to others, or to the fathers of others, also associated with the operation. Tzintzuntzeños are pragmatic in analyzing possible benefits and losses from any course of action, and they do not let sentiment, in the form of overriding family loyalty or long-standing grudges, stand in their way.

Again, the nuclear family as the basic unit of production, rather than a larger and more diffuse family group, and individual ownership of land and other property, rather than some communal form of holding, both seem to favor small ventures in new areas. An individual can decide to take a particular action — such as chicken ranching — which he sees as promising, without having to obtain the approval or participation of a wider kin group or a family patriarch. And the strong commitment to the private property principle is consistent in a national economy in which, apart from public utilities and certain large-scale manufacturing activities, private initiative is the rule.

In its efforts to change, Tzintzuntzan is also favored because it has no vested interests that try to maintain the status quo for their own gain. There are no large haciendas in the area whose owners could significantly influence people's decisions. Within the village professional money lenders are absent, so that government credit schemes, simply administered, in language villagers can understand, should meet no opposition. In the health field, the curanderos and curanderas do not see themselves in competition with physicians, and the three midwives have not objected to the new health center's pre- and postnatal and delivery services.

Despite these favorable factors, the ideal man of earlier years will probably continue to display traditional personality characteristics for a long time to come. But the decisive break whereby the village commits itself to step forward will come, not when traditional personality disappears, but rather when the negative sanctions the community has used to ensure that everybody con-

357

forms to this type no longer inhibit the progressive individuals from behaving otherwise. This point is close at hand, as evidenced by the breakdown of the economically leveling mayordomía system, and by the rise of a group of people who openly compete for status and prestige with material possessions, and who are no longer afraid to flout this superiority in their neighbors' eyes.

WORKING WITH, NOT FOR, VILLAGERS

The weakening of sanctions, which have held back progressive individuals, combined with developing confidence in government, and a growing hope of greater municipio independence in conducting its internal affairs, means that the present, and the next few years, are particularly critical in the village's history. Wise planning and thoughtful, sympathetic application of aid, can spell the difference between success and failure. The CREFAL experiment represented generally a sympathetic application of aid, but this good was compromised by poor and inadequate planning. The following example, on the other hand, was well planned, but suffered a setback because of thoughtless application.

In June of 1963 a tent appeared on the roadside opposite Carichuato Hill, a jealously treasured possession of the Indigenous Community, purchased with monies collected with great effort on a voluntary basis. Shortly thereafter tiny seedlings began to appear on the badly eroded slopes of the hill. People still were not much preoccupied, although most opined that the trees would not live. But then fence posts appeared, and people learned that the hill was to be fenced, and cattle kept out. The work was being done by the technically excellent Forestry Service of the State of Michoacán. The villagers' concern was quite logical: apart from a number of milpas on Carichuato, the slopes form an important dry-season grazing area for animals, so that it is basic to the community's economic life.

Forestry officials had, it turned out, approached the president of the Indigenous Community. He, perhaps feeling he had no alternative before a powerful government agency, had signed a permit for the program but then, doubtless fearing the consequences, he failed to inform his fellows. A revolution nearly

358

broke out when it was learned what had happened. The following Sunday five engineers came from Morelia, and in a public meeting in the plaza they explained in great detail, and very clearly, I thought, the threat to the land and the need for reforestation. An elderly, bald engineer talked eloquently, but simply and slowly, about land, trees, water, and the balance of nature. "What would the Emperor Tangaxoan think if he were to return?" asked the engineer, appealing to local pride. "He wouldn't stay. He'd ask, 'what have you done with all of those wonderful forests I left you?' "

Bernardo Zaldívar replied: the problem was not that the village was opposed to reforestation, he said, but that it had not been consulted beforehand, and that the villagers were disturbed when they saw their lands being fenced in, so they would have no access to them. There were other village lands, said Bernardo, which were of less economic value, but which could be reforested. Why not use some of them? Ultimately a compromise was reached. Not all the land originally selected would be fenced, and that fenced would have a wide gate so animals could be driven in and out for plowing. The village acquiesced, because it felt it had no alternative — as probably it hadn't — but by this time almost all men were sure this was a government plot to rob them of their lands, and very few believed that Tzintzuntzan would ever profit by the timber, when and if it grew.

Had the Forestry representatives taken the time and effort to discuss the project in an open village meeting before taking action, and had they been willing to modify their technical conclusions, according to village problems and needs, it is quite possible they would have had active village support instead of sullen opposition.

THE CULTURAL SIDE OF DEVELOPMENT

This incident illustrates what seems to me to be one of the basic flaws in much planning: the assumption that developmental problems are purely technical, that answers are equally technical, and that the economic and engineering sciences alone are qualified to carry out the work. Yet even the simplest device, which appears to be purely technical, may have its psychological or social concomitants which restrict, or even prohibit, the adoption of new ways. When aid was offered a few Tzintzuntzeños to install hot showers, the goal was seen as involving small amounts of money, and simple plumbing operations. The technician had to build a bath house, bring water from the main, install the little wood-fired heater, and connect the parts. But to Micaela and her family, accepting a hot shower meant a whole review of the causes of illness, and learning how to bathe without risking sickness each time. When the body is warmer than normal, in this case because of hot water, it is particularly vulnerable to cold both from air and from standing on a cold floor. Only when these dangers were countered could the family bathe with impunity. The problem was solved by several steps. To prevent "risen heat" from the cold floor, a bath mat was purchased, on which the bather stepped to dry. After showering the bather dressed slowly, allowing his body to cool gradually. Then, when finally emerging from the shower room, he wrapped his head in a towel, turban-like, and dashed for the bedroom, thus minimizing the danger of breathing cold air or being struck by a draft. Only when this sequence was figured out did people feel comfortable bathing in hot water. To Micaela and her family, technology was the most minor aspect of this new custom.

Or take glass windows opening to the street. Although these cost money, the resistance to their installation has not been primarily economic. Nor has it been the fear that robbers could more easily enter a house. The problem is psychological: the blank walls that protect one from the envy of others are breached, and people feel exposed to the dangerous gaze of all passersby. Only when this psychological hurdle is overcome do people feel comfortable with windows.

In spite of the kinds of miscalculation and lack of comprehension of both technical and social factors evidenced by CREFAL and the Forestry Service, it is clear that a happy future for Tzintzuntzan will depend on sound economic and social planning, and on the effective execution of the programs that are decided upon. Skilled and sympathetic outside guidance, from specialists who work with, and not just for, the local people, will be required for these enterprises. The kinds of outside change agents that are essential are varied. Some must have human skills that will enable them to aid Tzintzuntzeños to build a greater feeling of community identity and responsibility, and who will be able to assist in breaking down the traditional world view of Limited Good. Others will require the knowledge, and where necessary the authority, to take action, to bring Tzintzuntzeños out of their intellectual isolation, and into a relationship with town and city dwellers in which something like legal equality can prevail. Still others must have the technical skills to improve agriculture and arts and crafts, and the marketing knowledge and resources that will make possible an orderly disposition of Tzintzuntzan's production.

A NEW VILLAGE HELPER

In one ministry or another, all these specialists exist, although not all have directed their efforts toward Tzintzuntzan. But what is needed in the worst possible way is a new kind of developmental specialist not previously, to my knowledge, a part of any community development program. This individual, who might be called the *amigo del pueblo*, the friend of the community, should be a university graduate, a high-level official in a program of such national importance that he would not look upon his job as a stepping stone to more profitable employment. He should live, not in a village, but in a town or small city — in the case at hand, Pátzcuaro — the economic and political hub of a rural area, to which villagers come to buy, sell, and transact legal and other business. He should be "the man who knows the answers," the person who can help the villager bridge the chasm that separates him from city ways and national laws. A farmer has amassed sufficient funds to think of purchasing a used pickup truck. He needs advice on a fair price, on deferred payment, on the problems of obtaining a license, advice to avoid the many pitfalls that lie in wait for him. Nothing in his village experience, nothing in school, nothing on the radio prepares him to attempt this new venture. The amigo del pueblo can give him disinterested and honest counsel. A villager is sold shoddy merchandise or tricked into installment buying, or told that he will be prosecuted if he does not deliver a certain amount of money by a certain date. What is the truth? What are the villager's rights? The amigo del pueblo could be his advocate, his helper. A relative is ill, but there is no government hospital in the village. Are there other government medical services to which the villager may have access, if he but knows about them? All these circumstances have occurred in Tzintzuntzan. To city dwellers, with greater sophistication, they are hardly problems. To Tzintzuntzeños they often seem insurmountable. A knowledgeable, sympathetic, available specialist, a source of information on all manner of things, would do as much as any other project to aid villagers in facing the problems of the modern world.

PLANNING MUST BE INTEGRATED

With respect to the strategy of planned assistance of the types envisaged, it is clear that effective programming should not be attempted within the narrow traditional boundaries of the professional fields of health, education, community development, agriculture, and forestry, as it has been in the past. Every new project in the village, to be fully successful, must find its place in the community's total way of life, and not simply represent a transplant of a technical operation that has worked well elsewhere under very different circumstances. Social goals must be related to economic reality: the successful training of weavers and carpenters depends on the development of sound marketing. And technical goals must be related to social reality: reforestation that ignores the social context in which it is carried out is not likely to succeed.

Effective planning in every professional field must involve many aspects of village life — social, religious, technical, economic — and it must relate these factors to the nation at large. Moreover, sound planning involves step-by-step consultation with the people who are to be affected by new programs. It means ability on the part of planners to modify their preconceived ideas according to new knowledge obtained from village people. It means, on occasion, a willingness to sacrifice some part of technical perfection when the social toll of this excellence is excessive.

Sound and sympathetic planning and action are now imperative, for already the lives of the villagers are more inextricably bound up with the complexities of the nation than they realize, and much of their old independence, however limited it was, is gone. One morning the electric power failed. For me it meant the nuisance of not shaving. But for the village the entire day's work was thrown off schedule, for the nixtamal mills didn't work. This forced women to revert to hand grinding, a time-consuming process for which, moreover, their shoulder muscles are no longer toughened. Meals were delayed, tempers were short, and frustration was felt.

Tzintzuntzan is now vulnerable to events beyond its borders, and over which it has no control, in a way unknown a generation ago. With the disappearance of pack animals, a truck or bus strike disrupts pottery marketing. Once people are accustomed to consulting physicians, they cannot return to home remedies; they depend on continued access to modern medicine. The depth of this commitment is reflected in the popular belief that once the body has been invaded by modern medicine, the old medicine loses its powers. Tzintzuntzan depends much more on economic factors in the nation at large than formerly. Not only does it buy many more manufactured products, but its pottery market extends far beyond the former trade area. A good chunk of the village is now at the mercy of the tourist trade. Roadside pottery stands have brought prosperity to many people, and they assume this outlet will continue to grow. But a recently completed direct highway from Morelia to Pátzcuaro will certainly divert the bulk of tourists who now pass through the village. Will the market for specialized pieces of pottery disappear? Will most of the stands be forced to close up for lack of business? It is quite possible.

NEW SOURCES OF INCOME

What can make up for this loss of independence, the loss of bracero earnings, and the possible loss of pottery sales? To what

363

extent can basic economic problems be solved? The problem was forcefully thrust upon me one afternoon when Salomón Villagomez, a former mayor and bracero, asked "What can be done to bring industry to Tzintzuntzan?" I mumbled platitudes about water supply, land, a railroad, but Salomón kept pressing me, asking if in my capacity as anthropologist who had studied the village for many years I didn't know what should be done. To gain time I asked him what *he* thought the changes had been in Tzintzuntzan that might make it attractive to industry. He had no doubts. Now that so many men have travelled to Mexico City and the United States the village knows things about which it formerly was ignorant. People have seen things that are new, both customs and material items, and they want them. The village is *más abierto* said Salomón, more open and receptive to new ideas and ways. The people have more confidence in their government, too, he said. He remembered how people used to run when smallpox vaccinators appeared; now they line up to await their turn.

Salomón's conviction that people are now ready for major steps forward is, it seemed to me, still a bit premature, but he posed the basic question: in the new world it is entering, what does the future hold for the village? The outlook can be either hopeful or depressing, according to the color of the spectacles the viewer wears. The inherent economic restrictions around Tzintzuntzan are quite obvious; it can never be a great city, or even a large town. But to say that economic and ecological factors will prevent Tzintzuntzan from industrializing does not mean that nothing can or should be done, nor that the villagers are condemned to live out marginal existences. Many improvements can be brought about by changes in attitudes and aspirations of the villagers, aided by the growing developmental services of their national government.

With respect to national developmental action, two steps should be taken at once. One is to give attention to the agriculture of the community, analyze soils, determine proper fertilizers, develop hybrid seeds suitable to the lake region, and make available the other extension services currently lacking. Perhaps

364

20 per cent of Tzintzuntzan families could enjoy a reasonably good living from efficient farming. The other step is to vastly increase educational efforts, within the village at the primary and perhaps soon the secondary level, and in neighboring towns at more advanced levels, so that growing numbers of village young people can be trained both for careers outside their natal community, and to be leaders in it, should they return home.

Rationalized pottery production should enable a great many potters to enjoy significantly improved levels of living. This is particularly true of those potters who have special artistic capabilities, and who can produce wares for which tourists will pay premium prices. But fully exploiting the pottery potential will require outside aid in marketing. Many American tourists would order pottery shipped to their homes (as they do from Tlaquepaque and Guadalajara) if local merchants understood how to prepare customs' declarations, and how to ship via customs' brokers. Simple legal recourse in cases of victimization, such as that of Adolfo Delgado, should also be provided by the national government. With all its limitations, pottery must continue to be the major source of income for Tzintzuntzan.

With marketing help for pottery, there is no reason why weaving and woodworking should not be reactivated. Tzintzuntzan is as favorably located as other Michoacán weaving and woodworking villages, and with the extra attraction of pottery as well, to draw tourists, its high-quality hand-loomed textiles and furniture should sell well. If these products, too, could be shipped directly to the United States, there could be a market large enough to mean a great deal to the local economy.

Because of its lovely location, Tzintzuntzan may become a weekend resort for Morelia families. Already a few cottages have been built. If this trend develops, numbers of people may find employment as cooks and caretakers. An attractive lakeside restaurant, and even a small inn, might prove economically feasible. Tzintzuntzan, with the lake, archaeological remains, colonial monuments, arts and crafts, and colorful fiestas, has resources that should enable it to share in the benefits from the tourism which seems bound to increase in Michoacán.

Rather unexpectedly in late 1964 a new opportunity of a different type appeared. Alliance for Progress funds were made available through Morelia banks for loans to villagers for productive enterprises, at the very modest interest rate of 6 per cent annually. For the first time in their lives people now had access to credit at a price they could afford to pay. Moreover, the credit was supervised by responsible specialists, so that the possibilities of careless use of the money were greatly reduced. Father Fuentes spoke of the advantages of these loans in his Sunday sermons, and urged those men he felt to be most competent to have confidence in themselves, and to take advantage of this new credit source. Himself a spare-time hog raiser, he had shown people by example that keeping pedigreed stock offered good financial opportunities, and he had shared his technical knowledge with all those who had asked for help. By mid-1965 eight or nine men had taken out loans to go into hog raising on a modest scale, two had borrowed money to acquire pedigreed cattle, and others were contemplating similar steps. Although it is too early to assess the consequences of this action, stock raising may very well prove to be a decisive factor in the village's future welfare.

Thus, in various ways, in the bits-and-pieces fashion that characterizes an individual family's approach to solving economic problems, a Tzintzuntzan of modest size should enjoy a standard of living appreciably higher than that known today. But I foresee no developments that can support a much larger population than that of the present, at the level people are surely going to demand. By extensive emigration and smaller families the population stabilization problem must be solved. The present rate of growth, if continued, will prevent any significant improvements in standards of living.

Whatever happens, or does not happen, it is evident that the next ten to fifteen years will be the most critical in the life of the village since the Spaniards arrived almost 450 years ago. The past no longer affords security; willy-nilly, the villagers are being forced to seek new answers to both old and new problems. By 1980 we should know what is possible, and what is likely to happen.

Works Cited

Ammar, Hamed
  1954 *Growing up in an Egyptian Village: Silwa, Province of
         Aswan.* London: Routledge & Kegan Paul
Banfield, Edward C.
  1958 *The Moral Basis of a Backward Society.* Glencoe, Illinois:
         The Free Press
Caro Baroja, Julio
  1963 "The City and the Country: Reflexions on Some Ancient
         Commonplaces," in *Mediterranean Countrymen* (Julian Pitt-
         Rivers, ed.). Paris: Mouton & Co., pp. 27–40
Carstairs, G. Morris
  1958 *The Twice-Born: a Study of a Community of Highcaste
         Hindus.* Bloomington: Indiana University Press
Dube, S. C.
  1958 *India's Changing Villages: Human Factors in Community
         Development.* London: Routledge & Kegan Paul
Foster, George M.
  1961 "The Dyadic Contract: a Model for the Social Structure of
         a Mexican Peasant Village." *American Anthropologist* 63:
         1173–1192
  1963 "The Dyadic Contract in Tzintzuntzan, II: Patron-Client
         Relationship." *American Anthropologist* 65:1280–1294

367

1964a "Treasure Tales, and the Image of the Static Economy in a Mexican Peasant Community." *Journal of American Folklore* 77:39–44

1964b "Speech Forms and Perception of Social Distance in a Spanish-Speaking Mexican Village." *Southwestern Journal of Anthropology* 20:107–122

1965a "Cultural Responses to Expressions of Envy in Tzintzuntzan." *Southwestern Journal of Anthropology* 21:24–35

1965b "Peasant Society and the Image of Limited Good." *American Anthropologist* 67:293–315

1966 "Euphemisms and Cultural Sensitivity in Tzintzuntzan." *Anthropological Quarterly* 39:53–59

Foster, George M., assisted by Gabriel Ospina
1948 *Empire's Children: the People of Tzintzuntzan.* Mexico, D.F.: Smithsonian Institution, Institute of Social Anthropology, Publication No. 6

Friedmann, F. G.
1953 "The World of 'La Miseria.'" *Partisan Review* 20:218–231

Kroeber, A. L.
1948 *Anthropology.* New York: Harcourt, Brace and World

Lewis, Oscar
1951 *Life in a Mexican Village: Tepoztlán Restudied.* Urbana: University of Illinois Press

Maccoby, Michael
1964 "Love and Authority: a Study of Mexican Villagers." *The Atlantic* 213 (3):121–126

Rea, Alonso de la
1882 *Crónica de la Orden de N. Seráfico P.S. Francisco, provincia de San Pedro y San Pablo de Mechoacán en la Nueva España.* México Imprenta de J. R. Barbedillo y Gª

Redfield, Robert
1950 *A Village That Chose Progress: Chan Kom Revisited.* Chicago: University of Chicago Press

Redfield, Robert, and Alfonso Villa R.
1934 *Chan Kom: a Maya Village.* Washington, D.C.: Carnegie Institution of Washington, Publication No. 448

Simmons, Ozzie G.
1959 "Drinking Patterns and Interpersonal Performance in a Peruvian Mestizo Community." *Quarterly Journal of Studies on Alcohol* 20:103–111

Smith, William C.
1961 "Hens That Laid Golden Eggs." *International Development Review* 3(3):2–5.

Villa-Señor y Sánchez, Joseph Antonio de
1748 *Theatro Americano.* Segunda Parte. México

Wolf, Eric
1959 *Sons of the Shaking Earth.* Chicago: University of Chicago Press

Epilogue, 1979

INTRODUCTION

In a development-conscious, development-desiring world in which planned change is the keystone to most national policies, peasant conservatism has been a thorn in the side of technical specialists anxious to achieve change, and has been a topic of lively debate among anthropologists seeking explanations. That until comparatively recently most peasants have appeared to be noninnovative and resistant to change needs no documentation. For years preceding the Green Revolution new agricultural practices routinely were rejected, immunization was looked upon with fear, and new educational opportunities were spurned. Community development goals, including wells, latrines, smokeless *chulas*, and adult literacy more often than not fell short of initial hopes. The accounts of anthropologists and other observers of the rural scene were nearly unanimous in their conclusions: peasant villagers are suspicious of outsiders and neighbors alike; they are noncooperative and noncompetitive; gossip, backbiting, and fear of witchcraft characterize interpersonal relations; individual progress is viewed

369

with disfavor, and negative sanctions discourage progressive individuals. Economic surpluses are redistributed through ritual expenditures rather than accumulated for capital investment.

Common explanations of this behavior have invoked such things as economic irrationalism and psychological factors—such as the absence of a "need for achievement" (McClelland 1961). Although I found the forms of behavior described in the first paragraph during the early years of my research in Tzintzuntzan, these "explanations" seemed inadequate to me, and in "Peasant Society and the Image of Limited Good," I suggested a psychosocial zero-sum game model of cognitive orientation in their stead (Foster 1965). This model served as the theoretical basis for my interpretation of the culture of Tzintzuntzan as it is found in this book. The traditional peasant world view, it seemed to me, was one in which all good things in life were preceived to exist in finite, unexpandable, and insufficient quantities to satisfy individual and group needs and desires. In a closed system (which is how peasants have perceived their environments), individual progress could be based only on a redistribution of this "Limited Good," logically and inevitably at the expense of others. I argued that this is why peasant normative behavior discouraged attempts at and the show of an interest in change, modernization, and individual progress. Far from being irrational, I believe that a Limited Good outlook is a realistic appraisal of, and reaction to, the economic and social conditions that have long prevailed in peasant societies. Throughout history most peasant societies have had limited resources not easily expanded, and genuine economic and social opportunities to progress have been rare—for the individual and for the group.

Contrary to the interpretation of some critics, the model does not imply absolute restraint on change. Rather, it explains behavior as a function of perceived lack of opportunity, and predicts change when the reality of growing opportunity is perceived by potential peasant entrepreneurs. Specifically, I wrote: "The problem of the new countries is to create economic and social conditions in which this latent energy and talent [of peasant entrepreneurs] is not quickly brought up against absolute limits. . . . Change cognitive orientation through changing access to opportunity, and the peasant will do very well indeed" (1965:310). And again, "The primary task in development is to try to change the peasant's view of his social and economic universe . . . toward that of expanding opportunity in an open system, *so that he can feel safe* in displaying initiative. . . . Show the peasant that initiative is

370

profitable, and that it will not be met by negative sanctions, and he acquires it in short order" (*Ibid.*).

These predictions have been borne out insofar as they apply to Tzintzuntzan. In recent years production has increased, incomes have risen, and people eat and dress better than formerly; they live in more comfortable homes; they receive more schooling; they enjoy higher levels of health and live longer, and increasing numbers face the future with still higher expectations. A Limited Good mentality, although still found among many of the older people, is no longer a significant brake on change, as it certainly was in 1945. Genuine and significant increases in economic and social opportunities, coupled with the villagers' realization that these opportunities are available to them, underlie these dramatic developments.

In this epilogue I describe in some detail the forms of progress just ennumerated, discuss the new opportunities that have made them possible, and then attempt to relate the model of Limited Good to the realities of life in Tzintzuntzan in 1978. In doing the latter I will be concerned with a broader theoretical point about anthropological models: since most of them are static, rather than dynamic, can they be reconciled with the fact of the contemporary rapid change that is occurring in almost all formerly traditional societies?

POPULATION GROWTH

The physical boundaries of Tzintzuntzan remain essentially unchanged as compared to 1965 and, as far as that goes, 1945 and before. A half-dozen very poor houses have sprung up on the east side of the Pátzcuaro highway, just above the cemetary; known informally as *La Colonia*; they represent the only extension of traditional boundaries. But within these boundaries, population density is more than double the 1231 inhabitants counted in 1945. Fifteen years later this figure had risen to 1877, and in 1970 it was 2253. As of 1979, I estimate the figure at between 2500 and 2600. Were it not for the massive emigration that began about 1965, the figure would be substantially higher, perhaps as much as 3500, for the birth rate remains high, around 40 per 1000, and the death rate—8.7 per 1000 for the decade centering on 1960—shows no sign of rising.

While increasing numbers of parents recognize the relationship between many mouths to feed and bodies to clothe, and the cost of educating children, and while many parents know that family size depends on more than God's will, these facts have yet to make a major dent in rate of population growth. A formal government-sponsored family planning program was initiated in 1975; it has attracted a number of the more progressive women, mostly mothers who already have six or more children. Birth rates for the foreseeable future will remain high in the village.

ECONOMIC AND MATERIAL GROWTH

In spite of its rapid population growth, Tzintzuntzan has made remarkable material progress in recent years. In 1965 it boasted five trucks, six television sets, 16 propane gas stoves, one refrigerator and one washing machine. By contrast, in 1979 there were over 40 trucks, most of them new, in addition to 12 automobiles, a luxury earlier unknown. Television sets and propane stoves had become too numerous to count easily, but it is safe to say they were found in at least 40 percent of all homes. Elaborate hi-fi consoles, costing as much as U.S. $500, unknown in the earlier year, numbered over 40 in 1979. Refrigerators and washing machines, in contrast, have not been highly valued: there are still less than a dozen of each. A great many new houses have been constructed, and even more old ones have been significantly improved. As centrally located properties have been divided and subdivided between heirs, additional space has been obtained by going *up* instead of *out*, and two-story houses, a symbol of prestige as well as a family home, now number more than 25. Reinforced concrete and brick construction has largely replaced adobe, usually still found only in simple houses on the outskirts of the village. Tile floors, large windows, showerbaths, and hot water heaters are increasingly common in these new buildings. In 1972, a sewer system was laid under the main highway, and in subsequent years extensions have been made to other streets. This eliminated much of the constant runoff of waste water down streets and in theory has opened the way to flush toilets, locally known as *tazas inglesas,* "English bowls." A few have been installed. But they are not popular, at least in part because the village's antiquated water system is unable to supply the abundance of water that would be required for their general use.

Modern home construction is not unalloyed progress, for the most economical construction—flat roofs of concrete—has none of the charm of the traditional architecture. A few builders, with a sense of the appropriate, combine colonial styles with the new, but increasingly

Tzintzuntzan architecture is coming to resemble that of the drab villages that are all too well known to the casual tourist. As traditional peoples progress economically, they seem to lose the ability to distinguish between the modern and the aesthetically satisfying. Even as building design in American cities is determined by "economic reality," so is the same process at work in Tzintzuntzan.

Material progress is also reflected on the municipal level. In 1970, the dilapidated state-supported "2 de Octubre" school was demolished, after 30 years of service, to be replaced by a new primary school of several independent, simple, prefabricated units of the design found in all Mexico. A *kinder* (kindergarten) was built in 1973, and has proved highly successful. And, wonder of wonders, through local initiative a secondary school was organized in 1974. The *presidencia* (town hall), years under construction, has been completed—a fine, modern building—and two popular art market buildings have, with the aid and prodding of government agencies, been constructed—the more recent one in 1978. In 1972 the Federal Commission of Electricity extended its lines to peripheral areas of the village and to La Vuelta, the Tarascan settlements along the lake shore, and today more than 90 percent of all homes have this convenience. More and more streets have been cobbled, all with sidewalks. More than a luxury, paved streets are now essential for the villagers' cars and trucks, and to permit passage of the commercial vehicles that bring beer, soft drinks, and packaged goods to local stores.

Dress styles are increasingly those of the same social classes in the cities; the changes are nowhere more striking than among adolescent girls and young women, who have moved from the miniskirt of a decade ago to a near-uniform of slacks, with tight sweaters or blouses. Leather *huaraches* are still used by men working in fields, but store-bought shoes are worn on most other occasions. For women, plastic sandals are the single most common form of footwear. *Rebozos* and aprons, once the mark of the proper woman, are rarely seen on females under 30 years of age.

Much more money than formerly is spent on clothing. The same is true of medical care, which now takes a significant bite out of most family budgets. Thirty years ago the "hierarchy of resort" in seeking medical help was that found in all parts of the world where Western medicine was beginning to be available: first, home remedies; next, the traditional curer; and finally—and as a last resort—the desperate gamble of the physician. Today the hierarchy of resort for most illness is that of the

373

United States: first, home remedies; next the physician; and finally—usually only if the physician is unable to work a miracle—the traditional curer (increasingly a spiritualist or other form of faith-healer). Medical doctors in Quiroga, Pátzcuaro and Morelia are routinely consulted, and surgery has become common.

A majority of births now occur in the local health center, built with the aid of the national government in 1964; mothers are attended by a nurse-midwife (a young woman of the village) sometimes overseen by a physician. Herbal medicine has largely disappeared except for a few common household teas, and most members of the younger generation know very little about traditional etiologies, especially the hot/cold dichotomy of humoral pathology. No new midwives or *curanderas* have appeared during the past 34 years, and most of the old ones have died. Doña Natividad Peña still does a considerable business treating children for *empacho* and fallen fontanelle, and until recently Don Marcos Alejandre was visited by patients who believed themselves bewitched or afflicted with the evil eye. He is now too old to continue to practice and, in any event, belief in, or at least fear of, witchcraft and the evil eye has declined dramatically, and progressive people now dismiss them as simple superstitions.

In enumerating these material advances and the economic outlays they represent, it suddenly strikes one that Tzintzuntzan has become a consumer society in the real sense of the word, a distinction no traditional peasant society ever achieved. In addition to the major improvements just noted, a majority of homes now have at least one innerspring mattress bed, with pillows, sheets, and blankets. Many homes have factory manufactured furniture, including kitchen and dining room sets. Local stores offer a bewildering variety of foods, drinks, and drugs. In 1945 the best stocked store had about 100 items; today's best stocked store offers 500, and clerks sometimes use hand-held electronic computers to total buyers' purchases. Local butchers slaughter cattle and hogs daily, and meat is no longer a once-a-week luxury. Consumption of fruits and vegetables has also increased significantly, bringing greater variety to the traditional beans and tortilla diet. A generation ago no one worried about the disposal of refuse; everything was recycled. Today it is a major problem dealt with, unfortunately, in the same way as in larger towns. Villagers load refuse in pickup trucks, cart it to the edge of town, and dump it along the roadside. As in other heavily populated parts of Mexico, roadsides have become linear garbage dumps.

The new opportunities that underlie these startling changes in village life are in part the product of village initiative, and in part a spin-off from Mexico's dramatic economic growth manifest in recent years in an extensive infrastructure of highways, railways, rural electrification, supervised credit, health and educational facilities, and the stimulation of tourism. As Tzintzuntzeños have become convinced of the reality of new opportunities presented by this infrastructure, they have shown ingenuity in responding to them. These opportunities are not all of a kind; some are close at hand and others are more distant. Among the former is the phenomenal growth of national and international tourism in Michoacán. Tzintzuntzan, on the shores of Mexico's loveliest lake, in an area long known for scenic beauty, archaeological remains, picturesque Tarascan Indian villages, colonial buildings, and varied arts and crafts, draws hundreds, and sometimes thousands, of tourists daily. They visit the pre-Conquest pyramids and the colonial churches and open air chapel, but above all they stop to buy popular arts and crafts, for which the village has become a major emporium.

Among the latter is the capacity of Mexican cities to absorb vast numbers of rural migrants, and of the United States to accept, as legal and illegal immigrants, millions of Mexican workers. These two safety valves relieve (but do not solve) population pressure and underemployment in rural areas. Many of the material changes I noted between 1945 and 1965 were made possible by *bracero* savings. But with the last batch of Tzintzuntzan contract migrants in 1965, this source of funds was cut off sharply. Writing at that time, I anticipated a major economic, and perhaps social, crisis in Tzintzuntzan (and rural Mexico in general) because of loss of this source of income. Fortunately this did not come to pass, for immediately following cessation of the *bracero* program, Mexico City (and to a lesser extent other industrial cities) began to sop up surplus rural population on a scale no one could have believed possible. The participation of Tzintzuntzeños in this process has been well documented by Kemper (1977). In more recent years the United States has again become a major destination for migrants. For many years a dozen Tzintzuntzan men have had legal papers to work in California; some have left their families in the village, returning once a year to visit and to sire the next child. Others have moved permanently to *el norte*. At present, scores of village men migrate to the United States as "undocumented workers" where, however low the wages may seem by American standards, they earn money on a scale impossible for all but a few in Mexico.

Another significant "outside" source of village income is the remittances of young people who have become professionals, working away from home. In countries in the initial stages of industrialization, the population explosion is viewed as a deterrent to economic progress. Paradoxically, however, Mexico's booming population has benefited Tzintzuntzan by creating great demand for school teachers. Young people of both sexes, after six years of primary, three of secondary, and three of normal school (teacher training school), can become rural school teachers at salaries that are, by traditional standards, exceedingly good. For perhaps 15 years the career of rural school teacher has been looked upon by young people—realistically—as the greatest single opportunity for individual success; it has been embraced by perhaps 150 scholars. Parental investment in tuition and other expenses is high, especially when children must live in more distant cities. But secondary graduates admitted to normal schools usually obtain complete scholarship support, so when viewed against the return, the monetary outgo is seen as a sound investment. Many young teachers continue to regard Tzintzuntzan as their home: they build houses, to which they return on weekends in their new cars, or they contribute to the improvement of their parents' home, in which they maintain a room. Many also give money to younger siblings to help them continue their education. Lesser but growing numbers of young people now aspire to careers as medical doctors, lawyers, engineers, and bank employees. The demands of their employment mean that they are effectively lost to the village as residents, but they too more often than not remit money to their parents.

Local, intermittent wage-earning opportunities have also presented themselves within the village. During 1973 and 1974, the National Institute of Anthropology and History carried out a major reconstruction of the decaying Franciscan monastery adjacent to the parish church. Well over U.S. $100,000 went into local wages. Likewise, continuing excavation and reconstruction of the *yácatas* has provided several weeks of work almost annually for from 20 to 50 men. Collectively, all forms of cash income have spawned a building boom, unparalled in earlier years, and the number of masons and their helpers has multiplied several times over.

But it is not outside resources alone that explain the material progress of the community. In 1965, I found only slight increases in pottery productivity as compared to 1945. Today, although precise measurement is difficult, I estimate that productivity per potter has increased at least 50 percent, and possibly as much as 100 percent. The family workshop is still the basic unit of production. But with the wide-scale introduction of trucks in the village, most potters have given up keeping pack animals to transport clay and to market their wares. Instead, they buy truckloads of clay from other villagers, who mine it and distribute it in their trucks. Or they mine the clay themselves and hire a truck to cart it to their homes. Firewood has all but ceased to exist in the hills around Tzintzuntzan, and today sawmill slash from as far away as Santa Clara de los Cobres—about 35 miles—is trucked in and sold. All glazes now are sold commercially pulverized, a convenience that alone saves at least a half-day in a week's work. Potters who have had artistic success increasingly buy greenware, from widows and other elderly people, which they paint, glaze and fire. This provides economic opportunities on a piecework basis for people—mostly women—who could not otherwise make pottery, and it allows the artists to concentrate on what they do best.

Even greater efficiencies have been realized in the sale and transportation of pottery. Literally all pottery is taken to local markets, especially Pátzcuaro, in local trucks. Long before dawn every Friday morning, drivers pass through the streets, honking loudly, to announce they have space for transport of ware to market. A dozen potters-turned-merchants have large vans or smaller Volkswagen wagons in which they deliver pottery and other arts and crafts to stores in all parts of the republic. The 1,800 mile journey to Tijuana, with two drivers relieving each other so that rest stops are unnecessary, is now routine; wives sometimes also go along, just for the pleasure of the trip. Much pottery, of course, is sold in the 60 or more stores or stalls that now line the main highway, up in numbers from 15 in 1965, but representing an increase of several thousand percent in capacity and variety of wares offered. In short, increasing numbers of potters—especially those with artistic ware—make a good living, and pottery merchants do even better.

A new and major source of income is the weaving of *popote* wheat straw figures. The weaving of tule reeds has, of course, been known for centuries. But only in the 1960s did Tarascan Indians in the lakeshore villages take up the weaving of wheat straw, in forms such as boats, airplanes, trains, merry-go-rounds, and Christmas tree ornaments. Many of these were sold in the Tzintzuntzan stalls. Villagers were quick to realize the economic possibilities, and since 1970 more and more families have taken up wheat straw weaving, often abandoning their pottery work. *Popote* work is perceived to have many advantages over the older craft. It is clean and it can be done in odd moments of respite from other tasks. Storekeepers awaiting tourists can tend store and weave simultaneously, an impossibility for potters. Straw, too, is much more easily carried by merchants who distribute their wares by bus, as many still do. For tourists, too, and especially foreigners who travel by air, *popote* art can be carried home without the inconvenience of heavy pottery. *Popote* ware is beginning to rival pottery as a village source of income.

In other traditional areas, increased productivity is less marked. Fishing has essentially disappeared; only one elderly man still has his canoe and *chinchorro* net. Because of overfishing, absolute production in the lake appears to be dropping, and the famed white fish, now a common delicacy on menus in fine Mexico City restaurants, has quintupled in price in recent years. Agriculture, never a major activity in Tzintzuntzan, has made modest advances. All farmers now use chemical fertilizers, and most use steel plows for the first "breaking" of the earth. But subsequent tilling is still done with the ancient wooden plow, and oxen provide all power. Only one farmer has a tractor, and it is usually hired out to farmers in other villages with more flat land. Harvesting and threshing are still done in the traditional way—the former with a hand-held toothed sickle and the latter by animal hoofs.

Equally impressive as this absolute material growth is the realization on the part of many people that money is capital that can be invested to bring even greater returns. Large amounts of money continue to be spent on the traditional fiesta system, but the percentage of total village income allocated to fiestas is less than formerly. Capital investment, in goods and in education, is now realized by a great many people to be essential to major economic progress; the most important forms are trucks, stores, maize mills, automatic tortilla machines, and higher education for children. "Time is money," a concept incomprehensible a generation ago, is taken for granted by growing numbers of people, and cultural values are sacrificed to gain time for productive work. Those who have achieved the greatest economic success realize that it has meant sacrifices in social relations: "Many people no longer come to visit us," is the way one storekeeper put it, a tinge of regret in her voice. "They know we are too busy to talk with them." Other values are also sacrificed: machine-made tortillas, for example, are much less tasty than the hand-made variety, yet entrepreneurially-minded families almost without exception buy them. To make them at home takes time that can be spent more profitably on other activities.

SOCIAL AND POLITICAL CHANGES

Not all villagers have shared in the increased well-being I have described. Some families—maybe 10 percent of the total—still live at the poverty line—cooking and sleeping on the floor, dressing in rags, living with little hope. An additional 15 percent have made only modest progress. With rising affluence the incipient class differences of a generation ago have become more marked, but I am reluctant to speak of the village as having a genuine class system. Certainly class distinctions are not entrenched, and no one is excluded from progress—or even marriage to anyone else—by rigid social barriers. The remarkable thing is not that differences in levels of living have become more marked than formerly, but that such a high proportion of the community has increased its well-being, viewing the future with optimism.

Tzintzuntzeños are an increasingly mobile people, and the expanded environment from which spouses and *compadres* are drawn reflects the great distances people travel—to work, to study, and to engage in commerce. An overnight bus trip to Mexico City is routine and hundreds of villagers have traveled the 1,800 miles to Tijuana, the major port of entry for California. Perhaps 400 villagers, children included, now reside in Mexico City, and lesser but significant numbers live and work in such major cities as Toluca, Uruapan, and Tijuana. Today it is widely felt that advanced schooling is essential for success in life. As recently as 1960 less than a dozen young people were studying beyond the primary level; today the number exceeds 200.

This greater mobility is reflected in changing marriage and *compadrazgo* patterns. While still predominantly endogamous, increasing numbers—perhaps a fifth—of Tzintzuntzeños now marry outside the community. *Compadres* likewise are chosen from more distant places: for children baptised 1975–1977, only 70 percent of godparents were from the village and its immediate environs. In contrast, during the period 1958–1967, 94 percent of godparents were from the village or close by.

A social change only now coming to the fore is the rapidly increasing number of "senior citizens," villagers past the age of 60 who, although they usually continue to work, have passed their reproductive years and have made their major economic contributions. In 1945, only 3.7 percent of the population was 61 years of age or older. In 1960, this figure had risen to 4.4 percent, and in 1970 to 6.9 percent. In 1979, the figure was about 9 percent. Will the elderly, who until recently have not been a major economic drain on family resources, come to be considered a social problem? Will children be reluctant to assume the responsibility for years of support of elderly parents? Will useful work continue to be found, as at present, for almost all oldsters—work commensurate with their physical abilities? It is too early to tell.

With changing opportunities and growing material well-being, community leadership has strengthened. In recent years *presidentes municipales* (mayors) have more actively concerned themselves with civic improvements, such as the sewer system, street lighting and cobbling, and fiesta organization. They continue to be criticized, of course, but more things get done. Cooperation among villagers for the common good is less looked upon as involving personal risk than in an earlier period. This new spirit is most dramatically illustrated by the decision in 1974 of the mayor and a group of concerned citizens to establish a secondary school. They raised an impressive sum of money (by local standards) and by concerted action badgered state and national ministries of education to match this sum, thereby making possible the first three-room unit. A subsequent campaign produced a second comparable building, and the third unit is on the drawing board. When the success of the new school seemed assured, it was "federalized" by the national government, thus ensuring attractive teachers' salaries and the maintenance of national educational standards.

CHANGING PRESTIGE SYSTEMS: RELIGION AND ECONOMICS

Until quite recently, as we have seen, the only socially approved manner in which Tzintzuntzeños could compete for prestige was via the *carguero* system, in which wealth was exchanged for religious merit. By 1965, however, new roads to prestige were beginning to open up. One major road was that of competition to be the first or among the first to acquire visible symbols of material welfare, in large measure items of household use. A second major road was that in which the function, but not the form, of religious ritual was turned to the status quest: ritual expenses, instead of serving as an economic leveling mechanism, became a device for competition through conspicuous consumption. By 1979, these roads had become broad boulevards. With their newfound prosperity, increasing numbers of villagers have crossed the psychological threshold to where they seem no longer worried by the fear of nega-

tive sanctions if they spend conspicuously. Perhaps in part this is because they are sufficiently numerous to constitute a sizeable group
within which envy works as a stimulant to ever greater acquisitions,
rather than as a threat to one's self and possessions. New houses increasingly have two stories, and furnishings, as we have seen, are store-
bought rather than village-made. The simple weddings of yesterday are
becoming elaborate fiestas in which the ability to attract a preponderance of outside, city guests is the measure of competitive success. In one
recent wedding the bride wore an elaborate silk bridal gown, and the
groom full morning dress. Their future happiness was toasted with
sparkling wine in champagne glasses.

Death, too, is no longer a private sorrow for relatives and friends of
the deceased; a pine box in a grave marked by a wooden cross is no
longer adequate honor to the departed. Coffins increasingly are of expensive metal, lined in the same elaborate fashion as their American
counterparts. Tombs are, at the very least, topped with a concrete slab
with the particulars of the deceased scratched in it; and more and more,
elaborate engraved tombstones mark the spot of interment. Death, in
short, can be and often is an occasion to flaunt wealth, or at least a
chance to keep up with the Garcías.

Another religious ritual is not costly, but it can be very painful.
Hooded penitents, who for untold years on Good Friday have paid their
vows to the Virgin by wearing leg irons or shouldering heavy wooden
crosses, have proliferated in numbers. To become a penitent is the "in"
thing for young men to do. Elderly men who continue to make the penitent's rounds through the village streets are spoken of with admiration,
and when they are no longer able to do so, they are still praised for their
religious devotion. For many years penitents were few in number; a
single cross sufficed. By 1965 there were three. When, in 1978, I was in
Tzintzuntzan for Easter Week for the first time in some years, I was
dumbfounded to find that the number had risen to 11, which were in
constant use all Good Friday night, until well after dawn the following
morning. Well over 100 pentitents "paid" their vow that night—at the
same time acquiring status and prestige.

Another form of prestige competition is village-wide, directed at other
communities rather than at individuals. In most Mexican communities
rising standards of living and greater commercialization have been accompanied by a decay in the traditional fiesta system. This is not the
case in Tzintzuntzan. While the elaborate cargo organization of earlier
years has been simplified, with fiesta costs spread between larger num-

bers of encargados, the fiestas themselves are more animated and more interesting than 20 years ago. The *Judea* Passion Play grows in elaborateness, with new scenes added every year. The annual fiesta in honor of *Nuestro Señor del Rescate* now has a splendid group of at least 50 local dancers, who perform on three successive days. Corpus Christi, too, continues to be a major event. Even more striking has been the ritual (and commercial) florescence of All Souls Day, a trend just beginning to be apparent in 1965. About 1970 both the Michoacán Department of Tourism and the National Bureau of Arts and Crafts decided to feature Tzintzuntzan in their tourist advertising. In that year the "First Annual Arts and Crafts Fiesta" was held, with an exposition of local and regional arts and crafts in the plaza in front of the town hall. Prizes were offered for the finest work, as well as for the finest *arcos* (flower and fruit-adorned arches) traditionally placed over childrens' graves in the candle-lit cemetery vigil. The fiesta has continued to grow in importance, to include government-sponsored folkloric music and dancing, and the presentation by a professional troupe of the Spanish and Mexican dramatic classic, "Don Juan Tenorio." Yet when the tourists are gone, the villagers quietly adjourn to the cemetery "to accompany" the spirits of their departed relatives who annually return to earth on this occasion.

The villagers are fully aware of the economic importance of fiestas which draw both village and city tourists. But this alone is not sufficient to explain why Tzintzuntzan today has a more vigorous fiesta cycle than 20 years earlier. The ritual florescence has been made possible by economic prosperity, but at a deeper level it reflects a remarkable community commitment to religion. Tzintzuntzan, as we know, has been a religious ritual center since before the Conquest, when the Tarascan deities were housed in wood and thatch buildings on top of the five *yácatas*. During the colonial period, and into the present century the village has been a pilgrimage destination, especially since the miracle of the *Señor del Rescate* eight decades ago. The elaborate cargo system likewise bound together people who otherwise were atomistic in community-wide ties. Tzintzuntzan's collective commitment to Catholicism remains strong. I believe that all women and most men confess regularly and attend mass at least weekly. Their religion is important to them, and support of and participation in the annual religious cycle is a visible symbol of this commitment. The villagers enjoy their fiestas and are willing to spend huge sums of money on them because they sense in them a collective espirit lacking in nearby communities. A

382

vigorous fiesta system will, I believe, continue for the foreseeable future.

New opportunities can present themselves without necessarily producing significant change; individuals must be motivated to take advantage of them, to innovate, to try new ideas, to set new goals for themselves. The latent entrepreneurial energy that can be released by new opportunities (something probably present in all peasant societies) is abundantly apparent in Tzintzuntzan, where people avidly embrace every conceivable activity that promises success. The dominant force in changing production-related behavior is certainly the perception of likely economic gain. As we have seen, the tourist market has stimulated a profusion of popular arts and crafts; artists experiment to produce new forms and designs that catch the buyer's eye, and when they are successful they are immediately imitated by their co-producers. While utilitarian pottery has changed little if at all during the past 34 years, artistic pottery has taken a variety of forms undreamed of in an earlier period. And the tule reed and wheat straw figure industry is entirely new, the product of tourist demand—an activity that developed from the experiments of a single talented individual who first found a market with visiting anthropologists. The prospect of economic gain also explains the proliferation of stores and traveling middlemen. Likewise, economic advantage is an important factor stimulating young people to become school teachers or other professionals. In their case, however, the desire to know a wider world and to escape from what they see as the drudgery of traditional occupations is also a significant motivation.

The desire to achieve prestige is a second and related factor explaining innovation. Fearing envy, a few older people still hesitate to improve their houses, but most families routinely remodel old homes or build new ones, complete with gas stove, television set, expensive hi-fi radio-phonograph combinations, hot water shower baths, and other products of a commercial age. Open competition now occurs in dress, hair styles, in weddings and baptisms, and in shows of "knowing city ways" such as the sending of Christmas and birth announcement cards, and an occasional *quinceañera* "coming out" party for a 15-year-old girl.

Knowledge of city ways comes through a variety of channels: attending school in cities, visits with urban relatives, and travel and residence in the United States. Above all else, the most important source of knowledge of the urban world is television. Through it people learn of new commercial products, blatantly advertised, that they want to buy and try; they also learn of cultural activities, of national and international sports, and of current events. Television also has had a negative impact; prior to its arrival people were beginning to read a newspaper delivered daily from Morelia, the state capital; readership had reached more than 30 families. Today no one receives a newspaper; its place is taken by the TV screen.

Because of their many sources of information about the modern world, growing numbers of Tzintzuntzeños are no longer country hicks, ignorant of events beyond their local setting. They are becoming knowledgeable Mexican citizens. In Mexico, as in the United States, hard-surface roads, rural electrification, telephones, radio and television, motor vehicles, and schooling have in great measure erased ages-old rural—urban differences. In general knowledge, Tzintzuntzeños today are but little behind their urban counterparts. They no longer fear cities; they know them, and they know how to cope with them. Many even have learned the principal tramway, subway, and bus numbers and their routes in Mexico City.

LIMITED GOOD IN A CHANGING WORLD

Of the theoretical ideas advanced in *Tzintzuntzan*, the Image of Limited Good has been the most hotly debated. It has been strongly criticized by many anthropologists; it has also been discussed approvingly by other anthropologists, and by scholars in sociology, psychology, and political science. As we near the end of this Epilogue, a major question remains: To what extent, if any, is Limited Good a valid model to explain contemporary behavior and institutions in Tzintzuntzan? In attempting to answer this question we must remember that a collective cognitive orientation is never absolute; a spectrum of belief will be found. Moreover, in a rapidly changing community this spectrum will be broader than in a traditional, slowly changing community. With respect to Limited Good in Tzintzuntzan, it is helpful to visualize a continuum, the two poles of which are Limited and Unlimited Good. In theory, at least, every member of the community can be spotted on this continuum, his position depending on his personal mix of Limited and Unlimited Good thinking. A couple of decades ago, the dots representing individual positions clustered near the Limited Good pole. But as new opportunities have been perceived, and exploited, and as thinking has become more open, the cluster has begun to stretch out toward the opposite pole. Erosion of a Limited Good outlook therefore implies a gradual shifting of individual positions along the continuum.

Although the degree of collective shift in any community does not lend itself to precise measurement, it is readily apparent to a long-term observer. The evidence given in this Epilogue makes clear that in Tzintzuntzan a great many individual dots have moved a long way from the traditional toward the modern pole. Young people who have grown up in an environment of opportunity are quite different in their views from their elders. The Limited Good outlook, still reflected in the words and behavior of many of the older villagers, has essentially disappeared among members of the younger generation. They recognize and can discuss the zero-sum thinking of their parents and grandparents, but they know that this does not apply to them.

In trying to understand contemporary change, anthropologists are handicapped because our models have tended to be static rather than dynamic; we emphasize continuities at the expense of change. Our predilection for static models stems at least in part from our usual data-gathering exercise: a year or two of intensive residence in a single community, but little follow-up in subsequent years. Consequently, I believe, many anthropologists do not fully realize how rapidly contemporary societies can and do change, and what these rapid changes mean for our models. In 1945, few anthropologists anticipated the dramatic changes of subsequent years in the communities they had studied. Yet the changes have come, and they have often badly outdated our interpretations of earlier years. Or, put in another way, the models of earlier years, appropriate to conditions as they then existed, apply less and less well with the passage of time, because the facts on which they were based have changed. Limited Good was an attempt to explain Tzintzuntzan and peasant behavior in general as it was being reported during the first generation of peasant studies, from about 1940 to 1965. In these reports one finds remarkable unanimity about peasant character and behavior: a reserved people, suspicious of the motives of fellow villagers as well as outsiders, reluctant to cooperate, given to gossip and backbiting—in short, "atomistic" in outlook. These accounts also described the "leveling" mechanisms, such as costly fiesta systems, that promoted a shared-poverty style of life.

Contrary to what some critics appear to believe, the model does not say that behavior changes cannot occur. On pages 350–351 of this book one reads, "Cognitive orientations change, and an Image of Limited Good sets no absolute limits to a village's advancement. Basic as it is at the present time [i.e., 1965] in preventing villagers from taking advantage of the opportunities that already exist, it is not a perpetual part of life, and as time passes, and especially with sympathetic and understanding outside aid, it will melt away."

This has proven true in Tzintzuntzan, which, like most other formerly traditional peasant communities, has changed dramatically in recent years. What do these changes mean with respect to the applicability of the Limited Good model to explain behavior? Obviously, it is less appropriate than when it was formulated. Among the older people, raised at a time of little opportunity, it still fits. These are the people represented by the dots clustered near the traditional pole of our continuum. They still explain sudden and puzzling wealth as due to finding buried treasure, and they still criticize and gossip about their neighbors. Among the younger people, raised during a time of growing opportunity, Limited Good is inadequate to explain their behavior, and new models will have to be drawn up to account for it.

Some anthropologists, finding that Limited Good does not explain behavior in the contemporary peasant villages they study, jump to the conclusion that the model is erroneous. They fail fully to appreciate the nature of an anthropological model. Like other models, an anthropological model is timeless: it is designed to account for relationships between specified variables. When the variables are altered the model becomes inappropriate to account for the new variables, but in no way does it become a "bad" model. A young anthropologist going to a contemporary Mexican community that has experienced great recent change is unlikely to find that the Limited Good cognitive orientation explains the observed behavior as well as I believe it explained behavior in Tzintzuntzan two decades ago. The anthropologist can quite correctly say that the model does not fit the data he has gathered. But he cannot correctly say that the model is wrong. A model must be evaluated on the basis of the variables that it specifies, not on the basis of a time scale. Limited Good is, I continue to believe, a valuable model to explain behavior in Tzintzuntzan during the period 1945—1965. It partially explains contemporary behavior, especially that of members of the older generation. But with each passing year it becomes less and less appropriate, and in another decade few traces of it may remain. This prediction assumes continuing growth of opportunity. Should this growth cease, and should scarcity again become the rule, Limited Good thinking may well reverse its trend and become more common than it is today. The cognitive orientation continuum is a two-way street; depending on conditions, the dots can flow either way.

WORKS CITED IN EPILOGUE

Foster, George M.
  1965 Peasant Society and the Image of Limited Good. *American Anthropologist* 67:293–315.
  1969 Godparents and Social Networks in Tzintzuntzan. *Southwestern Journal of Anthropology* 25:261–278.
  1973 Dreams, Character, and Cognitive Orientation in Tzintzuntzan. *Ethos* 1:106–121.
  1979 Fieldwork in Tzintzuntzan: The First Thirty Years, in *Long-Term Field Research in Social Anthropology* (George M. Foster et al., eds.). New York: Academic Press, pp. 165–184.
Kemper, Robert V.
  1977 Migration and Adaptation: Tzintzuntzan Peasants in Mexico City. Beverly Hills, CA: SAGE Publications.
Kemper, Robert V. and George M. Foster
  1975 Urbanization in Mexico: The View from-Tzintzuntzan, in *Latin American Urban Research* (Wayne A. Cornelius and Felicity M. Trueblood, eds.). Beverly Hills, CA: SAGE Publications, vol. 5, pp. 53–75.
McClelland, David C.
  1961 *The Achieving Society.* Princeton, NJ: D. Van Nostrand Co.

Afterword, 1988

INTRODUCTION

Viewed in long-range perspective, the most notable events that have transpired in Tzintzuntzan during the nine years since the 1979 Epilogue was written have been a peaking, at least temporarily, in the rate of economic development, a possible easing in demand for higher education, growing population pressure, and the effects of rapid devaluation of the Mexican peso accompanied by run-away inflation. These are the topics dealt with in the following pages.

DEMOGRAPHIC DEVELOPMENTS

As noted in the Preface, 1988, in February of 1980, Robert Kemper, Stanley Brandes and I took a 100 percent census of the village. This census, like its three predecessors, includes not only a basic count of population but also a great deal of information on houses, furnishings, personal possessions, occupations, travel, migration and the like. These rich data provide a basis of comparison with the past and, since 1980-81 was the high point of Mexico's post-World War II growth, a basis against which to measure future developments. In 1979, I estimated the population of Tzintzuntzan at between 2500 and 2600, a considerable increase over 1970's 2253, but a figure suggesting a slowing in earlier growth rates. Our 1980 census confirmed this estimate. Yet it also threw into relief a new problem that makes it impossible to say exactly what the population of Tzintzuntzan is on any given date, namely who is to be counted? A number of men with legal immigration papers spend nine months or more a year in the United States, returning home for Christmas, or other holidays for a few weeks, usually to father another child and to renew their acquaintance with those already born. Tzintzuntzan is their only permanent home, and wives and children are there the year around. Are they to be counted as residents? A great many schoolteachers, born and raised in Tzintzuntzan, have jobs from fifty to a hundred miles distant. A number of them have built or are building homes in the village. They return on weekends and for long vacations, staying in their own or in parental homes. Should they be counted? Students in high school and the university in Morelia usually live in that city, returning home weekends; in 1986, they numbered 59. They are dependent on their parents for support, move from boarding house to boarding house, and are away more nights during the year than they are at home. How should they be classified? In short, we found it necessary to make two counts: a "core count," which gave 2507 people who, apart from an occasional journey away from home can usually be found in the village. An "extended count" added 142 or 143 people in the above categories for a total of 2650. This count includes all people who judge Tzintzuntzan to be their permanent home or who are largely dependent on it for support and who will, in many but not all, cases return to live there permanently.

In the anthropological literature on peasant communities of a generation or more ago, stability of population was one of the commonly noted characteristics, a feature that contributed to the concept of the "closed-corporate" village. However accurate this stereotype may have been (and I believe that movement in and out of peasant communities may always have been greater than commonly supposed), it is clear that Tzintzuntzan, and other communities like it, are now marked by significant population movements, with emigration exceeding immigration by a wide margin. I suspect that Tzintzuntzan is now close to its maximum population, which seems unlikely ever to reach 3,000. It is approaching the point where, even with remittances from workers in the United States and in Mexican cities, it can no longer support an ever-larger population.

The population problem will be met in part with a lower birthrate. The birthrate has declined slightly in recent years, but it is difficult to say by how much. Since beginning my research, I have recorded all baptisms and church marriages, as well as all births, marriages and deaths recorded in the civil registry. Twenty-five years ago, these reports gave a highly accurate count. This is no longer true, especially with respect to births. Parents have become increasingly lax in registering births; sometimes a father will register four or five at a time, births occurring over a ten- or twelve-year period. In earlier years, such dilatory practices usually could be compensated for by the baptismal records, but today one cannot be certain for, with increased frequency, infants are baptized away from Tzintzuntzan. Again, with many young people being emigrants, one cannot always be sure that a child was born in the village, even though registered and/or baptized there.

Whatever the exact figure, the modest decline in the birthrate appears to be due to formal family planning measures, pushed by the Mexican government with varying degrees of vigor during the past decade. A good many young people now talk openly about birth control, and my records on birth intervals and total numbers of children in sample families confirm that the better educated young people – schoolteachers and other professionals especially – are limiting families to from two to four children. In other families, eight and even ten children are not exceptional; unlike former times, almost all of them are protected by immunization against the common diseases of childhood, and they can be expected to reach adulthood. So, about all that can be said about family planning is that it is having a moderately positive effect on the village population problem but not enough in itself to solve the problem.

EMIGRATION

Emigration has had, and will continue to have, a much greater effect on slowing and eventually stopping village growth than will family planning. Given the nature of emigration from rural communities, however, it is difficult to give precise figures as to its magnitude. People go, and they return home. If they find work they often become permanent out-migrants, or if, as "undocumented" aliens in the United States, they escape detection, they may remain for five years or longer before risking a return home. Although we read most about Mexican migrants coming to the United States, and assume that this country absorbs most of the excess rural population that cannot find work at home, in fact, most emigration is to Mexican cities. Robert Kemper, who runs a 100 percent check on emigration figures biannually, found in 1986 a total of more than 350 adult emigrants who had left the village since the 1980 census. Of these, Mexico City accounted for over fifty, followed by Tijuana, Guadalajara and other cities for an additional 200. In contrast, the United States count showed only 107 new emigrants away at the time of his count. Minor children swell these figures in undetermined degree. These are not all permanent migrants of course; many will return to the village, their places to be taken by other emigrants anxious to try their luck. It must be emphasized that these figures are for *new* emigrants. The figures do not include the hundreds of migrants who left the village, temporarily or permanently, during pre-1980 years.

During 1987, a larger-than-usual number of illegal migrants returned to Tzintzuntzan from the United States, because of uncertainty about the new immigration law that provides amnesty for those who can prove at least five years residence north of the border and penalities for United States employers who hire illegal immigrants. Many migrants have adopted a wait-and-see policy. One can predict, however, that on balance there will always be more migrants leaving than returning to the village.

While population pressure has been eased largely by emigration, the 1979 spawning of a suburban daughter colony has also had a measurable effect. In that year, a number of potters and would-be arts and crafts merchants who lacked highway fronting houses permitting them to sell directly to tourists, squatted on community-owned land two miles from Tzintzuntzan on the highway to Pátzcuaro. The village government initially tried to dislodge them, since they had occupied communal grazing lands. These efforts proved unsuccessful, but no further action was taken since it was assumed that, in the absence of electricity, water and other amenities of life, the settlement would wither away. To the astonishment of almost everyone, this has proven not to be the case. The "Colonia Lázaro Cárdenas," named after Mexico's great liberal president (1934-1940) has grown from fifty-six inhabitants in 1980 to 142 in 1986. Many of its twenty-seven houses are of concrete block construction and most have electricity. There is also a full primary school (six years) with four teachers and more than sixty students. Pottery is made here, tule reed and wheat straw figures are woven, and with every house facing the highway, sales are sufficient to maintain the viability of the community. Although life presents difficulties, especially in the absence of a water supply system, it is clear that this is now a permanent settlement.

STANDARDS OF LIVING

To judge a standard of living, one must factor in such variables as material possessions, access to health care, educational and employment possibilities, travel opportunities and the like. Of these, material possessions are the most visible and easily measured items. Nothing more dramatically illustrates the rise in the standard of living in Tzintzuntzan since 1945 than a comparison of basic material possessions as reported in the 1945, 1960, 1970, and 1980 censuses. Table 1 shows the growth in ownership of selected items that lead to a rising standard of living.

By 1987, the numbers of some of these items had significantly increased over those of 1980. During the period 1980-86, seventy-four new homes were constructed (while twenty-five were abandoned or left unoccupied), and many additional homes underwent major reconstruction. In almost all of these new and rebuilt homes, flush toilets and hot water (usually

Table 1

Tzintzuntzan Material Possessions: 1945 to 1980

	1945	1960	1970	1980
Total Population	1231	1877	2253	2649
No. of Houses	248	319	358	448
Percent of Houses with:				
Electricity	14%	52%	65%	81%
Piped Water	22%	50%	62%	71%
Raised Bed	57%	69%	77%	94%
(Innerspring mattress)	0	3%	24%	60%
Radio	2% (?)	41%	70%	85%
Television	0	0	11%	54%
Stereo	0	0	0	21%
Telephone	0	0	0	9%
Sewer	0	0	0	30%
Hot Water Shower	0	(one)	5%	10%
Flush Toilet	0	0	1%	10%
Propane Stove	0	(two)	14%	49%
Electric Blender	0	(two)	4%	34%
Refrigerator	0	0	0	11%
Washing Machine	0	0	2%	5%
Truck or Car	0	(one)	7%	13%

Note: "One" and "two" indicate number of items.

automatic) for shower baths have been installed. Propane stoves and television sets probably are found in seventy percent of all houses, and the number of cars and trucks has increased by half or more. The count of telephones would have tripled had the company been able to meet the demand. The number has been frozen at forty-nine since the initial 1979 installation of an antiquated manual system; only when this system is replaced with automatic dialing will all families desiring an instrument be able to obtain one.

EDUCATION AND EMPLOYMENT

Large numbers of young people continue, like their parents, to farm, to make pottery, to work as day laborers or as masons, and to migrate legally and illegally to the United States. In addition to following these traditional occupations, however, significant numbers of young people have become real professionals. The initial opportunity for professional advancement was provided by Mexico's need for schoolteachers, particularly in rural areas. The first young man to follow this career received his teacher's certificate about 1950. Before his death thirty-five years later, he had risen to the rank of principal of a secondary school in Mexico City. A few additional teachers graduated during the late 1950s and early 1960s, but the great surge has been during the past twenty years when, by a conservative estimate, more than 200 young people have become teachers. Many, by taking summer courses, have furthered their careers and qualified for openings in secondary schools. One, a young woman, has taken an advanced degree in psychology at the university in Morelia.

Most Tzintzuntzeños who become teachers covet jobs in the village, but relatively few achieve this goal. In 1986, of the forty teachers in kindergarten and the primary and secondary schools, only fifteen were natives of the village, but an astonishing ninety-six additional teachers count the village as their home. The majority of these commute daily by bus or private car to schools five to fifty miles distant, while the remainder, in more distant communities, return for weekends and long vacations. Until recently, teacher salaries have been relatively good, and teacher income has been a significant economic factor in community life. Unlike some other professions, almost all teacher graduates can obtain employment.

Next to teaching, nursing has been the career most often followed by students, but a career limited to young women. Since about 1970, perhaps fifty nurses have received their professional credentials. Unlike teachers, not all nurses have been able to obtain work, and some have married and settled down to the roles of housewives and mothers.

Smaller, but significant, numbers of young people have entered professions requiring university or technical school degrees. To-date, five men have become medical doctors, two women and one man dentists, two men and one woman veterinarians, two men agronomists, two men architects, and four men and two women lawyers. At least six men are graduate engineers. One, the son of potters, lives in Mexico City, works for a multinational company, flies to all parts of the country on business, and, in appearance, is indistinguishable from other sophisticated city professionals. Another, the son of storekeepers and also a Mexico City resident, is a skilled computer specialist. Oddly, and in view of the strong religious sentiments of most villagers, only one young man has completed seminary training to become a priest. A good many others have fallen by the wayside.

More clearly than almost anything else, the story of professional success reveals how the relatively "closed" peasant communities of fifty and more years ago can no longer be meaningfully studied as isolated entities. Tzintzuntzan has, of course, like other peasant communities long had meaningful contacts both with urban centers and other villages. These contacts have been essentially commercial and social, involving the selling of village products, the purchase of items locally unavailable, the establishment of godparent relationships in other communities, and the like. Today, Tzintzuntzan's extra-village ties are not simply with Pátzcuaro, with Quiroga, with Morelia, and adjacent villages; on the contrary, they are with the nation as a whole. It is not a special local demand that has created professional opportunities (even though there is a need, obviously, for medical care, teachers, veterinarians and even lawyers); it is a national demand, which reflects the remarkable social and industrial progress that Mexico has made since the end of World War II. In 1945, when I began my research in Tzintzuntzan, there was *no* demand for professional candidates from rural villages. What has been described is a phenomenon of only forty years, and the changes experienced by the villagers seem to me to be far greater than those most Americans have faced during the same time period. That they have faced them successfully is a remarkable tribute to a people who were viewed in earlier decades as apathetic, traditional, even lethargic, unable to comprehend the possibility of a better life. Presented with new opportunities, and perceiving these opportunities to be realistic goals, Tzintzuntzeños (like other former peasants) have responded eagerly to the benefit of individuals and the community alike.

THE ECONOMIC CRISIS

It would be nice to close this Afterword on the note of uninterrupted progress and the belief in a bright future. Unfortunately, this cannot be done without qualification. Mexico's economic success of past years has presented Tzintzuntzan with the opportunities just described, but Mexico's recent economic problems have also diminished these opportunities, have threatened village standards of living, and have made it more difficult for parents to educate their children. Devaluation of the peso and the resultant run-away inflation are, as far as the villagers are concerned, the causes of these problems. From the end of World War II until early 1982, Mexico enjoyed remarkable price stability as compared to much of the Third World. In 1945, the peso traded at 4.85 to the U.S. dollar. Following a drop to 8.50, it settled down in 1952 at 12.50 to the dollar, where it remained until the mid-1970s. During that period, the peso was considered to be one of the "strong" world currencies. Between 1976 and early 1982, there were two additional devaluations, with the peso fluctuating between eighteen and twenty-six to the dollar. At the time, these devaluations were deemed regrettable but were not generally seen as catastrophic. Then, beginning in February, 1982, the peso began its long slide — first to thirty-eight, then a week later to forty-five, and, with increasing rapidity, to about

1,450 pesos to the dollar in July, 1987. This long-term stability, followed by the rapid decline in the value of the peso, is reflected in the prices of staples over the period 1945-1987 (see Table 2).

Table 2

Prices of Staples in Tzintzuntzan: 1945 to 1987 (In Pesos)

Item	1945	1960	1970	1980	1987
Maize, 4 liters	.90	1.25	3.00	20	480
Beans, liter	1.30	1.50	3.50	30	1000
Sugar, kilo	1.00	1.80	2.50	16	250
Beef, kilo	2.00	10.00	20.00	120	2200
Whitefish, kilo	5.00	20.00	30.00	160	6000
Milk, liter	-	-	1.80	9	250
Quaker Oats, package	1.20	2.00	2.30	30	840
Bolillos (bread)	.05	-	1.50	3	55
Beer, bottle	.40	.60	2.00	7	300
Soft drinks, bottle	.15	.50	1.50	8	140
Cigarettes, pack	.20	.70	.70	8	280
Hot Sauce, bottle	.60	-	1.40	18	340
Laundry Soap, bar	.50	-	1.10	28	500
A Band-aid	.05	.15	.25	2	40
Flashlight Battery	.42	1.20	2.30	12	390
Lead Glaze, kilo	1.05	3.20	4.20	30	2000
Propane Gas, tank	-	-	34.00	200	3800
Pátzcuaro, Bus to	-	-	1.00	7	370
Mexico City, Bus to	-	-	28.00	120	4500
Mason, daily wage	5.00	-	-	300	7000
Day Laborer, daily wage	2.00	-	-	150	3000
Pesos to the Dollar	4.85	12.50	12.50	26	1450

Faced with inflation of this magnitude, it is hard to see how a community can escape total collapse. Yet, in spite of obvious hardships, most people continue to live as well, or nearly as well, as five years earlier. When prices on any item rise in stores, purchases drop off for a few days, but, as buyers become reconciled to the new prices, they return. Some economies are effected by returning to earlier practices which, with relative prosperity, had been abandoned. For example, most mothers had adopted disposable diapers. Some mothers continue to use them, but many more have returned to the handwashing of cloths. Similarly, although tortilla dough (*masa*) continues to be ground from *nixtamal* in commercial electric mills, in many homes, housewives have reverted to making tortillas by hand rather than buying them ready-made in *tortillerías*. Consumption of hard liquor appears to have declined somewhat, and less expensive brands now substitute for the prestige brands of a few years ago. Since the price of candy has risen more rapidly than that of fruit, more children spend money on the latter than formerly (a silver lining, nutritionally speaking, to the cloud of inflation).

Perhaps the maximum economic squeeze is experienced by parents who wish for their children to continue their studies beyond the secondary level. Although many students continue to commute to Quiroga, Pátzcuaro and even Morelia, the astronomical rise in bus fares, coupled with decreased and inconvenient service, make such travel increasingly difficult. Perhaps in the future, fewer professionals will emerge from the village than in the recent past. Professional employment is also harder to come by than formerly, a fact that may discourage some young people from continuing their studies. The income of people on fixed salaries, such as schoolteachers and other government employees, has not kept up with inflation. Families where both parents teach continue to do fairly well, especially if one or both have a second "turn"; i.e., moonlighting by teaching two complete schedules, one in the morning and the other in the afternoon or evening. Yet young teachers tell me that increasing numbers of their ranks are giving up academic life for more remunerative occupations such as driving a taxi or entering the United States as "undocumented" workers.

In spite of the economic crunch, the building of new houses and the remodeling of old houses continues at a feverish pace. Much of the necessary money comes from workers in the United States who are, of course, favored by devaluation. The principle middlemen who carry arts and crafts in their trucks to major Mexican cities and to the United States border also continue to do well. Even less fortunate people continue to be as well-dressed as in recent years, and the same level of fiesta expenditures is maintained. Most friends tell me they eat as well as before, and perhaps better, since fruits and vegetables are now widely available in local stores, and more beef and pork are slaughtered than ever before.

In general, people feel they are less affected by the economic crisis than are their fellows in big Mexican cities. Tzintzuntzan, like all peasant communities, has always led a hand-to-mouth existence in the sense that people do not acquire liquid capital. In a time of rapid inflation, this is an advantage. Prices rise but so does non-wage income, for the prices received for agricultural produce, pottery, and woven straw and reed curios advance at roughly the same rate as other merchandise. The few people who once had savings accounts in Pátzcuaro banks have wisely dropped them, so that their capital is not eaten away by inflation.

In attitude and outlook, there have been great changes since I began research in Tzintzuntzan more than forty-two years ago. The zero-sum game cognitive orientation that I have called "The Image of Limited Good" has, in the face of genuine opportunity and improvement in life, largely disappeared among the younger people, and many of those approaching middle age as well. Yet traces remain, especially among older individuals, occasionally manifested in new forms. Middlemen with trucks have been economically the most successful people living in the village. Some less fortunate individuals still find it hard to see how they can do so well. They no longer assume, however, that the truckers have found buried treasure, for a new, more sinister explanation is at hand: they traffic in marijuana, *la mala hierba*. For villagers who watch television programs about marijuana, and who see soldiers checking on potential traffickers at every crossroad, it is easy to believe that everyone with a truck must certainly carry marijuana to the frontier, hidden beneath a load of pottery and wheat straw figures. Yet I believe this is not the case, and young friends who know the merchants well tell me they believe them to be "clean." To traffic in marijuana is simply – for those who need such an explanation – the contemporary equivalent of stories about finding buried treasure, a device to explain rapid economic improvement.

TZINTZUNTZAN: A POST-PEASANT COMMUNITY

In my earlier research and writing, I viewed Tzintzuntzan as a peasant community, using the term in the sense first brought to anthropology by Robert Redfield in the 1940s and in the sense that Eric Wolf, Oscar Lewis and others interpreted peasant society in the 1950s. While far from isolated, the village in 1945 was relatively "closed," suspicious of outsiders (including me, initially), and uncertain of how to deal with a culturally distant and little understood world. The gap between the city and the village, in occupation, education, clothing, access to health care and the like, was very great. People assumed that their children would lead very much the same lives that they led, that they would remain in the village, and that the outside world would go on, little influencing the village. Information about Mexico was hearsay and rumor. In 1945, no one read a newspaper, and there were so few radios in the village (perhaps five) that I did not think to include the item on the census.

All of this has changed beyond anything I would have dreamed possible forty years ago. As in the United States several decades earlier, the gap between rural and urban has, at least in the case of Tzintzuntzan, all but disappeared. Perhaps the best way to describe contemporary Tzintzuntzeños is to say that they are Mexicans who happen to live, geographically, farther from Mexico City's central plaza than do their fellow countrymen who live and work in the capital city. They watch the same television programs, drive the same cars and trucks, wear the same clothes, attend schools that conform to national models, experience the same medical care (but often in lesser degree and at greater personal expense), and hold similar hopes and aspirations for themselves and for their children. In short, the local community is no longer perceived by anyone to constitute a closed system. With large numbers of legal and illegal workers from the village in the United States, and many more migrants in major Mexican cities, with children in school in Morelia and Mexico City, and with merchants who travel to all parts of the Republic to sell arts and crafts, it is clear that the line between outside and inside, national life and closed-corporate community has long since disappeared.

For fifteen, perhaps twenty, years, it has been incorrect to think of Tzintzuntzan as a peasant community. If it is not peasant, however, what is it? Although it has butcher shops, grocery stores, and two pharmacies, it lacks clothing, furniture, and hardware stores, as well as restaurants and most of the other services found in traditional small towns. It is still a village and it will remain a village, for the urban products and services increasingly needed are available from fifteen to thirty minutes away in Quiroga and Pátzcuaro. So, how do we describe the Tzintzuntzan of today? For newly transformed traditional communities, we have no term as precise, as satisfying, as "peasant" was for their earlier forms. We read that traditional communities have become "post-peasant" or "post traditional," but these are awkward expressions at best. In spite of its proximity to Pátzcuaro, an urban center of 60,000 inhabitants, and its dependence on this city for many goods and services, Tzintzuntzan cannot be thought of as suburban. It is, in fact, an older community than Pátzcuaro, and it maintains an organic integrity that is quite distinct from new, amorphous suburban centers. Its inhabitants are proud of their church, proud of their ritual life, proud of their history. The frequency with which Tzintzuntzeños living outside the village build and maintain homes in it reveals a pride of, and loyalty to, the community that is quite distinct from the attitudes of most suburban dwellers toward their bedroom towns.

Terminology is not the important issue. What is striking about this overall situation is that Tzintzuntzan, and thousands of similar communities in the Third World, has, since World War II, demonstrated a remarkable vitality, a remarkable adaptability, an astonishing ability to take advantage of the new opportunities that developing national economies have presented to them. In spite of the hardships occasioned by *la crisis*, I am optimistic about the future of Tzintzuntzan.

Index

neighbors, 74–75; nuclear, 55–56; parent-child relationships, 62–65; patrilineality, 58; role behavior, 59–65; sibling relationships, 65–67; structure, 57–59
fears, basic, 103–108
fiscal, 198
fishing, 45
folk medicine, 9 (*see also* health)
folklore, 64–65, 145–150
foresight, lack of, 114–117
food, 52–53; role in dyadic contract, 221–223
fresco, 186
friendship, 100–103; Limited Good, 128–129; social structure, 74–75
frío, 186
Fromm, Erich, 13
"Fulano (-a)," 100

godparents, 77–79
gorda del perrito, la, 65–66
grado, de, 76
group responsibility, absence of, 178–179
"Gusta Ud?" 162

hábito, 235
health: causes of illness, 188–190; curing techniques, 190–191; emotions affecting, 191; hot and cold items, 185–188; Limited Good, 129–130; theory, 184–188, 192–193
hechicería, 140
hijo (-a), 65
hoarding, 13
hospital, el, 23–25
hospitality, 162–163
hot and cold theory, 185–188
housing, 48–51
hunting, 45

Ichupio, 34
Indigenous Community, 172; decision making, 172–175; elections, 175–177
innovation: clothing, 307–309; curiosity, role of, 310; friendship, role of, 309–310; psychological stimuli affecting, 304–306; resistance to, 300–304

innovators: characteristics, 295–297; identifying, 293–295; occupational differences, 297–300
irresponsibility, 111
irritante, 186

juez, 198

kenguería, 196
kenguí, 196
kinship: terminology, 58–59, 73; ties, and compadrazgo, 85
kwashiorkor, 129

Limited Good concept, 123–125; cargos, 205–206; economic behavior, 125–127; envy, 153–156; equilibrium theory, 136–141; friendship, 128–129; health beliefs, 129–130; inability to cooperate, 136; luck and fate, 145–152; love, 128–129; machismo, 130–133; resulting behavior, 133–134
living conditions, 20–21 (*see also* standard of living)
love, and Limited Good, 128–129
loyalty, 100–103
lucha, una, 135

Maccoby, Dr. Michael, vii, 143
machismo, 61; and Limited Good, 130–133
macho, 13
madrina, 76
manda, 207
mano, 52
marriage, 63, 67–74; age at, 71–72; birth statistics, 72–73; compadrazgo, 71; expenses, 71; kinship terms, 73; outside community, 72; social structure, 73–74
masa, 50
mayordomía, 195
mayordomía system, 194–196; cargos, 198–206; drain on economic system, 209; election, role in, 207; end of, 313; origin, 210; prestige, 207–211
mayordomo, 198
medicine (*see* health; folk medicine; population)
metate, 50
mestization, 25, 35, 37

403